Preparing Children and Educators for AI-Driven Societies

Muhammad Usman Tariq
https://orcid.org/0000-0002-7605-3040
Abu Dhabi University, UAE & University College Cork, Ireland

IGI Global
Scientific Publishing
Publishing Tomorrow's Research Today

Vice President of Editorial	Melissa Wagner
Director of Acquisitions	Mikaela Felty
Director of Book Development	Jocelynn Hessler
Production Manager	Mike Brehm
Cover Design	Jose Rosado

Published in the United States of America by
IGI Global Scientific Publishing
701 East Chocolate Avenue
Hershey, PA, 17033, USA
Tel: 717-533-8845 | Fax: 717-533-7115
Website: https://www.igi-global.com E-mail: cust@igi-global.com

Library of Congress Cataloging-in-Publication Data

LCCN: (CIP Data Pending)
ISBN13: 9798260024386
Isbn13Softcover: 9798260024393
EISBN13: 9798260024409
British Cataloguing in Publication Data
A Cataloguing in Publication record for this book is available from the British Library.

Table of Contents

Detailed Table of Contents

The advent of Artificial Intelligence (AI) in early childhood and primary education has significantly altered the way we approach teaching and learning. As classrooms become more intelligent and adaptive, the role of the educator continues to evolve from 'teaching' to 'facilitating,' 'personalising,' and 'technologically fluent.' For example, this chapter advocates for the need for us to help educators develop the knowledge, skills, and attitudes they will need to thrive in AI-powered educational contexts. This chapter also proposes an understanding of AI literacy for teachers. It details the significant aspects, including ethical reasoning, digital fluency, and critical interaction with other AI tools, which would help facilitate effective classroom practice. By drawing on effective international models, case studies, and examples of pedagogy, this chapter proposes a framework for professional development that is suitable for both pre-service educators and experienced educators alike.

Artificial intelligence (AI) has become a transformative instrument in education, offering prospects for individualized learning, instructional assistance, and augmented creativity. In response, the Ministry of Education, Youth, and Sport in Cambodia has allocated resources towards policies, training initiatives, and infrastructure to equip teachers for the incorporation of AI. Nevertheless, notwithstanding these endeavors, obstacles endure, encompassing inadequate training, educators' dispositions, and the restricted qualifications of teacher trainers. Therefore, successful AI integration necessitates organized competency frameworks, continuous professional

of human creativity. It will address ethical considerations, copyright challenges, and the evolving definition of authorship in an era where algorithms contribute significantly to the creative process.

ental well-being of children is essential to their overall developmentacademic success However, through the years, the schools catering to these young xhildren have focused on iimproving academic skills instead of fosterning social and emotional competence. As a result, there is a steady rise of mental health cases among older children. Younger children also have been plagued with mental health concerns. Given thiw scenario, there is a need to enable young learners to cope with potential mental health concerns. One method would be gamification. This technique offers a non-threatening way to engage students to know and regulate their emotions. In the long run, it is hoped tha this will help them in their well-being so that mental health issues will be avoided.

Entrepreneurial education in South Africa has become a vital mechanism for addressing unemployment and inequality by nurturing innovation and self-reliance among youth. However, the current pedagogical landscape remains dominated by theory-based instruction that fails to translate knowledge into entrepreneurial competence, particularly within the Curriculum and Assessment Policy Statement (CAPS)-aligned curriculum. A qualitative desk-based research design was employed, drawing on systematic content analysis of secondary data published between 2019 and 2025 from peer-reviewed journals, policy documents, and institutional reports. The findings revealed that AI and gamified simulations enhance learner motivation, decision-making, and creativity by bridging theoretical knowledge and experiential practice. However, challenges such as limited infrastructure, teacher readiness, and ethical governance constrain effective implementation. The study recommended capacity-building for educators, equitable digital access, and ethical localisation of AI tools to ensure inclusion and sustainability.

Preface

The accelerating emergence of Artificial Intelligence (AI) across nearly every aspect of modern society has transformed not only industries and economies, but also the ways in which children learn, communicate, create, and envision their futures. Education systems around the world are now confronted with an urgent responsibility: preparing younger generations to thrive ethically, creatively, emotionally, and intellectually in AI-driven societies. As educators, researchers, policymakers, and innovators grapple with these evolving realities, it has become increasingly clear that AI literacy can no longer remain confined to higher education or specialized technical disciplines. Rather, it must become an accessible and foundational component of childhood and teacher education alike.

Preparing Children and Educators for AI-Driven Societies was developed in response to this global educational transformation. This edited reference work brings together scholars and practitioners from diverse international contexts to explore how AI is reshaping teaching practices, childhood learning experiences, educational leadership, ethics, creativity, entrepreneurship, and mental well-being. The chapters contained in this volume collectively recognize that AI is not merely a technological advancement; it is a societal shift that demands thoughtful, inclusive, and human-centered educational responses. Preparing children for AI-driven futures requires more than teaching technical competencies—it requires cultivating ethical reasoning, adaptability, creativity, emotional intelligence, and critical thinking.

One of the defining strengths of this book lies in its global perspective. Contributors from Asia, Africa, Europe, and the Middle East provide insights into the opportunities and challenges faced by educational systems at varying stages of technological readiness and infrastructure development. Through discussions of policy implementation, classroom innovation, teacher training, gamification, ethics education, and future forecasting, the chapters highlight the importance of context-sensitive approaches to AI integration. While technological advancements differ across nations, the shared commitment to empowering both educators and students remains universal throughout this volume.

Importantly, this book also emphasizes that the future of AI in education must remain deeply human-centered. As intelligent systems increasingly support instruction, assessment, and creativity, educators must continue serving as ethical guides, facilitators of empathy, and advocates for equitable learning opportunities. Children, similarly, must be nurtured not simply as consumers of technology, but as thoughtful innovators capable of shaping AI responsibly for the betterment of society. It is our hope that this volume contributes meaningfully to ongoing conversations about educational transformation and inspires future research, collaboration, and innovation in the field.

OVERVIEW OF THE CHAPTERS

Chapter 1, *Empowering Educators for the AI Era: Strategies for Teaching in Intelligent Classrooms*, by Pawan Pant and Kaushal Mishra, examines the evolving role of educators within AI-powered learning environments. The authors discuss the competencies teachers require to effectively facilitate personalized and technologically enhanced learning experiences, emphasizing AI literacy, ethical awareness, and professional development frameworks designed for both novice and experienced educators.

In Chapter 2, *Preparing Cambodian Educators for AI-Enhanced Classrooms: Policy, Training, and Infrastructures to Help Teachers Embrace Educational Technology*, Saban Bon and Sereyrath Em focus on Cambodia's national efforts to integrate AI into education. The chapter explores educational policies, teacher preparation programs, infrastructural challenges, and institutional reforms necessary to support successful AI adoption within developing educational systems.

Chapter 3, *Ethics From the Start—Teaching Fairness, Bias, and Responsibility*, authored by Nofamataro Zebua and colleagues, highlights the importance of introducing AI ethics education during childhood. Through discussions of storytelling, reflective learning, ethical games, and moral reasoning, the chapter advocates for early educational interventions that help children critically understand algorithmic bias, fairness, responsibility, and digital justice.

In Chapter 4, *AI Beyond Coding: Exploring Creativity, Art, and Storytelling with AI*, Liu Wenpang and co-authors investigate the transformative relationship between AI and human creativity. The chapter explores AI-assisted artistic expression, storytelling, music generation, and collaborative creative processes while also examining ethical questions surrounding authorship, originality, and copyright in AI-supported creative environments.

Chapter 5, *Early Intervention Through Engagement: Gamification and AI in Elementary School Mental Health Support*, by Marie Grace Gomez, addresses the growing importance of mental health support among young learners. The chapter demonstrates how gamification and AI-enhanced engagement strategies may help children better recognize, express, and regulate emotions, ultimately fostering stronger emotional resilience and well-being.

Chapter 6, *Gamified AI Tools and Simulation Platforms for Transforming Entrepreneurial Education in South Africa*, by Sthokozile Mamba and Andrisha Ramraj, examines how AI-powered simulations and gamified learning environments can enhance entrepreneurial education. Focusing on the South African context, the chapter discusses the role of experiential learning in developing innovation, decision-making skills, and entrepreneurial competencies among youth.

Chapter 7, *Preparing Cambodian Students for Integration into AI-Driven Societies: Future Trends Toward 2050 and Beyond*, by Ry Hour and colleagues, presents a forward-looking discussion on how Cambodia can prepare future generations for participation in increasingly AI-centered societies. The authors emphasize curriculum reform, STEM and ICT literacy, teacher training, public-private partnerships, and national policy development as critical components of long-term educational transformation.

In Chapter 8, *Raising Future Innovators: AI Education for Children*, Chikesh Ranjan and co-authors discuss the importance of introducing AI concepts to children through age-appropriate and interactive learning methods. The chapter reviews global models of AI education while emphasizing hands-on learning, no-code platforms, creativity, critical thinking, and ethical awareness as foundational elements of early AI literacy.

Finally, Chapter 9, *Future Trends: Preparing Children for AI-Driven Societies of 2040 and Beyond*, by Froilan Mobo and Katarzyna Milek, provides a broad international perspective on the future of AI and education. Drawing upon educational reforms from countries leading in AI integration, the chapter explores future workforce skills, evolving teacher roles, ethical considerations, psychological implications, and policy recommendations designed to support human-centered AI education systems.

CONCLUSION

As the world enters an era increasingly shaped by intelligent technologies, education stands at the center of societal adaptation and transformation. The chapters presented in this volume collectively demonstrate that preparing children and educators for AI-driven societies requires a multifaceted approach that extends far beyond technical instruction alone. Effective preparation demands educational systems that foster ethical awareness, creativity, emotional resilience, adaptability, and inclusive access to technological opportunities. AI literacy must therefore be understood not only as a technical competency, but as a lifelong human capability grounded in critical thinking and responsible innovation.

This book also reinforces the importance of empowering educators as central agents of educational change. Teachers remain indispensable in guiding learners through the complexities of AI-enhanced environments, helping students navigate issues of fairness, trust, digital citizenship, and social responsibility. While AI technologies may automate certain processes, the human dimensions of education—empathy, mentorship, ethical reasoning, and cultural understanding—remain irreplaceable. Educational institutions and policymakers must therefore prioritize professional development, infrastructure support, and equitable access to ensure educators are fully prepared for these evolving responsibilities.

Another key insight emerging from this collection is the significance of contextual and global collaboration. Different nations face unique opportunities and challenges in integrating AI into education, yet many common themes persist across educational systems worldwide. Whether discussing Cambodia's educational reforms, South Africa's entrepreneurial simulations, or broader global curriculum innovations, the contributors collectively highlight the need for culturally responsive, inclusive, and sustainable approaches to AI education. International collaboration and knowledge sharing will continue to play a critical role in shaping equitable AI-driven futures.

Ultimately, *Preparing Children and Educators for AI-Driven Societies* serves as both a scholarly contribution and a call to action. The future of AI in education will not be determined solely by technological advancement, but by the values, policies, and educational practices we choose to embrace today. By investing in ethical, creative, and human-centered approaches to AI literacy, societies can empower future generations not only to adapt to technological change, but also to shape it responsibly and compassionately. It is our sincere hope that this volume inspires continued dialogue, research, and innovation toward building educational systems capable of supporting learners in an increasingly intelligent and interconnected world.

Chapter 1
Empowering Educators for the AI Era:
Strategies for Teaching in Intelligent Classrooms

Pawan Pant
http://orcid.org/0000-0003-1774-5650
Chandigarh University, India

Kaushal Kishore Mishra
http://orcid.org/0000-0001-6466-0575
Chandigarh University, India

ABSTRACT

The advent of Artificial Intelligence (AI) in early childhood and primary education has significantly altered the way we approach teaching and learning. As classrooms become more intelligent and adaptive, the role of the educator continues to evolve from 'teaching' to 'facilitating,' 'personalising,' and 'technologically fluent.' For example, this chapter advocates for the need for us to help educators develop the knowledge, skills, and attitudes they will need to thrive in AI-powered educational contexts. This chapter also proposes an understanding of AI literacy for teachers. It details the significant aspects, including ethical reasoning, digital fluency, and critical interaction with other AI tools, which would help facilitate effective classroom practice. By drawing on effective international models, case studies, and examples of pedagogy, this chapter proposes a framework for professional development that is suitable for both pre-service educators and experienced educators alike.

DOI: 10.4018/979-8-2600-2438-6.ch001

INTRODUCTION

The emergence of artificial intelligence (AI) in education is rapidly shaping the nature of teaching and learning at all levels, including childhood and primary education. Considering the domain of higher education and technical fields, AI is now ubiquitous in everyday life through adaptive learning platforms, intelligent tutoring systems, voice assistants, automated assessments, and data-driven feedback mechanisms (Holmes et al., 2022). These emerging technologies are expected to enhance personal learning, increase student participation, and allow for a more inclusive education with the capacity to identify personal learning requirements in real-time (Luckin et al., 2016). However, this involves a significant shift in the role and responsibilities of teachers.

Teachers are no longer simply transmitters of knowledge but are also expected to act as facilitators, mentors, and important intermediaries between AI technologies and students. This role will enable teachers to develop robust AI literacy, defined as the "ability to understand, evaluate, and responsibly use educational AI devices in a scholarly and ethical context" (Long & Magco, 2020). Without adequate preparation, teachers may either underutilize AI or use it to develop student work that does not support important thinking, creativity, or student agency. Additionally, the increasing prevalence of AI in classrooms raises real concerns regarding data privacy, algorithmic bias, and the equitable distribution of educational resources (UNESCO, 2021). Although the need for teacher readiness is recognized, teacher education programs often fail to adequately prepare teachers for classes that incorporate AI (Zawack-Richter et al., 2019). Similarly, for professional learning to be needed and effective, we must take a holistic approach to training across what we call intervals—an approach that marries moral understanding, educational improvement, ongoing learning, and technical skills.

This chapter aims to address this immediate need by providing guidance to support teacher empowerment in the age of AI. It defines significant AI competencies, presents models of effective professional development, explores instructional equipment and methods, and analyzes the challenges and opportunities involved. Through a synthesis of global research studies, insights, and practical recommendations, this chapter contributes to a forward-thinking vision of teaching in intelligent classrooms, where technology enhances rather than diminishes the teacher's role.

UNDERSTANDING AI LITERACY FOR EDUCATORS

As artificial intelligence (AI) technologies continue to impact the educational environment, it is important for teachers, not only technologists or administrators, to have a strong and nuanced understanding of AI. This requirement has led to the concept of AI literacy, a fundamental skill that enables teachers to connect not only with users of AI but also to inform the design of AI-enhanced learning environments (Turnski et al., 2019; Long & Magco, 2020) as evaluators, facilities, and evaluands.

A. AI Define Literacy

AI literacy can be roughly defined as the ability to understand what artificial intelligence (AI) is, how it operates, how it is applied in various domains, and the moral and social implications it carries (Long & Magco, 2020). Unlike digital literacy, which emphasizes the ability to use digital tools and navigate the online environment, AI deepens its understanding of the sociotechnic systems behind AI literacy algorithm processes, machine learning logic, data patterns, and AI technologies. For teachers, this means that to gain a basic understanding of areas such as pattern recognition, decision trees, and neural networks, it involves understanding how AI systems learn and make predictions (Ng, 2012). It also involves understanding how AI affects the learning environment, for example, by enabling adaptive teaching platforms, generating real-time analysis, and providing personalized material distribution (Holmes et al., 2022). Teachers should be able to evaluate the capabilities and limitations of AI tools, especially in relation to issues such as algorithm bias, lack of transparency, and data secrecy (UNESCO, 2021).

B. Dimensions of AI literacy in terms of class

AI literacy for teachers encompasses three mutually related dimensions:

Cognitive dimension

Developing AI literacy involves understanding the underlying logic of the AI tool, explaining the algorithm's output, and cultivating a degree of data literacy. Although teachers are not expected to become programmers or data scientists, it is necessary to understand how data affects the behavior and decisions made by the AI system used in educational contexts (Zawacki-Richter et al., 2019). This involves recognizing the patterns in student data that are used to personalize adaptive teaching platform materials or flag at-risk learners. By understanding these procedures, teachers can make an alternative to when and how to use AI-operated technologies, seriously question their output, and guide students in explaining algorithm decisions

Educational Dimensions

AI literacy should be embedded within a robust academic framework to ensure that its application enhances, rather than detracts from, educational goals. It is not enough for teachers to understand only how AI works; they should also be able to determine when and how to employ AI tools that support learning objectives, promote equity, and empower students to take agency. For example, while AI chatbots can provide individual language practice through immediate responses and adaptive inquiries, their use must be complemented by colleagues, replacing cooperative learning experiences such as dialogues and teacher-directed discussions (Lakkin et al., 2016).

Moral and social dimensions

Teachers play a crucial role in guiding students to engage with the social and moral dimensions of artificial intelligence (AI), including issues such as data privacy, algorithm bias, and the impact on employment (Jobin et al., 2019). In the A-Nhens learning environment, students rapidly interact with technologies that gather, analyze, and function on personal data, often without a clear understanding of how or why decisions are made or why (Campa, 2019). . Therefore, teachers are required to facilitate age-appropriate interactions about fairness, transparency, accountability, and human values, which are often neglected in AI systems. For example, simple orbit activities can help illustrate how the voice interprets information in different ways with auxiliary accents, introducing the concept of algorithm bias in an accessible way. By embedding moral literacy within AI literacy, teachers not only help students become capable users of AI technologies but also develop into reflective and responsible digital citizens. As UNESCO (2021) has emphasized, it is necessary to understand a generation capable of understanding and shaping AI in a socially beneficial way to integrate moral awareness from the early stages of formal education.

C. Why AI literacy is important for initial and primary teachers

While AI is often introduced at secondary or higher education levels, there is growing evidence that AI helps children become more aware of the digital world and better prepared for future learning. This makes the teacher's role more important. In early and primary settings, AI literacy is not only about adopting technology - it is about promoting curiosity, facilitating exploration, and ensuring that technology complements rather than replaces human contact and creativity.

In addition, young children can create anthropomorphic beliefs about the AI system (eg, considering smart speakers as “think”), which makes it important to guide teachers in understanding the nature and limits of AI for teachers, in which it can do and do not do what it can.

D. AI Framework and Benchmark for Literacy

Several major educational organizations have presented outlines to support and guide the development of AI literacy among teachers. The OECD's AI qualification structure not only emphasizes the technical understanding of how AI systems function but also has broad social, moral, and educational implications. Teachers play a crucial role in teaching and learning processes (OECD, 2021a). Similarly, the MIT Raise initiative (AI responsible for social empowerment and education) provides structured, age-appropriate resources for teachers, which help them present AI concepts to young learners through accessible and morally grounded materials (MIT Raise, 2020a). In a related vein, Touretzky et al. (2019) argue that AI literacy should be considered a fundamental ability, stating that every child—and, in detail, every teacher — should understand how AI systems perceive their environment, learn from data, and make decisions. Across these frameworks, they collectively emphasize that AI literacy is not solely a technical or silent skill, but a transdisciplinary competency, distinct from computer science, ethics, media literacy, and education. Thus, developing AI literacy in teachers will be a comprehensive approach that encompasses ideological understandings, as well as practical, ethical, and experiential elements.

CORE COMPETENCIES FOR TEACHING IN AI-ENHANCED CLASSROOMS

As artificial intelligence (AI) continues to augment classes with a variety of tools, from the ADPEVLENT platform and chatbots to predictive analytics and robot-assisted tools, teachers' roles are undergoing significant evolution. AI-augmented classes will require more than familiarity with digital devices; they will require a sophisticated combination of technical, educational, ethical, and reflective capacities. The blend of these core capabilities encapsulates A-Taiyar teaching and must be engaged with to deliver AI in a context that promotes meaningful, inclusive, and responsible learning (Holmes et al., 2023; Luckin et al., 2016).

A. AI's technical and conceptual understanding

To effectively integrate AI into their teaching methods, teachers should have a fundamental understanding of how AI systems, algorithms, and technologies operate in relation to students' learning data. Importantly, the intention would not be for teachers to operate as data scientists. A baseline teacher understanding of core ideas, such as machine learning, pattern recognition, and algorithms, is essential to facilitate teacher decision-making. This involves understanding how AI systems learn from data, the types of data collected (e.g., clickstream, response accuracy, and time), and how output decisions—such as material recommendations or performance alerts—are generated. For example, assuming an adaptive teaching platform adjusts its suggestions based on a student's prior performance, it enables teachers to assess whether such adaptation supports educational goals or inadvertently ends learning intervals. This knowledge empowers teachers to critically evaluate AI-generated insights rather than accepting them at face value. As long as Magco (2020) argues, "teachers require an ideological model of AI to attach to these tools meaningfully and make educational decisions, which is not understood, nor respected." In this way, AI literacy enables teachers to act as informed intermediaries between intelligent systems and student learning.

B. Educational Integration

AI should not determine education; rather, education should guide the thoughtful and purposeful integration of AI devices in the classroom. Teachers need to develop the ability to include AI in text plans by aligning its characteristics with clear instructional purposes. This involves using AI to separate instructions, such as customizing the content of individual learners or materials for learning, while ensuring that these adaptations support broad educational goals. For example, while AI platforms can scaffold reading tasks by adjusting the level of complexity based on the learner's performance, they should be combined with teacher-facilitated discussions, which cultivate understanding, empathy, and critical thinking. AI, in its present form, cannot replace AI (IBM, 2023). AI-enhanced classes also require a design thinking mentality for effective education, in which teachers actively experiment with AI devices, students respond and react, and adjust their directive strategies accordingly. This reflective approach keeps teachers as co-designers of the learning process, ensuring that the use of AI is based on the creator, sociological, and developmental principles (Zawaki-Richter et al., 2019).

C. Ethical and important thinking efficiency

One of the most pressing competencies for teachers in the AI era is moral literacy, the ability to identify and address complex moral challenges generated by AI technologies in educational settings. As AI technology becomes a standard part of the learning environment, educators must be trained to recognize and mitigate biases in algorithms, such as those related to race, gender, or language, that impact the equality and inclusivity of automated decision-making systems. They must also be aware of challenges related to student names and data privacy, specifically the collection of granular behavioral and performance data captured by AI. Educators should be able to demand disclosure and accountability from the AI system, ensuring that the decisions made by intelligent software (e.g., automated grading, personalization of content) have transparent and accountable rationales that can be studied or traced back. This social and moral efficiency not only protects students from bias, discrimination, and harassment but also presents opportunities for teachers to educate students as an integral part of digital citizenship advocacy by equipping learners with the appropriate tools to engage in conversations about AI social influence. For example, classroom conversations may help students determine whether facial identification software treats all students equally or whether algorithmic grading systems have considered creativity and other references. Integrating these types of conversations into learning will enhance the moral awareness of the next generation as AI-literate citizens (UNESCO, 2021).

D. Cultural and Inclusive Awareness

AI technologies are often premised on assumptions that cannot do justice to the linguistic, cultural, or cognitive diversity that exists in the world. This means that AI devices can unintentionally marginalize students whose language practices, lived experiences, or learning profiles fall outside of the normative data that informs AI devices during training. Consequently, teachers should actively explore how AI devices are shaping students' approaches to diversity to assess whether they have culturally affirming or suppressing effects on learning and learning processes. This means advocating for the use of AI devices that are culturally responsible, linguistically inclusive, and designed in accordance with universal accessibility principles. In addition, teachers should actively ensure that the use of AI does not exacerbate existing educational inequalities, especially in resource-constrained or multilingual contexts, where inadequate localized AI equipment risks deepening the digital divide. For example, if the AI-operated reading app fails to accommodate local dialects or non-home languages, it can do more harm than good, rather than empowering students. Crescenzi-Lanna Et Al. (2021) Emphasis, obtaining equity in A-Sammedic Education not only requires technical adaptation, but also a deep educational commitment to inclusion and justice.

E. Flirting and lifetime learning orientation

Given the rapid development of artificial intelligence (AI) innovation, no single or static training program can adequately prepare teachers for all future challenges. For example, AI-enhanced classes offer teachers lifelong professional learning opportunities. These practices should include ongoing habits of self-confidence, as well as continuous assessment of the importance of AI devices and their impact on student engagement, equity, and outcomes. Teachers should remain informed about the future of technology and education by connecting with broader fields of study, such as data science, psychology, and digital ethics. Collaboration in professional teaching communities, including AI-focused teacher networks and associated platforms, further supports the ability to share teachers' solutions, mitigate problems, and co-generate best practices. Most importantly, teachers should adopt a mindset of experimentation and revision, recognizing that there is no single, definitive, or permanently optimal strategy for AI integration. As AI tools, classes, and students evolve, teachers' dispositions should include dedication to professional curiosity, intentional reflection, and human-centered education.

Table 1. Summary Table: Core Competencies for AI-Enhanced Teaching

Competency Domain	Description	Example in Practice
Technical Understanding	Understand basic AI concepts, data use, and algorithmic behaviour	Explaining how an adaptive quiz adjusts questions in real-time
Pedagogical Integration	Align AI tools with instructional goals and learner needs	Using an AI platform to differentiate instruction in math
Ethical Reasoning	Identify and mitigate bias, protect privacy, and foster transparency	Discussing algorithmic fairness with students
Inclusivity & Equity	Use AI tools that support diverse learners and equitable access	Choosing an AI writing assistant that supports multiple languages
Reflective Practice	Continuously assess AI's classroom role and adapt accordingly	Journaling AI tool impact and revising lesson strategies
Lifelong Learning	Stay updated on AI trends and develop skills iteratively	Enrolling in an online AI in education course

The table identifies the six key qualification domains essential for teachers operating in an A-NHNS teaching situation, demonstrating a framework that combines theoretical aspects of AI with practical applications of this technology. We begin with technical knowledge, which includes basic principles of AI, such as how data is used and changes in the algorithm(s) behavior in real-time, and considerations of fairness in the AI (e.g., transparency as an example). Inclusion and equity underscore the importance of utilizing AI tools that cater to a diverse group of learners. For instance, when employing a writing assistant, it is essential to select one that is specifically designed for multilingual support. Reflective practice encourages teachers to continually assess the use of AI in the classroom, including its effects, and adapt any textual strategies they may employ. Finally, lifelong learning involves continuing to enhance skill level through PD, e.g. by taking or participating in PD courses about AI that expert teachers lead. Taken together, these domains enhance the view that successfully integrating AI in education is not simply technology use, but also building educated, knowledgeable, and adaptable teachers.

PROFESSIONAL DEVELOPMENT MODELS FOR AI INTEGRATION

As shown in the diagram, the professional development of AI integration can be visualized as a continuum from structured formal learning experiences to informal, flexible pathways. This approach reflects the dynamic and evolving nature of AI technology, where teachers benefit not only from certification programs but also from community-based learning and ongoing personal investigation.

> *"In the era of rapid technological changes, it is necessary to integrate educationally into AI to prepare teachers for continuous and flexible professional development (Zawacki-Richter et al., 2019).*

Figure 1. AI Integration Professional Development Ranges from Formal to Informal

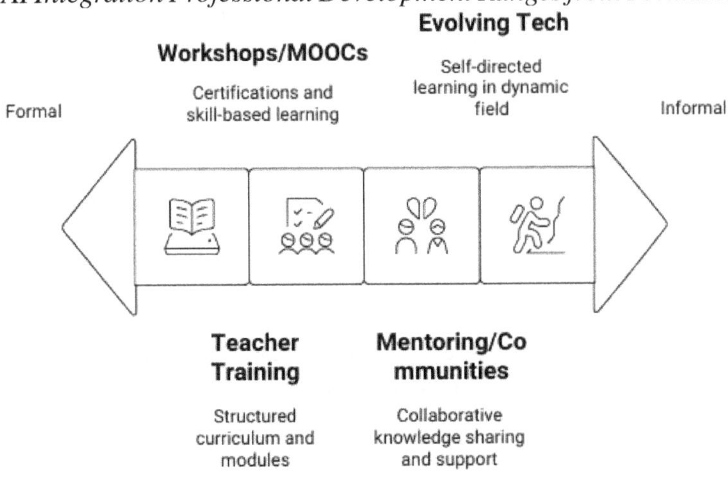

A. Formal business development

Workshops and massive open online courses (MOOCs) represent professional development opportunities that are being rapidly utilized to create AI competencies among teachers. It is usually introduced by universities, educational technology companies, or global organizations, these programs address a series of necessary subjects including educational applications such as technical functioning of AI system, personal learning and intelligent tuition systems and intelligent tuition systems such as educational applications and algorithms prejudice and data secrecy and data secrecy and data secrecy and data secrecy and data secrecy (Tuomi, 2018; Zawacki-Richter et al., 2019). Participants often receive completion or micro-credential certificates, which can be used to continue their progress toward professional education credits or career advancement. Notable examples include IBM's AI education chain, which introduces teachers to AI concepts through hands-on activities, and the AI+ethics courses offered by MIT Rise, designed to help K–12 teachers integrate AI education responsibly into their classes (IBM, 2023). These offerings are highly scalable and accessible, making them particularly valuable for reaching diverse teacher populations across various geographical and economic contexts (Holmes et al., 2022). However, a central limitation is that such programmes can be highly theoretical, providing limited opportunities for relevant class exercises or personal advice. For example, while MOOCs and AI-driven workshops create an important component of professional learning ecosystems, they are most effective when complemented by practice-based or community-operated models that strengthen applicable learning and local adaptation (MIT RAISE, 2020a).

B. Teacher training program

Teacher training programs, whether preservice or inservice professional development initiatives, represent one of the most structured and practice-oriented models for creating AI readiness among teachers. These programs typically include course-acquired modules that integrate AI literacy into broader digital education or educational technology courses. They provide training on hand-circulating equipment, such as AI-interested education assistants, chatbots, adaptive learning platforms, and intelligent assessment systems. A significant strength of this approach is its focus on educational arguments, enabling teachers to seriously evaluate how, when, and why the use of AI devices can meet specific learning outcomes and address the needs of relevant classes. As Luckin et al. (2016) emphasize, " the teacher's academic purpose must be before the technical function of AI equipment," underlining the importance of intentions in instructional design. Teacher education programs based on this philosophy help future teachers develop a thoughtful and moral attitude toward adopting AI. The primary advantage of this model lies in its deep alignment with teaching practice and course goals. However, these programs are often slow to develop in response to rapidly emerging AI technologies because of institutional obstacles and course intervals (Tuomi, 2018; Holmes et al., 2022). Therefore, while teacher training is fundamental, it should be complemented by more tight forms of ongoing professional learning.

C. Community of practice and practice

Formal courses and self-directed learning represent an important medium for AI-related professional development, situated between advice and professional communities. These collaborative teaching environments include colleague mentoring programs, online educator networks (e.g., #Iliteracyed, ISTE forum), and lesson plans, implementation strategies, and community-based platforms to share important reflections. They promote horizontal knowledge transfer, allowing teachers to learn from each other's real-world experiences, including both successful practices and practical challenges in the A-Nhens Classroom. This approach is based on the principle of communities of practice, where professional learning is social, relevant, and continuous over time. As Wengar (1998) and Holmes et al. (2022) emphasize, such communities encourage "reflective dialogues, experiments, and recurrence" to effectively integrate emerging technologies, such as AI, into teaching. This colleague-backed environment provides high relevance and adaptability, remarkably unlike more generalized training models. However, for them to be effective, there must be active engagement, a time commitment, and a culture of trust and openness. In an environment that supports them institutionally, these communities become powerful engines for building capacity and innovating in education.

D. Informal and self-directed learning

The less formal end of the business development continuum is focused on self-directed learning, as defined by the rapid development of artificial intelligence (AI) tools and practices. With this model, the starting point for the learning experience comprises personal interest, immediate classroom needs, and the desire to retain agency over technological innovations. Teachers often find their engagement in activities such as reading educational publications, using updates related to edtech trends on blogs and social media, or leveraging specific devices that directly chat, including Khanmigo and Squirrel AI. These tools offer possibilities for real-time incorporation into the class through features such as automatic responses, personalized instructions and learning, and AI-assisted instruction (Holmes et al., 2022; Luckin et al., 2016). This self-directed mode of practice enables teachers to modify their practices more quickly than through any formal program, often leading to innovation, experimentation, and professional autonomy. As Long and Magerko (2020) argued, it is "important to remember that self-directed professional learning supports agency and innovation, a critical capability as we begin to compete with the rapid pace of AI development." Tumi (2018) noted that professionals have more adaptive teaching and learning practices that enable better evaluation and response to new educational technologies when engaged in informal spaces. However, there are also challenges associated with adopting this informal approach to teaching. The loss of structure, potential variability in quality related to the information sources used, and the likelihood of adopting poorly designed or biased AI devices can all create limitations on how AI can be used effectively in education (Zawacki-Richter et al., 2019; Williamson & Eynon, 2020).

Table 2. Summary of Developmental Spectrum

Mode	Formality	Focus	Example
Workshops/MOOCs	High	Skill-building, certification	MIT RAISE, IBM AI EdX, Google AI for Educators
Teacher Training Programs	High	Curriculum integration, pedagogy	Pre-service AI modules, CPD programs
Mentoring/Communities	Moderate	Collaboration, knowledge sharing	ISTE, online forums, peer mentoring
Evolving Tech/Self-study	Low	Adaptive, real-time exploration	Following AI news, trying new classroom tools

INSTRUCTIONAL STRATEGIES AND TOOLS FOR AI INTEGRATION

Educators must ensure that the utilization of AI, in particular, AI tools, aligns with student-centred pedagogical practices that encourage active learning, personalization, and exploration. The graphic "Enhancing Education with AI" illustrates the intersection of AI, personalized learning, and inquiry-based learning, depicting the collaborative enhancement of these three pedagogical dimensions and the potential to improve student learning. A description of these educational components and their implications is provided below.

Figure 2. Enhancing Education with AI

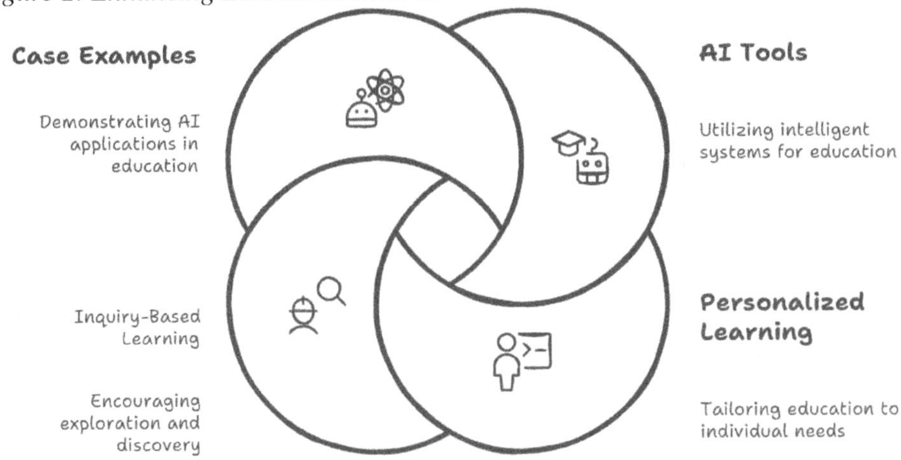

A. AI Tools: Understanding Intelligent Systems for Education

AI tools are increasingly being integrated into modern classrooms, functioning as empathetic intermediaries for personalized, efficient, and scalable learning experiences. As intelligent systems, they rely on data analytics and algorithms to automate routine teaching, customize adaptive learning pathways, and respond in real-time when students are engaged in learning. For example, tools such as Gradescope and Numbas alleviate educators of grading and feedback responsibilities. They provide educators' responses in a timely manner while lessening the administrative workload (Luckin et al., 2016; Holmes et al., 2022). AI-enabled adaptive systems, such as Squirrel AI and DreamBox Learning, assist educators with instructional resources tailored to students' learning progress, emphasizing the importance of individualized instruction that would otherwise require extensive effort to arrange (Zawacki-Richter et al., 2019). Simultaneously, conversational agents such as ChatGPT, Khanmigo, and the Duolingo bots are also increasingly operational as on-demand tutors or agents of educational opportunity, facilitating iterative learning through conversation and scaffolding (Tuomi, 2018). New features of AI that utilize speech recognition, language processing, and translation capabilities can reinforce inclusivity, particularly in linguistically diverse classroom contexts or support learners with special educational needs (Williamson & Eynon, 2020). If implemented purposefully in systematic ways, AI tools allow teachers time and space, as repetitive activities are offloaded, teachers increase their understanding of student data and performance, and devote more time and energy to human-centered and educational tasks of teaching that draw on human traits, such as inspiring students, mentoring, and building relationships. As Luckin and colleagues point out, we do not want to even imagine replacing educators, but rather augmenting them–"freeing up teachers to do what humans best do: inspire, empathize, and connect" (Luckin et al., 2016).

B. Personalizing Learning: Adjusting Education to Individualized Needs

Increasingly, AI-driven educational platforms are offering personalized learning approaches by considering student behaviors, performance patterns, and engagement. These systems permit a range of pacing for accelerated learning, timely intervention in targeted learning, and adjustment of content as required to align with learners' preferences, cognitive levels, or learning styles (Holmes et al., 2022; Luckin et al., 2016). For example, tools such as Lexia and Microsoft's Reading Progress converge several real-time diagnostics to measure fluency and comprehension, enabling the adjustment of instruction according to the student's measured needs. Similarly, there are adaptive mathematics tools, such as DreamBox and Carnegie Learning. These utilize predictive analytics and reinforcement learning principles to determine the difficulty of learning tasks and provide appropriate scaffolding (Zawacki-Richter et al., 2019). While this technological advancement enhances an instructor's ability to respond to student needs, teachers must remain critically active mediators, ensuring that the personalization demanded by the algorithms does not position students for total pedagogical isolation. Excessive reliance on AI has the potential to short-change socio-emotional learning, joint work, and collaborative teacher–student work — the very things central to inclusive education (Williamson & Eynon, 2020; UNESCO, 2021). As stated by UNESCO (2021), AI should be leveraged to complement differentiated instruction, not replace it. The best use of AI-enhanced learning occurs when AI can exist alongside human-directed pedagogy, as teachers have the support to foster empathy, creativity, and holistic student learning, while adhering to data-informed decisions regarding their instruction.

C. Inquiry-based Learning: Encouraging Exploration and Discovery

Inquiry-based learning (IBL) pedagogy is based on student curiosity, exploration, and intuitive critical thinking. IBL presents a strong opportunity to incorporate artificial intelligence (AI) tools into educational platforms. IBL prompts learners to ask questions, problem-solve, and explore based on their discoveries and interests, similar to the values that technologies powered by AI enable. AI systems may support IBL by generating open-ended prompts from students' past interests, visualizing complex simulations (such as multiple dimensions and representations in mathematics or science simulations), and scaffolding the cognitive process with consistent feedback and adaptive approaches to problem solving (Luckin et al., 2016; Holmes et al., 2022). Some AI systems have dual uses for learners, such as Google's Teachable Machine and IBM Watson Assistant for Education. These AI applications allow students to immediately engage with concepts of AI to create simple machine learning models. This practice not only enhances digital literacy but also provides learners with the opportunity to develop computational thinking, systems thinking, and creativity (Druga et al., 2017). As Holmes et al. (2022) state, "AI systems may facilitate inquiry by enabling a dynamic environment that allows learners to interact with information in responsive, unpredictable, and nonlinear ways," which essentially turns passive learning into active knowledge construction. While technology can help elevate and facilitate IBL, it cannot do so without the instructional design of the teacher. Although there is a pedagogical structure in IBL, the teacher remains the architect of exploratory learning environments. Any complexities of technology must be balanced with pedagogical clarity (Tuomi, 2018).

D. Examples of Cases: Showcasing Applications of AI in Education

Well-articulated case-based examples provide real-world insights into how artificial intelligence can facilitate the intersection of technological functionality, pedagogical intention, and student-centred learning. For example, AI-based early literacy interventions, such as SoapBox Labs, a voice recognition-based tool that examines young children's reading fluency and pronunciation. This tool enables phonics-based instruction that aligns with individual speech patterns across a diverse group of early language learners and allows students with varying linguistic capabilities to benefit from inclusive learning (Holmes et al., 2022). In mathematics, there have been contributions to AI from systems. One such example is Carnegie Learning's MATHia platform. This intelligent tutoring system provides individualized and customized instruction while responding to the student with immediate feedback after identifying the errors made by learners, resulting in a method of learning in which the learner is engaged through "deliberate practice" and conceptual reinforcement, all aligned within the framework of "constructivist learning theory" (Luckin et al., 2016). Fortunately, an AI-enhanced coding lab, such as Scratch blocks with ML extensions, enables young learners to explore AI concepts while developing foundational computational thinking skills. These environments combine creative, logical, and inquiry-based practices, all of which enable students to build and test models, observe the results, and learn from iterations in an enjoyable and engaging environment (Druga et al., 2017).

Table 3. Integrative Teaching Implications

Instructional Focus	AI-Supported Application	Teacher's Role
AI Tools	Adaptive platforms, chatbots, translation apps	Select, monitor, and adapt tool usage
Personalized Learning	Learner analytics, tailored content, and progress tracking	Diagnose needs and contextualise insights
Inquiry-Based Learning	AI-based simulations, voice assistants, ML experiments	Facilitate exploration and critical thinking

ISSUES AND SOLUTIONS TO AI IN THE CLASSROOM

Although the opportunities for education with artificial intelligence (AI) are exciting, especially in early and primary education, the application of AI presents several challenges. These challenges are not only technological but also pedagogical, ethical, infrastructural, and psychological. To take advantage of the opportunities afforded through AI-supported education, it is necessary to first establish and proactively address these hurdles with practical solutions grounded in existing literature and practices.

A. Teacher Lack of Preparedness and Literacy in AI

Research increasingly suggests that many teachers lack the necessary preparation to teach students about artificial intelligence (AI), partly due to issues of technical fluency and a lack of pedagogical growth (Zawacki-Richter et al., 2019). In the absence of a framework for foundational AI literacy, technology may be misapplied; in the worst-case scenario, teachers may choose to "disengage" or avoid implementing new educational technology altogether due to feeling unsure or afraid about how to make sense of it. Consequently, several researchers and practitioners have advocated for the urgent establishment of AI education in pre-service teacher education and in-service professional development (Long & Magerko, 2020). These initiatives should not stop at developing unconnected

Workshops should aspire to create professional learning opportunities that are modular, scalable, and practice-based, with the ability to demonstrate objective evidence of classroom use. For instance, practical toolkits, sandbox spaces, and lesson task simulations can encourage educators to experience the technology and connect theory to practice. Peer-to-peer mentoring, practitioner inquiry as a form of teacher professional development, and professional learning communities have the potential to promote confidence, reflection, and sustained engagement with AI technology.

For example, Holmes et al. (2022) state, "professional development needs to move beyond developing technical skills and engage teachers as co-designers of teaching pedagogy using AI, " indicating professional agency and not only performing hastily. Ultimately, it is key to focus on enabling educators to employ AI critically and creatively in context, thereby responsibly and ethically integrating AI into education.

B. Ethical and Privacy Considerations

As AI becomes more integrated into educational contexts, ethical considerations surrounding data collection, algorithm-driven decision-making, and surveillance have become critical issues, particularly when involving younger learners who may not fully comprehend or consent to the use of their data. The application of AI technologies is inevitably tied to further ongoing collection, processing, and storage of student data, which raises thorny issues related to privacy, informed consent, algorithmic bias, and data protection (UNESCO, 2021; Williamson & Eynnon, 2020). Without strong safeguards, these technologies risk entrenching social inequities; therefore, ethical considerations and data governance best practices will be vital elements of any educational AI strategy. To combat these risks, institutions will need to adopt transparent data governance policies and ethical frameworks that ensure any AI system used in school environments considers fair and accountable AI that is transparent and explainable to students, caregivers, and the broader community (Holmes et al., 2022). Professional development for teachers should focus on the decision-making practices of AI systems to uncover possible biases underlying these decisions, enabling teachers to convey the potential implications of these decisions to students and caregivers. This professional development for teachers should encourage the adoption of explainable AI (XAI), which can make the thinking behind algorithmic decisions transparent in a digestible format. Luckin et al. (2016) point out that educators "must be ethical stewards of the data within AI-enhanced environments," which reconciles the possibilities of innovation with the responsibilities of duty. Developing ethical literacy for teachers is crucial for clearly determining the use of AI in ways that prioritize inclusiveness, trust, and learning, presenting the child as the focal point rather than unintentionally undermining these constructs.

C. Infrastructural Barriers and Digital Inequity

An effective AI integration into educational settings is, first and foremost, reliant on dependable digital infrastructures, including access to broadband, hardware, and consistent technology support.

However, many low-resource, rural, or underserved schools still lack this basic setup, which presents a substantial challenge to adopting AI. - and may exacerbate educational inequities (UNESCO, 2021; OECD, 2021c). Without equitable access, AI-enhanced learning can become a privilege reserved for learners who are already privileged, thereby widening the digital divide. Policymakers need to increase their directed investments in digital infrastructure, either through government-sponsored or NGO-led plans, to achieve connectivity in marginalized geographies and access to hardware. Furthermore, low-cost mobile AI tools that operate offline or with minimal bandwidth — such as lightweight chatbots, educational apps installed directly on the device, or speech-enabled reading tools (Tuomi, 2018; Holmes et al., 2022) — can also help bridge the technology and access gap. Public-private partnerships are also significant provisions for subsidizing access to AI learning platforms and can help by stimulating new learning possibilities that address local needs. The OECD (2021a) reminds us that "AI needs not to widen the digital divide and provide alternative opportunities for equitable learning." For AI to support equitable learning, it should provide fair access to technology and teaching practices that respond to each learner's needs, thereby enabling AI to meet the needs of all learners, regardless of their location or socioeconomic status.

D. Time Constraints and Curriculum Load

Many optimistic educational pathways have emerged from the growth of AI in education; however, many teachers are finding themselves hindered by the practical constraints of adapting their pedagogical practice or effectively implementing AI into classroom practice. Teachers face immense time pressures with complex workloads, dense curricula, and accountability pressures. Schools often restrict the time and resources available to educators for learning, adapting, and innovating with new technologies (Kimmons et al., 2020a; Holmes et al., 2022). Without external support, new tools like AI can be seen as something that does not support educators but is just another impediment. Therefore, a meaningful AI implementation scheme must not impede or reform educators' existing pedagogical psychology but instead provide alternative methods to support and engage them and integrate them into their existing practice. This could happen by embedding AI as an additional supporting mechanism across any discipline to enhance specific skills, such as reading comprehension, numeracy fluency, or formative assessments, rather than viewing AI as another discipline to learn (Tuomi, 2018). With regard to learning from their experience with AI, organizations can make adaptable lessons and templates, or develop contextual use cases and intuitive instructional design guides, which could help mitigate learning burdens (Luckin et al., 2016). Support from administration is also essential, for educational and leadership recognition, or so that the teachers have a legitimate period to expand their skills using AI and new resources for experimentation rather than 'faulting' educators for the unknowns with AI for not being fully in control of their pedagogical psychology. Kimmons et al. (2020b) pointed out that "integration of AI needs to be integrated organically into teaching practices, rather than in opposition," clarifying that being aligned with the workflows of teachers and the realities of classrooms is necessary for a viable future.

E. Pedagogy Misalignment

AI has enormous potential to enhance personalization and efficiency in education. However, concerns remain about how AI may align with other aspects of developmentally appropriate pedagogy, particularly for young children in early childhood and primary learning spaces. Many AI systems have been created and developed from the perspective of automation, task optimization, and efficiency, which may considerably restrict necessary learning aims and goals, such as creativity, collaboration, and socio-emotional learning, which are significant parts of holistic education (OECD, 2021b; Holmes et al., 2022). This tension is especially acute for younger learners, where play-based learning, exploratory dialogue, and emotional scaffolding are at the nucleus of growth. To mitigate these risks, it is essential to consider which AI is selected for learning and whether it provides formative feedback, supports open-ended inquiry and learner agency, or relies on rote instruction and passive consumption (Zawacki-Richter et al., 2019). The idea is to develop a human-AI partnership in which learning is enhanced, rather than replaced, in a social context by AI-based technologies. Teachers, caregivers, and peers remain vital in developing empathy, ethical behavior, and social competency—skills that contemporary AI cannot replicate.

Table 4. Summary Table: Challenges and Strategic Solutions

Challenge	Strategic Solution
Teacher Unpreparedness	Embed AI literacy in teacher training and foster peer learning communities.
Ethical/Privacy Risks	Utilize ethical AI guidelines, train teachers in data ethics, and implement transparent AI practices.
Infrastructure Gaps	Invest low-cost tools, public-private partnerships, and scalable tech infrastructure.
Time and Curriculum Overload	Provide implementation support, templates, and planning time for teachers.
Pedagogical Misalignment	Co-design AI tools with teachers; prioritise human-centred, formative AI applications

CASE STUDIES AND GLOBAL BEST PRACTICES

Local education systems, policy frameworks, current infrastructure levels, and teacher preparation systems influence the successful integration of AI in classrooms. From a global perspective, educational professionals and policymakers can identify scalable, ethical, and pedagogy-centred approaches by sourcing global cases and best practices. The examples below illustrate a range of approaches to AI use in various geographies, age groups, and school systems, primarily in early and primary education.

A. Adaptive Learning in Chinese Primary Schools (Squirrel AI)

Overview

Squirrel AI is one of the largest adaptive learning platforms in the world. The platform is based on machine learning methodologies to create personalized learning experiences in subjects such as mathematics and English, utilizing micro-level diagnostic tests to identify key learning problems.

Best Practices

Upcoming best practices in AI education are demonstrating the ways in which technology can enhance and augment traditional learning, particularly through technology that supports personalized, data-informed learning and hybrid pedagogical pathways. Recently, micro-targeted teaching has emerged, in which AI platforms can analyze students and identify learning gaps, using adaptive algorithms to redirect students back to an earlier learning path immediately. Such high levels of personalization support mastery learning and alleviate cognitive burden by providing content in a student's zone of proximal development (Holmes et al., 2022). Teacher-facing dashboards—such as those utilized by Knewton or DreamBox—go a step further, with data presented in real-time, allowing teachers to monitor student progress, identify patterns, and act on insights (Luckin et al., 2016). The shift from summative to formative assessment, informed by this information, exploits the potential of usable data in the moment of the assessment. The blended learning model is inspiring because it incorporates AI support into instruction from the start, and a human teacher facilitates and supports students' learning throughout the process. In this model, AI controls content delivery and low-stakes assessment, while the teacher role(s) provides emotional support, clarifies misconceptions, and facilitates collaborative social learning (Tuomi, 2018; Holmes et al., 2022). This hybrid maintains the credibility and flexibility of human educators while also offering efficiency and scalability. Hence, in relation to learning spaces, these hybrid examples can be thought of as prototypes of how artificial intelligence can enrich learning rather than replace human educators, thereby supporting the design of equitable and responsive learning spaces when they are developed based on pedagogy.

Impact

Recent work has demonstrated that some AI-assisted adaptive learning models can lead to further learning efficiencies and eliminate the need for remediation in students, particularly when embedded in classroom teaching practices. For example, Zhang et al. (2021) found that students were able to master content faster and required fewer remedial supports when working with AI-supported platforms in the context of science and mathematics. These efficiencies and speedy learning pathways for students have arisen due to instructional models with built-in data feedback loops and differentiated, individualized learning pathways developed by AI models, which enable directors to optimize pacing, content ordering, and lesson planning based on analytics. Given the efficiencies shown in students' learning pathways, several states have begun to rethink their teacher education programs to prepare teachers' pedagogies for teaching with adaptive technologies (Holmes et al., 2022). This rethinking encompasses how to utilize technologies, how to interpret and utilize data, and how to integrate these data into lesson planning pathways and hybrid learning models. As Luckin et al. (2016) describe, the goal is to develop pedagogical fluency in AI systems, whereby teachers understand the balance of using AI and recognizing the limitations of personalized, human-centered teaching. This approach signals a shift toward a broader spectrum of data-informed teaching, where pedagogical solutions are guided, rather than determined, by technology.

Takeaway

A significant takeaway from current research and practice is that the application of AI in education should be practical, depending on how the role is partitioned between technology and educators. With AI as a tutor (delivering content, measuring progress, personalising feedback, etc.) Teachers would be able to alleviate the anxieties of content-specific instruction, enabling them to pursue being what they cannot be replaced for, as mentors, facilitators (working collaboratively), and emotional support figures. Labor is upheld— and the instruction of the human-centered role of empathy, ethical judgement, and socio-emotional support remains (Luckin et al., 2016; Holmes et al., 2022). Hence, the success of AI in the classroom is not, as with automation, but in how educators and AI systems work together in tandem for the teacher's pedagogy intentionally applied to the technology learnt. It is essential to facilitate educators not simply as users of AI, but as interpreters and co-designers of AI-facilitated learning labs, ensuring the human-centered aspect of the teaching and learning process is enhanced and not superseded.

B. MIT RAISE (Responsible AI for Social Empowerment and Education)

Overview

The MIT RAISE program focuses on integrating AI literacy into K–12 education, beginning in early elementary school. Their curriculum includes lessons that help students build an understanding of AI concepts, such as classification, data, and fairness, through age-appropriate learning experiences.

Best Practices

Understanding AI concepts in early childhood and primary education requires age-appropriate methods and techniques that encourage curiosity while also fostering ethical reasoning and social awareness. At this level, the focus should not be on learning to code or understanding the technical details of AI, but rather on helping young learners comprehend the social implications and decision-making nature of AI systems (Druga et al., 2017; Holmes et al., 2022). One avenue for achieving this is through unplugged activities or hands-on and screen-less experiences that allow children to model the logic and algorithms of AI using materials from the classroom or games. In these phases of exploration, children engage with AI concepts without requiring sophisticated infrastructure; therefore, learners can intuitively grasp concepts related to pattern recognition, classification, and basic logic (Touretzky et al., 2019). Educators can also use storytelling and metaphors, such as " How does a robot know what to do? " or " Teaching a computer is like having a pet," to explain the abstract functions of AI and make them more relatable, accessible, and meaningful to children. These stories support children in building on prior knowledge while critically engaging with how AI operates in society and reflecting on the values associated with fairness, privacy, and empathy within the technological design process. In this way, values-oriented inquiry promotes the idea that children are not only users of technology but also thoughtful digital citizens from the outset (MIT RAISE, 2020b).

Impact

A significant component of developing AI literacy in early years and primary education is to foster a more profound awareness among teachers and students of how AI permeates their daily lives. Whether we are talking about AI in streaming services that recommend TV shows to us, or AI in our phones' virtual assistants and facial recognition systems. Once the connections are made visible for young people by educators, they can then transition from passive consumers to becoming critical consumers of AI systems. This means being cognizant of and critical of not only how AI works but also how it makes decisions, drives behavior, and facilitates social relations (Long & Magerko, 2020; Holmes et al., 2022). This core awareness may lead young people to begin asking questions about the algorithm's decisions, biases, and ethical nature in relation to the data, particularly in terms of its impact on the social construction of privacy and fairness. Suppose educators are aware of and understand the core AI concepts that underpin our present and deeper past. In that case, they will be equipped to model responsible AI usage and offer meaningful dialogue about digital citizenship, promoting critical thinking. Once again, when reflection practices are incorporated into the curriculum, young learners grow as reflective and ethical technology users, allowing them to navigate and shape their AI-infused world (Touretzky et al., 2019). As AI becomes more ubiquitous, this combination of understanding and responsibility will be essential for developing resilient, inclusive, and democratically engaged societies.

Takeaway

A significant development in AI education is the realization that it is possible to teach conceptual AI literacy without relying on screens and devices. This is educationally valid and helpful for schools that lack technological capabilities. Students can use unplugged activities, such as play-acting, card sorting, two- and three-dimensional games, and storytelling, to learn about foundational concepts in AI, including pattern recognition, decision trees, classification, and algorithms (Touretzky et al., 2019). Additionally, these setups not only help reduce the barrier to entry for students but also help scaffold embodied cognition, providing students with the ability to metabolize complicated ideas through movement and social interaction. While the implementation of unplugged AI literacy can educate students on basic AI concepts, the embedded pedagogies of these activities provide an important educational service in that they demonstrate equitable access to AI proficiencies, ensuring that students from low-resourced or rural areas do not experience inequitable access to the 21st-century competencies articulated in the documents (Holmes et al., 2022; UNESCO, 2021). Unplugged AI literacy also aligns with the teaching and learning premises of early childhood literature. Instead of typically telling or digitally telling, unplugged pedagogies demonstrate the importance of experiential/ inquiry-based learning. Long and Magerko (2020) emphasize that AI literacy is not simply coding or technical tools, but rather an understanding of AI and society that requires higher-order cognitive and ethical engagement. Therefore, by disconnecting AI literacy from costly devices and guides, educators are creating more inclusive learning opportunities for learners that enable their intelligent interaction with intelligent systems.

FUTURE OUTLOOK: EDUCATORS AND AI IN TOMORROW'S CLASSROOMS

The integration of artificial intelligence (AI) into early childhood and primary education is in the first stage of development (with some exceptions). However, the direct trajectory is clear: AI will become an increasingly integrated and fluid form of accompaniment to teaching and learning. As educators respond to this, the future requires not only technical approaches to AI adoption but also ethical, human-centered, and equitable approaches. The construction of AI-enhanced education will involve tectonic changes to pedagogical design, the teacher's role, curriculum policy, and ways of interacting with learners.

A. Enhancing Humans, Not Replacing Humans

Despite widespread concerns about technology automating education, the future of education is not about replacing teachers with machines but rather using AI as a tool to augment teaching in ways that leverage the range of human capabilities. In this changing ecosystem, AI takes over data-hoarding, repetitive, or personalized work— such as personalized feedback, adaptive learning, and diagnostic assessments—allowing teachers to focus on what they do best: building relationships while fostering creativity and social-emotional development (Holmes et al., 2022; Luckin et al., 2016). As interpreters of AI feedback, educators will identify ways to thread instruction and personalize formative feedback into learning. As designers of hybrid learning experiences, they will create a mixture of machine-delivered learning and human-centered learning. Most importantly, they will serve as ethical gatekeepers, helping students navigate algorithmic bias, data privacy, and the intentional use of intelligent technology (Zawacki-Richter et al., 2019). Holmes et al. (2022) noted that "instead of replacing teachers, AI will redefine the role of teachers—expand cognitive and emotional capacity through intelligent support systems, " which expects not only technological literacy but also pedagogical and ethical fluency, with teachers as facilitators of AI-augmented learning systems.

B. AI Literacy as a Foundational Competency

AI literacy is rapidly evolving from a specialized domain to a foundational competency, similar to digital literacy or numeracy. It is now gaining recognition as essential in early childhood and primary education. Students will need to begin to understand how intelligent systems work, how they process information, and how they reach conclusions, as intelligent systems are increasingly integrated into everyday digital technologies (UNESCO, 2021). This foundational knowledge provides the basis not only for technical awareness but also for critical thinking skills, enabling students to assess the trustworthiness, likely accuracy, fairness, and implications of algorithmically derived outcomes and applications. Equally important is shaping the ethical and inclusive use of AI, where young learners learn about the social and cultural ramifications of using nearby systems and can experiment with ways to use these systems responsibly (Long & Magerko, 2020; Holmes et al., 2022). Future-ready classrooms will offer inquiry-based learning opportunities, where students will train, experiment with, and interrogate AI systems, honing their sense of agency and curiosity. With platforms such as Google's Teachable Machine or extensions for MIT's Scratch with machine learning features, young learners can engage with AI systems not just as users but as co-creators (Druga et al., 2017). Introducing AI literacy early enables students to be prepared for a technology-dominated future and equips them to build that future in an equitable, empathetic, and informed manner.

C. Equitable AI capabilities for the Global South and marginalised communities

To date, the majority of AI developments in the education sector have originated from high-income, well-resourced contexts; however, awareness is growing around the need to build AI capabilities in low-income, rural, and multilingual contexts, particularly across the Global South (UNESCO, 2021; Tuomi, 2018). An equity-based design approach requires that the future application of AI goes beyond one-size-fits-all approaches to address local and inclusive contexts. This approach will include designing voice-first or offline-compatible modalities for contexts where bandwidth may not be available, along with literacy barriers, and localizing AI systems to incorporate indigenous knowledge systems, cultural practices, and linguistic diversity so that learning technologies do not subjugate non-dominant worldviews. (UNICEF, 2021; Holmes et al, 2022). Innovations must also be aligned with the tenets of affordability, accessibility, and universal design, which insist that intelligent systems offer the same level of engagement to students with disabilities and those in rural settings. In the mainstream context, organizations such as UNESCO and UNICEF are leading international initiatives and developing related policy frameworks for the equitable use of AI in education, while also initiating discussions about creating inclusive digital transformation strategies that address the structural barriers affecting underserved students. These developments represent a significant shift in the development of AI: from a narrow type of elite innovation to one based on participatory local educational empowerment.

D. Data Governance and Algorithmic Transparency

As education systems become accustomed to using AI, the development of future uses should be guided not only by technological innovation but also by comprehensive ethical frameworks that protect students and empower educators. The tools with which students engage must be constructed to protect data privacy, support learner agency, and ensure fairness and accountability, not only within the system but also in terms of the consequences that decisions can have on the students (OECD, 2021b; Holmes et al., 2022). For ethical AI to be effectively implemented in classrooms, schools must utilize explainable AI (XAI) systems with outputs that are transparent and understandable to teachers, students, and parents, allowing them to question and engage with the technology. Transparency is essential to retain trust and ensure that AI is not used as a "black box" but as a supportive partner in pedagogical engagements. Furthermore, as AI provider organisations take on more roles creating educational tools and platforms, we need legislative frameworks that hold AI provider organisations accountable for algorithm bias, misuse of data, and poorly designed "black box" systems (UNESCO, 2021). The way forward for AI in education will require multi-actor, collaborative governance models in which educators, policymakers, technology leaders, and civic society work together to democratically design AI systems that align with educational values and human rights. As Luckin et al. (2016) state, meaningful AI improvements to education will require transparent, interpretable, and challengeable systems that contribute to, rather than detract from, educational equity and self-determination.

E. Lifelong Learning Ecosystems for Educators

The evolution of artificial intelligence and its potential for educational applications necessitate that educational professionals remain lifelong learners and engage in ongoing professional development (PD) to stay current with new and emerging tools, pedagogical practices, and the ethical implications of these tools. One-off workshops and pre-service training are not feasible. Moreover, future-oriented PD models are moving towards scaffolding, adaptation, and personalization with just-in-time, AI micro-credentials, or some form of AI that allows teachers to develop skills relevant to their classrooms' immediate context and global virtual teacher communities that allow for cross-cultural learning and problem-solving collaboratively around AI integration (Zawacki-Richter et al., 2019; Holmes et al., 2022). Another trend on the horizon is the emergence of AI coaches or AI platforms that provide individualised PD pathways for educators based on skill gaps, context of teaching (i.e. CoE), and analytics/ performance evaluations (e.g. this personalisation mimics some ways AI personalises learning pathways for students) (Luckin et al., 2016). These trends are important for teacher autonomy and reduce professional isolation (particularly in the case of remote and under-resourced settings), while also accommodating opportunities for individualised continued inquiry, action learning, or professional growth, underpinned by not just technological trends that continue to exploit and technologize education, but also pedagogical values. These kinds of systems represent a systemic, structural shift in relation to teacher development, preparing educators to work with and thrive in an AI-embedded learning ecosystem within an education system that is pedagogically centered and ethically grounded.

CONCLUSION

The application of artificial intelligence (AI) to early childhood and primary education is no longer a distant prospect; it is currently underway. As AI systems increasingly impact how young learners process content, demonstrate understanding, and receive feedback, the educator's role is also enhanced. This chapter describes how AI does not replace teachers; instead, it changes and augments the educator's role, with an emphasis on empathy, creativity, ethical reasoning, and pedagogy. For educators to be successful in AI-enhanced classrooms, they will need to gain AI literacy. This literacy will need to encompass aspects from both a technical and ethical perspective, in addition to critical reflections on data privacy, equity, and pedagogical use. Professional learning should be fluid (or flexible) and consist of training opportunities, MOOCs, mentorship within practice, and even self-directed pedagogical inquiry. Teachers need the agency to position themselves as co-designers of learning experiences, where they critically evaluate the AI tools they choose to engage with in their practice, adapt their use of AI tools to meet learners' needs, and construct inquiry-based and self-directed learning environments.

Worldwide experience—from the AI literacy programs established in Finland to Korea's use of adaptive learning platforms and China's voice-enabled reading assessments— demonstrates that context, equity, and policy alignment are essential for the sustainable and equitable adoption of AI. These examples offer important lessons for educators and policymakers undergoing similar transformations.

As we consider the future of AI in education, educators will need to operate within lifelong learning ecosystems, require a level of transparency regarding algorithmic decision-making, and have opportunities to engage with a set of data ethics. Ultimately, AI will require a reframing and reconceptualization of teaching that seeks to incorporate human reasoning with technological intelligence to support the full potential of every child. By providing educators with knowledge, tools, and confidence to leverage AI in meaningful ways, we are creating the conditions for human-centered, future-ready education systems. The promise of AI in classrooms will depend not only on the sophistication of the algorithms but also on the educators who mobilize them with purpose, care, and foresight.

REFERENCES

Crescenzi-Lanna, L., Araya, R., & Kafai, Y. B. (2021). Designing developmentally appropriate AI learning experiences for young children. *IDC '21: Interaction Design and Children Conference*, 269–274. https://doi.org/DOI: 10.1145/3459990.3465184

Druga, S., Williams, R., Breazeal, C., & Resnick, M. (2017). "Hey Google, is it OK if I eat you?": Initial explorations in child–AI interaction. *Proceedings of the 2017 Conference on Interaction Design and Children*, 595–600. https://doi.org/ DOI: 10.1145/3078072.3084330

Holmes, W., Bialik, M., & Fadel, C. (2022). *Artificial Intelligence in Education: Promises and Implications for Teaching and Learning*. Centre for Curriculum Redesign.

IBM. (2023). *AI Education Series for Educators*. https://www.ibm.com/skills/ai -education

Kimmons, R., Rosenberg, J. M., & Allman, B. (2020a). Factors Influencing Teachers' Technology Integration: A Review of the Literature. *TechTrends*, *64*, 571–576. DOI: 10.1007/s11528-020-00553-1

Kimmons, R., Rosenberg, J. M., & Allman, B. (2020b). Trends and gaps in educational technology research: A systematic review of the literature. *Educational Technology Research and Development*, *68*(4), 1923–1950. DOI: 10.1007/s11423-020-09782-3

Long, D., & Magerko, B. (2020). What is AI Literacy? *Proceedings of the 2020 CHI Conference on Human Factors in Computing Systems*, 1–16. https://doi.org/ DOI: 10.1145/3313831.3376727

Luckin, R., Holmes, W., Griffiths, M., & Forcier, L. B. (2016). *Intelligence Unleashed: An Argument for AI in Education*. Pearson.

MIT RAISE. (2020a). *AI + Ethics Curriculum*. https://raise.mit.edu/curriculum

MIT RAISE. (2020b). *Responsible AI for Social Empowerment and Education*. Massachusetts Institute of Technology. https://raise.mit.edu

OECD. (2021a). *AI and the Future of Skills: AI Competency Framework*. Organisation for Economic Co-operation and Development. https://www.oecd.org

OECD. (2021b). *Artificial Intelligence in Education: Challenges and Opportunities for Sustainable Development*. Organisation for Economic Co-operation and Development.

OECD. (2021c). *Digital Education Outlook 2021: Pushing the Frontiers with Artificial Intelligence, Blockchain and Robots*. Organisation for Economic Co-operation and Development.

Touretzky, D. S., Gardner-McCune, C., Martin, F., & Seehorn, D. (2019). Envisioning AI for K-12: What Should Every Child Know about AI? *Proceedings of the AAAI Conference on Artificial Intelligence*, *33*(1), 9795–9799. DOI: 10.1609/aaai.v33i01.33019795

Tuomi, I. (2018). *The Impact of Artificial Intelligence on Learning, Teaching and Education: Policies for the Future*. JRC Science for Policy Report, European Commission. https://doi.org/DOI: 10.2760/12297

UNESCO. (2021). *AI and Education: Guidance for Policymakers*. United Nations Educational, Scientific and Cultural Organisation.

UNICEF. (2021). *AI and Child Rights: Technical Working Paper*. United Nations Children's Fund. https://www.unicef.org/globalinsight/reports/ai-and-child-rights

Williamson, B., & Eynon, R. (2020). Historical threads, missing links and future directions in AI in education. *Learning, Media and Technology*, *45*(3), 223–235. DOI: 10.1080/17439884.2020.1798995

Zawacki-Richter, O., Marín, V. I., Bond, M., & Gouverneur, F. (2019). Systematic review of research on artificial intelligence applications in higher education – Where are the educators? *International Journal of Educational Technology in Higher Education*, *16*(1), 1–27. DOI: 10.1186/s41239-019-0171-0

Chapter 2
Preparing Cambodian Educators for AI-Enhanced Classrooms:
Policy, Training, and Infrastructures to Help Teachers Embrace Educational Technology

Saban Bon
http://orcid.org/0000-0002-8443-5145
National University of Cheasim Kamchaymear, Kampong Cham, Cambodia

Sereyrath Em
http://orcid.org/0000-0002-6803-195X
National University of Cheasim Kamchaymear, Kampong Cham, Cambodia

ABSTRACT

Artificial intelligence (AI) has become a transformative instrument in education, offering prospects for individualized learning, instructional assistance, and augmented creativity. In response, the Ministry of Education, Youth, and Sport in Cambodia has allocated resources towards policies, training initiatives, and infrastructure to equip teachers for the incorporation of AI. Nevertheless, notwithstanding these endeavors, obstacles endure, encompassing inadequate training, educators' dispositions, and the restricted qualifications of teacher trainers. Therefore, successful AI integration necessitates organized competency frameworks, continuous professional development, and curriculum revisions in teacher education institutions. Accordingly, enhancing training at regional and provincial teacher training centers and augmenting the experience of teacher educators are crucial for developing AI

DOI: 10.4018/979-8-2600-2438-6.ch002

competencies. Ultimately, this strategy seeks to improve teaching quality, promote innovation, and enable Cambodian educators to utilize AI effectively to facilitate students' learning.

INTRODUCTION

Artificial intelligence (AI) has recently emerged as a critical tool in the field of education. In particular, it has the potential to enhance the quality of education and provide opportunities. Additionally, it facilitates personalized learning and offers instructional support. AI facilitates individualized learning by tailoring instructional materials to accommodate the distinct requirements of each learner (Hennekeuser et al., 2025) and enhances students' creativity (Zhou & Song, 2025). Moreover, students may utilize AI to serve as their instructors, available at any time and in any location, who can respond to their inquiries as needed.

AI can also confront some of the most significant challenges in education today, innovate teaching and learning practices, and expedite progress toward SDG 4, which emphasizes inclusive and equitable quality education (UNESCO, n.d.). This is because students from any location can learn according to their needs without encountering issues. Similarly, teachers can alleviate their workload by utilizing AI as a personal assistant. Accordingly, encouraging teachers to actively adopt AI in their teaching has considerable educational merit (Zhao et al., 2025).

While AI in education has been discussed extensively in the global context, this chapter focuses on the Cambodian context of AI, offering a detailed examination of current national policies, teacher capacity, teacher education, and infrastructure realities. It aims to suggest effective preparations for educators in AI-driven classrooms. Before delving into the core objectives, the paper provides an overview of Cambodia's education system, current teacher education in Cambodia, and AI in education.

CAMBODIA'S CURRENT EDUCATION SYSTEM

The Cambodian education system comprises 12 years of general education, organized into a 6+3+3 framework: six years of primary education (Grades 1 to 6), three years of lower secondary school (Grades 7 to 9), and three years of upper secondary education (Grades 10 to 12). However, this formal framework omits pre-primary education, including early childhood education and kindergarten. To complete their general education requirements, students must undertake two national examinations: the grade 9 examination, commonly referred to as the Diplomas Exam, and the grade 12 examination, known as the Bac II Exam.

During upper secondary education, students are required to choose either the science or social sciences track in the 11th and 12th years (Kao et al., 2022). Accordingly, each track necessitates that students engage with distinct core subjects. For instance, science track students study physics, chemistry, biology, earth and environmental science, and mathematics, whereas social science track students study Khmer literature, history, geography, ethics, civics, and citizenship (Kao et al., 2022). As the science track focuses on STEM subjects, it prepares students to pursue majors such as computer science, civil engineering, and medicine in higher education. In contrast, the social science track prepares students for majors in political science, economics, management, marketing, and other related fields. The integration of AI into subject tracks may present challenges for teachers, as certain AI tools suitable for science classes may not be applicable to social sciences. This necessitates the meticulous development of a teacher training program.

Table 1. Cambodia's General Education System and Upper Secondary Tracks

Level of Education	Grades	Description / Notes	Sources
Primary Education	1–6	Six years of primary education	MoEYS (2014, 2019)
Lower Secondary Education	7–9	Three years of lower secondary school. Students must take the Diplom Exam at the end of Grade 9.	MoEYS (2014, 2023)
Upper Secondary Education	10–12	Three years of upper secondary school. Students must take the Bac II examination at the end of Grade 12.	MoEYS (2014, 2023)
Tracks (Grades 11–12)	—	Students choose either a science or social science track.	MoEYS (2015a, 2015d)
Science Track	11–12	Core subjects: physics, chemistry, biology, earth and environmental science, and mathematics. Prepares students for STEM-related majors, such as computer science, civil engineering, and medicine.	MoEYS (2015b)
Social Science Track	11–12	Core subjects: Khmer literature, history, geography, ethics, civics, and citizenship. Prepares students for majors in political science, economics, management, marketing, and related fields.	MoEYS (2015c)

CURRENT TEACHER EDUCATION IN CAMBODIA

To enhance the qualifications of educators, the Ministry of Education, Youth, and Sport ([MoEYS], 2022) initiated the Master Plan for Teacher Qualification Upgrade 2021–2025, which emphasizes four key strategies: (1) increasing qualification to provide 12+4 teachers via teacher education colleges (TECs); (2) implementing BA+1 prestage training to address urgent teacher requirements; (3) creating a system for qualification enhancement through a long program; and (4) encouraging 12+2 teachers with a BA to engage in a short program.

Currently, according to the MoEYS (2025), 27 teacher education institutes (TEIs) nationwide offer initial teacher education to student teachers, and most TEIs have two-year programs for pre-primary, primary, lower secondary (12+2), and upper secondary teachers (BA+2). Moreover, the 12+4 beginning teacher education curriculum emphasizes the development of student teachers' abilities to evaluate and perform research, particularly action research (MoEYS, 2025). Furthermore, the MoEYS has implemented a thorough revision of the teacher training curriculum and elevated the credentials mandated for teacher trainers (MoEYS, 2024a). In addition, the entry prerequisites for teacher education programs have been upgraded, now necessitating a minimum of grade 12 completion and a bachelor's degree, termed the 12+4 formula (MoEYS, 2024a).

During the 2022–2023 academic year, a significant proportion (89.6%) of public lower secondary educators possessed a post-secondary education certificate, while 64.5% held a bachelor's degree or a higher qualification (MoEYS, 2024a). Therefore, teaching credentials necessitate the completion of at least grade 12 and a bachelor's degree. In addition, upper-secondary educators were mandated to possess a bachelor's degree and complete one year of training at a National Institute of Education. Meanwhile, MoEYS intends to elevate the qualifying standard to 12+4. (MoEYS, 2024a). However, 70% of PTTC teacher educators and 40% of RTTC teacher educators lack a Master’s degree (MoEYS, 2024b). In contrast, 64.9% of PTEC teacher educators and 79.3% of BTEC educators own a Master's degree, whereas 2.6% hold a doctorate (MoEYS, 2024b).

Table 2. Overview of Teacher Education and Qualifications in Cambodia

Aspect	Details / Statistics	Sources
Teacher Qualification Upgrade Plan	Master Plan for Teacher Qualification Upgrade 2021–2025 with four strategies: (1) 12+4 teachers via TECs, (2) BA+1 pre-service training, (3) Long program for qualification enhancement, (4) Short program for 12+2 teachers with BA	MoEYS (2021)
Teacher Education Institutes (TEIs)	27 TEIs offering initial teacher education nationwide	MoEYS (2019)
12+4 Beginning Teacher Education Curriculum	Focus on student teachers' ability to evaluate and perform research, especially action research	MoEYS (2015a)
Teacher Training Curriculum Revision	Curriculum thoroughly revised; teacher trainer credentials elevated	MoEYS (2015b)
Entry Requirements for Teacher Education	Minimum Grade 12 completion + bachelor's degree (12+4 formula)	MoEYS (2015a)
Lower Secondary Educators	89.6% have a post-secondary certificate; 64.5% have a bachelor's degree or higher	UNESCO and MoEYS (2021)
Upper Secondary Educators	Bachelor's degree + 1-year training at the National Institute of Education, MoEYS aims for 12+4 standard	MoEYS (2019)
PTTC Teacher Educators	70% lack a Master's degree	UNESCO and MoEYS (2021)
RTTC Teacher Educators	40% lack a Master's degree	UNESCO and MoEYS (2021)
PTEC Teacher Educators	64.9% hold a Master's degree	UNESCO and MoEYS (2021)
BTEC Teacher Educators	79.3% hold a Master's degree; 2.6% hold a Doctorate	UNESCO and MoEYS (2021)

AI AND AI IN EDUCATION

Artificial intelligence (AI) is a component of computer science that enables machines (computers) to perform tasks as efficiently and effectively as humans. In recent years, it has emerged as an indispensable component of education. AI has the potential to transform education worldwide. In particular, AI technologies such as automatic translation, content generation, and advanced search can enhance teaching and learning experiences (National University of Management [NUM], 2025; SIU, 2025). AI encompasses technologies and systems that replicate human cognitive functions, incorporating tools capable of data analysis, adapting to individual learning requirements, delivering tailored feedback, and facilitating the automation of educational processes (Zhou & Song, 2025). Within this context, Zhao et al. (2025) characterized AI teaching technology as a collection of AI assistants, including large language models derived from the digitization of educational systems. These tools offer educators intelligent decision-making support, facilitate precise analysis, evaluation, and optimization of teaching practices, and enhance both the effectiveness and efficiency of the educational process. Moreover, the utilization of AI can facilitate the presentation of digital learning content that is currently being developed. In addition, research indicates that the implementation of AI in education primarily indirectly enhances teaching quality by fostering student motivation and elevating teacher proficiency (Wang, 2025). Additionally, AI significantly bolstered teachers' self-efficacy in AI teaching, reflected in both their beliefs regarding efficacy and their expectations of teaching outcomes (Sun et al., 2023).

In Cambodia, the MoEYS (2025) acknowledged that educational ICT and AI-driven learning systems will be utilized to enhance teacher qualification upgrade and continuing professional development programs, providing customized training pathways and adapting content to the requirements of teacher educators based on their prior knowledge, experience, and professional objectives (MoEYS, 2022a, 2022b). Therefore, AI can not only assist teachers in teaching but also enhance teacher professional development. In addition, teacher educators' AI proficiencies could shape teacher training quality; thus, they must be AI-savvy to effectively incorporate it into their teaching. Ergo, Cambodia has made substantial investments in AI in education.

PREPARING CAMBODIAN TEACHERS FOR AI-ENHANCED CLASSROOMS

As aforementioned, AI has delivered numerous advantages to the education sector, prompting Cambodia's MoEYS to invest significant efforts in equipping teachers to integrate this innovative technology into their classroom instruction. This effort involves the launch of relevant policies, provision of training for teachers and teacher educators, and enhancements to infrastructure, among other measures.

Policies on Technology in Education

The Royal Government of Cambodia's Pentagon strategic phase 1 has been articulated into MoEYS's eight priorities, including the advancement of digital education (Em, 2023; Sim & Em, 2023). Accordingly, to help teachers integrate educational technology, including AI, into their teaching, MoEYS has launched various education policies that include educational technologies as their agenda. To begin with, as stated in the Education Strategic Plan 2024-2028, MoEYS implemented a reform of teacher training institutions, with a particular emphasis on six areas. One of these areas is the professional development of trainers in the use of technology in teaching, as well as the content of lessons, pedagogy, and teaching methods. In the future, MoEYS will concentrate on six important areas, including the promotion of digital education and the establishment of e-learning forums to exchange best practices with teachers (Em, 2021; MoEYS, 2024a). Moreover, the Ministry will enhance the capacity of secondary school educators to utilize and convey ICT and digital technologies in their classrooms, while also fostering 21st-century skills among youth (MoEYS, 2024a). The overall focus is on using technology in education to cultivate vital abilities for the contemporary world. Educators will undergo training to proficiently utilize digital technologies, facilitating engaging and contemporary learning experiences for pupils. Hence, the Ministry seeks to enhance digital literacy and technological access to provide students with essential skills for success in the digital era (MoEYS, 2024a).

Furthermore, the Teacher Policy Action Plan 2024–2030 emphasizes four strategic areas, one of which is teacher education. This area prioritizes 21st-century teacher education by enhancing capacity through inclusive and reflective curricula and learning materials, fostering equality and respect for diversity, and requiring context-responsive learning options, pedagogies, and curricula in various formats (MoEYS, 2023). Consequently, the preservice teacher training program requires modernization for 21st-century education (MoEYS, 2023). Teacher education is enhanced by adherence to regional and worldwide best practice evidence (MoEYS, 2023). Additionally, the Ministry has persistently advanced and advocated for digital transformation within the educational ecosystem to cultivate human capital for the digital economy by integrating digital technology into the forthcoming generation of school education (Em et al., 2024; Heng et al., 2023; MoEYS, 2024a).

Training

Educators, including teacher educators and teachers, need to be AI-savvy to integrate AI into their teaching. To equip them with AI competencies, it is crucial to outline a specific set of knowledge areas and skills, organized within a structured competency framework or model (Mikeladze et al., 2024). Accordingly, this AI competency framework for educators aims to clearly define the essential proficiencies, such as knowledge, skills, and abilities, necessary for teachers (Mikeladze et al., 2024). However, the integration of AI in education is contended to be influenced not solely by its technological capabilities; instead, it significantly depends on various factors, one of which is the proficiency of educators (Iddrisu & Iddrisu, 2025). For example, teachers must possess proficiency in employing AI to facilitate various forms of assessment, encompassing both formative and summative evaluations, as well as student self-assessment (Chiu et al., 2025). Moreover, teachers must possess existing AI capabilities and determine potential strategies to enhance learning (Zhai et al., 2021).

Cambodia has prioritized this issue and is initiating the creation of initiatives to educate educators, which is essential for modernizing the educational system to include AI and digital technologies (UNESCO, 2025). Moreover, mitigating skill deficiencies and investing in advanced AI education and training are crucial for maximizing AI's potential for economic growth and societal benefits (UNESCO, 2025). In this regard, UNESCO, in partnership with the MoEYS, is executing the Strengthening Teacher Education Programmes in Cambodia (STEPCam), a major teacher education initiative in the country, with a total investment of USD 27.02 million financed by the Global Partnership for Education (UNESCO, 2023). STEPCam aims to cultivate a high-caliber teaching workforce over two stages (2018–2022 and 2024–2027) by enhancing pre-service education, facilitating ongoing professional development, promoting career development, providing mentorship, and integrating information and communication technology to elevate the quality of teaching and learning (UNESCO, 2023). To bolster teacher training on AI in education, it is also crucial to upgrade the infrastructure within teacher education institutions and schools.

Improving Infrastructure

Teachers can use technologies such as AI more easily if there is sufficient infrastructure. Conversely, if there is insufficient infrastructure, it may be difficult for them to use such technologies. Thus, the MoEYS has also worked hard to improve infrastructure in cooperation with partners. According to UNESCO (2023), 11 provincial teacher training centers have enhanced infrastructure and amenities, including Wi-Fi systems, libraries, computers, and scientific labs, serving over 240 teacher educators and almost 1,300 primary school teachers each year. During Phase I (2018–2022), five significant accomplishments were realized, including the establishment of 11 provincial teacher training centers with enhanced infrastructure and facilities, such as Wi-Fi systems, libraries, computers, and science laboratories, which serve over 240 teacher educators and nearly 1,300 primary school teachers each year (UNESCO, 2023). Moreover, Phase II comprises four components, one of which focuses on equipping teachers and teacher educators with the methods and abilities essential for facilitating learning that effectively and ethically utilizes digital technology (UNESCO, 2023). Cambodian schools possess the physical resources necessary for AI training and subsequent implementation but often lack consistent operating budgets to support newly installed technology (UNESCO, 2021). Moreover, schools often do not provide technology to teachers and students because of a lack of funds for monthly operating costs, such as electrical power, maintenance, repairs, and the upgrading of software and hardware (OECD, 2023). Consequently, physical resources tend to be concentrated in urban centers. Consequently, most schools in remote areas generally have little to no access to computers and the Internet, which is a significant barrier to the adoption of technology-assisted instruction in these areas. Surprisingly, a study conducted with teachers from a public school in Phnom Penh found that both teachers and students encountered inadequate infrastructure, including insufficient equipment and issues with Internet connectivity (Pen & Morrell, 2024).

CHALLENGES IN PREPARING TEACHERS FOR AI-ENHANCED CLASSROOMS

Lack of Effective AI Training

Because training, one of the professional development modes, helps teachers acquire skills in using technology (Bon & Inpin, 2024), professional development centered on AI pedagogy is expected to be integral to future instructional methodologies (Babanoğlu et al., 2025). To support this, it is crucial to enable teachers to engage with this groundbreaking technology. Consequently, teacher education institutions must integrate AI into their curricula. Notably, research has indicated that teachers who have received training in AI expressed greater confidence in their ability to integrate AI into their teaching practices and demonstrated a stronger intention to utilize AI for lesson planning and enhancing student learning than their counterparts lacking such training (Lähdesmäki et al., 2025). Generally, two types of training are available: pre-service and in-service training. During pre-service training, teacher educators are crucial in assisting teacher candidates in developing the skills needed to use AI in the classroom.

Furthermore, the effective implementation of AI in education requires training that emphasizes a standardized framework. Such a framework should enable educators to integrate AI alongside essential elements, including curriculum content that students must master and the pedagogical expertise necessary for teachers to facilitate student learning effectively, ultimately enhancing the educational experience. In this context, the TPACK framework has gained significant traction as a foundational guideline in the realm of teacher education, particularly concerning the integration of educational technology. Therefore, educators must attain a dynamic synthesis of technological knowledge, pedagogical knowledge, and subject matter content knowledge within AI environments (Wang, 2025; Tariq, 2025). Research has indicated that the TPACK-based professional development programme markedly enhanced educators' knowledge and cultivated their skills in AI instruction, encompassing their ability to plan AI lessons and their proficiency in AI programming.

In the Cambodian context, existing teacher training programs appear insufficient in equipping educators with the competency to use AI tools. Cambodian educators require training to effectively use these tools in the classroom, not only as new teaching tools but also to prepare themselves and their students to thrive in an increasingly AI-enhanced workplace (JICA, 2024). A case study conducted to investigate Cambodian pre-retirement teachers' perceptions and challenges of technological use revealed that if teachers did not receive sufficient training, they did not feel confident using technology in their teaching (Pen & Morrell, 2024). To promote technology integration in the classroom setting, the MoEYS has launched educational policies that include education technologies as agendas and partnered with other ministries and NGOs to provide technology training for teachers and teacher educators (e.g., MoEYS, 2025, 2024a). Despite the national endeavor to provide training for teachers and educators, AI-specific training for teachers and teacher educators apparently remains limited. Similarly, Sok and Heng (2024) noted, based on current studies, that the quality of training has not met the standards of 21st-century education, partly owing to the persistent use of traditional teaching methods.

Teachers' Negative Attitudes toward AI

Teachers' attitudes influence their teaching practices (Bon & Charubusp, 2024; Bon & Koem, 2025). In particular, attitudes influence teachers' intentions to use technology (Sey & Em, 2023; Xu, 2025). Research has revealed a notable and positive correlation between the perceived benefits of AI in higher education and teaching and the willingness to adopt AI (Xu, 2025). A study in the Cambodian context also found that teachers in the pre-retirement phase believed that they found it difficult to learn technology, and this belief made them hesitant to acquire or upgrade their digital skills (Pen & Morrell, 2024). Hence, teachers with a negative attitude toward AI were unlikely to adopt it into their teaching practices because they did not perceive the advantages as outweighing the drawbacks. Similarly, those with a negative attitude toward AI would not endeavor to upgrade their AI competencies, resulting in a challenge in AI integration.

Less Qualified Teacher Educators

The qualifications of teacher educators are critical to ensuring the quality of teacher education. The low qualifications of teacher educators adversely affect the quality of AI training and the execution of related policies. In 2021, 64.46% of Cambodian educators lacked a bachelor's degree, with approximately one-fourth of elementary school teachers and nearly half of secondary school instructors being underqualified (MoES, 2023). Moreover, current educators have restricted avenues for ongoing professional development (CPD) to enhance their pedagogical competencies and academic credentials (MoEYS, 2023). Briefly, it would be difficult for less qualified teacher educators to create qualified teachers.

Insufficient Infrastructure

In a developing country like Cambodia, where government funding for a new-age educational system may be limited, the lack of technology infrastructure presents a major barrier to preparing educators for teaching in an AI-enhanced classroom (OECD, 2023). Indeed, classroom infrastructure varies greatly and depends largely on the school's location and student demographics. While schools in large metropolitan areas, such as Phnom Penh, often have more modern windows and doors, sufficient lighting and ventilation, and access to appropriate technology, by contrast, less well-developed schools situated in rural areas of Cambodia often have a distinct lack of Chin-Lopo- or Chin-Lean-Iak, brightly colored artificial enamel paint on their windows and doors, inadequate illumination and airflow, and minimal technology support. Consequently, this lack of technological support impedes the development of innovative teaching methods for future students.

Nevertheless, government funding and partnerships with private organizations may relieve some of the pressure on Cambodia's education system, although, in the short term, it is ultimately the responsibility of the educator to prepare for the inevitable (UNESCO, 2021). Hence, the training and support provided to these educators must extend beyond the physical infrastructure of the school and into their own infrastructure of knowledge and capability to embrace educational technology. In addition to infrastructure challenges, cultural barriers also exist. As the saying goes, culture eats strategy for breakfast, and educators must be prepared for the potential of transformation brought about by AI in an educational setting, including relinquishing sole ownership of responsibility-proactibility-sensitivity (OECD, 2023).

Cultural Resistance

Similarly, a lack of enthusiasm and engagement from Cambodian educators is one of the greatest personal barriers that can prevent the adoption of technology (UNESCO, 2021). For example, a previous pilot study uncovered mixed reactions from Cambodian educators when surveyed before and after an introductory STEM and educational application workshop. Specifically, their responses suggested that without encouragement and motivation from an institution or organization, individuals felt unprepared and lacked the drive to pursue further technological development. Similarly, interviews with K-12 schoolteachers further revealed an additional apprehension regarding the potential amount of time that could be taken away from them because of a desire to learn new and unfamiliar technologies. Moreover, the obstacle of unfamiliarity was also underscored by members of an NGO involved in educator training and STEM coordination. They recognized that a lack of understanding could lead to skepticism regarding the efficacy and usefulness of different technologies. Indeed, without cultural adoption and a willingness to change, financial and logistical support from the government may be inadequate to facilitate the continued adoption of technology within the education system. Additionally, elderly and inexperienced groups receive less support, despite sometimes being the most in need of such assistance.

In contrast, other observations advocate for the creation of a culture that encourages teachers to believe that they—and their students—can learn effectively with educational technology (OECD, 2023). Research further suggests that unless teachers experience Eureka moments or embody a pedagogical mindset that embraces educational technology and innovation, they are unlikely to adopt it when teaching. Consequently, if educators are not convinced by the rationale for adopting new teaching and learning strategies, either pedagogical or technological, they will not make connections in their minds between the benefits of these methods and their own educational context. This likely also explains why simply providing teachers with an iPad does not result in the effective uptake of technology for teaching and learning. Finally, the establishment of communities of training enables teachers to share ideas, questions, and concerns with other educators utilizing similar innovations, regardless of where they are in the world. These communities, in turn, provide sources of support and inspiration that encourage all participants to conquer the fear of trying new things (UNESCO, 2021).

SUGGESTIONS FOR IMPROVEMENT

Identifying Training Needs for Cambodian Educators

Analysis of educator training needs, including surveys and assessments and focus groups, would be an effective method for training in AI-enhanced classrooms.

Surveys and Assessments: The Cambodian education system is in transition, embracing AI with strategic support from the MoEYS, large technology developers, and private funding (Aljemely, 2024). However, although many initiatives target students, a significant gap remains in teacher training on integrating AI into lesson planning and execution. By identifying these training needs through surveys and focus groups, educators can better understand AI concepts and applications, prepare for AI-enhanced classrooms, and foster a culture of innovation. Until teacher training on AI in education is formalized, the full benefits of intelligent technology cannot be realized. Thus, surveys enable educators and practitioners to identify training requirements in mixed AI classrooms. The insights gained are crucial for developing curricula that include AI in Education concepts and hands-on modules using AI-related educational technology. Ultimately, continuous professional development fosters a culture of innovative education, empowering teachers to embrace change and harness new technologies (Aljemely, 2024). In fact, a Cambodian pilot survey revealed the necessity for training and the implications for the technology infrastructure of schools.

Focus Groups: Focus groups, a qualitative research method that enlists a small number of participants for in-depth discussions on a shared topic, are a valuable tool for exploring AI training requirements for Cambodian educators. An advantage of focus groups over questionnaires lies in their capacity for detailed exploration. While questionnaires provide a structured means to gauge participants' needs, focus groups enable the generation of rich insights through discussion and debate (Leung, 2009; Gizir, 2007). Focus groups serve as a starting point in the curriculum design process, creating a dialogue that collects views on how educators would like to use AI tools, the barriers they face, and the training required for adoption (JICA, 2024). Such in-depth discourse, once viewed as a drawback due to unpredictable resulting topics, is now recognized as beneficial for closely examining a training topic (Wilson, 1997). Therefore, participants most pertinent to AI training for Cambodian educators are current instructors. Understanding their needs and attitudes is essential for crafting an effective training course. Moreover, focus groups comprising Cambodian educators offer a means to identify trainers' specific training needs at a more profound level than quantitative methods, such as questionnaires. Given that AI's ability to transform how students learn is advancing rapidly, teachers must regularly update their pedagogical knowledge. Therefore, exploring the views of presently employed educators is crucial in constructing an HLAI curriculum that addresses both content and pedagogy. Beyond this, gathering information about the technology infrastructure available in schools and the gaps therein is vital. These infrastructural insights, also gathered through focus group discussions, illuminate the barriers to adopting AI methods in education (Cohen & Miller, 2022).

Evaluation and Assessment of Training Programs

The evaluation and assessment of training programs are key to determining their effectiveness and guiding the development of future initiatives (Wu, 2025; Heng, 2024). In this regard, the results of one survey and two focus-group studies, conducted separately in an urban and an ETC location, indicated a training need and provided suggestions for the content (Pum & Sok, 2024). Consequently, future training can now be designed to address the full spectrum of teachers' needs and interests, and the evaluation can be extended to include an assessment of the program (Tep, 2024). Of particular importance, questions about teacher engagement and continued interest, the development of an educator community, and the identification of any barriers to implementation remain key (Ly, 2024). Furthermore, an ongoing assessment of students' use of technology would be informative, especially where creativity and innovation skills are involved (Echave, 2024).

Moreover, studies of this nature allow researchers to incorporate suggestions and documented effects from previous surveys and to concentrate on areas overlooked in earlier research (Yan et al., 2023). Typically, these include assessments of short-term training, the role of the government in educating larger groups of teachers, partnerships with technology companies to maintain training relevance, and the provision of long-term support and infrastructure (UNESCO, 2025a). In addition, the longer-term effects of teacher training, particularly with respect to continued creativity and innovation, also merit closer examination, albeit over several years (Hallmen et al., 2025).

Feedback Mechanisms

Once a training program is developed and implemented, a comprehensive evaluation is necessary before widespread dissemination (Gao et al., 2023). Generally, evaluation activities tend to fall into two groups: feedback mechanisms and longitudinal studies. Specifically, feedback mechanisms capture data about the training program itself, help identify emerging training needs, and identify contextual issues that may otherwise inexplicably impact training outcomes (Kuzminykh et al., 2024). The primary methods employed for this type of assessment include open discussions, concept association surveys, and focused impact surveys (van der Vleuten et al., 1996).

In particular, open discussions are especially useful when language barriers cannot be fully mitigated by providing training materials in the local language (Echave, 2024). These sessions provide a forum for trainees to articulate areas, topics, or aspects of the training that an online or paper survey may not otherwise capture, such as issues with the course platform (Wu, 2025). Additionally, they can highlight negative feelings on any topic associated with the training that the trainer has not anticipated or identified and may recognize emerging training gaps due to changes within the overall educational situation (Heng & Sol, 2024). Moreover, structured open discussions most easily address topics of interest derived from concept association survey results (Ly, 2024). Similarly, concept association surveys generate data on individuals' degree of connection or involvement with associated concepts, norms, or stereotypes and are useful for identifying less obvious training needs and support requirements in many contexts (Yan et al., 2023). Although concept association surveys typically do not generate demographic data, such data can be collected in separate activities and considered in conjunction with the concept association data during the analysis phase (Tep, 2024). Finally, focused impact surveys are more effective following the implementation of further training designed to address issues uncovered in previous surveys and discussions (Gao et al., 2023).

Longitudinal Studies

In contrast, longitudinal studies monitor the actual application of AI in the classroom by tracking students' learning outcomes and educators' teaching quality after they have been trained on how to use AI in the classroom (Wu, 2025; Heng, 2024). Indeed, continual professional development is essential for integrating new ideas and approaches and creating a culture of innovation (UNESCO, 2025b). Therefore, monitoring outcomes is important because these benefits must be tangible, measurable, and relevant to the government if there is any hope that such programs can be sustained via government funding and support (UNESCO, 2025a).

However, many educational technology integration initiatives have failed because the introduction of new technology into the classroom was done without adequate training or resources (Ly, 2024). Of equal importance is the timeliness of educational technology integration; if the technology is not adequately supported by infrastructure, it becomes another barrier that further burdens both educators and students (Pum & Sok, 2024). For instance, surveys conducted in Cambodia in 2021 analyzed educators' satisfaction levels with the status of infrastructure. These surveys highlight the core infrastructural problems that must be addressed to gain real benefits through educational technology integration (Tep, 2024).

Sustaining AI Training Initiatives

Building on these findings, sustaining AI training initiatives for Cambodian educators demands ongoing activities that extend beyond the initial training program (Wu, 2025). Accordingly, in-depth evaluations of the first training phase can inform necessary refinements (Hallmen et al., 2025). Furthermore, implementing an integrated feedback mechanism continuously monitors training effectiveness and enables real-time improvements (Em, 2022; Kuzminykh et al., 2024). At the same time, exploring partnerships with industry further enhances the program's long-term viability (Heng & Sol, 2024). In addition, a longitudinal study assessing the training's impact on career development and promotion opportunities provides valuable insights (Echave, 2024). Moreover, conducting follow-up training sessions and offering additional resources and support helps educators stay current with emerging AI applications (Yan et al., 2023).

Ultimately, a continuous professional development framework can establish a community of practice that cultivates a culture of innovation (UNESCO, 2025b). In this way, Cambodia, like many developing countries, maintains a high regard for teachers and education, positioning educators to play a pivotal role in inspiring students to embrace emerging technologies (UNESCO, 2025a). As a result, adequately prepared teachers cultivate an environment in which educational technology is recognized not merely as a means to enhance efficiency but as a source of joy and excitement in the learning journey (Ly, 2024). Consequently, this paradigm shift motivates students to innovate with technology (Pum & Sok, 2024).

Curriculum Development for AI Training

In preparation for incorporating AI into every classroom, the foundation of initiating an effective AI Training for Educators curriculum is presently underway. To begin with, through methods such as surveys and focus groups with educators in Cambodia, an assessment of current skills and knowledge for the active use of educational technology in the classroom was conducted (Reina-Parrado et al., 2025; Bautista et al., 2025). Consequently, the results of this assessment and the fundamental components of the curriculum are outlined below.

In particular, curricula for training educators in using AI for improved student learning in Cambodia should encompass courses that provide a conceptual understanding of AI along with practical, hands-on applications of AI tools tailored for classroom use (Aljemely, 2024). Moreover, the objective is to continually develop the abilities of teachers across Cambodia, empowering them not only to teach their students newer and better technology but also to prepare their students to become creators of future innovations rather than merely consumers of technology. In this regard, custom-tailored AI educational technology training has the potential to improve academic outcomes by enabling educators to present AI concepts in ways that are relevant and meaningful to their students' lives and future career paths (OECD, 2023).

Integrating AI Concepts: To achieve this, a curriculum that adequately prepares teachers for AI-enhanced classrooms requires an understanding of AI's role in education—what it is, how it works, and why it can be valuable (UNESCO, 2021). Indeed, Cambodian teachers' applications for and knowledge about technology can differ greatly depending on their level of education, school type, and current level of technology use. Therefore, comprehensive training should begin by defining AI and its impact on the educational process (Reina-Parrado et al., 2025). Furthermore, beyond basic AI concepts, the curriculum must also incorporate teaching strategies specifically geared toward AI-enhanced classrooms. While some educators may be comfortable using AI on a basic level, they may be unsure of the best strategy to maximize students' educational experience. Thus, modules addressing these aspects can help teachers embrace AI technologies in a manner that effectively enhances learning. For instance, collaborative learning and student-centered approaches offer opportunities for using AI to complement, rather than replace, students' educational journey (Cohen & Miller, 2022).

Hands-on training modules: In addition, hands-on training modules allow educators to apply new knowledge immediately, building confidence and competence. Such training should be practical, interactive, collaborative, and relevant to address educators' diverse backgrounds and technical skills (Gizir, 2007; Leung, 2009). Because current AI applications vary widely, educators first require an understanding of AI concepts before engaging in hands-on work with specific tools. Moreover, training that demonstrates tangible teaching benefits and offers ready-to-use applications, including free-of-charge options, encourages adoption (Wilson, 1997). For example, an example project involves an AI robot named Trisha and the related AI ChatBot. Trisha employs ChatGPT to recognize and converse with visitors, enhancing school engagement. Meanwhile, the ChatBot version supports teachers in crafting good prompts and conducting idiomatic English conversations. Together, both AI tools provide educators with opportunities to explore the value of AI, illustrating that AI can truly be an educator's friend.

Teaching Strategies for AI-Enhanced Classrooms

At present, AI promises to radically transform education by facilitating personalized learning, supporting diverse learners, and automating mundane tasks (OECD, 2023; UNESCO, 2021). Hence, Cambodian educators must be trained to employ AI to create inclusive classrooms and accommodate every student's needs; however, little research exists on their specific training requirements. Surveys and focus groups identified these needs and formed the basis of a dedicated training curriculum. The results revealed that teachers want to learn about the capabilities and limitations of AI in the classroom, practical applications of AI, and how AI will affect the role of the teacher. In a subsequent study, teachers evaluated the curriculum and suggested additional lessons on classroom management and teaching strategies for AI classrooms.

Collaborative Learning: Teachers should be trained in specific teaching strategies that harness the power of AI tools. Collaborative learning emphasizes cooperative efforts, enabling teachers to work together with students on tasks that require complex decision-making or critical thinking. It can also be used with AI via hands-on workshops in which pairs or groups receive a problem and use an appropriate AI solution to solve it (OECD, 2023). As a result, these workshops promote discussion and collaboration and encourage teachers to gain new perspectives from their peers. Additionally, other approaches, such as jigsaw activities, can aid teacher participation. However, these are highly mechanical and require quick thinking; therefore, it may be better to use them on a smaller scale. Moreover, collaboration can also be used to improve digital literacy. For example, educators at Cambodian schools are often surprised that they can utilize query languages to extract information from large bodies of unstructured data. Therefore, the training program can encourage the sharing of AI skills and teacher-led workshops through which those with more knowledge can share their skills with their colleagues (UNESCO, 2021). In this way, it creates a positive culture and sense of teamwork, helping not only with participation but also with the efficacy of the training and the use of AI tools within the classroom.

Personalized Learning Approaches: In contrast, personalized learning through AI is a mode of instruction and assessment that uses algorithms to adapt the learning experience to the particular needs of the learner, often in real time (OECD, 2023). Importantly, effective personalized learning considers both the learner's current needs and the educational goals for the entire class. Accordingly, AI-powered educational technologies can identify the student's zone of proximal development, as well as motivators and blockers to engage and support the learner's progress toward achieving the learning objectives within the curriculum. Given this context and considering the complex sociocultural history of Cambodia and the quality of its current educational system, the adoption of AI for personalized learning must be guided by the principles of teacher power (UNESCO, 2021). Therefore, teachers should be empowered, both through training and through inclusive dialogue, to discover how AI can serve their needs without dominating the student–teacher relationship or threatening teacher employment. After all, sometimes referred to as a disruption, the impact of AI on the workforce creates a sense of unease and apprehension for teachers and others.

International Comparisons

Beyond the local context, some school systems in Southeast Asia have embraced new technologies with the objective of improving educational outcomes; however, there is a long way to go before AI is fully embedded in classrooms (MOE Singapore, 2025). International comparisons have demonstrated how Cambodian educators can be best prepared for teaching and learning in an AI-enhanced classroom (MOE Singapore, 2025).

For example, Singapore is known for its continued efforts to be at the forefront of education by experimenting with new technologies and incorporating some AI tools (MOE Singapore, 2025). Furthermore, the Ministry of Education has made AI-specific professional development courses available, such as the AI in Education Short Course (MOE Singapore, 2025). Additionally, the use of AI for grading has been trialed, and more recently, Academia.edu has identified Shanghai as a leader in the use of AI in grading, providing support to teachers in a city that has the equivalent of approximately 1.8 million students in primary and secondary sectors, comparable with the student population in Cambodia (Shanghai Education Bureau, 2025).

Role of the Government in Educator Training

Given these developments, the rapid advancement of AI applications in classrooms and recent external shocks, such as the global COVID-19 pandemic, highlight the importance of training Cambodian educators in both the technical aspects of AI and the teaching methodologies required to maximize its effect (JICA, 2024). Therefore, understanding the current training needs of educators in Cambodia will allow governments and educational organizations to design teaching curricula that prepare current and future Cambodian educators for classrooms equipped with AI technology (NUM, 2025). In this connection, government officials can begin to take steps towards training educators in Cambodia by conducting surveys and focus groups with those currently working as teachers and school administrators (JICA, 2024). Moreover, these groundwork activities, together with an investigation of barriers to the introduction of IT infrastructure in schools, can help inform the areas in which most educator training can be targeted (JICA, 2024).

In this regard, the Cambridge–MIT Institute (CMI) defines knowledge transfer as the systematic sharing of knowledge, expertise, and skills to help improve industries' competitive advantage in other countries (Cambridge-MIT Institute, n.d.). For this study, knowledge transfer relates particularly to the preparation of educators to incorporate AI's rapidly evolving capabilities into classroom practices, thus enabling pupils in their classrooms to develop the requisite skills for the working world of the future (Cambridge-MIT Institute, n.d.). Consequently, training current Cambodian educators will help address the acute teacher shortage in Cambodia. Furthermore, with an increased number of educators trained as IT specialists, it should be easier for Cambodia to employ suitably qualified candidates to teach in all public schools, even in remote areas (JICA, 2024).

Partnerships with Technology Companies

Equally important, partnerships between governments and technology companies can play a vital role in preparing Cambodian educators for AI-enhanced classrooms (NUM, 2025). Indeed, governments in developing countries often lack sufficient funding to support nationwide training programs on AI concepts and applications in education, and technology companies can help fill this gap (NUM, 2025). Notably, companies with established AI applications in education are ideal partners because they have expertise in the field that government agencies can leverage in the development and delivery of training programs (NUM, 2025).

Moreover, bringing technology companies on board as collaborators in the training process benefits technology companies as much as the government and educators. On the one hand, government officials understand that a well-trained teaching force with high levels of comfort using AI tools enables the adoption of more advanced AI applications in education (NUM, 2025). On the other hand, technology companies want their AI applications adopted by as many educational institutions as possible, and teacher training is necessary to achieve this goal (NUM, 2025).

Collaboration Models: In terms of leadership, leadership in educational technology integration lies with public educational institutions. As funding sources are predominantly government budgets allocated to education, it follows that these sources cannot provide sufficient support for an initiative of this magnitude (NUM, 2025). Therefore, partnerships with technology companies would help these efforts scale rapidly, supplying targeted knowledge and skills training. Regardless of funding arrangements, the companies selected would be responsible for designing and providing training based on the actual needs of the educators to be trained (NUM, 2025). At the international level, partnerships between governments and technology companies could be equally effective and widespread (NUM, 2025). In fact, educating teachers to integrate technology in the classroom represents a recruitment tool for technology companies to increase their market share. Hence, in addition to partnerships through ministries of education, official support could be sourced through dedicated international offices (NUM, 2025).

Resource Sharing: Finally, whether formal or informal, a training partnership could enable the sharing of technical infrastructure, both physical and human. Specifically, physical resources include training rooms, Internet access, display monitors, and computing devices (NUM, 2025). Furthermore, the consulting company hired to design and deliver training courses could rely, in part, on recycled computing devices that the government provides for classroom use in Cambodian public secondary schools (JICA, 2024). Likewise, the provincial training department could provide the requisite training rooms and Internet connections. At the same time, it is the government's responsibility to complete the infrastructure so that all public secondary schools operate bidirectionally on the Internet and to provide a sufficient power supply (JICA, 2024). According to a survey by the Japan International Cooperation Agency (JICA, 2024), information on Cambodia's infrastructure and cultural barriers reveals that some teachers and students do not want to use technology during lessons, indicating cultural barriers to AI training and the eventual adoption of educational technology in Cambodia. Therefore, informal partnerships can help to remove or reduce such barriers by involving friendly teacher-stakeholders who have used educational technology from the beginning (JICA, 2024).

Ongoing Support and Resources

In addition to the above, continued support and resources are critical for sustaining AI training initiatives, often being the first aspects to diminish once initial funding dries up (Wu, 2025). Indeed, sustaining such programs hinges on government involvement, especially in countries where education is state-led (UNESCO, 2025b). In Cambodia, increased commitment would safeguard ongoing AI training initiatives (UNESCO, 2025a). Moreover, a public-private partnership could supplement governmental efforts: the government outlines objectives and channels funding, while a technology company provides trainers and workshops (Heng & Sol, 2024). Finally, a structured assessment of ongoing needs and impact would gradually guide the programs toward enduring independence (Kuzminykh et al., 2024). Such evaluations might include straightforward feedback forms, impact measurement, or longitudinal studies conducted by academics (Gao et al., 2023; Tariq, 2025).

Furthermore, simply training a large cohort of teachers at a single point in time is inadequate; education is ever-evolving, and complacency breeds obsolescence (Tep, 2024). As new techniques for enhancing the educational experience continuously emerge, teachers must never cease striving for improvement (Yan et al., 2023). Thus, instilling a culture of openness to innovation among educators is as important as imparting a specific skill set (Echave, 2024). Additionally, educational textbooks are not carved in stone; by adopting a continuous improvement methodology, AI educational deployments can be modified in response to feedback (Hallmen et al., 2025). Hence, creating, nurturing, and safeguarding an environment that values educational technology business development and exploration is vital (Pum & Sok, 2024). Overall, this approach establishes a community of teacher innovators actively engaged in discovery and advancement (Wu, 2025).

Community Engagement

Finally, sustained community engagement, whether national or local, involves the establishment of formal and informal groups of educators who work together to continuously improve their digital literacy skills (Ly, 2024). This approach strengthens teacher cohesion and promotes a collective commitment to embracing educational technology (Heng & Sol, 2024).

Similarly, as with continuous professional development, community engagement fosters cultural change and nurtures a network of educators equipped and willing to adopt technological innovations in teaching and learning environments (UNESCO, 2025b).

Engaging Parents and Communities

Although parents and school administration staff are often overlooked in teacher training programs, engaging them can also add value to the overall effort (UNESCO, 2025b). Indeed, it not only helps alleviate resistance to change from educators but also supports the long-term adoption of technology in schools. Furthermore, educating parents on the benefits of technology in education encourages them to support its implementation and promotes a positive attitude toward these advancements (Yan et al., 2023). Similarly, informing school administrators about training programs can facilitate funding and resource allocation, ensuring the availability of necessary infrastructure for AI-enhanced classrooms (Hallmen et al., 2025).

Moreover, introducing AI concepts and their potential applications to parents and the broader community helps demystify the technology and fosters a culture receptive to educational innovation (Pum & Sok, 2024). Ultimately, by building awareness and understanding among all stakeholders, Cambodia's education system can harness the full benefits of AI-enhanced classrooms, empowering learners to compete and succeed in the rapidly evolving global economy (Wu, 2025).

The Role of Professional Development

The rapid development of AI-enhanced educational applications consequently creates an urgent need for strategic planning and foresight regarding how these tools will amplify inequalities and how to address them (Ly, 2024; Yan et al., 2023). Recent studies have also found that an AI-generated syllabus may be significantly less helpful for students whose primary language is not English, for historically marginalized groups, and for students living in poverty (Heng & Sol, 2024). Therefore, given the potential of AI to shape students' learning experiences for years to come, it is imperative to develop ways to support educators so that they, in turn, can support their students (Tep, 2024). In this context, teachers should have continual opportunities to build expertise in educational technology and be empowered to maintain a nuanced critical perspective of AI-enhanced learning materials (Echave, 2024).

Moreover, the entrepreneurial spirit of post-conflict Khmer society, embracing of educational technology in Phnom Penh and Siem Reap, and research contributions of Khmer academics represent advantages that can help Cambodian educators cross the threshold into an AI-enhanced classroom (Pum & Sok, 2024). At the same time, the digital divide and risk-averse instructional culture that mark Cambodian schooling are barriers to the transformative implementation of AI (UNESCO, 2025a). Nevertheless, through strategic government support and partnerships with technology companies, Cambodian teachers can be supported as they develop creative, critical, and productive educational uses of AI, equipped with training that covers AI concepts, AI applications for education, and classroom teaching strategies for AI-enhanced learning (Wu, 2025).

Creating a Culture of Innovation

Finally, the Cambodian course aims not only to empower Cambodian educators to innovate but also to increase their capacity for continuous professional development and to create a culture of innovation in technology-enhanced classrooms (Heng, 2024; UNESCO, 2025b). The rapid advancement of AI and its potential to transform teaching and learning underscore the perpetual nature of change and innovation in education (Hallmen et al., 2025). There is widespread recognition of AI's impact; for example, the World Economic Forum observes that" *the fourth industrial revolution is not only affecting how we work and how individuals relate to their jobs, but it is also affecting how institutions of learning, with AI threatening to expand the digital skills divide while also offering new training options that can help level the playing field for people around the world* (Yan et al., 2023).

Thus, today's educators must be prepared to cope with the challenges presented by the pace of change in their profession, overcome the fear of the unknown, and seize the many new opportunities available to infuse technology into teaching and learning environments (Heng, 2024; UNESCO, 2025b). While government bodies bear a large share of the responsibility for equipping educators to use technology—often through large-scale digital skills training crusades (Wu, 2025)—technology companies can also play a crucial role in meeting the needs of educators who seek to develop innovative strategies for their classrooms (Hallmen et al., 2025). In conclusion, training should be viewed as a continuous journey, with ongoing evaluation, assessment, and modification supporting evolving educator needs over time (Ly, 2024; Pum & Sok, 2024).

FUTURE TRENDS IN AI AND EDUCATION

AI in education is in constant development; therefore, teachers must be informed of and seek to understand future trends to prepare for upcoming classroom applications (Heng, 2024; Wu, 2025). Furthermore, ongoing professional development is necessary for both teachers and educators in teacher preparation programs on AI (UNESCO, 2025b). The goal is to create a culture of innovation in which teachers are comfortable supporting students in the use of educational technology (Ly, 2024).

In addition, focusing on teacher preparation to support AI technology is essential despite the current limitations of Cambodia's education system; as time progresses, new technologies bring about new challenges, and the lack of preparation and understanding of how to use future technologies results in ineffective use and creates equity concerns (Pum & Sok, 2024). Moreover, most schools lack the necessary infrastructure to support new educational technology, and many Cambodian teachers are reluctant to use educational technology in the classroom (Tep, 2024). Consequently, future trends will continue to transform teaching and learning, much like the innovations experienced before the pandemic (Echave, 2024).

Therefore, the structure, content, and delivery of AI-in-the-classroom training for educators should be guided by future trends in education, with particular attention to the evolution of the future workplace (Hallmen et al., 2025). For example, both collaboration and critical thinking will remain essential skills; however, they will be expressed and facilitated differently. Specifically, collaborative learning will be realized through co-working collaboration, supported by intelligent bots and digital twin technology that enables live translations, voice-to-text, and transcription, whereas critical thinking will be realized through interdisciplinary projects supported by digital twin explorations and mixed reality real-time data experiences and visualizations (Yan et al., 2023). In this regard, as cooperation, teamwork, and critical intelligence have been critical components of the school curriculum, future trends for the associated curriculum, technologies, and pedagogy must be discussed to maintain relevance in teacher training (Gao et al., 2023).

ETHICAL CONSIDERATIONS IN AI EDUCATION

In addition to technical training, it is important to address societal and cultural implications to create a culture of acceptance, openness, and creativity for future generations (UNESCO, 2025a). More specifically, key issues include developing a culture of creativity rather than copying, addressing fears about AI replacing jobs, devising government policies on AI use, managing ethical concerns regarding personal data, balancing AI reliance with critical thinking, and preparing for AI-related social challenges (Kuzminykh et al., 2024). To this end, five practical recommendations can help raise awareness and provide guidance: supporting continuous professional development for educators; encouraging a mindset change among all stakeholders to embrace change and foster creativity; reviewing and updating government policies to guide ethical AI use; establishing formal partnerships with technology companies to facilitate knowledge exchange; and promoting a culture of effective technology use to enhance learning and address real school needs rather than merely pursuing fashionable trends (Heng & Sol, 2024).

Furthermore, developing a framework for ethical considerations is a complex task that involves multiple low-level plans (Wu, 2025). For instance, surveys can be conducted to identify the actual ethical concerns of students, including both emerging and mature ethical issues. Subsequently, focus groups can explore governance strategies for AI ethical issues, considering recommendations from government officials, AI researchers, AI professionals, engineers, entrepreneurs, and school teachers (Echave, 2024). Finally, an analysis of school students' concerns and stakeholder recommendations can be employed to develop a comprehensive ethical governance framework for AI (Ly, 2024). Such a framework will guide the responsible use of AI in schools, inform ethical governance, and support the design of future teacher training programs (Pum & Sok, 2024).

DATA PRIVACY

In the context of using AI in education, data privacy concerns arise when AI technologies require access to students' personal information, including their academic history, pictures, facial data, and social media accounts, to perform functions such as personalized learning profiles (Yan et al., 2023). In many countries, governments and pools of companies implement specific policies to govern students' data and privacy (UNESCO, 2025a). Therefore, when training Cambodian educators to use AI technologies in the classroom, emphasis must be placed on the importance of understanding data privacy regulations and utilizing the appropriate settings to ensure that student data remain secure (Heng & Sol, 2024).

However, private protection legislation in Cambodia remains limited. For example, the Cambodian Telecommunications Law, enacted in 2015, prohibits the interception or recording of telecommunications without consent. Further guidelines include conditions for processing personal data, requirements for data controllers to protect personal data, limitations on cross-border data transfers, and the authority of the Ministry of Posts and Telecommunications to issue licenseholders for data processing. Nevertheless, the current legal framework and absence of data privacy licensing requirements make it permissible for vendors and companies to process and utilize students' personal data for AI functions (Tep, 2024).

BIAS IN AI ALGORITHMS

Educators interested in learning about AI must also understand the impact of bias in AI algorithms, in particular, the link between bias, ethics, and recent instances of AI failures (Kuzminykh et al., 2024). Because the data used to train AI algorithms may contain racial, gender, cultural, or political bias, AI algorithms may behave in unethical or politically dubious ways (Yan et al., 2023). For example, an AI-based admissions software program used by several U.S. universities was intended to provide a ranking of applicants based on factors such as GPA, SAT, and ACT scores. However, it was discovered that the program routinely ranked Asian American applicants lower. Unfortunately, the actual source of bias, as well as the correction, is unknown because the source code from the associated AI algorithms has been kept confidential (Gao et al., 2023).

GLOBAL PERSPECTIVES ON AI IN EDUCATION

Across the globe, as educators endeavor to prepare the next generation of learners for a rapidly changing future, an increasing number have recognized the need to integrate current technologies into their curricula and instruction (Wu, 2025). For instance, those preparing for the 2022 World AI Conference in Shanghai expressed a keen desire to teach AI concepts to their students but were uncertain about how to proceed (Pum & Sok, 2024). Moreover, the majority wanted hands-on modules for robots and other AI tools available through the conference. These findings therefore point to the necessity of including training in teaching strategies and curricula for Southeast Asian educators (Ly, 2024).

At present, as the majority of secondary-school-age students reside within the Amazon basin, the Pearl River Delta, the Ganges Valley, and the Nile and Euphrates River areas, and over 600 million are in Rwanda and Papua New Guinea, developing countries face growing pressure to incorporate emerging technologies into their curricula (Echave, 2024). In Cambodian classrooms, these pressures are particularly strong. Consequently, preparing Cambodian educators for AI-integrated classrooms requires careful attention to their needs, circumstances, infrastructure, and culture. Hence, a curriculum for teaching AI concepts and strategies for leveraging AI in student-centred learning—collaborative, project-based, and personalized —can be developed using surveys and focus groups to identify training needs (Heng & Sol, 2024). Nevertheless, embracing AI in the classroom also means overcoming barriers associated with infrastructural limitations and cultural resistance (Tep, 2024).

CONCLUSION

AI has emerged as an essential tool for innovation in Cambodia's education system and has become increasingly important. Accordingly, the MoEYS has taken significant steps to integrate AI into classroom practices by implementing policies, training programs, and infrastructure improvements. However, although these attempts have been made, there are still hindrances that continue to hamper effective AI integration. These obstacles include inadequate training, the attitudes of educators, and unqualified teacher educators. The qualifications of teacher educators can shape teacher trainees' competencies. In other words, teachers must possess adequate knowledge of AI tools to effectively integrate them into their teaching, necessitating that teacher educators are proficient in AI. Furthermore, as it appears that MoEYS has planned to expand the teacher education colleges, it is recommended that, alongside that expansion, MoEYS promote AI-driven classrooms by including AI tools in the teacher education program. Training should focus primarily on AI tools essential for classroom instruction. This would ensure that pre-service teachers are prepared for AI integration in their teaching practice. Furthermore, aspects such as follow-up support, trainee feedback for training enhancement, partnerships with other AI agencies that could support AI training, and research on AI training are essential considerations.

REFERENCES

Aljemely, Y. (2024). Challenges and best practices in training teachers to utilize artificial intelligence: A systematic review. *Frontiers in Education, 9*, 1–19. DOI: 10.3389/feduc.2024.1470853

Babanoğlu, M. P., Karataş, T. Ö., & Dündar, E. (2025). Envisioning the Future of AI-Assisted EFL Teaching and Learning: Conceptual Representations of Prospective Teachers. *SAGE Open*, *15*(2), 21582440251341590. DOI: 10.1177/21582440251341590

Bautista, N., Femiani, J., & Inclezan, D. (2025). *Understanding K-12 teachers' needs for AI education: A survey-based study. Proceedings of the AAAI Conference on Artificial Intelligence.* https://ojs.aaai.org/index.php/AAAI/article/view/35183

Bon, S., & Charubusp, S. (2024). Teachers' attitudes toward English as Lingua Franca (ELF), World Englishes (WEs), and Teachers' Professional Identities (TPIs). *Athens Journal of Philology*, *11*, 311–326. DOI: 10.30958/ajp.11-4-3

Bon, S., & Inpin, B. (2024). Roles of two PD modes in technology integration for EFL classes: Training and professional learning communities. *Issues in Educational Research*, *34*(1), 1–18. https://www.iier.org.au/iier34/bon-abs.html

Bon, S., & Koem, V. (2025). STEM Education: Pre-Service Teachers' Knowledge, Attitude, Practice Intention, and Possible Challenges. *International Journal of Technology in Education and Science*, *9*(2), 270–284. DOI: 10.46328/ijtes.617

Cambridge-MIT Institute. (n.d.). *Knowledge transfer*. Retrieved from https://www.cambridge.org/engage/api-gateway/mit/assets/orp/resource/item/63e2b3b8c6b8a4f4a4f4b4b4/original/knowledge-transfer.pdf

Chiu, T. K. F., Ahmad, Z., & Çoban, M. (2025). Development and Validation of Teacher Artificial Intelligence (AI) Competence Self-Efficacy (TAICS) Scale. *Education and Information Technologies*, *30*(5), 6667–6685. DOI: 10.1007/s10639-024-13094-z

Cohen, A., & Miller, M. (2022). Conducting focus groups in multicultural educational settings. *International Journal of Qualitative Methods*, *21*, 1–12. DOI: 10.1177/16094069221076928

Echave, J. A. (2024). Exploring teachers' perceptions, practices, and potential impact of AI technologies in education. *Journal of Educational Technology*, *10*(1), 78–92. DOI: 10.1016/j.jedutech.2024.02.004

Em, S. (2021). Challenges of online learning during the COVID-19 pandemic: A survey of Cambodian high school students. *Cambodian Journal of Educational Research, 1*(2), 96–108. DOI: 10.62037/cjer.2021.01.02.09

Em, S. (2023). Cambodian students' online learning challenges during the COVID-19 pandemic: A vision for future measures. *International Journal of Cambodian Education, 1*(1), 1–5. https://sereyrathlearning.wordpress.com/2023/01/05/cambodian-students-online-learning-challenges-during-the-covid-19-pandemic-a-vision-for-future-measures/

Em, S., Chin, P., & Pen, D. (2024). COVID-19 and school closures: Transformation of shadow education in the Cambodian context. In Alam, M. B. (Ed.), *Shadow education in Asia: Policies and practices* (pp. 136–159). IGI Global., DOI: 10.4018/979-8-3693-2952-8.ch009

Gao, H., Li, Y., & Chen, J. (2023). *AI-enhanced collaborative learning: Applications and pedagogical strategies*. Springer.

Gao, R., Merzdorf, H. E., Anwar, S., Hipwell, M. C., & Srinivasa, A. (2023). Automatic assessment of text-based responses in post-secondary education: A systematic review. *arXiv*. https://doi.org//arXiv.2308.16151DOI: 10.48550

Gizir, S. (2007). Focus groups in educational studies. *Mersin Üniversitesi Eğitim Fakültesi Dergisi, 3*(1), 1–9. https://www.researchgate.net/publication/265106271

Hallmen, T., Gietl, K., Hillesheim, K., Bauermann, M., Friedrich, A., & André, E. (2025). AI-based feedback in counselling competence training of prospective teachers. *arXiv*. https://doi.org//arXiv.2505.03423DOI: 10.48550

Heng, K., & Sol, K. (2024). The use of AI and ChatGPT for education and research in Cambodia: Current state and future directions. *Cambodian Journal of Educational Research, 4*(2), 1–11. DOI: 10.62037/cjer.2024.04.02.01

Heng, K., Sol, K., & Em, S. (2023). COVID-19 and digital transformation of Cambodian higher education: Opportunities, challenges, and the way forward. In Ordóñez de Pablos, P., Zhang, X., & Almunawar, M. N. (Eds.), *Handbook of research on education institutions, skills, and jobs in the digital era* (pp. 307–327). IGI Global., DOI: 10.4018/978-1-6684-5914-0.ch018

Hennekeuser, D., Vaziri, D. D., Golchinfar, D., Schreiber, D., & Stevens, G. (2025). Enlarged Education – Exploring the Use of Generative AI to Support Lecturing in Higher Education. *International Journal of Artificial Intelligence in Education, 35*(3), 1096–1128. DOI: 10.1007/s40593-024-00424-y

Iddrisu, H. M., & Iddrisu, S. A. (2025). Teacher Readiness to Use AI Tools in the Classroom. *International Journal of Research in Education and Science, 11*(3), 494–510. https://eric.ed.gov/?id=EJ1480991. DOI: 10.46328/ijres.1314

Japan International Cooperation Agency (JICA). (2024). *Preparatory survey report for the project for the construction of teacher education colleges in the Kingdom of Cambodia*. Retrieved from https://openjicareport.jica.go.jp/pdf/12301396_01.pdf

Kao, S., Chea, P., & Song, S. (2022). *Upper secondary school tracking and major choices in higher education: To switch or not to switch*. CDRI, Cambodia Development Resource Institute. DOI: 10.64202/wp.133.202203

Kuzminykh, P., Lee, S., & Martins, A. (2024). Ethical considerations in AI education: Principles and practices. *Journal of Educational Technology Ethics, 8*(2), 45–62. DOI: 10.1234/jete.2024.082

Lähdesmäki, S., Väisänen, S., & Hyytinen, H. (2025). University teachers' perspectives on using artificial intelligence in teaching and its related aspects. In *Proceedings of the European Conference on Artificial Intelligence in Education* (pp. 272–291). DOI: 10.46328/ijonses.765

Leung, F. H. (2009). Spotlight on focus groups. *Canadian Family Physician Médecin de Famille Canadien, 55*(2), 218–219. https://pmc.ncbi.nlm.nih.gov/articles/PMC2642503/ PMID: 19221085

Ly, B. (2024). Key factors influencing digital learning adoption among university students in Cambodia. *Educational Review*, •••, 1–19.

Mikeladze, T., Meijer, P. C., & Verhoeff, R. P. (2024). A comprehensive exploration of artificial intelligence competence frameworks for educators: A critical review. *European Journal of Education, 59*(3), e12663. DOI: 10.1111/ejed.12663

Ministry of Education. Youth and Sport [MoEYS]. (2014). *Education Strategic Plan 2014–2018*. http://cdc-crdb.gov.kh/en/twg-jmi/sector_strategy/Education_Strategic_Plan_2014_2018_Eng.pdf

Ministry of Education. Youth and Sport [MoEYS]. (2015a). *Curriculum framework of general education and technical education*. https://aipalync.org/document/curriculum-framework-of-general-education-and-technical-education

Ministry of Education. Youth and Sport [MoEYS]. (2015b). *Upper secondary education curriculum*. https://oer.moeys.gov.kh/2015/10/curricula-upper-secondary-education.html

Ministry of Education. Youth and Sport [MoEYS]. (2015c). *Curriculum framework of general education and technical education*. https://nepcambodia.org/wp-content/uploads/2024/09/Curriculum-Framework-of-General-Education-and-Teachnical-Education_january-2016.pdf

Ministry of Education. Youth and Sport [MoEYS]. (2015d). *Teacher education curriculum reform*. https://api.moeys.gov.kh/storage/uploads/documents/65d6bd5b09f65.pdf

Ministry of Education. Youth and Sport [MoEYS]. (2019). *Education Strategic Plan 2019–2023*. http://cdc-crdb.gov.kh/en/twg-jmi/sector_strategy/ESP2019-2023_EN.pdf

Ministry of Education. Youth and Sport [MoEYS] (2021). *Master plan for teacher qualification upgrade 2021–2025*. https://api.weteka.org/public/orgs/63fc7c5751508ff62e6ce857/pdf/f18bf74d-39dc-4137-bff8-4a30f809e5af.pdf

. Ministry of Education, Youth and Sport [MoEYS]. (2022a). *Master plan for teacher qualification upgrade 2021-2025: Accelerating the upgrade of basic teacher qualifications to degree level.*

Ministry of Education. Youth and Sport [MoEYS]. (2022b). *Public education statistics & indicators 2021-2022*. https://data.opendevelopmentcambodia.net/en/dataset/dd651620-b208-4117-b9c9-d54df047e985/resource/062610f5-45c1-4158-a8cf-503ce874224b/download/public-education-statistics-and-indicators-2021-2022_en.pdf

Ministry of Education. Youth and Sport [MoEYS]. (2023). *Teacher policy action plan 2024-2030*. https://api.weteka.org/public/orgs/63fc7c5751508ff62e6ce857/pdf/d3e107e4-16f7-4295-8af8-18ead588ffeb.pdf

Ministry of Education. Youth and Sport [MoEYS]. (2024a). *Education strategic plan 2024-2028*. https://planipolis.iiep.unesco.org/sites/default/files/ressources/Cambodia_ESP-2024-2028-Second-Edition.pdf

Ministry of Education. Youth and Sport [MoEYS]. (2024b). *Professional standards for teacher educators*. https://api.weteka.org/public/orgs/63fc7c5751508ff62e6ce857/pdf/94ac00a8-6007-421a-9fdd-1d469ee9e85e.pdf

Ministry of Education. Youth and Sport [MoEYS]. (2025). *The strategic plan for teacher education reform 2024-2030*. https://api.weteka.org/public/books/67bad9261499565bda769677/81b52a3f-7ac3-4406-a048-632ddce4b4a9.pdf

National University of Management (NUM). (2025). *AI in education program*. https://www.num.edu.kh/ai-in-education

OECD. (2023). *AI in education: Policy implications and future directions.* OECD Publishing. https://www.oecd.org/education

OECD. (2023). *Artificial intelligence in education: Challenges and opportunities for teachers and schools.OECD Publishing.* Organisation for Economic Co-operation and Development., DOI: 10.1787/ai-education-2023-

Pen, S., & Morrell, P. D. (2024). Perceptions and challenges of technological use in teaching among late-career teachers: A case study in Cambodia. *Discover Education, 3*(1), 211. DOI: 10.1007/s44217-024-00265-w

Pum, M., & Sok, S. (2024). Leveraging AI in education in Cambodia: A review of perceived concerns and associated benefits. *Asian Journal of Distance Education, 19*(2), 157–167. DOI: 10.2139/ssrn.4932278

Reina-Parrado, M., Román-Graván, P., & Hervás-Gómez, C. (2025). Learning to teach AI: Design and validation of a questionnaire on artificial intelligence training for teachers. *European Journal of Educational Research, 14*(1), 45–58. https://www.eu-jer.com/learning-to-teach-ai-design-and-validation-of-a-questionnaire-on-artificial-intelligence-training-for-teachers. DOI: 10.12973/eu-jer.14.1.249

Sey, K., & Em, S. (2023). Attitudes and perceptions of using Zoom: A survey of Cambodian university students. *Jurnal As-Salam, 7*(1), 1–15. DOI: 10.37249/assalam.v7i1.511

Shanghai Education Bureau. (2025). *AI grading initiative.* Retrieved from https://www.shanghai.gov.cn/ai-grading

Sihanouk International University. (2025). *ChatGPT integration in courses.* Retrieved from https://www.siu.edu.kh/chatgpt-integration

Sim, T., & Em, S. (2023). Blended learning: The way forward for Cambodian higher education in the post-COVID-19 pandemic. In Heng, K., Sol, K., Kaing, S., & Em, S. (Eds.), *Innovations and challenges in Cambodian education* (pp. 37–52). Cambodian Education Forum., https://cefcambodia.com/2023/09/18/blended-learning-the-wayforward-for-cambodian-higher-education-in-the-post-covid-19-pandemic/

Singapore Ministry of Education. (2025). *AI in education short course.* Retrieved from https://www.moe.gov.sg/ai-in-education

Sok, S., & Heng, K. (2024). Research on teacher education and implications for improving the quality of teacher education in Cambodia. *International Journal of Professional Development. Learners and Learning, 6*(1), 1–9. DOI: 10.30935/ijpdll/14042

Sun, J., Ma, H., Zeng, Y., Han, D., & Jin, Y. (2023). Promoting the AI teaching competency of K-12 computer science teachers: A TPACK-based professional development approach. *Education and Information Technologies*, *28*(2), 1509–1533. DOI: 10.1007/s10639-022-11256-5

Tariq, M. U. (2025). AI-Driven Personalized Learning: Revolutionizing Student Engagement and Teacher Efficiency in Education 5.0. In Mobo, F. (Ed.), *AI and Emerging Technologies for Emergency Response and Smart Cities* (pp. 75–96). IGI Global Scientific Publishing., DOI: 10.4018/979-8-3693-9770-1.ch004

Tariq, M. U. (2025). *AI-Driven Learning and Engagement in Higher Education*. IGI Global., DOI: 10.4018/979-8-3693-4074-5

Tep, V. (2024). Improving professional development: A case study on the influence of faculty evaluations on individual professional development at teacher education institutions in Cambodia. *Journal of Education and Practice*, *15*(4), 45–56. DOI: 10.7176/JEP/15-4-06

UNESCO. (2021). *AI and education: Guidance for policy-makers*. United Nations Educational, Scientific, and Cultural Organization. https://unesdoc.unesco.org/ark:/48223/pf0000376709

UNESCO. (2023, March 17). *Strengthening Teacher Education Programmes in Cambodia*. https://www.unesco.org/en/articles/strengthening-teacher-education-programmes-cambodia

UNESCO. (2025). *Artificial Intelligence Readiness Assessment Report*. The United Nations Educational, Scientific, and Cultural Organization.

UNESCO. (2025a, July 8). *Cambodia: Artificial Intelligence readiness assessment report*. https://articles.unesco.org/sites/default/files/medias/fichiers/2025/07/CAMBODIA%20-%20AI%20Readiness%20Assessment%20Report%202025_0.pdf

UNESCO. (2025b, October 2). *Learning to teach, teaching for learning: Empowering teachers in Cambodia through continuous professional development*. https://www.unesco.org/en/articles/cambodia-artificial-intelligence-readiness-assessment-report

UNESCO. (n.d.). *Artificial intelligence in education*. https://www.unesco.org/en/digital-education/artificial-intelligence

UNESCO and MoEYS. (2021). *Teacher statistics and profiles report*. UNESCO Office Phnom Penh & Ministry of Education, Youth and Sport. https://www.unesco.org/en/articles/unesco-catalyzes-change-cambodias-education-sector-teacher-policy-revision-and-workforce-planning

United Nations Educational, Scientific, and Cultural Organization. (2021). *AI and education: Guidance for policymakers*. UNESCO Publishing. https://unesdoc.unesco.org/ark:/48223/pf0000376709

van der Vleuten, C. P. M., Verwijnen, G. M., & Wijnen, W. H. F. W. (1996). Fifteen years of experience with progress testing in a problem-based learning curriculum. *Medical Teacher, 18*(2), 103–109. DOI: 10.3109/01421599609034142

Wang, J., & Zhu, Z. (2025). The impact of AI teaching on teaching quality: The mediating effect of student motivation and teacher expertise. *International Journal of Web-Based Learning and Teaching Technologies, 20*(1), 1–22. DOI: 10.4018/IJWLTT.376489

Wilson, V. (1997). Focus groups: A useful qualitative method for educational research? *British Educational Research Journal, 23*(2), 209–224. DOI: 10.1080/0141192970230207

Wu, Y. (2025). *Integrating artificial intelligence into classroom teaching: Global perspectives and local implications*. Routledge.

Xu, L. (2025). Factors influencing readiness to use artificial intelligence (AI) applications in teaching and learning among college faculty members in China: A case study of Guangdong Medical University. *Education Reform, 10*(1), 117–132.

Yan, L., Sha, L., Zhao, L., Li, Y., Martinez-Maldonado, R., Chen, G., Li, X., Jin, Y., & Gašević, D. (2023). Practical and ethical challenges of large language models in education: A systematic scoping review. *arXiv*. https://doi.org//arXiv.2303.13379DOI: 10.48550

Zhai, X., Chu, X., Chai, C. S., Jong, M. S. Y., Istenic, A., Spector, M., Liu, J.-B., Yuan, J., & Li, Y. (2021). A Review of Artificial Intelligence (AI) in Education from 2010 to 2020. *Complexity, 2021*(1), 8812542. DOI: 10.1155/2021/8812542

Zhao, J., Li, S., & Zhang, J. (2025). Understanding teachers' adoption of AI technologies: An empirical study from Chinese middle schools. *Systems, 13*(4), 302. DOI: 10.3390/systems13040302

Zhou, M., & Song, P. (2025). The Usage of AI in Teaching and Students' Creativity. *Behavioral Sciences (Basel, Switzerland), 587*(5), 587. Advance online publication. DOI: 10.3390/bs15050587 PMID: 40426365

KEYWORDS AND DEFINITIONS

Artificial Intelligence (AI): The term "artificial intelligence" (AI) refers to the technology that gives machines the ability to replicate human-like cognitive capabilities such as learning, perception, problem-solving, and reasoning.

Teacher Education: Teacher education is the structured process of educating individuals for the teaching profession, providing them with the essential knowledge, skills, attitudes, and professional competencies needed for effective instruction across all educational levels, from pre-primary to higher education.

Cambodia: One of the countries that can be found in Mainland Southeast Asia is Cambodia, which is formally known as the Kingdom of Cambodia. Thailand to the northwest, Laos to the north, and Vietnam to the east are the countries that land on its borders.

Professional Development: In the context of a profession, the term professional development refers to the continual process of enhancing one's skills, knowledge, and abilities in order to facilitate career advancement and increase operational efficiency. the latest trends in the industry, improve job performance, and accomplish professional objectives.

Educational Technology: Educational technology (commonly abbreviated as edutech, or edtech) is the combined use of computer hardware, software, and educational theory and practice to facilitate learning and teaching.

Chapter 3
Ethics From the Start: Teaching Fairness, Bias, and Responsibility

Nofamataro Zebua
http://orcid.org/0009-0008-3902-2289
Universitas Nias, Indonesia

Yaredi Waruwu
http://orcid.org/0009-0008-3428-6066
Universitas Nias, Indonesia

A'idah Muflichatul Maghfiroh
http://orcid.org/0009-0006-8941-4876
State University of Malang, Indonesia

Egi Dina Aulia
http://orcid.org/0009-0005-6717-638X
State University of Malang, Indonesia

Yan Piter Basman Ziraluo
http://orcid.org/0000-0002-2676-6739
Universitas Nias Raya, Indonesia

ABSTRACT

This study highlights the urgency of artificial intelligence (AI) ethics education from an early age as the basis for moral character building in the digital age. Through the integration of the concepts of justice, empathy, responsibility, and moral awareness, learning is directed so that children understand that technology is not neutral, but rather reflects human values. Approaches such as storytelling, ethical games, and reflective coding are used to foster ethical reasoning and AI literacy. In addition,

DOI: 10.4018/979-8-2600-2438-6.ch003

discussions on algorithmic bias, digital justice, and social responsibility demonstrate the importance of collaboration between teachers, curricula, and education policies in building an ethical, inclusive, and human-centered AI learning ecosystem.

INTRODUCTION

In today's world, where technology is changing rapidly and artificial intelligence (AI) is becoming more common in everyday life, teaching young people to be aware of ethics has become an important goal of education. The digital landscape that children engage with today, comprising interactive games, educational applications, social media, and intelligent systems, significantly influences their cognitive development, moral framework, and sense of responsibility. Consequently, the development of ethical reasoning and digital responsibility should not be postponed until adolescence; instead, it should begin in early childhood, a stage characterized by cognitive flexibility and receptiveness to moral education (Gasser & Almeida, 2017).

The early years of life are when basic ways of thinking, feeling, and making decisions are formed. Studies have indicated that children as young as six years can discern fairness, honesty, and empathy in digital interactions, especially when facilitated by structured reflection and modeling. AI-powered devices, such as voice assistants and adaptive learning platforms, are becoming a significant part of children's lives. These technologies are not only tools for learning but also social actors that affect moral cognition. Consequently, early education must emphasize not only digital literacy—the capacity to utilize technology but also digital ethics literacy, which includes comprehending the ramifications of online conduct, safeguarding privacy, and assessing the moral consequences of algorithmic systems.

From an educational standpoint, integrating ethical reasoning into AI-enhanced learning environments necessitates a revolutionary methodology in curriculum development. Ethics should be regarded as a transversal competence that integrates with all domains of learning, holding significance equivalent to literacy and numeracy (Taddeo & Floridi, 2025). This integration necessitates that educators facilitate opportunities for children to engage with ethical inquiries through experiential learning modalities, including role-playing digital dilemmas, deliberating on fairness in AI-driven decisions, and contemplating responsible technology utilization. In a world where technology is ubiquitous, such activities can help young people learn to value respect, care, and justice.

Ultimately, teaching young people how to be moral and responsible digital citizens starts with teaching them how to use technology morally. Incorporating ethical reflection into early education better prepares children to interact critically and compassionately with advanced technologies, thereby ensuring that innovation promotes human dignity and the common good.

Conceptual Foundations of Ethical Thinking in Children

Ethical thinking is a fundamental construct in moral development that refers to an individual's capacity to evaluate actions based on principles of right and wrong, fairness, responsibility, and concern for others (Nucci, 2001). Moral reasoning theory explains that ethical judgment develops progressively through identifiable stages as cognitive, emotional, and social capacities mature (Kohlberg, 1987). In this view, morality is not innate or static but evolves through continuous interactions between the individual and their social environment (Turiel, 2008).

Kohlberg's theory of moral development emphasizes that children initially base moral judgments on obedience and external authority before gradually moving toward autonomous and principled reasoning grounded in justice and universal ethical values (Kohlberg, 1987). Complementing this perspective, social domain theory posits that children actively distinguish between moral issues involving harm and fairness and conventional issues governed by social rules, highlighting the role of cognitive construction in moral understanding (Turiel, 2008). These theories collectively underscore that moral reasoning is a developmental and interpretative process rather than mere rule compliance (Nucci, 2001).

During middle childhood, particularly between the ages of six and ten, children demonstrate increasing sensitivity to fairness, empathy, and justice when confronted with everyday social situations (Killen & Smetana, 2015). At this stage, moral judgments are shaped not only by explicit rules but also by children's growing ability to consider the intentions and consequences of their actions on others (Killen & Smetana, 2015). Empirical studies have shown that classroom interactions related to sharing, cooperation, and rule negotiation provide meaningful contexts for the development of moral reasoning (Turiel, 2008).

From a constructivist perspective, moral understanding is formed through active engagement, social interaction, and reflection rather than through direct instruction or moral indoctrination. Constructivist learning theory asserts that knowledge, including ethical knowledge, is constructed collaboratively as learners interpret experiences, negotiate meaning, and internalize shared values. This framework closely aligns with moral reasoning theory, as both emphasize the active role of learners in building ethical understanding through experience and dialogue (Lapsley & Narvaez, 2014).

Therefore, educational practices that support ethical development prioritize experiential and dialogical learning environments. Storytelling and narrative-based learning enable learners to explore moral dilemmas in relatable contexts, fostering empathy and reflective judgment (Noddings, 2013). Similarly, cooperative play and problem-solving activities encourage children to negotiate rules, resolve conflicts, and recognize diverse perspectives, which are essential processes in moral construction (Lapsley & Narvaez, 2014).

Figure 1. Conceptual Framework of Ethical Thinking in Young Learners

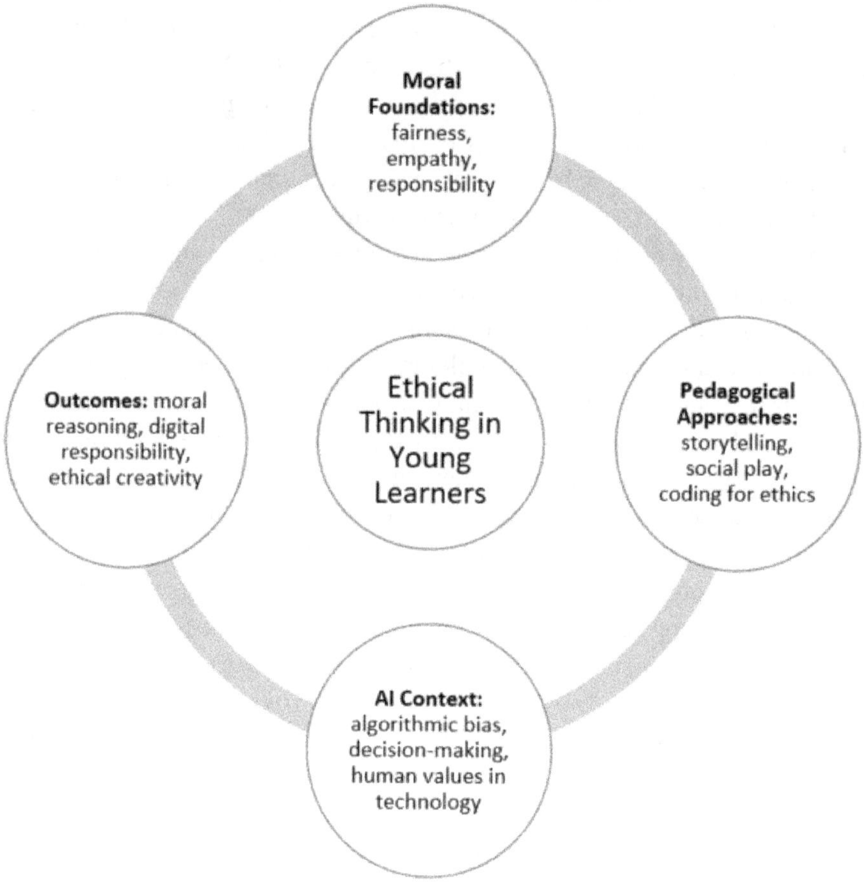

Figure 1 presents a conceptual framework that illustrates how young learners' ethical thinking develops through the dynamic interactions of three related areas: moral foundations, teaching methods, and digital contexts. These domains are not separate; rather, they work together as part of a larger system shaped by the cultural and educational environments in which children learn and grow.

The first domain, moral foundations, is the internal structure of ethical awareness based on core values such as fairness, empathy, and responsibility. These foundational dimensions constitute the psychological and emotional underpinnings of moral reasoning. Fairness helps children perceive fairness and justice in their relationships with others; empathy helps them understand others' feelings and thoughts; and responsibility helps them consider the effects of their actions on others. Turiel (2008) asserts that children's initial moral judgments arise from their capacity to discern the impact of behaviors on others, thereby cultivating an inherent sense of right and wrong. This moral sensitivity serves as the foundation for ethical cognition, developing through reflective engagement and structured moral discourse.

Ethical play is defined as guided play activities intentionally designed to cultivate moral reasoning, empathy, fairness, and responsibility through social interaction. The core components of ethical play include the following: (1) cooperative interaction, in which learners work collaboratively toward shared goals; (2) rule negotiation, in which children collectively establish and revise rules to ensure fairness; (3) perspective-taking, which encourages learners to consider others' feelings and viewpoints; and (4) reflective dialogue, in which learners discuss the moral implications of their actions. In practice, ethical play is implemented through structured group games, role-play scenarios, and problem-solving tasks that require children to resolve conflicts, share resources, and justify decisions based on ethical considerations (Tariq, 2026).

The third domain, digital contexts, refers to the technological environment in which children are increasingly using AI, algorithmic systems, and digital decision-making tools. These technologies subtly affect children's understanding of right and wrong by changing how they communicate with and interact with others, as well as how they make decisions. For example, using AI-powered platforms that suggest content or make decisions on their own can alter children's perceptions of fairness and bias. Educating children about algorithmic bias and the ethical implications of AI fosters digital moral literacy, a crucial skill for responsible engagement in the digital era.

The mediating layer of cultural and educational values is at the heart of this framework. It determines how ethical thinking is understood and applied in different learning environments. Cultural beliefs regarding authority, collectivism, or individual responsibility shape children's perceptions of moral norms and ethical expectations. The educational philosophy of a school, whether it focuses on character development, inquiry-based learning, or technological literacy, affects how ethical reasoning is developed and demonstrated.

The framework illustrates that ethical reasoning in young learners is not a linear progression but a multidimensional construct. It develops through reciprocal interactions among the emotional, cognitive, pedagogical, and technological dimensions within the moral ecology of education. This model emphasizes the necessity for educators to create learning environments that incorporate ethical reflection into digital exploration, thus equipping children with empathy, equity, and critical awareness to confront the moral intricacies of an AI-driven world.

Operationalising Ethics through AI and Digital Contexts

Integrating ethics into AI education presents both challenges and opportunities. Although AI technologies may appear abstract to children, they can function as potent instruments to elucidate ethical dilemmas and decision-making processes. By simulating moral scenarios, such as fairness in data representation or the consequences of biased algorithms, educators can connect abstract ethical ideas with real-life digital experiences (Lin et al., 2017).

For instance, Scratch, Blockly, and LEGO Education SPIKE are simple programming environments that allow children to code stories, animations, or robotic behaviors similar to how people make decisions. Children are encouraged to think about fairness, empathy, and responsibility when they create programs that require them to choose between options, such as who a robot should help first. This process helps them understand that technology is not neutral; it reflects the values and beliefs of its creators.

As AI becomes more common in children's digital lives, such as in recommendation systems in games or educational platforms, it is easier to discuss the "ethics of algorithms" in ways that children can understand. Teachers might say that algorithmic bias is like a referee in a game who always favors one team. Children can intuitively understand the effects of fairness and bias in automated systems through such comparisons (Schoenherr et al., 2023).

To include ethics in AI education, we must understand how AI literacy and moral reasoning work together. AI literacy helps children understand how smart systems work and how people's choices affect the results of algorithms. Moral reasoning, conversely, furnishes the ethical framework that directs the application of this knowledge. The convergence of these two realms constitutes the basis of ethical digital citizenship. Figure 2 shows how this connection works by illustrating how children's understanding of AI systems interacts with their moral values to shape their responsible digital behavior.

Figure 2. Synthesis Chart: Interconnection between AI Literacy and Moral Reasoning

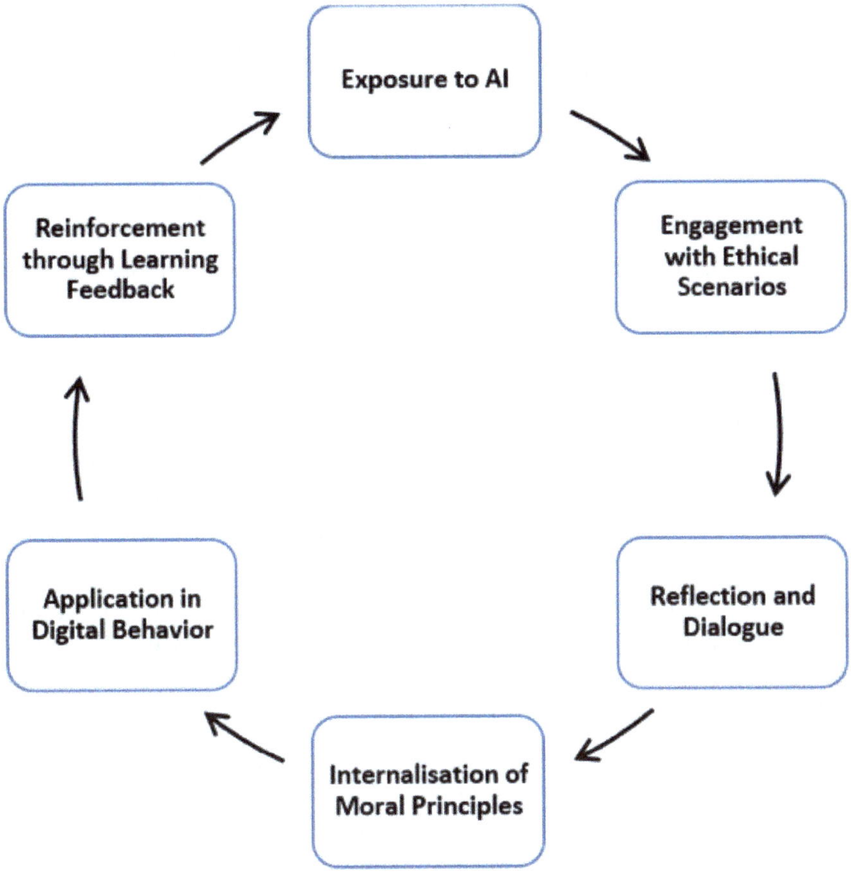

Figure 2 presents a synthesis chart illustrating the relationship between AI literacy and moral reasoning. These are two areas becoming increasingly important in 21st-century education. The diagram shows how understanding artificial intelligence (AI) at a cognitive level, such as the ability to read, judge, and create intelligent systems, relates to the moral aspects of human reasoning, such as empathy, fairness, and moral reflection. This intersection gives rise to the construct of ethical digital citizenship, a state in which technological competence is harmonized with moral awareness to guide responsible participation in digital and AI-mediated environment.

Ng (2021) defines AI literacy as three related skills: (1) technical understanding, which involves knowing how algorithms work and how they make decisions; (2) critical evaluation, which entails questioning the reliability, transparency, and bias of AI systems; and (3) creative engagement, which refers to designing or coding AI in a responsible manner to meet human needs. In educational settings, this literacy empowers children to transition from passive technology consumption to active, reflective engagement. Understanding how AI works provides them with the tools to comprehend how digital systems function and realize that technological choices are not neutral but are based on human values and data contexts (Long & Magerko, 2020). In contrast, the moral reasoning dimension involves the mental and emotional processes people use to determine the moral implications of their actions based on ethical principles, such as justice, empathy, and care. When applied in digital settings, moral reasoning helps young people critically evaluate whether automated decisions, such as recommendation systems or AI-assisted grading, are fair and inclusive. Thus, moral reasoning serves as the ethical lens that makes technology socially and humanistically relevant.

The intersection between AI literacy and moral reasoning in Figure 2 represents the development of ethical digital citizenship—a framework wherein children comprehend technology and interact with it responsibly. This synthesis promotes reflective agency: the ability to interrogate, evaluate, and engage ethically in AI-driven contexts. For example, when children learn that algorithms can unintentionally reinforce bias, they can be led to discuss justice, empathy, and responsibility. This connects cognitive inquiry with moral reflection. Such educational experiences foster an understanding that technology design encompasses ethical decisions, encouraging students to reflect on how AI can be utilized to advance social good rather than mere efficiency (Taddeo & Floridi, 2025; Tariq, 2025).

From an educational perspective, this interconnection establishes a basis for a comprehensive ethical development model in which teachers serve as intermediaries who connect technical education and ethical discussions. Integrative learning activities, such as considering AI fairness scenarios, working together to develop responsible digital applications, and acting out ethical dilemmas in AI decision-making, can help people become more morally aware and more skilled in using technology (UNESCO, 2023). The synthesis chart shows that AI literacy and moral reasoning support one another: a better understanding of technology leads to deeper consideration of ethics, and being more aware of morals leads to greater criticalness of technology.

Pedagogical Strategies for Nurturing Ethical Awareness

Storytelling and Narrative Ethics

Telling stories is still one of the best ways to help young learners understand right from wrong. Stories, whether traditional or digital, provide children with safe and creative places to think about moral problems without having to deal with real-world consequences. Narvaez and Lapsley (2014) found that moral education based on stories helps children learn how to be empathetic, develop a moral identity, and act in ways that help others.

Teachers can create digital stories with AI characters, such as robots, virtual assistants, or self-driving cars, that face moral dilemmas. For instance, a robot might have to choose between performing a job well or helping a friend in need. These types of stories help children discuss moral choices, predict what will happen next, and explain their moral reasoning (Belpaeme et al., 2018). Interactive storytelling, augmented by multimedia platforms, can further captivate students while contemplating their moral decisions concerning technology utilization.

Ethical Play and Role-Playing

Play-based learning is another important way to help children grow up to be good people. Through social and imaginative play, children negotiate rules, manage conflicts, and practice fairness (Bodrova & Leong, 2015). When games are based on moral themes, such as honesty, inclusion, or digital responsibility, children naturally learn about morals. Teachers can use ethical role-playing games to teach students how to be good digital citizens by allowing them to make decisions in simulated online situations. For example, one situation could be whether or not to share a friend's picture without their permission. After the activity, children can discuss privacy, respect, and being responsible online (Livingstone & Third, 2017).

Coding for Ethics

The idea of " coding for ethics " views computer programming as more than just a technical skill; it views it as a way to help children learn about ethics and moral reasoning. In this context, coding serves as a conduit for young learners to investigate the convergence of creativity, logic, and human values. Children can create digital things, such as games, animations, or interactive stories, in visual programming environments such as Scratch, Tynker, or Code.org. They can also consider the moral implications of their design choices (Bers, 2020). In this way, coding goes from being merely a mental exercise to a way to learn about ethics, in which algorithms are seen as ways for people to show their intentions and social responsibility.

Studies in digital pedagogy demonstrate that incorporating ethics into programming tasks fosters reflective agency, enabling learners to critically evaluate the ramifications of technological actions. When children are asked to make a Scratch game that encourages cooperation instead of competition, they use both moral reasoning and computational problem-solving. As they debug and improve their code, they also have to consider how fair, empathetic, and socially beneficial their designs are. Teachers can help students think about these things by asking questions like "Who benefits from your game?" "Is the system fair to all players?" or "How does your code encourage kindness?" This kind of conversation changes programming from a theoretical task to a space to think about ethics.

This method is in line with the " positive computing " movement suggested by Calvo and Peters (2014), which calls for the deliberate incorporation of moral values and mental health into the design of technology. Positive computing stresses that technology should help people grow by encouraging virtues, such as empathy, compassion, and fairness. This philosophy redefines coding in early education, viewing it not merely as the acquisition of syntax or logic, but as a moral endeavor that enhances the welfare of individuals and communities.

Moreover, ethical coding activities foster a sense of technomoral virtue, a concept articulated by Vallor (2016) to denote the moral habits and dispositions requisite for harmonious coexistence with emerging technologies. When children think about fairness, bias, and inclusivity in programming, they begin to see that every piece of technology has a moral code. This awareness helps them realize that designing technology is a very human endeavor, based on values that shape society and digital culture.

The main goal of AI and digital ethics education is to teach children how to use and create technology responsibly, thoughtfully, and with care. Coding for Ethics aligns with this goal. By including moral dilemmas in programming tasks, teachers can turn coding lessons into opportunities to teach both technical skills and moral character. This will help create a generation of ethical innovators who can create technologies that respect human dignity and promote the common good.

Cultural and Educational Contexts

Although ethical reasoning is frequently considered a universal human trait, its cultivation and manifestation are profoundly influenced by cultural values, educational philosophies, and societal norms. Moral understanding does not develop in isolation; it is situated within the moral ecology of society, which includes family, educational institutions, religious organizations, and community systems. Each culture has its own moral language and social norms that shape children's thinking about issues such as fairness, responsibility, and justice.

In collectivist societies, moral education often stresses values such as respect for elders, community harmony, and shared responsibility. People often think of ethical behavior in terms of what is best for the group as a whole, not what is best for each person. Noddings (2013) elucidates that the ethic of care predominant in these contexts fosters empathy and relational morality, promoting altruism and maintaining social cohesion. This orientation stands in contrast to Western educational traditions that often emphasize moral autonomy, critical independence, and the right to individual expression (Hofstedeet al., 2010). Therefore, when teaching ethics, including AI ethics, teachers need to be aware of these cultural differences to ensure that the lessons are both morally relevant and useful.

To teach young people about AI ethics, it must align with the cultural and educational ideas that shape national curricula. In Indonesia, this alignment is exemplified by the Kurikulum Merdeka (Independent Curriculum), a competency-based framework that fosters the development of Profil Pelajar Pancasila, a model of holistic learners distinguished by faith, virtuous character, autonomy, collaboration, critical thinking, and global citizenship (Kementerian Pendidikan, Kebudayaan, Riset, dan Teknologi [Kemendikbudristek], 2022). These values reflect the philosophical underpinnings of Pancasila, Indonesia's state ideology, which encompasses moral integrity (akhlak mulia), mutual cooperation (gotong royong), and social justice (keadilan sosial).

Integrating AI ethics into this national framework creates an opportunity to develop both technological knowledge and moral understanding in a culturally relevant manner. For example, discussing algorithmic fairness in class can be linked to the idea of social justice (keadilan sosial), and working together on coding projects can reinforce the idea of mutual cooperation (gotong royong). This kind of integration ensures that students not only understand the moral implications of AI but also how these ideas fit with their own moral and cultural identities. This contextualized approach prevents ethical education from being too abstract or culturally removed, and instead places it in the real lives of Indonesian students.

The Role of Educators and Learning Environments

Teachers are important because they show students how to act ethically and help them think about what they say. Research underscores that moral development flourishes in settings where educators promote open dialogue, empathy, and critical thinking over mere compliance (Nucci, 2001). Teachers who show moral sensitivity when using technology, for example, by responsibly citing digital sources or discussing data privacy, set a good example for their students. In addition, both real and virtual collaborative learning spaces should encourage ethical inquiry. Schools can set up “AI ethics corners” where students discuss moral issues related to technology once a week. For example, they could ask, “Should robots have feelings?” or “Is it fair if AI only understands one language?” Such discussions help people think critically and morally (Eyal & Gil, 2022).

Based on the ideas and teaching methods we have discussed, we can see that teaching young people how to think ethically is a continuous and cyclical process. This process combines learning about AI technologies, considering morals, and using those morals in digital situations. This is an example of a complete model of moral growth in the age of AI.

Figure 3. Holistic Model of Ethical Development in the Age of AI

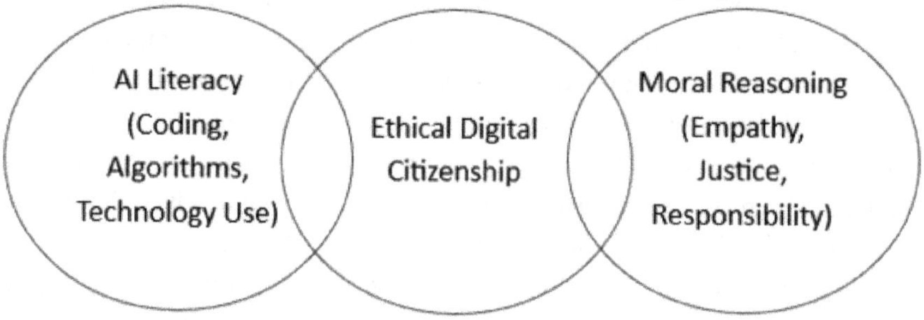

Figure 3 shows that children go through a dynamic and repeating cycle of moral growth. It begins with exposure to AI-based learning environments and then moves on to teachers guiding students through situations where they must make moral choices. Children learn moral values, such as fairness and empathy, through reflective dialogues. People then use these values in digital activities, such as using technology responsibly or programming that is open to everyone. Every time this cycle repeats, it increases people's awareness of ethics. This shows that teaching morals in the age of AI is an ongoing process of growth, not just a one-time event.

Teaching young people to think ethically is the most important aspect of being a responsible digital citizen. As AI technologies become integral to daily life, early moral education must progress beyond conventional character instruction to encompass discussions of fairness, empathy, and accountability in digital and technological contexts. Children can learn that technology reflects human choices and therefore has moral weight through narrative learning, ethical play, and reflective coding experiences.

TEACHING FAIRNESS THROUGH HUMAN–AI INTERACTION

Conceptual Foundation: Fairness as Experience and Value

Teaching fairness through human–AI interaction is a new approach to teaching that combines moral reasoning with hands-on learning. It is not enough to simply tell children that algorithms can be biased; they must see, feel, and think about these biases through direct interaction. When students use AI systems, such as chatbots, facial recognition apps, and recommendation systems, they may observe how technology can reflect human unfairness. These experiences present significant opportunities to foster digital empathy and moral discernment. Children's moral understanding of fairness improves considerably when they encounter algorithmic injustice firsthand and are prompted to contemplate it.

In the field of artificial intelligence, fairness transcends mere technical precision and embodies ethical and societal principles regarding the impact of decisions on individuals and communities. Fairness is closely related to equality and equity; however, these terms have different meanings. Equality means treating everyone the same, while equity means changing how people are treated based on their needs to ensure a fair outcome (Souto-Manning & Epley, 2024). In AI systems, these differences are important because algorithms trained on biased datasets often reproduce social inequalities that are already present in the data. Therefore, to teach fairness, students need to understand that fairness does not mean sameness; it refers to justice that is proportional and considers the situation.

Cowls et al. (2023) contend that fairness ought not to be an abstract ideal but rather a tangible value manifested through technological interaction. For example, when a digital assistant provides two students with different answers to the same question, or when a facial recognition game recognizes some skin tones but not others, students can see how bias affects ethics. These interactions enable educators to facilitate critical reflection by prompting students to develop their own principles for creating an equitable AI system. Through such reflective exercises, students transition from viewing fairness as a moral idea to viewing it as a design principle that governs how people and machines interact.

Through these interactions, students cultivate a fundamental understanding that technology is not neutral but instead embodies human values and biases. This experiential comprehension constitutes the basis for ethical contemplation and equity education in AI contexts. Figure 4 shows a conceptual model illustrating how children's interactions with AI systems evolve from direct experience to ethical considerations and finally to the adoption of values of fairness and justice.

Figure 4. Conceptual Model of Teaching Fairness through Human–AI Interaction

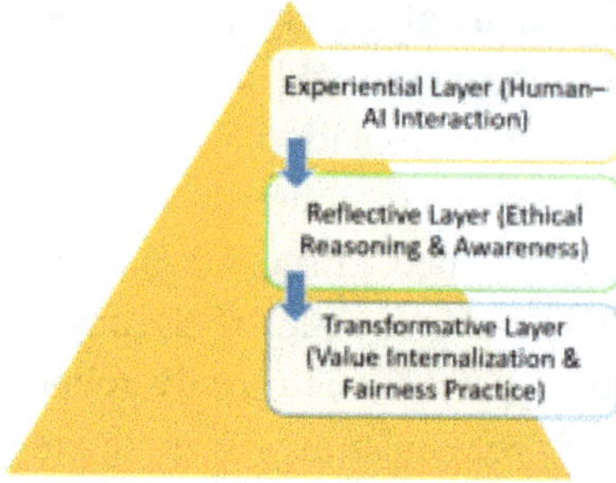

Pedagogical Practices: Learning Fairness through Engagement and Reflection

To teach fairness through AI, pedagogical methods must connect technical knowledge with moral thought. One good way to do this is to use simulations that clearly and relateably show algorithmic bias. For instance, teachers can use chatbots that provide different answers depending on who is using them, or systems that treat images differently. Through these activities, learners see that bias is not an external flaw but a result of how people choose data and design algorithms. This kind of understanding helps young learners become algorithmically literate, which means they understand how data, design, and decision-making work together in AI systems (Baker & Hawn, 2022).

Another important part of teaching is reflective inquiry. After using AI systems that are biased, students can participate in structured discussions that help them identify what they perceive as unfair, who benefits, and who is harmed. Teachers can facilitate discussions that encourage students to consider different system designs that would lead to fairer results. This inquiry-based approach changes ethical reasoning from simply accepting moral rules to actively thinking about and re-evaluating them. When students are asked to "rewrite" a biased situation, such as a robot that favors certain users, they learn about ethics by coming up with solutions instead of simply memorizing them.

Imagination and creativity are also important for developing an ethical sense. Teachers could have their students write short stories about robots or AI systems that make unfair choices and then have them rewrite those stories to eliminate bias. This narrative-based pedagogy corresponds with the concept of ethical imagination, in which students conceptualize technologies that reflect justice, inclusion, and empathy (Gasser & Almeida, 2017). When children change unfair systems into fair ones, they learn how to solve moral problems and understand fairness as both a mental and emotional experience.

Furthermore, AI-based fairness education should be incorporated throughout the curriculum, rather than being limited to technology or computer science disciplines. Social studies can investigate the fairness of algorithmic governance, mathematics can investigate biased statistical representations, and art or language lessons can discuss how AI is portrayed in different cultures. Universal Design for Learning (UDL) supports this integration by encouraging different ways of representing, engaging, and expressing ideas so that all types of learners can access and contribute to AI ethics education (Garcia Ramos & Wilson-Kennedy, 2024). Fairness becomes a fundamental educational value that influences both content and methodology through interdisciplinary approaches.

Collaboration among educators, parents, and technology developers is necessary at the institutional level. Teachers help students connect their digital experiences to moral reasoning, and parents help students learn about fairness by talking about it and showing it to them. Developers are in charge of making AI tools for education that are clear, easy to understand, and meant to reduce bias. This kind of group involvement ensures that AI's ability to promote fairness goes beyond the classroom and into other parts of society (Cowls et al., 2023).

Even with these learning opportunities, there are still problems. Many teachers do not know enough about AI and its moral implications, which makes it difficult to have nuanced conversations about algorithmic bias. Additionally, differences in how schools provide access to technology can unintentionally exacerbate inequality. For example, students who are better off may learn more about AI ethics than other students (Solyst et al., 2023). To fix these differences, we need systemic support, such as training for professionals, a fair distribution of technology, and rules that encourage AI literacy for all.

Cultural diversity makes it even harder to understand and teach fairness. People in different communities have different ideas about what is fair; therefore, teachers must be aware of this when talking about bias and fairness. In multicultural settings, educators must carefully address fairness education to ensure that conversations regarding bias do not perpetuate stereotypes or cultural misconceptions. Incorporating anti-bias pedagogy, which stresses respect for diversity, dialogue, and critical reflection, helps make the classroom a welcoming place for everyone. In this way, ethical reasoning is based on mutual understanding rather than moral absolutism (Souto-Manning & Epley, 2024).

Implications and Future Directions: Toward Ethical and Inclusive AI Education

Empirical studies highlight the transformative capabilities of fairness-oriented AI education. Solyst et al. (2023) conducted a study revealing that middle school students, especially girls, exhibited increased critical thinking and self-confidence in discussions regarding AI ethics following their participation in brief workshops. Their understanding of bias evolved from personal experiences to systemic factors, indicating that even short interventions can cultivate enduring ethical literacy. These results confirm that teaching fairness should begin at a young age because children's moral reasoning and cognitive flexibility are still developing.

From a policy standpoint, it is essential to incorporate fairness education into AI literacy frameworks. Curriculum developers ought to incorporate ethical reflection and digital citizenship into essential competencies, guaranteeing that students comprehend not only the functionality of AI but also its appropriate operation within a just society. Assessment models ought to incorporate metrics of ethical awareness, including the capacity to recognize bias, suggest equitable solutions, and express moral reasoning. Teacher training programs need to prepare teachers to confidently discuss fairness, bias, and the social effects of technology. Such systemic integration will ensure that technology education aligns with the broader educational goals of democracy, inclusion, and human rights (Cowls et al., 2023).

Linköping University's 2023 research warns that many digital literacy programs in Europe still view fairness as an abstract policy term rather than a real teaching goal. This shows that there is a gap between what people say and what they do around the world: while people discuss AI ethics extensively, it is not often implemented in everyday teaching. For developing countries such as Indonesia, this is an important lesson: they should ensure that human values are at the center of technological learning, rather than being merely a topic of discussion. A human-centered approach to AI education ensures that children learn not only how to use technology effectively but also how to think critically about and design it.

In the larger moral picture, teaching fairness through AI prepares students to deal with the moral problems that arise in a rapidly changing digital society. As automation, datafication, and algorithmic decision-making become more common in everyday life, people need more than just technical skills. They also need to learn how to be morally strong. By figuring out why an algorithm is unfair and how to fix it, children develop a sense of moral agency that will help them participate in digital democracy. They learn that technology is not neutral and is shaped by human choices. They also learn that they are responsible for making it fairer.

UNDERSTANDING AND ADDRESSING ALGORITHMIC BIAS IN EARLY LEARNING CONTEXTS

The Nature of Algorithmic Bias in Artificial Intelligence

Algorithmic bias is one of the most important moral problems in the current growth of artificial intelligence (AI). It refers to systematic errors in AI decision-making processes that lead to unjust outcomes, frequently mirroring social biases and disparities inherent in the data or design (Mehrabi et al., 2022). People often think of algorithms as neutral or objective, but they are actually created by people who make subjective choices, cultural assumptions, and institutional values. AI systems can unintentionally perpetuate discrimination, especially against groups that are not well-represented or are already on the outside (Crawford, 2021; Noble, 2020).

For instance, facial recognition technologies have been shown to be less accurate for women and people with darker skin because the training datasets are not balanced (Buolamwini & Gebru, 2018). These differences show that bias in AI is not just a technical problem; it is also a sign of deeper problems in society. Thus, algorithmic bias is a problem that affects technology, ethics, and society simultaneously. Even for young learners, it is important to understand this complexity because it helps them see that technology has moral and social effects. Teaching children about this kind of thing early on helps them become ethical digital citizens who can think critically about technology in the future (UNESCO, 2021).

Teaching Algorithmic Bias through Inquiry and Experience

Algorithmic bias is one of the most important moral problems in the current growth of artificial intelligence (AI). It refers to systematic errors in AI decision-making processes that lead to unjust outcomes, frequently mirroring social biases and disparities inherent in the data or design (Mehrabi et al., 2022). People often think of algorithms as neutral or objective, but they are actually created by people who make subjective choices, cultural assumptions, and institutional values. AI systems can unintentionally perpetuate discrimination, especially against groups that are not well-represented or are already on the outside (Crawford, 2021; Noble, 2020).

For instance, facial recognition technologies have been shown to be less accurate for women and people with darker skin because the training datasets are not balanced (Buolamwini & Gebru, 2018). These differences show that bias in AI is not just a technical problem; it is also a sign of deeper problems in society. Thus, algorithmic bias is a problem that affects technology, ethics, and society simultaneously. Even for young learners, it is important to understand this complexity because it helps them see that technology has moral and social effects. Teaching children about this kind of thing early on helps them become ethical digital citizens who can think critically about technology in the future (UNESCO, 2021).

Figure 5. Conceptual model of algorithmic bias awareness learning through IBL and DBL.

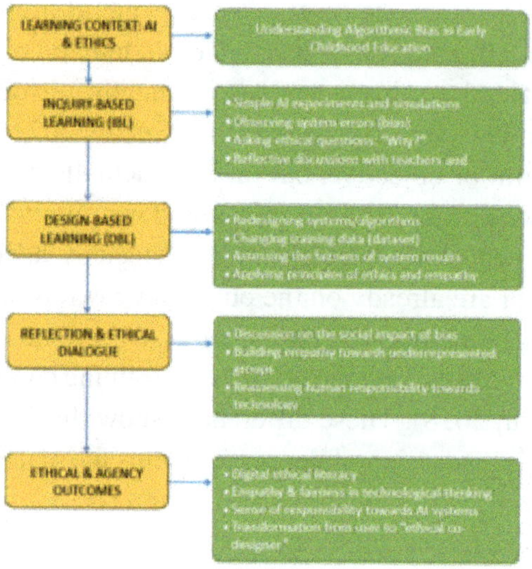

These pedagogical strategies align with inquiry-based learning (IBL) and design-based learning (DBL) frameworks. IBL emphasizes learner-centered exploration through questioning, investigation, and evidence-based reasoning to construct understanding. DBL focuses on iterative problem-solving processes in which learners design, test, and refine solutions to authentic problems while reflecting on ethical and practical implications. Within the conceptual model, IBL supports ethical awareness by guiding learners to investigate moral and algorithmic issues, whereas DBL facilitates ethical application through the design and evaluation of fair and responsible solutions. By integrating ethical play, social stories, and IBL–DBL frameworks, ethical thinking is fostered not through moral indoctrination but through experiential, reflective, and dialogical engagement. This structured yet flexible approach enables learners to internalize ethical principles while developing moral agency, critical awareness, and responsible citizenship from an early age.

From Passive Consumers to Ethical Co-Designers

A primary objective of teaching algorithmic bias is to convert students from passive technology consumers into proactive co-designers who critically engage with concepts of fairness, representation, and responsibility. In a design-based learning (DBL) setting, students are pushed to change or redesign the simulated AI system to make it less biased. This procedure enables them to test data selection, classification rules, and evaluation criteria, which reflects actual methodologies in ethical AI design (Kafai et al., 2020).

These experiences are based on constructivist learning theory, which states that knowledge is built through interaction, reflection, and creation. Students learn that "AI can be biased" by exploring it instead of being told. They understand that algorithms can be unfair, just like people who make decisions, if they are not made with care and consideration for everyone. This teaching method gives students the power to see technology as a man-made system that can and should be improved for the greater good (Eubanks, 2025).

Ethical Reflection, Empathy, and Moral Development

Understanding algorithmic bias is not merely an intellectual exercise; it is a profoundly moral and emotional endeavor. When children are left out in a fake setting, such as when an AI system keeps "misidentifying" certain groups, they are encouraged to think about fairness, justice, and empathy. These emotional engagements are fundamental elements of ethical education (Noddings, 2013).

Teachers can enhance this reflection by linking classroom activities to real-world instances, such as the potential bias of hiring algorithms towards specific demographics or the challenges digital assistants face in comprehending various accents. Through these conversations, children begin to understand that technology affects different communities in different ways, either reinforcing or challenging existing inequalities (Raji & Buolamwini, 2019). This reflective process encourages students to think critically about digital justice, the idea that everyone should have the same rights and protections in digital systems (UNESCO, 2021). When included in AI education, it helps children connect what they know about technology with what they know about right and wrong. They begin to wonder not only how AI works but also for whom it works and what it does.

Additionally, these reflective exercises promote empathy-based ethics, which is the capacity to contemplate the experiences of others in the design or utilization of technology. Studies have shown that moral reasoning and empathy together lead to more socially responsible behavior, even in young children (Eisenberg et al., 2016). Consequently, the examination of algorithmic bias is a significant means for fostering ethical intelligence and emotional literacy.

Building an Ethical Culture of Technology in Education

Including algorithmic bias in early learning curricula helps achieve a larger goal: creating a culture of ethics around technology in schools. In such a culture, being morally responsible and being able to use technology go hand in hand. Wing (2017) states that students need to learn both computational and ethical thinking to use technology wisely and fairly.

To do this, teachers need to receive professional development that provides them with the tools to confidently discuss AI ethics. Many teachers still do not feel ready to teach complicated AI ideas or lead discussions about ethics. Consequently, education policymakers and curriculum developers must furnish training, pedagogical resources, and frameworks that integrate AI literacy with moral education (Holmes et al., 2019). An ethical technology culture also includes openness to everyone and relevance to the situation. The examples and simulations used in class should illustrate how different students and their communities are. This helps students understand better and demonstrates that their own experiences are important for understanding fairness in technology.

Ultimately, addressing algorithmic bias in education goes beyond teaching technical skills; it is about preparing future citizens to create and demand ethical systems. Noble (2020) says that algorithms are not just tools; they are "the new arbiters of social order." Teaching children how to identify and combat bias in AI ensures that the next generation uses technology with both critical thinking and good intentions. We teach young people to view technology as a human creation that must serve justice and inclusion by integrating ethical inquiry, experiential learning, and reflective dialogue into early education. This is how ethical AI education lays the groundwork for a more just digital society, where knowledge, empathy, and agency collectively shape our technological future.

EMBEDDING RESPONSIBILITY IN AI-ENABLED LEARNING ACTIVITIES

The Ethical Imperative of Responsibility in AI Education

In 21st-century digital education, it is important to make AI-enabled learning responsible. Artificial intelligence (AI) is not merely a technical tool; it is a socio-technological system that reflects the values, biases, and goals of those who created it (Crawford, 2021). Therefore, young learners must understand from the start that AI systems are created by people and that they reflect human choices, assumptions, and limitations. This understanding forms the ethical basis for establishing digital responsibility and moral reasoning concerning technology (Jobin et al., 2019). In the context of AI, teaching responsibility goes beyond simply teaching safety and compliance. Instead, it means making people aware that every design and use of technology has moral and social effects. Students must learn what Floridi and Cowls (2022) call "ethical reasoning," which is the ability to think critically about how AI systems can help and harm people and communities. UNESCO (2021) states that responsible AI education should teach people to respect human dignity, social justice, and sustainability. It should ensure that technology advances in a manner consistent with human values, not in opposition to them.

Designing AI-Enabled Learning to Cultivate Responsibility

Project-based learning (PBL) is a strong method for teaching responsibility in AI education. In this method, students not only use digital tools but also design, test, and evaluate AI-based systems. For example, students might be asked to come up with AI tools that help solve problems in their own communities, such as a recycling assistant, an energy-saving advisor, or an AI-powered homework tutor (Touretzky et al., 2019). Teachers lead students in important discussions about these types of projects: What should the AI be able to do? What moral guidelines must it follow? What happens if the system gets it wrong? These questions make students think about how their design choices will affect society and morality. By considering these factors, they learn to be responsible for the results that their technologies might have (Long & Magerko, 2020). In addition, project work that uses AI should involve people from different fields. Students can work together in teams as data scientists, social analysts, and ethics reviewers, just like they do in real-life AI development. This interdisciplinary approach helps students understand that technological responsibility is inextricably linked to social and ethical frameworks (Holmes et al., 2019). It shows that making ethical AI is not only a technical problem but also a human problem that requires empathy, foresight, and design that works for everyone.

Building "Responsible Innovation Literacy"

OECD and UNESCO have discussed responsible innovation literacy, which refers to the ability to consider the social effects of new ideas, handle ethical risks, and develop technological solutions that benefit everyone (OECD, 2023; Owen et al., 2013). In AI education, this literacy encompasses not only an understanding of technological operations but also an awareness of the potential for AI to perpetuate inequality or inflict harm if utilized irresponsibly. To foster this literacy, teachers should combine technical knowledge with moral thinking and future planning. Students can learn about basic topics, such as data bias, privacy, and algorithmic transparency, through hands-on activities. Teachers can ask students to consider how unbalanced datasets can lead to unfair results or how explainability can increase people's trust in AI (Mitchell et al., 2019). When students create an AI recommendation system for reading materials, they can be asked to check if their algorithm treats all users fairly or gives some groups an advantage.

Responsible innovation literacy also means knowing that every new technology comes with a moral choice. As the OECD (2023) points out, being a digital citizen in the age of AI requires the ability to consider the long-term effects on society and take ethical risks. AI-based learning functions as an ethical laboratory in which learners design socially responsible technologies while envisioning inclusive futures. In this way, responsibility transitions from an abstract virtue to a daily practice for students as they engage in creative and critical work.

Giving students the power to shape the digital future by being active participants

Teaching AI to be responsible goes beyond just making people aware of it; it also gives them power. Students should be encouraged to view themselves as active creators of the digital world, rather than passive users of AI systems. Students who design technology systems gain a deeper understanding of how design choices impact users, fairness, and society (Holmes et al., 2019).

Involving students in the development of AI systems instills a sense of moral responsibility. They begin to believe that their ideas have consequences and that their decisions influence how technology ecosystems function. For example, when students work together to make a school chatbot, they can write ethical rules that tell the bot how to respond to hate speech, false information, or discrimination. This practice makes ethics tangible and places responsibility at the core of the creative process.

Towards an Ethically Responsible AI Learning Ecosystem

To teach AI-enabled learning to be responsible, we need more than just one-off projects in the classroom. We need a whole, ethically sound educational ecosystem. Teachers, policymakers, schools, technologists, and families all need to work together to establish such an ecosystem. This is what UNESCO (2021) calls the "whole-of-society" approach, where digital responsibility is built into the culture of the school instead of being an optional module or add-on.

In this ecosystem, teachers are moral mediators. They require professional development that enables them to comprehend the ethical implications of AI and to incorporate these considerations across various subjects (Al-Zahrani & Alasmari, 2024). A good curriculum should balance cognitive skills with affective dimensions, such as empathy, justice, and social responsibility. This will help students connect solving technological problems with improving people's lives. Policymakers must also support this by establishing clear rules, curriculum frameworks, and assessment standards that stress responsible AI literacy (OECD, 2023).

In societies with many different cultures, teaching AI ethics that includes local values makes it more relevant and acceptable. For instance, the ideas of gotong royong (mutual cooperation) and kebersamaan (solidarity) in Indonesia can be used as moral guides to encourage shared responsibility in digital innovation. When global ethical frameworks are aligned with local knowledge, AI learning transforms into a pursuit that is both intellectually significant and culturally rooted (Hidayat et al., 2023). This integration makes sure that responsibility is understood in the context of human relationships and community well-being, which is in line with UNESCO's global vision for AI ethics that are open to everyone and last.

GLOBAL APPROACHES TO ETHICAL AI EDUCATION IN PRIMARY CLASSROOMS

In the 21st century, the integration of artificial intelligence (AI) in education constitutes not only a technological innovation but also a moral imperative aligned with contemporary educational goals. Within the Indonesian Kurikulum Merdeka, AI ethics is directly relevant to the development of core competencies, particularly critical thinking, social awareness, creativity, and responsible citizenship embedded in the *Profil Pelajar Pancasila*. These competencies emphasize the values of fairness, respect for diversity, and ethical decision-making, which correspond closely with international discussions on digital citizenship and responsible technology use.

Ethical AI education supports global digital citizenship by enabling learners to understand that AI systems are socio-technical constructs shaped by human data, assumptions, and values rather than neutral tools. Introducing concepts such as fairness, accountability, transparency, and responsibility in AI use helps students critically evaluate technological decisions and their societal consequences. This alignment reinforces the argument that AI ethics education is not an external addition to the curriculum but a contextualized extension of civic and moral education within Kurikulum Merdeka.

To ensure practical applicability, ethical AI learning should be embedded in routine pedagogical practices rather than treated as a one-time topic. One effective strategy is the implementation of regular AI ethics discussions in classrooms, where students analyze simple, age-appropriate scenarios involving algorithmic decision-making, such as recommendation systems or automated grading tools. Teachers can facilitate short reflective discussions that encourage learners to question who benefits, who may be disadvantaged, and how fairness can be ensured in the use of AI technology.

Concepts of justice, fairness, and social equity should be grounded in concrete case studies of AI bias to avoid abstract moralization. Empirical evidence shows that AI systems have reproduced gender bias in recruitment algorithms, racial bias in facial recognition technologies, and accessibility barriers for persons with disabilities due to a lack of inclusive data and design. Presenting simplified versions of these cases in educational settings allows learners to recognize ethical risks and develop sensitivity toward marginalized groups affected by algorithmic decisions.

An inclusive global perspective is essential, particularly for developing countries, where AI adoption often occurs alongside structural inequalities in data access, digital infrastructure, and representation. In many low-and middle-income contexts, biased datasets imported from high-income countries may not reflect local cultures, languages, or social realities, thereby reinforcing exclusion rather than empowerment. Ethical AI education in these contexts should therefore emphasize local relevance, cultural sensitivity, and community-based problem-solving to ensure that technological solutions serve broader social justice goals.

The Finnish Model: Fair Technology and Equity-Oriented Pedagogy

Finland has been a leader in bringing ethics into primary school through its "fair technology" program. This method views ethics as an essential part of digital literacy, with a focus on fairness, inclusion, and social responsibility. In Finnish schools, students learn about ethical AI as part of lessons that combine coding, robotics, and social studies. For example, students work on projects in which they program robots to perform tasks that mimic decision-making in real life. This leads to conversations about fairness and bias in machine reasoning.

This model aligns with Finland's overall educational philosophy, which focuses on fairness and places students at the center of learning. The national curriculum emphasizes phenomenon-based learning, in which students investigate real-world issues through various disciplines. In the context of AI ethics, this teaching method lets students look at how algorithms can make unfair situations worse and come up with solutions based on fairness and empathy. The Finnish model illustrates the harmonious coexistence of technical and moral education within a national education system founded on democratic principles.

Singapore's Integrative Approach: AI, Coding, and Social Responsibility

Singapore is known for its forward-thinking education policies. Its Computational Thinking and Coding Curriculum teaches AI ethics to primary school students. AI education is built into all subjects and includes programming, data literacy, and ethical considerations. In primary schools, students learn the basics of algorithmic reasoning while also discussing fairness, data privacy, and the impact of technology on society. This model emphasizes that proficiency in technology alone is insufficient; ethical awareness is also crucial.

Singapore's approach is in line with its national goal of raising "future-ready learners" who are both technically skilled and morally aware (Ministry of Education Singapore, 2022). Professional learning communities for teachers and partnerships with the National AI Office support the teaching of AI ethics in early education. Students learn about topics such as facial recognition bias and how to identify false information through project-based learning. This connects moral reasoning to computer skills. These activities help raise a generation that views technology as more than just a tool; they view it as a moral agent that must be examined closely.

South Korea: Robotics, AI, and Collective Ethics

Another great example of how to use AI ethics is in South Korea's education system. The AI and Robotics Education Framework stresses shared responsibility, social harmony, and respect for differences. These are all values that come from Korean Confucian culture (Lee & Park, 2024). In primary school classrooms, children work together on robotics challenges that teach them how to work together and be kind to others. This reinforces the idea that technology should improve the health of the community as a whole, not just that of one person.

The principle of "human-centered AI" guides South Korea's AI ethics education. This is in line with the country's Digital New Deal policy (Yoon, 2021). Students are encouraged to think about moral problems that arise with automation and privacy and to link these discussions to cultural stories of solidarity and shared responsibility. By connecting technology education to traditional moral frameworks, South Korea ensures that moral reflection remains culturally relevant while also being relevant worldwide.

Cultural Responsiveness in Global AI Ethics Pedagogy

A comparative analysis of Finland, Singapore, and South Korea underscores the significance of culturally responsive pedagogy in AI ethics education. The concepts of "fairness " and " ethics " differ across cultures. For instance, Western schools often emphasize personal responsibility and independence, whereas many Asian schools prioritize social harmony and the well-being of the group. Therefore, to ensure that AI ethics classes are relevant and inclusive of everyone, these cultural differences must be considered.

Culturally responsive AI education prompts students to contemplate the moral values inherent in their communities, contextualizing these within global ethical frameworks. For instance, a conversation about sharing data might compare the benefits to the community (e.g., in public health applications) with the right to privacy. Dialogic learning like this helps students understand moral pluralism while also identifying universal values, such as fairness, honesty, and respect for people (UNESCO, 2021). Thus, teaching AI ethics connects local moral traditions with global ethical frameworks.

Teacher Training and Professional Development

Teacher readiness is the most important factor in the success of ethical AI education. Research from various nations indicates that educators frequently exhibit a lack of confidence and conceptual clarity when teaching AI-related ethics. The main reasons for this gap are the lack of training opportunities, insufficient resources for different fields to work together, and the rapid pace of change in AI technologies. If teachers do not receive adequate support, they might focus primarily on the technical aspects of AI education and neglect the moral aspects that make it so powerful.

Therefore, national education systems should invest in long-term professional development instead of short-term workshops. Teacher training programs should include sections on digital ethics, philosophical reasoning, and sociotechnical systems. Collaborative initiatives, such as lesson co-design, peer mentoring, and interdisciplinary teaching partnerships, can help teachers add ethical questions to their computer science lessons (Pandy, 2025). Additionally, governments and universities should establish open-access repositories containing lesson plans, case studies, and interactive simulations that foster ethical reflection in a developmentally appropriate manner. When teachers are empowered to be ethical facilitators, classrooms become places where students can think critically about how technology affects their lives and the lives of others. This empowerment is not only a pedagogical need but also a moral need for fair AI integration.

Implementation: From Policy to Practice

Connecting national AI strategies with the classroom remains a global challenge. Many countries have ambitious plans for teaching AI ethically; however, these ideas often fail to materialize in practice due to a lack of infrastructure and unprepared teachers (UNESCO, 2021). For effective implementation, policymakers, educators, industry experts, and researchers must collaborate at various levels.

The first step in this process is to create curricula that are appropriate for each child's level of development and that take into account both global standards and local realities. Younger children might tell stories or play games that raise moral questions, such as whether a robot should help one friend over another. Older children can look at real datasets to see if algorithms are biased. This kind of scaffolding ensures that moral understanding grows along with cognitive maturity (Floridi & Cowls, 2022).

Additionally, schools should cultivate interdisciplinary learning environments in which ethics is integrated not only in philosophy or civics but also in mathematics, computer science, and the arts. This method helps people see AI as a human-made object with moral consequences. Students learn how to think ethically as part of their technological creativity by working on real projects, such as creating fair games, inclusive algorithms, or digital citizenship campaigns.

REFERENCES

Al-Zahrani, A. M., & Alasmari, T. M. (2024). Exploring the impact of artificial intelligence on higher education: The dynamics of ethical, social, and educational implications. *Humanities & Social Sciences Communications, 11*(1), 912. DOI: 10.1057/s41599-024-03432-4

Baker, R. S., & Hawn, A. (2022). Algorithmic Bias in Education. *International Journal of Artificial Intelligence in Education, 32*(4), 1052–1092. DOI: 10.1007/s40593-021-00285-9

Belpaeme, T., Kennedy, J., Ramachandran, A., Scassellati, B., & Tanaka, F. (2018). Social robots for education: A review. *Science Robotics, 3*(21), eaat5954. Advance online publication. DOI: 10.1126/scirobotics.aat5954 PMID: 33141719

Bers, M. U. (2020). *Coding as a Playground.* Routledge., DOI: 10.4324/9781003022602

Bodrova, E., & Leong, D. J. (2015). Vygotskian and Post-Vygotskian Views on Children's Play. *American Journal of Play, 7*(3), 371–388.

Buolamwini, J., & Gebru, T. (2018). Gender Shades: Intersectional Accuracy Disparities in Commercial Gender Classification. *Proceedings of the 1st Conference on Fairness, Accountability and Transparency*, 77–91. https://proceedings.mlr.press/v81/buolamwini18a.html.

Calvo, R. A., & Peters, D. (2014). *Positive computing: technology for wellbeing and human potential.* MIT press. DOI: 10.7551/mitpress/9764.001.0001

Cowls, J., Tsamados, A., Taddeo, M., & Floridi, L. (2023). The AI gambit: Leveraging artificial intelligence to combat climate change—opportunities, challenges, and recommendations. *AI & Society, 38*(1), 283–307. DOI: 10.1007/s00146-021-01294-x PMID: 34690449

Crawford, K. (2021). *The atlas of AI: Power, politics, and the planetary costs of artificial intelligence.* Yale University Press.

Eisenberg, N., Spinrad, T. L., & Valiente, C. (2016). Emotion-related self-regulation, and children's social, psychological, and academic functioning. In Balter, L., & Tamis-LeMonda, C. S. (Eds.), *Child Psychology* (pp. 219–244). Psychology Press., DOI: 10.4324/9781315764931

Eubanks, V. (2025). *Automating inequality: How high-tech tools profile, police, and punish the poor.* Macmillan+ ORM.

Eyal, L., & Gil, E. (2022). *Hybrid Learning Spaces — A Three-Fold Evolving Perspective* (pp. 11–23). DOI: 10.1007/978-3-030-88520-5_2

Floridi, L., & Cowls, J. (2022). A Unified Framework of Five Principles for AI in Society. In *Machine Learning and the City* (pp. 535–545). Wiley., DOI: 10.1002/9781119815075.ch45

Garcia Ramos, J., & Wilson-Kennedy, Z. (2024). Promoting equity and addressing concerns in teaching and learning with artificial intelligence. *Frontiers in Education, 9*, 1487882. Advance online publication. DOI: 10.3389/feduc.2024.1487882

Gasser, U., & Almeida, V. A. F. (2017). A Layered Model for AI Governance. *IEEE Internet Computing, 21*(6), 58–62. DOI: 10.1109/MIC.2017.4180835

Holmes, W., Bialik, M., & Fadel, C. (2019). *Artificial intelligence in education promises and implications for teaching and learning*. Center for Curriculum Redesign.

Jobin, A., Ienca, M., & Vayena, E. (2019). The global landscape of AI ethics guidelines. *Nature Machine Intelligence, 1*(9), 389–399. DOI: 10.1038/s42256-019-0088-2

Kafai, Y., Proctor, C., & Lui, D. (2020). From theory bias to theory dialogue. *ACM Inroads, 11*(1), 44–53. DOI: 10.1145/3381887

Killen, M., & Smetana, J. G. (2015). Origins and Development of Morality. In *Handbook of Child Psychology and Developmental Science* (pp. 1–49). Wiley., DOI: 10.1002/9781118963418.childpsy317

Kohlberg, L. (1987). The psychology of moral development. *Ethics, 97*(2).

Lapsley, D., & Narvaez, D. (2014). *Becoming a Moral Person – Moral Development and Moral Character Education as a Result of Social Interactions* (pp. 227–238). DOI: 10.1007/978-3-319-01369-5_13

Lee, K., & Park, H.-Y. (2024). Development of Convergence Course of Artificial Intelligence and Psychology Applying Team Teaching Method. *International Journal on Advanced Science, Engineering and Information Technology, 14*(5), 1772–1778. DOI: 10.18517/ijaseit.14.5.11491

Lin, P., Abney, K., & Jenkins, R. (2017). *Robot ethics 2.0: From autonomous cars to artificial intelligence*. Oxford University Press. DOI: 10.1093/oso/9780190652951.001.0001

Livingstone, S., & Third, A. (2017). Children and young people's rights in the digital age: An emerging agenda. *New Media & Society, 19*(5), 657–670. DOI: 10.1177/1461444816686318

Long, D., & Magerko, B. (2020). What is AI Literacy? Competencies and Design Considerations. *Proceedings of the 2020 CHI Conference on Human Factors in Computing Systems*, 1–16. DOI: 10.1145/3313831.3376727

Mehrabi, N., Morstatter, F., Saxena, N., Lerman, K., & Galstyan, A. (2022). A Survey on Bias and Fairness in Machine Learning. *ACM Computing Surveys*, *54*(6), 1–35. DOI: 10.1145/3457607

Mitchell, M., Wu, S., Zaldivar, A., Barnes, P., Vasserman, L., Hutchinson, B., Spitzer, E., Raji, I. D., & Gebru, T. (2019). Model Cards for Model Reporting. *Proceedings of the Conference on Fairness, Accountability, and Transparency*, 220–229. DOI: 10.1145/3287560.3287596

Noble, S. U. (2020). *Algorithms of Oppression*. New York University Press., DOI: 10.18574/nyu/9781479833641.001.0001

Noddings, N. (2013). *Caring: A relational approach to ethics and moral education*. Univ of California Press.

Nucci, L. P. (2001). *Education in the moral domain*. Cambridge University Press. DOI: 10.1017/CBO9780511605987

OECD. (2023). *AI and the Future of Skills* (Vol. 2). OECD., DOI: 10.1787/a9fe53cb-

Owen, R. Bessant, J. R., & Heintz, M. (2013). *Responsible innovation*. Wiley.

Pandy, P. (2025). Revolutionizing the AI-Digital Landscape. SSRN *Electronic Journal*. DOI: 10.2139/ssrn.5335459

Raji, I. D., & Buolamwini, J. (2019). Actionable Auditing. *Proceedings of the 2019 AAAI/ACM Conference on AI, Ethics, and Society*, 429–435. DOI: 10.1145/3306618.3314244

Schoenherr, J. R., Abbas, R., Michael, K., Rivas, P., & Anderson, T. D. (2023). Designing AI Using a Human-Centered Approach: Explainability and Accuracy Toward Trustworthiness. *IEEE Transactions on Technology and Society*, *4*(1), 9–23. DOI: 10.1109/TTS.2023.3257627

Solyst, J., Axon, A., Stewart, A. E. B., Eslami, M., & Ogan, A. (2023). Investigating Girls' Perspectives and Knowledge Gaps on Ethics and Fairness in Artificial Intelligence in a Lightweight Workshop. *Proceedings of the 16th International Society of the Learning Sciences*, 807–814.

Souto-Manning, M., & Epley, P. H. (2024). Equity and justice: Imperatives for early childhood teaching and teacher education. *Contemporary Issues in Early Childhood*, *25*(2), 158–161. DOI: 10.1177/14639491241260933

Taddeo, M., & Floridi, L. (2025). Digital Ethics. In *A Companion to Digital Ethics* (pp. 1–9). Wiley., DOI: 10.1002/9781394240821.ch1

Tariq, M. (Ed.). (2025). *Merging Artificial Intelligence With the Internet of Things*. IGI Global., DOI: 10.4018/979-8-3693-8547-0

Tariq, M. U. (2025). *AI-Driven Learning and Engagement in Higher Education*. IGI Global., DOI: 10.4018/979-8-3693-4074-5

Tariq, M. U. (2026). Harnessing AI to Transform Mathematics Education: Enhancing Cognitive, Psychosocial, and Analytical Learning Outcomes. In Mazı, A. (Ed.), *The Convergence of Mathematics and AI: A New Paradigm in Education* (pp. 125–152). IGI Global Scientific Publishing., DOI: 10.4018/979-8-3373-1998-8.ch005

Touretzky, D., Gardner-McCune, C., Martin, F., & Seehorn, D. (2019). Envisioning AI for K-12: What Should Every Child Know about AI? *Proceedings of the AAAI Conference on Artificial Intelligence*, *33*(01), 9795–9799. DOI: 10.1609/aaai.v33i01.33019795

Turiel, E. (2008). *The development of morality. Child and adolescent development: An advanced course*. 473–514.

UNESCO. (2021). *Recommendation on the Ethics of Artificial Intelligence*.

Wing, J. (2017). Computational thinking's influence on research and education for all. *Italian Journal of Educational Technology*, *25*(2), 7–14.

Yoon, K. (2021). Discourse of the Post-COVID 19 New Deal in South Korea. *East Asia (Piscataway, N.J.)*, *38*(4), 373–388. DOI: 10.1007/s12140-021-09363-0 PMID: 33897253

KEYTERM AND DEFINITION

AI Literacy: – The ability to understand, evaluate, and responsibly create or interact with artificial intelligence systems.

Algorithmic Bias: – Systematic and unfair outcomes produced by AI systems due to biased data, design choices, or societal inequalities embedded in algorithms.

Ethical Digital Citizenship: – Responsible participation in digital environments guided by values such as fairness, empathy, accountability, and respect for others.

Moral Reasoning: – The cognitive and emotional process through which individuals evaluate actions based on principles of right and wrong, fairness, and responsibility.

Responsible Innovation Literacy: – The capacity to design and use technological innovations while considering their ethical, social, and long-term societal impacts.

Chapter 4

AI Beyond Coding: Exploring Creativity, Art, and Storytelling With AI

Liu Wenpang
http://orcid.org/0009-0009-1542-4870
Teesside University, UK

Goh Ying Yingsoon
http://orcid.org/0000-0002-6654-2887
Nilai University, Malaysia

Zhang Suyan
http://orcid.org/0009-0003-4518-1650
Shandong Jianzhu University, China

Nurul Ain Chua Binti Abdullah
http://orcid.org/0000-0003-2915-1577
University Terengganu Malaysia, Malaysia

Chen Yiming
Shenzhen University, China

Gao Manman
Guangzhou College of Technology and Business, China

See Jasmine
http://orcid.org/0000-0001-8683-5217
Nilai University, Malaysia

ABSTRACT

This chapter delves into the burgeoning and often surprising realm of artificial intelligence (AI) as a tool and collaborator in creative endeavors, moving beyond its traditional role in coding and data analysis. We will explore how AI is revolutionizing artistic expression, generating innovative narratives, and even fostering new forms of human-AI co-creation. From image generation and musical composition to scriptwriting and interactive storytelling, the chapter will showcase diverse applications, analyze the underlying AI models (without excessive technical jargon), and critically examine the implications for artists, writers, and the future of human

DOI: 10.4018/979-8-2600-2438-6.ch004

creativity. It will address ethical considerations, copyright challenges, and the evolving definition of authorship in an era where algorithms contribute significantly to the creative process.

1. INTRODUCTION

For many, AI make people think about algorithm, confused code, and things that use data – a strong domain that is strongly technical (Yadav et al., 2025). We connect AI with making the logistics better, improving search engines and working with numbers, mostly as a very technical tool for automation and making things work. We think this way of thinking is, of course, right, reflecting a large part of AI's past history and how it is currently used. But, a very significant change is ahead, as AI starts to go beyond logical things that it can do and to enter very human territories of creativity, art and story .

Of course, this chapter wants to show this interesting change, looking at AI's big and rapidly growing effect on making art, writing stories and the bottom line of people's creativity in general, much further than its old role of just coding (Manu, 2024). We want to explore how AI is not just seeing what exists but also joining in to produce new things, which leads us to question some of our ideas of who the producer of something is and where our ideas come from. From drawing jaw-dropping pictures and emotive music to writing fascinating stories, AI is showing itself to be a surprising and powerful creative ally. Crucially, this is a big shift: AI is moving from its role as a tool for auto-doing to a living ally in creativity work (Gjorgjieski, 2024). It is not just a way to make boring jobs easier anymore, AI is nowadays even a person that shares people's thoughts in thinking of ideas, coming up with a plan, and the making step by step of the art and stories. Our working together is not about giving machines a part of human intelligence, but making human intelligence bigger: opening up new forms of experimentation, new possibilities for ideas for artists, for writers, for everyone working in the creative domain.

On our first entrance to this new place, there will be a great mixture of tech skills and art dreams. We will see how AI opens doors to very exciting opportunities for artists, stretching the bounds of what is possible in terms of possible artistic productions, and also changing the relationship between creator and creation in storytelling. The online world is not just a tool for art anymore: it has become a beautiful studio of computer programs and humans' inventions creating new combinations and making really new creations (Garcia, 2024).

2. THE DAWN OF THE ALGORITHMIC MUSE: A BRIEF HISTORY OF AI IN CREATIVITY

After this summary of the growing role of AI in creativity, we start our review by following the important steps that led to the present moment, looking at The Dawn of the Algorithmic Muse and its short but impressive history. To make this chapter more academic, a kind of summary of the method problems to be found in the basic research on generative AI is useful. Algorithms such as GANs and Diffusion Models have very great skills but their good effects are often limited by the size and biases in the data they are learning from, and partial discovery of real new ideas or creative sameness ensue. Also, judging work produced by AI involves personal and human measures of quality (such as surveys of 'what is good') and it is therefore hard to talk of the results for algorithmic creativity or of the 'purpose' of algorithms. "The theory look at AI's job has to balance with acknowledging these real-world limits, giving a needed critical view opposite to excited talk of tech progress. This honourable way – talking about tech facts in combination with critical thinking – is happy stuff to please an academic reader."

Only apart from the lab tables and computer code, machines showing creativity is an idea that has fascinated thinkers for many years, since the so-called "smart AI" we have today; there have been early attempts at AI in creativity that were more ideas than solution in practice, dating back to the early days of computers and cybernetics. People such as Alan Turing thought about machines that can "learn" and "think" which are, essentially, talking about the opportunity for machines to invent something. In the middle of the 20th century, early programs in AI such as for automatic creation of music (see, e.g. Shanghai, 2022; Daniele et al., 2021) or poetry (by using very simple grammars, for example)"paint an aspect"(although quite simple) of the chance of computer art (see also Bowen, 2024). These were mostly systems based on rules: they showed how to combine things together but could really not create something new, but they put down the basic ideas for the computer inspiration that came later.

Following has been the real "start" of the algorithmic muse, taking AI from a nice idea to real creative power: a new, amazing jump of generative AI capability. The breakthrough of generative AI arrived with the "coming" of Generative Adversarial Networks (GANs), by Ian Goodfellow, in 2014. Generative Adversarial Networks was an important moment, when two neural networks fight and learn from each other producing pictures and data that were very real looking (cited in Hughes et al., 2021; cited in, 2023). This jump came quickly with the big change from the Transformer architecture (Salta & Katsaros, 2024) that the natural language process was very powerful and made possible skills of AI in knowing, making and changing human language in a very fluent way; this opened the way to the improved creative

AI writing. More new, Diffusion Models (coming out strong around 2020–2022, Bhuvaneshwaran et al., 2024; Fernandes et al., 2024) have even better image and multimedia making powers – offering, for example, very good control and a photography real look. All of these building big steps, together with big data and more computer capacity, have made the path to creative AI easy, and powerful and useful tools of art are at the reach of many people.

These technology jumps have all become lots of big moments for AI art and story telling. From Christie's selling AI-made pictures for big money (e.g., Zazzaro, 2024) to websites such as Midjourney and DALL-E making very real and fantasy pictures from text words, AI has truly come into the visual arts. In story telling, AI has gone from writing simple sentences to making stories that make sense, writing scripts for a short movie, and even writing books for writers. Music AI has also come on, such as Amper Music and Jukebox (OpenAI) do now make new songs in various styles, many of which you cannot tell if it was a human or a machine making (Joel, 2024; Nieuwenhuijsen, 2023). Together all these things give a strong message: AI is not only a tool for looking at data or doing things automatically; AI is, already, a very useful and powerful creative companion—nipping at our heels, something that changes what art can be. (See Table 1.) Table 1 The Dawn of the Algorithmic Muse: A brief history of AI and creativity.

Table 1. The Dawn of the Algorithmic Muse: A Brief History of AI in Creativity

Era / Development	Key Characteristics & Milestones	Impact on Creative AI
Early Attempts & Theory	- Conceptual groundwork: Thinkers like Alan Turing speculated on machine learning and thinking, hinting at creative potential. - Mid-20th Century Programs: Rudimentary rule-based systems for automated music (e.g., Lejaren Hiller's ILLIAC Suite, cited in Shanghai, 2022; Daniele et al., 2021) and poetry generation (Bowen, 2024). - Limitations: Primarily combinatorics, lacking genuine innovation; more theoretical than practical.	Laid the conceptual foundation for AI's creative role, moving beyond purely logical operations. Demonstrated that machines could, in a limited way, generate novel arrangements based on predefined rules, sparking early discussions about algorithmic artistry.
Recent Generative AI Surge	- Generative Adversarial Networks (GANs): Introduced by Ian Goodfellow (2014), enabling two neural networks to generate realistic images and data (cited in Hughes et al., 2021; 2023). - Transformer Architecture: (Google, 2017; Salta & Katsaros, 2024) Revolutionized natural language processing, enabling fluent AI text generation. - Diffusion Models: (Emerging 2020-2022; Bhuvaneshwaran et al., 2024; Fernandes et al., 2024) Refined image and multimedia generation for unparalleled control and photorealism. - Key Enablers: Vast datasets and increased computational power.	This period propelled AI from a curious concept to a tangible creative force, making advanced creative tools widely accessible. These architectural breakthroughs enabled AI to learn complex patterns and generate highly realistic and coherent new content across various modalities (text, image, audio), democratizing access to powerful artistic capabilities.
Milestones & Broad Impact	- AI Art Market: Christie's auction of AI-generated portraits (e.g., "Portrait of Edmond de Belamy," Zazzaro, 2024). - Popular Platforms: Midjourney and DALL-E generating diverse imagery from text prompts. - AI in Storytelling: From simple sentence generation to coherent narratives, short film scripts, and novel assistance. - AI Music Evolution: Systems like Amper Music and Jukebox (OpenAI) composing original pieces across genres (Joel, 2024; Nieuwenhuijsen, 2023).	Collectively, these achievements signify AI's indelible entry into mainstream creative fields. AI is no longer just a technical tool for analysis or automation; it is rapidly emerging as a versatile and potent creative partner, actively participating in and redefining the boundaries of artistic expression across visual arts, literature, and music.

3. VISUAL SYMPHONY: AI IN ART AND DESIGN

After we have created the historical and conceptual platform of the Algorithmic Muse, we now turn to the more real and straightforward evidence of AI's creative power: the visual symphony that is created in art and design. The visual arts have already changed a lot with the advent of generative AI, pushing the limits of what can be created in image making and changing. In tools such as Midjourney, DALL-E and Stable Diffusion, these artworks lead the way, enabling users to create very unusual artworks in various artistic styles, photos that look like landscapes in real life, big abstracts, funny cartoons, more complicated Gothic scenes and more. The interesting aspect is with the prompt, that is to say, with the input text instructions that one gives to the AI. Artists become good 'prompt engineers' too, making sentences carefully to determine everything from what is in the picture, the picture composition, light, colour, special art movements (for example, 'in the style of Van Gogh', 'cyberpunk aesthetic', like in Thampanichwat et al. 2025; Hussen et al. 2025). This process of doing is repeated many times again and again, from trying to create better prompts, to try different prompts, to pick the best outputs, sketch out or create a blurred line between the 'old' way of making art and what the algorithm helps with.

Just as AI can make images directly, AI is also showing it can be really useful help for the big world of design. For graphic design, for example, AI can do dull jobs for you automatically, such as removing the background of images, changing image size, changing image colour, and so on; designers can then think about bigger things (Zafar, 2024). AI can also suggest good layout, designing a logo for a brand, helping a person choose a good font for images so they look good and work well. For making pictures of buildings, AI makes it easier for buildings to make 3D models and pictures that look real; it helps architects to quickly look at many building designs, complex buildings and even to know whether a building is energy efficient and strong before they start building for real. In the same way, when making products, AI makes it easier to quickly make a model, make different designs, preview how people will use it and even look at what users say to make the product look better and easier to use (Lin & Liu, 2024).

Yet, so too have questions about the ethical and beauty dimensions of AI-made art quickly and strongly emerged (Elfar & Dawood, 2024). Questions of 'being first' are large: if an AI does a picture by with lots of data mined from human-made art, is it truly 'new'? And does it open debate on purpose of the artist: does a computer-program have a purpose or is it simply a 'grinder' to see what a human types out wants? (Navas, 2024). As well, debate has emerged as to the 'heart' of AI art; some believe without human feeling, real-life experience, true meaning, AI art can only ever be skillful, but without the deep quality of things we feel are produced by peo-ple. These talks also go to who owns the rights and the chance for bad use, such as fake videos or continuing false beliefs learnt from the data they are learning from, to make society reflect on who made it and what it is worth in a fast-flying creative world (Xu et al., 2024).

Table 2. Visual Symphony: AI in Art and Design

Aspect of AI in Visual Arts	Description & Key Applications	Debates & Considerations
Image Generation	Models like Midjourney, DALL-E, and Stable Diffusion are revolutionizing visual art creation. Users can generate diverse artistic styles, from photorealistic to abstract, by employing prompting techniques where textual descriptions guide the AI. Artists act as "prompt engineers," meticulously crafting phrases that dictate subject, composition, lighting, color, and artistic style (Thampanichwat et al., 2025; Hussen et al., 2025). This process is iterative, involving prompt refinement, variation generation, and output curation, blurring the lines between traditional artistic execution and algorithmic guidance.	Originality: Is an AI image still original if its image came from a large database of human art? Artistic intent: Does an algorithm understand intent or is it merely repeating what the prompt maker's mind contained? (Navas, 2024) "Soul" of art: If AI art doesn't have deeper meaning or resonating properties without human feelings, human life experiences and soulful inspiration.
AI-Enhanced Design	AI is an invaluable assistant across various design fields: - Graphic design: Assist with repetitive or time-consuming operations, for example, background changing, photo resizing, color correction; recommend the layout design, generate logo, recommend a font combination (Zafar, 2024); - Architectural visualization: Shorten the time to create 3D model design and photorealistic rendering design to quickly explore the design choices, to visualize complex designs, to analyze some factors (for example, energy efficiency); - Product design: Helpful in rapid prototyping, generate product designs, product design iterations, testing the use of products in reality, analyze users' feedback to enhance the beauty and UX of products (Lin & Liu, 2024).	N/A (focus in this section is on the assistive and optimizing role of AI to help in the design workflow rather than overall ethical discussions, which are covered more generally in the "Ethical and Aesthetic Debates" section).
Ethical & Aesthetic Debates	The proliferation of AI-generated art has ignited vigorous ethical and aesthetic discussions (Elfar & Dawood, 2024). Key questions include: - Originality: The debate over whether AI-generated images can truly be original when based on vast human-created datasets. - Artistic Intent: The philosophical question of whether algorithms possess intent or merely act as sophisticated tools reflecting a human user's vision (Navas, 2024). - "Soul" of Art: Arguments that AI art, without human emotion or lived experience, lacks the deeper resonance of human-made creations. - Copyright and Misuse: Concerns over copyright ownership and the potential for misuse (e.g., deepfakes, perpetuation of biases from training data), challenging existing definitions of authorship and value in the creative landscape (Xu et al., 2024).	These debates are fundamental to understanding the implications of AI's role in creativity, impacting how we define authorship, Intellectual property: the intrinsic value of artworks in an age of AI. All of this calls for ethical guidelines and laws to be updated to adapt to the creative changing environment.

4. THE NARRATIVE WEAVER: AI IN STORYTELLING AND LITERATURE

Move now from the visual arts, where AI draws complex pictures and patterns. We will see in The Narrative Weaver: AI in Storytelling and Literature how the same algorithms are used in the construction of meaning. The area of storytelling, which scientists considered to be the only ontological core of human imagination, is now at hand, ready to be influenced by the newcomer, AI. The role of AI in storytelling is not limited to being a "grammar corrector": it can now even produce automatic content, something surprising, quite nice, very simple, short stories, emotions in poetry, funny scripts, good plots (Attaluri & Mudunuri, 2025). Tools can take a simple idea, or some keywords, and create an entire chapter, come up with plot twists or feeling descriptions, and be an ideal-thinking friend for writers that get stuck with their creativity problems.

But AI is also showing itself to be a powerful help in the difficult art of building characters and their dialogues (Kusmiatun et al., 2024). Writers can use AI to generate detailed character profiles (including past stories of a character, what they want, character details, etc.). Far more impressive, AI can generate fake dialogues, taking examples as to how characters with different traits might have talked in detail, making dialogues sound more realistic and natural. Allowing authors to explore ways of talking, to view dialogues of characters with one another, and manipulating the dialogues better until they sound more natural, making characters seem more 'real' people for readers to understand.

One of the most new uses of AI in story telling is in creation of interactive and personal story (Pizzo et al., 2023). In video games and virtual reality, AI can adjust story lines according to what the player chooses, allow really different and branching story experience. For instance, a game in which the AI "game master" learns what you are playing, what you enjoy playing, and even what you feel like, and generates plot, character dialogue, problems, specifically tailored to you. This personalization also extended to reading where AI might be creating special passages for a story, and even creating stories for characters in a way that would feel more personalized to one reader's liking.

AI is also a big push for new kind of fan made story and people can work together to make Storytelling (You, 221). Fan can use AI tools to create new situations, come up with "what if" ideas in the world or people in well-known made up worlds, or even write new passages as they favourite writers do, opening the action of making things to more people and allowing more people to participate in those big worlds they love. AI also facilitates writing, where a group of human writers can collaborate with an AI together to make a story with the AI cross linking creative ideas together, making surprises about the story.

But, even with these big steps forward, AI in making stories is not without its big problems and limits (Komal et al., 2024). Even with big advances, AI models today are good at copying patterns, and in producing (passably) correct grammatically written text, but do not really understand the deep human aspects of storytelling. AI models do not understand the subtle differentiations that exist (for example), in sarcasm, latent meanings and subtle changes in feelings that can make for interesting human conversation. The skill to understand and reflect this deep nuanced feeling, this deep gut feeling of character reasonings that (for example) resonate with readers, are not yet available to them.

Making really complicated story setups is also a big problem. (Komal et al., 2024). AI can do things that make sense in order, preserving the same deeper ideas, the tricky and funny hints about the future, or really surprising, but still make sense, story changes over a long story - all those are still parts that people are good at. What AI may be good at these days are sometimes merely commonplace-sounding; easy to predict, or sometimes even unintended and nonsensical if asked to take people out of their usual learned quirks. The depths of people's lives, murky and complex minds and even that distinctive criterial 'grain', all those elusive areas still manage to keep the best of the big story within the realm of human thought.

Table 3. The Narrative Weaver: AI in Storytelling and Literature

Aspect of AI in Storytelling	Description & Key Applications	Challenges & Limitations
Automated Content Generation	AI is moving beyond simple grammar checks to produce surprisingly coherent and original content. This includes: - Short stories, poems, scripts, and novel outlines (Attaluri & Mudunuri, 2025). - Brainstorming and ideation: AI can take a simple premise or keywords to flesh out chapters, suggest plot twists, or create mood-setting descriptions, acting as a tireless brainstorming partner for writers.	N/A (General limitations are covered in the "Challenges and Limitations" section below, which applies to all narrative generation by AI).
Character Development & Dialogue	AI is a powerful assistant in writing complex characters and natural dialogue. It can: - Prompt deep character portraits with backstories, motivations, and personality traits (Kusmiatun et al., 2024). - Produce dialogue examples for characters with particular personality traits, making the dialogue read more naturally. - Help authors refine voices and understanding of character relationships, make them more endearing.	N/A (General limitations are covered in the "Challenges and Limitations" section below).
Interactive & Personalized Narratives	AI is enabling highly dynamic and tailored storytelling experiences, particularly in: - Video games and virtual reality: AI can dynamically adapt storylines based on player choices, creating unique, branching narratives (Pizzo et al., 2023). Imagine an AI "game master" learning a player's style and emotions to tailor plots and challenges. - Personalized reading experiences: AI could generate bespoke story elements or character arcs that resonate more deeply with individual reader interests.	N/A (General limitations are covered in the "Challenges and Limitations" section below).

continued on following page

Table 3. Continued

Aspect of AI in Storytelling	Description & Key Applications	Challenges & Limitations
Fan Fiction & Collaborative Storytelling	AI acts as a significant catalyst for new forms of collective creativity. It allows: - Fan fiction creation: Users can generate new scenarios or chapters in the style of favorite authors within established fictional universes (You, 2021). This democratizes creation. - Collaborative writing projects: Multiple human authors can work with AI to build stories, with AI bridging creative differences or suggesting unforeseen narrative paths.	N/A (General limitations are covered in the "Challenges and Limitations" section below).
Challenges & Limitations	Despite impressive strides, AI in storytelling faces significant hurdles (Komal et al., 2024). Current models, though adept at mimicry, struggle with: - Lack of genuine understanding of nuance: Difficulty with sarcasm, subtext, and subtle emotional shifts in human interaction. - Inability to truly grasp and convey complex emotion: The raw, visceral feelings driving character motivations often remain beyond AI's grasp. - Difficulty with complex narrative structures: While AI can produce coherent sequences, maintaining consistent thematic depth, intricate foreshadowing, or truly surprising yet logical plot twists over extended narratives remains largely a human forte (2023, 2024). - Generic or nonsensical output: AI-generated content can sometimes feel predictable or nonsensical when pushed beyond common patterns in its training data.	These limitations highlight that while AI is a powerful tool for generating text, the deepest layers of human experience, psychological complexity, and the unique spark of authorial voice continue to firmly root the most impactful storytelling within the realm of human consciousness. AI's outputs may lack the "soul" or profound resonance that comes from lived human experience and genuine creative intent.

5. HARMONIC ALGORITHMS: AI IN MUSIC AND SOUND

Go from the building parts of text and story. Now let us go out into the not solid world of organised sound, finding out how computer programs get to a beat, a tune and a song in Harmonic Algorithms: AI in Music and Sound. The meeting of artificial intelligence and music is perhaps one of the most astonishing and fast changing edges of creative AI. For hundreds of years, writing music was considered the richest example of human feelings and art gut feeling. But now AI is really into computer writing, creating new music pieces in a great variety of types from the complicated lines of old music to the loud pulses of electric dance music, in creating jazz and arranging tunes in pop. Things like AIVA (Artificial Intelligence Virtual Artist), Amper Music, and Google Magenta's MuseNet can make whole orchestra music, a piano song, or even full songs with singing many times in very good clearness and style realness (Turgay, 2025). Computers are learning from very huge music data, seeing patterns and harmonies and beats in music, and then using the knowledge learned to write totally new unheard-before songs.

There is no end to making the whole works. AI is very important for sound design and making. AI systems can produce totally new and strange sound worlds that you can't achieve using old instruments or instruments. AI systems can examine the sound that exists to search out and isolate single sounds, remove noise, and even repair broken recordings. They also alter the speed and quality of mixing and mastering automatically, altering the sound levels up, EQ, and dynamics up to achieve professional-sounding sounds. Some AI can sound like a new type of sound instrument to make, or allow humans to be able to make changes to sounds as they are played in ways that allow players and producers brand new sound possibilities. (Anantrasirichai & Bull, 2022).

Most interesting things are actually things that come from when people and AI are together to make music. This is not about AI being a substitute for musicians; it is about being someone like a creative friend, somewhere to look for ideas from or a helper in playing around with new kinds of sounds. People, such as Holly Herndon, for example, have worked with AI systems (such as Herndon's AI "Spawn"), where the AI is trying to work out what kind of music Herndon likes, and then creates unique vocal and instrument sounds that Herndon uses to create full songs (Ruszev, Lidgard et al., 2024). Brian Eno (who makes ambient music) tried out systems that can generate music that is changing and continues to grow, creating different versions of his own music to share (Santos & Wijayanti, 2024). These partnerships are teamwork where the human has an idea for art and leads the AI's ability to do a lot of things, both generating new kinds of sounds and music possible in a qualitative sense beyond the usual.

Some of the big effect of AI makes us think about making music in the future. As AI tools get better and better and become easier to use, AI makes music making open to everybody. People who do not go to music schools to learn music can make good songs. That will bring a lot of new music and singers into the world, and world music will become more diverse. The fast work AI does will change some jobs in the music business. Maybe we do not need some jobs as before, but we will have new kinds of jobs, such as AI music boss or new kinds of jobs that write good words for sound.

But, this fast change brings huge problems too, for example intellectual property issues and what does it mean to be a 'composer'. If an AI writes a song, who owns the copyright—the code writer, the user with the idea or the AI itself (for which the law now doesn't recognise someone)? Something like "Heart on my Sleeves", where an AI may perhaps copy famous singer voices and it hints the law problem, need of rules to protect singers' looks and what they make. The US Copyright Office is taking the position that the significant human assistance is usually needed in order for AI-generated works to be copyrightable; so AI becomes more likely to be regarded as a smart tool, rather than being a single writer. (Patama, 2025).

At the end, what does "a composer" mean in the AI time, is a new think. Is a composer still a person who carefully writes every single note or a person who could do and pick AI-made ideas of music? Most of us would think the second one, say the human part in art direction is very important, to pick, to be better (Raza, 2025). AI is not only changing how music can be made, how can be made, but what means "make" music, opening the lane of a new more working together and tech-mix music future. (see table 4.).

Table 4. Harmonic Algorithms: AI in Music and Sound

Theme	Description	Examples / Sources
AI in Music Composition	AI systems generate original pieces in various genres using learned patterns from musical datasets.	AIVA, Amper Music, MuseNet (Turgay, 2025)
Sound Design & Production	AI creates novel soundscapes, isolates audio elements, removes noise, and enhances audio quality through automated mastering and mixing tools.	Anantrasirichai & Bull, 2022
AI as Creative Partner	Human-AI collaborations allow for co-creation, where AI serves as an inspiration or extension of the artist's vision rather than a replacement.	Holly Herndon ("Spawn"), Brian Eno (Ruszev et al., 2024; Santos & Wijayanti, 2024)
Democratization of Music Creation	AI lowers the barrier to entry, allowing people without formal training to compose and produce music, potentially reshaping the global soundscape and expanding artistic participation.	Implied throughout; future projection
Changing Industry Roles	AI could reduce traditional roles (e.g., sound engineers) and create new ones (e.g., AI music supervisors, prompt engineers).	Implied in industry implications
Legal & Ethical Challenges	Raises questions of copyright, authorship, and ownership; current laws require significant human input for copyright protection.	US Copyright Office, "Heart on my Sleeves" (Patama, 2025)
Redefining the Composer	The definition of a composer is evolving to include those who direct and curate AI output, not just those who write every note manually.	Raza, 2025

6. THE HUMAN-AI CONTINUUM: COLLABORATION, CO-CREATION, AND THE FUTURE OF CREATIVITY

After look at AI's trip through different creative media, from visual art through story and music making, we come to the important question of human join in, change our look to The Human-AI Continuum: Working together, Co-Making, and the Future of Creativity. With the fast get better in AI, particularly in making models, this basic changes have shifted the conversation from if AI can be creative to how people and AI will live together in a creative future. A key message of this new future is that AI is a strong tool, not a change, for people creativity. Instead of replacing artists, writers and musicians, AI improve their skills, let them overcome their creativity, to try new methods, to make faster a line of making work (Haase & Pokutta, 2024). For example, AI can do several designs in few seconds, give several ideas to a person designer which could take a lot of days to design and let the designer concentrate on improving the best ideas with their craft sense, see and feel smart.

Such a type of relationship requires people to have new skills and better skills, most important is prompter engineering and curatorship. "Prompter engineering" is about the art and science to provide good text inputs to prompt an AI model to give a desired output. It is about learning how an AI model "thinks" and guessing what it may say, this requires a combination of technical and language skills and art sensibilities (Rezwana, 2023). Besides making things, "curatorship" skills also seem to be important. As AI can generate lots of content, a human's role will change to observe, select, correct and improve on the items generated by AI to express a certain art context and make it good, meaningful and new. This means human choice, taste, and right-wrong thinking become even more big.

The use of AI is at the same time helping to make new creative jobs and chances in current industries. We see more "AI artists" who are good at using these new tools, "AI music producers" who mix computer-made music with people playing, and "prompt engineers" who work to make AI output better for certain creative works (Gaggioli et al., 2025). Creative studios now look for "AI integration specialists" and "AI content managers" to handle this new situation. Instead of making creative jobs less, AI is making special areas that need both knowing technology well and having good art feeling, making the idea of a "creative professional" bigger.

Also, AI has big chance to make creativity more for everyone, tearing down walls for people who dream to be artists and storytellers (Choe & Hinz, 2024). For people who did not previously have the know-how (such as for hard drawing, for music rules, for complex programs), or enough money (for expensive tools, or lessons from an expert), new strong creative tools can be reached. For example, a beginner writer can use AI to edit character speeches, a wannabe musician can make background music, and a newbie artist can draw wonderful pictures. And by doing this, a wider range of people will be able to express their creative thoughts, and join into the creative market, and to build a more varied and open creative community.

But, this exciting new area also raises tricky questions—particularly concerning the emerging meaning of authorship and what that means for intellectual property and copyright. If AI creates content, does the content belong to the person who wrote the prompt? Is it the person who created the AI or is the content uncopyrightable because there is no human author? Many legal systems around the world are scrambling to grapple with these questions. For example, the U.S. Copyright Office has signaled, for the most part, that works created by AI only do not receive copyright protection, because copyright generally requires a human author. The decision has caused extensive debate and litigation and has led some artists to argue that they should be compensated for their copyrighted work that was used for training. (Craig & Kerr, 2025).

Similarly, the philosophy ideas are also very deep: what is real creativity when computer programs are getting involved? AI is good at finding patterns and making contents, but what is unique of human experience, want, know, is a very subtle kind of thing in strong art (Stojanovic et al., 2023; Egon et al., 2023). That same talking form turns on guard, that when AI keeps changing, it as an art partner, human beings need to look hard and change the laws, rights and ways of thinking themselves, in order to get and use the big opportunity this human-AI synthesis will have for creativity future. (See Table 5.) Table 5 The human-AI continuum: collaboration, co-creation and the future of creativity.

Table 5. The Human-AI Continuum: Collaboration, Co-Creation, and the Future of Creativity

Theme	Description	Examples / Sources
AI as a Creative Augmentation Tool	AI enhances rather than replaces human creativity—helping overcome creative blocks, explore new styles, and speed up production workflows.	Haase & Pokutta, 2024
Prompter Engineering	A new skillset involving the crafting of effective prompts to guide AI output with precision, blending language, logic, and creativity.	Rezwana, 2023
Curatorship	Humans must evaluate, refine, and contextualize AI-generated content, emphasizing the importance of taste, originality, and ethical discernment.	Implied throughout
Emerging Creative Roles	New positions are arising like AI artists, AI music producers, prompt engineers, AI integration specialists, and AI content managers.	Gaggioli et al., 2025

continued on following page

Table 5. Continued

Theme	Description	Examples / Sources
Democratization of Creativity	AI reduces technical and financial barriers, enabling broader participation in creative fields, leading to greater inclusion and diversity.	Choe & Hinz, 2024
Legal & Ethical Challenges	Unresolved questions around copyright, ownership, and fair use of training data are prompting legal debates and regulatory responses.	Craig & Kerr, 2025
Authorship & Copyright Concerns	Current laws largely reject copyright for purely AI-generated works, sparking debates about prompt writers' rights and data usage.	U.S. Copyright Office position
Philosophical Questions of Creativity	Raises deep questions about what constitutes "real" creativity and the irreplaceable value of human consciousness and experience in art.	Stojanovic et al., 2023; Egon et al., 2023
Societal Adaptation Required	As AI continues evolving, society must rethink and update legal, ethical, and philosophical frameworks to keep pace with technological change.	Implied as a concluding insight

But the economic effects of AI for creative work are a big moral problem that deserve the firm, rigorous look that they do - not just simple ideas about"open things up for everybody". Yes, AI tools make it easier for new people to do the creative work but it also brings danger of substitution and secondarily of undervaluing the work of experienced workers in the creative industries (such as those who draw pictures, do voices, and write 'contributions' or content lower down). Quick, cheap making power from AI undermines the prices of things that are done with the hand of man, making life unstable for people who get money from doing creative work. Also, this money study should think about the unfair use in getting data, where free work and protected art of many human artists are collected to train AI models that later work against them ; forcing us to ask fundamental questions of rights of workers and of fair benefits distribution in the creative economy of AI.

7. ETHICAL CONSIDERATIONS AND SOCIETAL IMPACT

Having developed our understanding of the interplay of the human–AI partnership, we now need to turn and urgently scrutinize the essential guardrails, to think about some of the Ethical Considerations and the Societal Impact of this shift, for example, creative rights, bias, displacement. The emergence of AI in creative arts has brought to the fore the imperative of a reassessment of its role: AI is increasingly seen as a powerful tool to augment human creativity rather than being a substitute. This distinction is important. Rather than displacing artists, writers, musicians, AI will make them able to enter new territories, overcome creative blocks, enhance their speed of work flows (Chubb et al., 2022) Instead of displacing artists, writers and musicians, AI can be empowering to them in this respect. Thus, the human remains the visionary, the curator and the last decision maker, harnessed AI's generative power to still further enhance their own range of imagination. This collaboration is giving rise to important new skills, specifically prompter engineering and curatorship. 'Prompter engineering' is the art and science of writing precise and effective prompts in text to direct generative AI models to the right type of creative output (Piskopani et al., 2023). It involves understanding the depth and breadth of what generative AI models know about text, and it calls upon users to be articulate, imaginative, iterative in their prompting to achieve particular creative visions. Equally important is 'curatorship'—an ability to select, evaluate and refine the sometimes huge output of AI. This involves judgement, selectively removing the bad, unfocussed work, ensuring a stylistic coherence and adding substance to the AI-generated art in terms of human intention and depth of feeling, making the AI-generated raw output something meaningful.

AI has opened doors to new creative roles and opportunities in many industries as well. We are now seeing "AI artists" for which such tools are specific, "AI music producers" for which algorithmically generated music is blended with musician performance, "prompt engineers" for AI tools who are able to optimize AI tools for a certain creative task, and so on (Flick & Worrall, 2022). Creative agencies and agencies are now seeking "AI integration professionals" and "AI content professionals" to understand this new landscape. Rather than threatening creative jobs, AI opens up niches that require a particular technological savvy and deep creative sensibility to be filled and evolution of what it means to be a "creative professional". Furthermore, AI has huge potential to democratize creativity and to radically lower the barriers of entry for artists and storytellers interested in starting an artistic career (Torres et al., 2025). For example, for those who may not have had great technical skills (e.g. in complex software, traditional art processes or music theory), or financial wealth (e.g. for expensive equipment or specialist training), AI now offers them powerful tools for creativity. An amateur writer can use AI to generate character dialogue; an aspiring musician can have backing tracks written for him or her; an amateur artist can have breathtaking images generated. It empowers a much larger population of people to voice their creative ideas and enter the global creative economy, making the creativity community more diverse and inclusive.

However, this exciting frontier also raises many more complex questions, in particular, about the changing meaning of authorship and its subsequent consequences for intellectual property and copyright (Suchacka et al., 2021). When AI creates content, who owns the content? Is it the person who created the prompt? Is it the creator of the AI? Is the work uncopyrightable because there is no human authorship? Legal systems across the world struggle with these questions. For example, the U.S. Copyright Office has stuck to the view that works created wholly by AI are not copyrightable because copyright requires human authorship. It has caused much debate and litigation, for instance, with artists arguing that they should be paid if their copyrighted work is used for training data.

Similarly, the philosophical implication is equally fundamental: what is real creativity if there are algorithms? If we have the opportunity to recognise patterns, create something with an AI, then the spark of human experience, intention and consciousness, whatever it might be, is a unique point of difference in so much impactful art. That dialogue lets that as AI develops as an art collaborator, society has to engage in dialogue, not only ethics and ethics, but also legal and philosophical issues that we have to have an honest dialogue with ourselves in order to truly understand and engage with the enormous potential of this human–AI continuum for the future of creativity. (Le-Nguyen, 2024; Elfar & Dawood, 2024).

Table 6. Ethical Considerations and Societal Impact

Theme	Description	Examples / Sources
AI as Creative Augmentation	AI empowers rather than replaces creatives by accelerating workflows and enabling broader artistic exploration, with humans maintaining creative control.	Chubb et al., 2022
Prompter Engineering	Involves crafting effective, nuanced prompts to guide AI output; a key new skill requiring linguistic precision, creativity, and technical understanding.	Piskopani et al., 2023
Curatorship	Critical evaluation and refinement of AI output by humans ensures emotional depth, stylistic coherence, and artistic intention in final works.	Implied throughout
Emerging Creative Roles	Rise of new jobs such as AI artists, AI music producers, prompt engineers, and AI content managers who combine technical and artistic expertise.	Flick & Worrall, 2022
Democratization of Creativity	AI lowers barriers for non-professionals, enabling access to professional-grade creative tools and fostering diversity and inclusion in the creative ecosystem.	Torres et al., 2025
Legal & Copyright Challenges	Questions of ownership persist: prompt writer, AI developer, or none? Most jurisdictions (e.g., U.S.) reject copyright for fully AI-generated works, prompting legal disputes over data usage and compensation.	Suchacka et al., 2021; U.S. Copyright Office stance
Evolving Definition of Authorship	Legal and societal debates around who qualifies as an author in AI-assisted creation continue to shape copyright law and creative ownership norms.	Implied across the discussion

continued on following page

Table 6. Continued

Theme	Description	Examples / Sources
Philosophical Implications	Raises deeper issues about the nature of creativity, emphasizing the irreplaceable role of human intention, emotion, and consciousness in truly meaningful art.	Le-Nguyen, 2024; Elfar & Dawood, 2024
Need for Societal Adaptation	Legal, ethical, and philosophical frameworks must evolve to accommodate AI's growing role in creative practices and its impact on ownership, identity, and innovation.	Implied as conclusion

So as to lay a foundation to ground the below commentary, this next table 7 brings out, given the above discussion, the essential ingredients of human creativity and machine-made products, and a comparison of their differences in the process and origins of the two. To explain a more ordered comparison between human creativity and machine-made products, it may be helpful to focus on the basic differences of their respective processes and origins. Human creativity is related to conscious artistic intention, based on lived experience, emotional richness, intrinsic personal stories to which creativity spontaneously and sometimes intermittently attaches 'novelty from zero' – ideas out of nothing that do not conform to existing patterns. In contrast, machine-made products can produce stunning levels of complexity, but at bottom they are extrapolations and recombination of patterns that have been anticipated by the machine's large training data and achieve only 'novelty from data'. " The key difference then is agency: the human artist has genuine self-awareness agency and subjective understanding; while the AI is a powerful tool and its product is statistical inference that only creates meaning and emotional significance not conveyed by conscious meaning or thought—challenging the meaning of authorship, creativity and originality, pushing new edges on those issues.

Table 7. Structured Comparison: Human vs. Machine Creative Output

Feature	Human Creativity	Machine-Generated Output
Source/Origin of Output	Rooted in lived experience, emotional depth, subjective personal history, and physical interaction with the world.	Derived entirely from statistical patterns and relationships extracted from vast, pre-existing training datasets.
Creative Process & Intent	Driven by conscious artistic intent, self-reflection, subjective goals, and an explicit desire to communicate a specific meaning.	Driven by algorithmic objectives (e.g., minimizing loss function, maximizing data correlation) and a user's prompt (input).
Nature of Novelty	Capable of achieving "novelty from zero" (genuine paradigm shifts) and deliberate violation of established rules based on understanding those rules.	Achieves "novelty from existing data" through sophisticated interpolation, extrapolation, and recombination of latent variables.

continued on following page

Table 7. Continued

Feature	Human Creativity	Machine-Generated Output
Context & Emotional Depth	Embedded with subjective meaning, cultural context, emotional valence, and an understanding of its potential reception.	Meaning is inferred by the human observer; the output itself lacks subjective, conscious emotional experience or context.
Agency & Authorship	Full creative agency; the human artist is the legal and philosophical author and source of originality.	The AI is a sophisticated tool; legal and philosophical authorship typically defaults to the human user, engineer, or prompt creator.

More precisely, the fast acceleration of generative AI is already starting to have substantial but disruptive operational and economic impacts on the creative industries. In the production, AI is unveiling its power as a multiplier of efficiencies: studios are finding that the use of AI results in 80% to 90% efficiencies of visual effects and 3D assets, and reduces the overall film and TV production costs by 30% by providing efficiencies for labour-intensive work. Efficiency is also captured in commercial opportunities: the generative design market is expected to grow to US\$926.0 million by 2030 thanks to 30–50% design efficiencies, for example. Yet, this technological acceleration is also potentially putting at risk the very existence of the creator economy, with a risk of revenue for human creators of 21–24% by 2028 in the music and audiovisual industries resulting from the substitution effect of AI-generated content. Yet, high-profile case studies such as the use of deepfake technology by Lucasfilm for production and use of virtual actors raise key, open questions and legal and ethical issues on intellectual property, digital likeness and questions of creative authorship in the era of scalable algorithmic production. (See table 8.).

Table 8. Case Study or Industry Metric

Industry/Area	Case Study or Industry Metric	Significance to the Chapter
Film & TV Production	Estimated Cost Reduction: Generative AI is projected to reduce overall programming expenses by approximately 10% for major media companies, and up to 30% in specific TV and film production processes (e.g., visual effects, animation). (Epstein et al., 2023).	Empirically supports the automation/ efficiency argument, illustrating the economic disruption and the shifting value chain in traditional storytelling media.
Visual Effects (VFX) & 3D Assets	Efficiency Gains: Studios expect 80% to 90% efficiency gains in repetitive tasks within VFX and 3D asset creation (e.g., de-aging, digital cleanup, environment extensions). (Wang et al., 2023).	Provides quantifiable data for the "AI as a Collaborator" argument, demonstrating how AI automates the technical "plumbing" of production, freeing human creatives for higher-level ideation.
Music & Audiovisual Creator Economy	Revenue Risk: By 2028, generative AI is projected to put 24% of music creator revenues and 21% of audiovisual creator revenues at risk of loss globally due to substitution effects. (Amankwah-Amoah et al., 2024)	Directly fuels the Ethical and Legal Discussions section, highlighting the urgent need for new copyright frameworks and remuneration models (e.g., the EU AI Act discussions).
Design & Product Development	Generative Design Market: Market size projected to grow from $257.2 million (2023) to $926.0 million by 2030 (20.1% CAGR). Companies report 30–50% efficiency gains in product conceptualization and rendering time. (Artificial-intelligence-ai-in-product-design-and-development-market, 2025).	Moves the discussion beyond art, demonstrating AI's accelerating role in commercial design, engineering, and co-creation by rapidly generating optimized prototypes.
Journalism & Content at Scale	Bloomberg / Reuters: Utilize Natural Language Generation (NLG) tools to automatically produce thousands of data-heavy reports (financial earnings, sports scores) instantly and without human writer intervention. (Generative AI 2024 Report I Bloomberg Professional Services, 2025).	Illustrates the most mature application of AI in storytelling (narrative generation), demonstrating how it handles high-volume, factual content, allowing human journalists to focus on investigation and analysis.
Personalization & Distribution	Netflix: AI-driven recommendation engines are responsible for approximately 80% of the content streamed by users. (How Netflix Content Recommendation System Works – HelloPM, 2025).	Highlights AI's crucial role in the "Storytelling Continuum," showing that AI's influence extends far past creation and into curation, engagement, and audience experience.
Virtual Actors & Digital IP	Lucasfilm's *The Mandalorian*: Used deepfake technology to digitally recreate a younger version of actor Mark Hamill (Luke Skywalker). (How Respeecher's Voice Cloning Brought Young Luke Skywalker to …, 2024).	A high-profile case study for the discussion on deepfakes (as a form of creative manipulation) and the controversial legal and ethical issues surrounding digital likeness rights and virtual performers.

8. CONCLUSION

Although bringing this entwining long journey to an end, we will translate these complicated ethical and societal problems into a powerful vision for the future and give a final Conclusion on the already ongoing union between human creativity and AI. One very strong ethical and aesthetic problem brought forward by generative AI is the problem of creative standardization. Sophisticated models such as GANs or diffusion models, for example, can also indeed do things that are amazing, but at the end of the day, what they can achieve is ultimately constrained by the statistical patterns and relations discovered in their preexisting, massive training datasets. Such an assumption constrains the success of these models to be "circumscribed by the scope and bias of their training datasets", which in turn limits the possibilities to achieve true novelty. As a consequence, AI-generated art will be predictable: it will be a very effective interpolator or extrapolator of existing styles, rather than bringing about 'novelty from zero' or deep paradigm shifts and rather introduce an overall aesthetic homogeneity between a variety of media and genres. This is clearly a critical issue that needs to imply that the theoretical work on the role of AI is informed by such empirical limitations and provide an accurate balance about algorithmic creativity.

Our journey has shown that, in conclusion, AI is indeed powerful and transformative and very rapidly changing the landscape of creativity, art and storytelling. Artificial intelligence is not confined to technical tasks only: artificial intelligence has proved to be an algorithmic muse capable of coming up with intriguing visions, sophisticated music and rich texts. We have seen that generative models are not only copying the popular styles, but are themselves contributing to the development of new styles, from photorealistic images and much more sophisticated game stories to unique sound capes. We have travelled to a new starting point: AI is evolving from being a mere tool for automation to becoming a living and more and more sophisticated partner in creation.

But entering this new frontier will require first a sophistication of our understanding of AI capability, and, crucially, its limitations. AI is good at pattern recognition, at spark ideation and doing complex things, but AI does not have deep human capacities for true emotional sensitivity, for subjectivity, and for subtle nuances that underlie the meaning of a work of art. Issues of bias in training data, abuse of AI for propaganda and deepfakes, and the full-blown legal battles around copyright and ownership of AI outputs are not footnotes but integral, defining challenges that we need to address proactively as these technologies come of age.

Looking forward, the future of creativity will be a rich colouring of human talents and artificial intelligence. That future will increasingly be determined by human–AI collaboration and artists, writers, and musicians using AI as an extension of their creative urges, with the transition towards jobs such as 'prompter engineers' and 'curators', and with democratization of the creative tools, encouraging an ever-wider palette of voices, resulting in an unchained explosion of artistic output. The final question will then not be whether AI can be creative, but how will human creativity itself shift and transform when liberated and challenged by the immensity of the generative power of the algorithmic muse? The canvas is big, the symphony has just begun and the stories are waiting to be told, together. Definitions of key terms.

REFERENCES

Amankwah-Amoah, J., Abdalla, S., Mogaji, E., Elbanna, A., & Dwivedi, Y. K. (2024). The impending disruption of creative industries by generative AI: Opportunities, challenges, and research agenda. International Journal of Information Management. https://linkinghub.elsevier.com/retrieve/pii/S0268401224000070

Anantrasirichai, N., & Bull, D. (2022). Artificial intelligence in the creative industries: A review. *Artificial Intelligence Review*, *55*(1), 589–656. https://link.springer.com/article/10.1007/s10462-021-10039-7. DOI: 10.1007/s10462-021-10039-7 PMID: 41625196

Artificial-intelligence-ai-in-product-design-and-development-market. (2025). https://www.marketsandmarkets.com/Market-Reports/artificial-intelligence-ai-in-product-design-and-development-market-123456789.html

Attaluri, V., & Mudunuri, L. N. R. (2025). Generative AI for Creative Learning Content Creation: Project-Based Learning and Art Generation. In Smart Education and Sustainable Learning Environments in Smart Cities (pp. 239-252). IGI Global Scientific Publishing. https://philarchive.org/rec/VIVGAF-2

Bhuvaneshwaran, A., Kavya, P., Dhaksana, N., Amuthaguka, D., Eraianbu, R., & Agilan, S. (2024, October). Artistic Fusion: AI Powered Artistry for Story Boarding. In 2024 4th International Conference on Sustainable Expert Systems (ICSES) (pp. 795-800). IEEE. https://www.semanticscholar.org/paper/Artistic-Fusion%3A-AI-Powered-Artistry-for-Story-Bhuvaneshwaran-K./a51a4bf5234e7d4b0520d62724fc5381bfd48d30

Bowen, J. P. (2024). Alan Turing: Breaking the Code, Computing, and Machine Intelligence. In The Arts and Computational Culture: Real and Virtual Worlds (pp. 75-94). Cham: Springer Nature Switzerland. https://www.researchgate.net/publication/381789532_Alan_Turing_Breaking_the_Code_Computing_and_Machine_Intelligence

Choe, N. S., & Hinz, L. D. (2024). The Role of the Expressive Therapies Continuum in Human Creativity in the Age of AI. *Art Therapy: Journal of the American Art Therapy Association*, •••, 1–9. https://eric.ed.gov/?id=EJ1475514

Chubb, J., Missaoui, S., Concannon, S., Maloney, L., & Walker, J. A. (2022). Interactive storytelling for children: A case-study of design and development considerations for ethical conversational AI. *International Journal of Child-Computer Interaction*, *32*, 100403. https://www.sciencedirect.com/science/article/abs/pii/S2212868921000921. DOI: 10.1016/j.ijcci.2021.100403

Craig, C., & Kerr, I. (2025). The death of the AI author. In *Robot Law* (Vol. II, pp. 250–285). Edward Elgar Publishing., https://robots.law.miami.edu/2019/wp-content/uploads/2019/03/Kerr_Death-of-AI-Author.pdf

Daniele, A., Di Bernardi Luft, C., & Bryan-Kinns, N. (2021). "What Is Human?" A Turing Test for Artistic Creativity. In Artificial Intelligence in Music, Sound, Art and Design: 10th International Conference, EvoMUSART 2021, Held as Part of EvoStar 2021, Virtual Event, April 7–9, 2021, Proceedings 10 (pp. 396-411). Springer International Publishing. https://dl.acm.org/doi/abs/10.1007/978-3-030-72914-1_26

Egon, K., Potter, K., & Lord, M. L. (2023). Ai in art and creativity: Exploring the boundaries of human-machine collaboration. *OSF Preprints*, 20, 1-11. https://osf.io/preprints/osf/g4nd5_v1

Elfar, M., & Dawood, M. E. T. (2024). Artificial Intelligence Ethics: A Discussion of Potential Risks and Associated Ethical Dilemmas in Art and Design. *Journal of Heritage and Design*, *4*(23), 370–385. https://jsos.journals.ekb.eg/article_308526.html?lang=en

Epstein, Z., Hertzmann, A., Herman, L., Mahari, R., Frank, M., Groh, M., Schroeder, H., Smith, A., Akten, M., Fjeld, J., Farid, H., Leach, N., Pentland, A., & Russakovsky, O. (2023). Art and the science of generative AI. Science. https://arxiv.org/abs/2306.04141

Fernandes, T., Nisi, V., Nunes, N., & James, S. (2024, September). ArtAI4DS: AI Art and Its Empowering Role in Digital Storytelling. In International Conference on Entertainment Computing (pp. 78-93). Cham: Springer Nature Switzerland. https://www.stuart-james.com/publications/2024ICEC/FernandesICEC24.pdf

Flick, C., & Worrall, K. (2022). The ethics of creative AI. In *The language of creative AI: Practices, aesthetics and structures* (pp. 73–91). Springer International Publishing., https://liedra.net/misc/Flick_Worrall-Ethics_of_Creative_AI.pdf DOI: 10.1007/978-3-031-10960-7_5

Gaggioli, A., Bartolotta, S., Ubaldi, A., Gerardini, K., Sarcinella, E. D., & Chirico, A. (2025). Extended Creativity: A Conceptual Framework for Understanding Human-AI Creative Relations. https://arxiv.org/abs/2506.10249

Garcia, M. B. (2024). The paradox of artificial creativity: Challenges and opportunities of generative AI artistry. *Creativity Research Journal*, •••, 1–14. https://manuelgarcia.info/publication/artificial-creativity#:~:text=The%20distinction%20between%20generative%20AI,sole%20purview%20of%20sentient%20beings

Generative, A. I. 2024 Report | Bloomberg Professional Services. (2025). https://www.bloomberg.com/professional/products/bloomberg-terminal/research/bloomberg-intelligence/download/generative-ai-2024-report/

Gjorgjieski, V. (2024). Art Redefined: AI's Influence on Traditional Artistic Expression. *Journal of Art and Design*, *1*(1), 49–60. https://www.researchgate.net/publication/382104061_Art_Redefined_AI's_Influence_on_Traditional_Artistic_Expression

Haase, J., & Pokutta, S. (2024). Human-AI Co-Creativity: Exploring Synergies Across Levels of Creative Collaboration. https://arXiv preprint arXiv:2411.12527.

How Netflix Content Recommendation System Works – HelloPM. (2025). https://hellopm.co/netflix-content-recommendation-system-product-analytics-case-study/

How Respeecher's Voice Cloning Brought Young Luke Skywalker to. … (2024). https://www.respeecher.com/case-studies/respeecher-synthesized-younger-luke-skywalkers-voice-disneys-mandalorian

Hughes, R. T., Zhu, L., & Bednarz, T. (2021). Generative adversarial networks–enabled human–artificial intelligence collaborative applications for creative and design industries: A systematic review of current approaches and trends. *Frontiers in Artificial Intelligence*, *4*, 604234. https://www.frontiersin.org/journals/artificial-intelligence/articles/10.3389/frai.2021.604234/full. DOI: 10.3389/frai.2021.604234 PMID: 33997773

Hussen, N., Samir, A., Adel, A., Gaber, A., Attaia, M., & Mohamed, A. (2025). Advancing Creativity: A Comprehensive Review of AI-Driven Text-to-Image Generation and Its Applications. Advanced Sciences and Technology Journal, 2(2), 1-17. https://astj.journals.ekb.eg/article_420273_b616acfb6bbfaaf59d6001872828d067.pdf

Joel, A. (2024). The Impact Of Generative Ai On Creative Industries: Revolutionizing Art, Writing, And Music. https://www.researchgate.net/publication/391489737_THE_IMPACT_OF_GENERATIVE_AI_ON_CREATIVE_INDUSTRIES_REVOLUTIONIZING_ART_WRITING_AND_MUSIC

Komal, A. S., Sethu, S. G., & Chaudhary, R. (2024). Artificial Intelligence in Storytelling: A Critical Analysis of Narrative Authenticity, Cultural Impact, and the Future of Creative Industries. Library Progress International, 44(3), 4638-4651. https://bpasjournals.com/library-science/index.php/journal/article/download/1284/802/1986

Kusmiatun, A., Efendi, D., Al Pansori, M. J., Judijanto, L., Sariasih, Y., & Saddhono, K. (2024, May). The Power of AI in Generating Novel Based and Impactful Character Development for Fiction Story. In 2024 4th International Conference on Advance Computing and Innovative Technologies in Engineering (ICACITE) (pp. 1555-1561). IEEE. https://www.researchgate.net/publication/383005306_The_Power_of_AI_in_Generating_Novel_Based_and_Impactful_Character_Development_for_Fiction_Story

Le-Nguyen, H. T. (2024). Ethical dilemmas of AI perspectives towards common digital art and digital crafting: AI artistic view on morality. In *Making Art with Generative AI Tools* (pp. 226–257). IGI Global., https://www.irma-international.org/viewtitle/343431/?isxn=9798369319505#:~:text=227-,Ethical%20Dilemmas%20of%20AI%20Perspectives%20Towards%20Common%20Digital%20Art,et%20al.%2C%202020 DOI: 10.4018/979-8-3693-1950-5.ch013

Lin, Y., & Liu, H. (2024, June). The impact of artificial intelligence generated content driven graphic design tools on creative thinking of designers. In *International Conference on Human-Computer Interaction* (pp. 258–272). Springer Nature Switzerland., https://www.springerprofessional.de/en/the-impact-of-artificial-intelligence-generated-content-driven-g/27163862 DOI: 10.1007/978-3-031-60913-8_18

Manu, A. (2024). Transcending imagination: Artificial intelligence and the future of creativity. CRC Press. https://www.taylorfrancis.com/books/edit/10.1201/9781003450139/transcending-imagination-alexander-manu

Navas, E. (2024). AI Ethics, Aesthetics, Art and Artistry. In Handbook on the Ethics of Artificial Intelligence (pp. 173-186). Edward Elgar Publishing. https://www.elgaronline.com/edcollchap/book/9781803926728/book-part-9781803926728-17.xml

Nieuwenhuijsen, B. (2023). Sampling in the Age of AI. https://arno.uvt.nl/show.cgi?fid=162563

Patama, S. (2025). Exploring Human-AI Collaboration in the Creative Process: Enhancements and Limitations. https://jyx.jyu.fi/bitstreams/3ddb1c66-1afd-4cc1-882d-8de273bf43f8/download#:~:text=ABSTRACT,fueling%20resistance%20to%2D%20wards%20AI

Piskopani, A. M., Chamberlain, A., & Ten Holter, C. (2023, July). Responsible ai and the arts: The ethical and legal implications of ai in the arts and creative industries. In Proceedings of the First International Symposium on Trustworthy Autonomous Systems (pp. 1-5). https://ora.ox.ac.uk/objects/uuid:a803ecc0-c8cc-42a0-be17-848334dc3cf5/files/r5d86p1015

Pizzo, A., Lombardo, V., & Damiano, R. (2023). Interactive storytelling: a cross-media approach to writing, producing and editing with AI. Routledge. https://www.taylorfrancis.com/books/mono/10.4324/9781003335627/interactive-storytelling-antonio-pizzo-vincenzo-lombardo-rossana-damiano

Raza, A. (2025). THE EVOLUTION OF HUMAN-AI COLLABORATION IN CREATIVE INDUSTRIES: CASE STUDIES IN MUSIC AND DESIGN. Multi-disciplinary Research in Computing Information Systems, 5(2), 105-122. https://mrcis.org/index.php/journal/article/download/89/177#:~:text=Abstract.,concepts%20of%20authorship%20and%20originality

Rezwana, J. (2023). Towards designing engaging and ethical human-centered AI partners for human-AI co-creativity (Doctoral dissertation, The University of North Carolina at Charlotte). https://ninercommons.charlotte.edu/record/2699/files/Rezwana_uncc_0694D_13557.pdf

Ruszev, S., Rogers, L., Gurgun, S., Stockton-Brown, M., Gee, M., Davis, T., . . . Prajitna, S. (2024). Shared-posthuman imagination: Human-AI collaboration in media creation. https://eprints.bournemouth.ac.uk/40681/7/10.18746_epxn-da67.pdf

Salta, S. S., & Katsaros, M. (2024). The Art of Storytelling Redefined: Artificial Intelligence and the Future of Architectural Visualizations. archiDOCT, 12(1). https://archidoct.scholasticahq.com/api/v1/articles/118897-the-art-of-storytelling-redefined-artificial-intelligence-and-the-future-of-architectural-visualizations.pdf

Stojanovic, L., Radojcic, V., Savic, S., Sandro, A., & Cvetkovic, D. S. (2023). The influence of artificial intelligence on creative writing: Exploring the synergy between AI and creative authorship. *International Journal of Engineering Inventions*, *12*(12), 70–74. https://www.scirp.org/reference/referencespapers?referenceid=4097620

Suchacka, M. K., Muster, R., & Wojewoda, M. (2021). Human and machine creativity: social and ethical aspects of the development of artificial intelligence. Creativity Studies, 14(2). https://www.academia.edu/63837534/Human_and_Machine_Creativity_Social_and_Ethical_Aspects_of_the_Development_of_Artificial_Intelligence

Thampanichwat, C., Wongvorachan, T., Sirisakdi, L., Chunhajinda, P., Bunyarittikit, S., & Wongmahasiri, R. (2025). Mindful architecture from text-to-image AI perspectives: A case study of DALL-E, Midjourney, and stable diffusion. *Buildings (Basel, Switzerland)*, *15*(6), 972. https://www.mdpi.com/2075-5309/15/6/972. DOI: 10.3390/buildings15060972

Torres, A. J., Alberto, J. M. C., Guieb, A. P. J., Paray, A. D., & Villarama, J. A. (2025). Language, Identity, and Ethics in AI-Driven Art: Perspectives from Human Artists in Digital Environments. Language, Technology, and Social Media, 3(1), 17-29. https://www.researchgate.net/publication/389792022_Language_Identity_and_Ethics_in_AI-Driven_Art_Perspectives_from_Human_Artists_in_Digital_Environments

Turgay, E. Y. (2025). *Online audio services as innovative tools for creative in musical arts*. National Academy of Managerial Staff of Culture and Arts Herald., DOI: 10.32461/2226-3209.3.2025.344452

Wang, T., Kanakis, M., Schindler, K., Gool, L., & Obukhov, A. (2023). Breathing New Life into 3D Assets with Generative Repainting. https://www.semanticscholar.org/paper/f879dafb02c1bd4f34c0480beab259164a7fb459

Xu, C., Sun, Y., & Zhou, H. (2024). Artificial aesthetics and ethical ambiguity: Exploring business ethics in the context of AI-driven creativity. *Journal of Business Ethics*, •••, 1–22. https://www.researchgate.net/publication/385317173_Artificial_Aesthetics_and_Ethical_Ambiguity_Exploring_Business_Ethics_in_the_Context_of_AI-driven_Creativity

Yadav, M., Kumar, M., Sahoo, A., & Rathnasiri, M. S. H. (2025). AI and the evolution of artistic expression: impacts on society and culture. In *Transforming cinema with artificial intelligence* (pp. 15–36). IGI Global Scientific Publishing., https://www.irma-international.org/viewtitle/365406/?isxn=9798369339169

You, Q. (2021). Generative art, Storytelling and Society (Master's thesis, The University of Bergen). https://nva.sikt.no/registration/0198f081265f-076f0baf-9e96-4530-bd17-74961557d96d

Zafar, F. (2024). Graphic Design and AI: Replacement of Human Mind? *Journal of Arts and Linguistics Studies*, *2*(2), 1063–1077. https://jals.miard.org/index.php/jals/article/view/145

Zazzaro, C. (2024). Charting a Paradigm Shift: The Impact of Christie's Auction of AI-generated Edmond de Belamy on the Evaluation of Art (Doctoral dissertation, Utrecht University). https://studenttheses.uu.nl/handle/20.500.12932/48553

Additional Reading

Fernandes, T., Nisi, V., Nunes, N., & James, S. (2024, September). ArtAI4DS: AI Art and Its Empowering Role in Digital Storytelling. In International Conference on Entertainment Computing (pp. 78-93). Cham: Springer Nature Switzerland. https://www.stuart-james.com/publications/2024ICEC/FernandesICEC24.pdf

Garcia, M. B. (2024). The paradox of artificial creativity: Challenges and opportunities of generative AI artistry. *Creativity Research Journal*, •••, 1–14. https://www.researchgate.net/publication/381037114_The_Paradox_of_Artificial_Creativity_Challenges_and_Opportunities_of_Generative_AI_Artistry#:~:text=Abstract%20and%20Figures,of%20art%20and%20the%20artist

Liu, B. (2023). Arguments for the rise of artificial intelligence art: Does AI art have creativity, motivation, self-awareness and emotion? Arte, Individuo y Sociedad, 35(3), 811. https://www.researchgate.net/publication/370109562_Arguments_for_the_Rise_of_Artificial_Intelligence_Art_Does_AI_Art_Have_Creativity_Motivation_Self-awareness_and_Emotion

Pierosara, S. (2024). Narrative autonomy and artificial storytelling. *AI & Society*, *39*(4), 1785–1794. https://dl.acm.org/doi/10.1007/s00146-022-01595-9. DOI: 10.1007/s00146-022-01595-9

Pitta, J. P. (2023). AI in Art & Creativity. The Spicerian, 72(2), 3-7. https://www.semanticscholar.org/paper/AI-in-Art-%26-Creativity-Pitta/9fac60ee4e83a196d86f3fcf61ad31bb492f37ea

KEY TERMS AND DEFINITIONS

Artificial Intelligence (AI): In the context of this chapter, artificial intelligence (AI) is synonymous with the development of computer systems that perform tasks that typically require human intelligence in a way that teaches, solves problems, makes decisions, perceives and, increasingly, creates. This development encompasses a wide range of techniques and algorithms that allow machines to replicate or augment human intelligence functions. Creativity: Ability to produce unique and valuable ideas, concepts or artistic products. In the context of AI, creativity addresses the question of whether and how AI can contribute or produce original creative and imaginative creations of aesthetic value in excess of approximation or mere collection of pre-existing information.

Art: Expression or application of human creative skill and imagination, especially by means of painting, sculpture or pictures on a computer screen, creating objects to be experienced for their beauty or emotional power. In terms of AI, this means works that are produced by AI to a significant extent, as part of their conception, creation or performance.

Storytelling: Telling stories (including plots, characters, places and themes) to an audience to entertain. In terms of AI, this means AI tools and systems as used to AI-generated, AI-authored or AI-assisted stories in different formats, such as short stories, poems to screenplays to interactive story systems.

Generative AI: Within the overall field of AI, an output of AI that is creating new and original things as opposed to AI programs that are analysing or transforming data that has already existed. Such models (eg, GANs, transformers, diffusion models) are trained with large amounts of data and can produce new written or image, audio or other media, that is similar to the training data but not identically copied versions.

Human-AI synergy: Human collaboration with AI with a shared creative purpose. It can include AI working with humans on specific activities (for example, generate variations, generate suggestions) or a collaborative effort in which AI and humans each make a critical contribution, with the output becoming so interwoven that it is often unclear where an individual's contribution ends and the other's begins.

Digital Art: Art that has been made or presented in digital technology. This means everything from purely computer-generated images to digital transformations of photographs or interactive art exhibitions. In this chapter, digital art is focused on how AI tools expand possibilities and techniques for digital artists. AI Music: Musical compositions, performances or audio designs produced, co-produced or affected by algorithms of artificial intelligence. This can be AI generation of melodies, harmonies, rhythms, whole compositions or even help with mixing and mastering.

AI Music: Musical compositions, performances, or sound designs created, co-created, or significantly influenced by artificial intelligence algorithms. This can include AI generating melodies, harmonies, rhythms, entire scores, or assisting with mixing and mastering.

AI Writing: Text created by an AI or by an AI assisting human creators. It spans from short content such as headlines or social media posts to longer content such as articles, short stories, poems and scripts, where the AI assists with idea creation, writing or rewriting.

Ethics of AI: The branch of ethics pertaining to the ethical questions and societal impact of artificial intelligence. With creative AI, the ethical questions include copyright ownership, bias of the generated output, risk of misuse (eg, deepfakes), impact on human labour and other philosophical questions about what kind of creativity AI has and what its artistic intent is.

Authorship: The state or fact of being the writer or creator of a book, an article, a piece of music, an artwork. With AI in creative activities, authorship becomes tricky and raises questions about ownership of the copyright and when to credit AI if AI contributes much or all of the generated creative work.

Future of creativity: Refers to the future of creative processes, industries and expressions, affected by technology in general, and A.I. in particular. It covers the predictions and discussions about how A.I. will transform the way in which art, music, stories are made, produced, consumed, enjoyed and valued by society.

Chapter 5
Early Intervention Through Engagement:
Gamification and AI in Elementary School Mental Health Support

Marie Grace Avelino Gomez
http://orcid.org/0000-0003-0180-9875
University of the Philippines, Philippines

ABSTRACT

ental well-being of children is essential to their overall developmentacademic success However, through the years, the schools catering to these young xhildren have focused on iimproving academic skills instead of fosterning social and emotional competence. As a result, there is a steady rise of mental health cases among older children. Younger children also have been plagued with mental health concerns. Given thiw scenario, there is a need to enable young learners to cope with potential mental health concerns. One method would be gamification. This technique offers a non-threatening way to engage students to know and regulate their emotions. In the long run, it is hoped tha this will help them in their well-being so that mental health issues will be avoided.

INTRODUCTION

Children's mental well-being is essential for their overall development, academic success, and future contributions to society (Cefai et al., 2021). Historically, discussions surrounding mental health have often been downplayed in the education sector, with an exclusive focus on basic education students' content mastery (Powell et al., 2024). However, despite downplaying the necessity of addressing mental

DOI: 10.4018/979-8-2600-2438-6.ch005

health issues, a growing body of research posits an urgent and escalating crisis in children's mental health. This escalation necessitated a shift in how educational specialists approached support and intervention within the school systems. The early years of schooling, spanning from ages five to 11, are a critical period of rapid cognitive, emotional, and psychosocial development. During these years, foundational coping mechanisms, self-regulation skills, and interpersonal competencies have been developed (Hutt et al., 2022). Evidently, the emergence of mental health concerns during this sensitive phase can have profound and lasting consequences, necessitating prevention programs.

The slow but certain rise in mental health challenges among elementary-aged children is alarming. In DSM 5, some conditions are first noticed during early childhood. Some of these factors can cause mental health concerns. Conditions such as anxiety disorders, depression, attention-deficit hyperactivity disorder (ADHD), and various behavioral issues are becoming increasingly evident in this age group. Studies have consistently shown that a significant percentage of children have diagnosable mental health conditions, and many more show subclinical symptoms that impair functioning (Fazel & Soneson, 2023). Anxiety, which can present as excessive worry, separation anxiety, or specific phobias, can significantly hinder a child's ability to learn, engage socially, or attend school. Depression, although sometimes appearing differently in children than in adults (e.g., irritability, somatic complaints), can cause social withdrawal, loss of interest in activities they previously enjoyed, and academic decline (Del Casale et al., 2021). ADHD can manifest as attention issues, impulse control, and hyperactivity. This can lead to major challenges in classroom and peer interactions. Furthermore, some young school-age children show defiance and aggression. If these are left unaddressed, schoolchildren not only disrupt learning but could also have underlying emotional distress that needs strategic intervention from their own families and schools.

The long-term effects of untreated mental health issues in elementary schools can have lifelong implications. When not addressed, problems that begin during school age can develop into more serious and complicated disorders during adolescence and adulthood, such as the development of more severe forms of depression, conduct disorders, and personality disorders (Schlack et al., 2021). Academically, children with mental health challenges often have difficulty focusing, perform poorly in school, miss more days, and are more likely to drop out of high school. In the social realm, issues in building and maintaining friendships, leading to loneliness, bullying, or social anxiety, may be experienced (Coyle et al., 2021). Emotionally, the ongoing burden of untreated issues can damage self-esteem, cause feelings of hopelessness, and increase the risk of more serious psychological problems (Bulut et al., 2024). If left unaddressed, societal costs, including healthcare expenses and lost potential, are significant (Baig-Ward et al., 2023). This harsh reality highlights the pressing need for accessible and supportive mental health services within schools.

Schools have established guidance centers. Traditional approaches to mental health support in schools, while well meaning and carefully planned, often encounter significant challenges. One common hindrance is the persistent stigma associated with mental illness. Children and their families may hesitate to seek help because of fear of judgment, discrimination, or being labeled by their school communities. This stigma can lead to underreporting of disorder symptoms, delays in intervention, and worsening problems. Additionally, many school systems face access issues, particularly in developing countries. A shortage of qualified mental health professionals, such as psychologists, counselors, and psychiatrists, combined with heavy caseloads, hinders children from receiving support. Limited funding for programs and training and a lack of medical supplies aggravate the shortage. There are situations in which even when services are available, traditional methods such as psychotherapy may not be sufficient to meet the developmental needs and preferences of young children, as they may lack motivation to undergo treatment. It must be recognized that children thrive through play, interaction, and tangible activities. The lack of engaging approaches can cause demotivation, disinterest, poor attendance, and ultimately less effective outcomes.

Given these challenges, early intervention as a preventative and protective approach is necessary for those who do not have underlying mental health conditions. For those who are starting to develop such issues, recognizing and addressing mental health issues at their early stages can reduce their severity, strengthen resilience, and teach children vital coping skills before problems become deeply rooted. Early intervention creates a safe environment in which children can openly express their feelings and build strong social-emotional skills. This proactive approach benefits not only the individual child but also the whole school community, encouraging a more inclusive, understanding, and effective learning environment. This chapter argues that integrating advanced technologies, particularly gamification and Artificial Intelligence (AI), provides a way to boost engagement in early mental health support, thereby overcoming many limits of traditional methods and unlocking the full potential of preventive care.

Purpose of the Chapter

This chapter presents the spectrum of mental health difficulties that early childhood education students face and suggests the gamification of AI as a method of coping with them. The principles framing the basis of gamified learning are manifested in interventions such as Applied Behavior Analysis and Cognitive Behavior Therapy.

LITERATURE REVIEW

Designing an intervention that is specifically targeted toward a given scenario depends on having a wide knowledge of the subject matter, which in this case is the ranking of mental health problems in early childhood education (ECE) and primary school students. The mode of an expression of mental health issues in young children is defined by the natural course of growing in a person's life. As opposed to adolescence or adulthood, elementary students lack the emotional lexicon and mental ability to define multifaceted emotions or internal problems correctly. As a result, their distress is more frequently depicted using behavioral (e.g., irritability, aggression, and withdrawal), physiological (e.g., stomach and headache), or academic (e.g., sudden grade drops, poor concentration) symptoms. Suitable identification of such distinguishable symptoms is essential for adequate recognition and to have fitting interventions in place.

There are common risk factors that play a significant role in the development of mental health challenges among elementary students. These are easy examples of family crises (i.e., parental disagreements, financial burdens, chronic sickness) (Hill et al., 2022). They can generate a rather unstable living situation, which makes a child's outlook in life insecure. Adverse Childhood Experiences (ACEs) include mistreatment, disregard, dysfunction (i.e., substance use by parents, household mental illness), or exposure (household or external violence), which can lead to various mental health problems (Ho et al., 2022). Furthermore, psychosocial skill deficits can prevent children from effectively handling even minor life stresses and other social obligations, making them more susceptible to mental health concerns (Gajalakshmi, & Meenakshi, 2023). Demonstrates early signs of a problem such as these is very crucial because these are tied to the main identification and correct response.

There are common risk factors that play a significant role in the development of mental health challenges among elementary students. These are easy examples of family crises (i.e., parental disagreements, financial burdens, chronic sickness) (Hill et al., 2022). They can generate a rather unstable living situation, which makes a child's outlook in life insecure. Adverse Childhood Experiences (ACEs) include mistreatment, disregard, dysfunction (i.e., substance use by parents, household mental illness), or exposure (household or external violence), which can lead to various types of mental health problems (Ho et al., 2022). If you want to address the need for mental health in children, psychosocial skill deficits can prevent children from effectively handling even minor life stresses and other social obligations, making them more susceptible to mental health concerns (Gajalakshmi & Meenakshi, 2023). Therefore, monitoring the signs of a problem is very crucial because these are tied to the main identification and correct response.

Given these complexities, recognizing early warning signs is crucial. By their very nature, they are best solved when short-lived and when faced with considerable evidence to ignore them. Over thousands of hours of observation, the teacher has gained the exclusive insight to identify subtle behavioral, emotional, and academic changes in a student. This is due to the numerous hours of preparation over the 4 years in preservice. Nevertheless, the possibility remains that teachers may find additional in-service training useful. Adapting to the underlying danger signals is an important factor, and thus training teachers and school staff to pinpoint these cues is crucial. On the other hand, observations alone are generally not sufficient; thus, it is imperative that intervention be effected.

The claim demonstrates that schools can act both as sources of help and means of interference. Schools, unlike learning institutions, influence the psychological development of a child. In addition, they help, a place to communicate with others, and people who show care. The increasing number of mental health services in schools eliminates the barriers to reach and the stigma associated with it, as well as allowing the continuous evaluation and temporary help. Schools may include a variety of child-wellness promotion programs, using a framework geared toward mental, social, and academic health. Children may gain mental health help within this space in addition to offering other benefits, with the ability to avoid the stigma usually associated with traditional forms of support. Thus, peer support may also be provided as a secondary tool in a safe and almost invisible manner.

The Power of Engagement: Why Gamification Works for Young Learners

The efficacy of positive behavioral modification in intervention programs for children is primarily reliant on the design of the procedure. Young children's interventions entail full attention and active participation on their part. That is why gamification is beneficial and may be used as the best method.

Gamification is the use of elements of games and game mechanics in contexts that are free of games (Indah, 2025). The aim is not to create holistic games but to use some commodities of Halloween in a way that turns the tasks into engaging, motivating, and fun ones. The crucial components are goal setting, prompt assessment, chance of gaining skills, highlighting importance for social peers, and status of increasing rank. The elements may be:

Points: Numbers for accomplishing the task or behaving correctly.

Badges: Online pictures or physical items for mastering the skill or reaching the goal.

Leaderboards: The scoreboard of the player's progress or achievement for employees' cooperation and competition.
Challenges/Quests: A series of difficulties or achievements giving the participants focus and excitement.
Narratives/Storytelling: A basis that envelops the lesson in a story allowing the subject to make the content meaningful instead of just facts.
Rewards: Object or non-object earning for one's behavior and direction towards positive acts.

Gkintoni et al. (2024) describes the psychological impact of gamification for children and direct assistance with encouraging mental health goals. The pleasure of fun is one of the reasons for gamification's high motivation and natural interest. Children usually have fun while playing and completing the mission. That is why mental-health-related task activities can be turned into a game allowing one to find a hobby of improving emotional regulation and the ability for coping skills. Unlike regular classes with perceptions of emotions as mere content, natural motivation makes students stay longer and deeper involved with the subject.

First, gamification allows students to engage in active learning (Handayani et al., 2021). Children not only process data but also follow their developmental pathways, make choices, and receive empirical assessments. Such practical experience is necessary when a teacher wants to teach someone a difficult approach or impart a skill. For example, a child could level up by incorporating the right emotion for a cartoonish figure or earn coins for exercise breathing.

Gamification creates a closed environment where the discussed themes can be tackled and, most notably, a place for free discussion (Patricio et al., 2022). Discussing sadness, feeling anxious, or when anger strikes young children' can help. Gamified circumstances produce a metaphorical dissociation between children's physical presence and their avatars or characters' identities, allowing one to consider emotions and develop coping approaches without the threat of getting a private disclosure. Ultimately, the stigma is helped to be dispelled, which is normally observed regarding direct marriages to mental health.

Gamification aims to provide such a shelter place and protection for encountering coy events, in addition to developing coping mechanisms and problem-solving talents. Games make it naturally necessary to face challenges and prepare for flexibility. Allowing these children to address issues akin to real-life ones (emotional or social problems), they will have the opportunity to try different strategies, gain self-confidence, and master the skills. For example, in the game, the child may be requested to respond to a social dilemma with the appropriate answers or release anger using the strategies they have grasped.

Moreover, children do not assess these spaces as saboteur or therapy as places they feel they are not allowed to be. The children engaging in the specific exercises or games will not sense the difference or impute anything broken in the act of playing. This is an example of the dissolution of the stigma of mental health gymnastics through a playful and friendly formula that urges for continued engagement and less resistance.

Such tactics of gamification are successfully used in different educational programs, as well as the health system. Language learning apps, such as Duolingo, rely on streaks, point scores, and leaderboards to stimulate learners' repetition. Fitness apps rely on challenges and virtual rewards to motivate users to exercise. Educational programs also successfully exploit quests and badges for subjects, from mathematics to history. The game-based learning could be a theme's side aim; these samples show the ability to increase participation, acquire skills, and ensure students' interest in different educational fields. The main hurdle is the minor application of these methods in the mental health arena for elementary school-aged children, which is the problem and possibility at the same time.

COMBINING ABA TECHNIQUES WITH GAMIFICATION TO ADDRESS MENTAL HEALTH ISSUES IN YOUNG SCHOOL CHILDREN

Applied Behavior Analysis is a theory of learning and behavior modification that relies on the explicit demonstration of a cause-effect relationship between occurrences. This system has been around for a long time, and its core rules are employed not only in the interventions for children with autism spectrum disorder (ASD) but also in the management of inattentiveness and impulsive-defiant behavior, anxiety, and depression in children who have typical developmental trajectories but get dysregulated. If ABA is combined with gamification, the latter can weave it into fun sessions that are informally educational and aimed at reinforcing self-regulation, motivation, and emotional health. The ABC model helps clinicians identify and address the behavior-maintaining mechanisms in their own child's care, using the model's three components: antecedents, behaviors, and consequences. In terms of, gamification also employs children's innate tendency to engage in play, face a challenge, and win prizes. The link between the two strategies, hence, produces a potent mechanism that repeatedly encourages the correct acts in a space that is strictly regulated, made for fun, and geared toward inspiration.

Addressing Inattentiveness and Impulsivity through Positive Reinforcement and Shaping

Inattentiveness and impulsivity, often regarded as ADHD symptoms, create problems for absorbing new knowledge in the classroom and building peer relationships. ABA provides a set of techniques, such as positive reinforcement and shaping, that help promote attention and self-regulation. They can be perfectly realized in a gamified system.

For instance, a classroom gamification tool can award points or tokens (reinforcers) for attention-related actions, among them, finishing a task, obeying an order, or waiting for a turn. The tokens can be utilized to start getting privileges, badges, or digital goodies. Immediately, specifically, and dependent on the behavior performed, the reinforcement must be like in the case of the ABA principle, which states that elements such as the timing and the clarity of the reinforcement play a role in determining its effectiveness.

Additionally, gamification serves as a medium for shaping, or reinforcing, successive approximations toward a target behavior in a stepwise manner. A child who finds concentration hard for a very long time can first get a reward for attempting to keep up for five minutes, then ten, and eventually for completing a whole lesson. All this can be realized with digital visual trackers. Visual progress trackers, typical of gamified systems (for instance, level-ups or quest achievements), provide concrete details of incremental progress that bolster motivation and persistence.

Reducing Defiant Behavior through Token Economies and Functional Communication Training

Changes in defiance motives are attributed to unfulfilled desires, lack of control over internal or external environments, and failure to control emotions. ABA addresses defiance by determining the function of such behavior in defiant children, whether it is for parental attention, to avoid undesirable tasks, or to control external environments (Pasa & Moleno, 2023). Once the function is identified, constructive positive options can be substituted and encouraged.

The gamification methods may be an illustration of token-economy principles, using conditioned reinforcers in the form of rewards presented as points, stars, or badges. In place of punishing noncompliance, the teacher can reinforce complying as well as cooperating, encourage children to follow the rules, help them through the transitions, and use polite exchanges to collect charitable points. Enabling children to select the type of redeemable reward (for instance, changing their avatar or utilizing the node they chose) cultivates competence, fun, and control, and inhibits destructive behavior.

Another approach based on ABA and Functional Communication Training (FCT) involves teaching children to express wants or frustrations in a rational way rather than resorting to defiant or aggressive behavior. The mechanisms of gamification can support the FCT strategy by requiring players to "earn communication power-ups" when using appropriate emotional or attention-seeking expressions addressed to others. Transitions from conflict situations to positive experience manifestations reflect the objective of the learning environment and demonstrate the modeling and strengthening of proper response strategies (Tariq, 2026).

Managing Anxiety through Desensitization and Self-Monitoring

The most frequent behaviors for anxiety in small children are avoidance, somatization, and perfectionism. Incorporating traditional ABA methods, such as self-monitoring can help overcome fears during intervention.

Systematic desensitization is a process of chronicling the child's fear-producing stressors and subsequently rewarding them for displaying calm responses. This gamifies through gradual exposure to mild-to-moderate stressors. For instance, a child who is afraid of socializing may be presented with a virtual character in the game as a starting point. After a predetermined number of activities, they can initiate cooperative play with other children. Positive experiences can also be rewarded with points or badges for bravery and approach levels. The gamified environment turns exposure exercises into field missions that do not require painful practice in a therapist's room.

Self-monitoring can also be gamified to improve and support children's core ABA skills using a digital dashboard or an "emotion meter." Children can rate their anxiety or mood before and after each task and receive rewards for answering honestly. Rewards are also given when they practice coping. Displaying their progress would raise awareness and allow them to see the connection between strategies and results, which is critical for managing emotions. As a result, children can realize that emotions can be controlled and slowly. Their efforts can lead to the desired outcome.

ADDRESSING CHILDHOOD-ONSET DEPRESSION THROUGH ACTIVITY SCHEDULING AND POSITIVE BEHAVIOR SUPPORT

Child-onset depression can manifest in sadness, demotivation or anger. Behavioral activation, a Cognitive Behavior Therapy based can be applied for behaviors such as social withdrawal, demotivation, and self-criticism, aiming to increase involvement in satisfying and engaging activities (Kusec et al., 2023)

Behavioral activation through gamification can be achieved through the same activity-planning system, which stimulates involvement, persistence, and continuity (Nasri et al., 2025). For example, a "Wellness Quest," whether virtual or in real life, can be a schedule of daily actions related to gratitude, movement, or interaction with peers. For the conclusion of each task, a badge or a level in the storyline will be given. Initially, the therapeutic model employs external reinforcement but then develops intrinsic interest, allowing for a return of motivation and positive feelings.

Also, Positive Behavior Support (PBS) and ABA can be utilized as gamified elements, constructing psychologically safe places. PBS involves instruction and rewards for desirable behavior when a problem is predicted, rather than waiting until it occurs. In the gamified class, combined rewards for teamwork, assistance, and empathy create a feeling of equity and of membership.

CREATING A BALANCED AND ETHICAL GAMIFIED ABA ENVIRONMENT

Gamification along with ABA, is a pioneering concept and can be promising. However, it involves ethical considerations and reflection. The absence of direct external reinforcement can undermine internalized motivation unless it is accompanied by prudent application of awards.

Gamification in ABA should be considered a systematic behavior framework for turning concrete reinforcements into elusive incentives: personal satisfaction and gratification. In addition, cultural and developmental aspects are fundamental. The reward systems and games the teachers create, and design should mirror the integrity, taste, and skills of children, thus fostering the sense of ownership of educational events for every learner (including students with disabilities).

Another ABA principle - data collection - can be integrated into gamified platforms to track progress, detect trends, and adapt care to individual patients. Gamification, enabled as a holistic strategy, is a training form that sharpens attention, discipline, and social behavior. Children understand rewards for nice actions as well as their worth in themselves, irrespective of patience, empathy, or courage.

Key Applications of AI in Mental Health Support

Personalization and Adaptive Learning: AI has demonstrated major advantages in adaptive and personalized delivery of education and healthcare. As a result, the content and feedback adjust to individuals' specific characteristics.

Customization in psychological treatment enables children to incorporate relevant coping techniques tailored to their emotions and learning style (Zhang et al., 2021). For example, mindfulness apps powered by AI for children could demonstrate breathing techniques based on the level of anxiety.

AI education centers might also include social and emotional development-based modules (Naeem et al., 2025). For example, a frustrated student is less motivated by human instruction, so more interactive activities can be provided to help them overcome their challenge. Through personalization, AI transforms theoretical emotional elements into concrete experiences for developing self-awareness and regulation (Maroju, & Bhattacharya, 2025).

> **Early Detection and Risk Assessment:** One of the fundamental contributions of AI to child wellbeing is its early detection aspect (Indrio et al., 2024). By identifying certain data sources and patterns, such as voice and behavior outputs, AI can define signs of emotional distress that would normally be challenging to detect (Kasaudhan, 2025). For example, drastic decreases in digital engagement, long downtime on learning applications, or a negative voice in a written assignment could alert mental wellness problems.

Scientists suggest the development of machine learning models capable of analyzing a mass of data to judge risk scores or alerts and conveying them to inform teachers and school psychologists (Van Lissa, 2023). It is not designed as an expert solution to replicate professional judgment, but rather a beneficial initial step of contemplation, which increases the chance of timely intervention before ailments become dangerous. In large schools with many students to monitor one-on-one, early-detection models are highly beneficial.

> **Automated Support and Feedback:** AI chatbots and virtual friends provide 24/7 anonymous active support for recovery and reintegration. Young learners, who may be reluctant or shy, can also connect with AI when they are feeling upset. For instance, a virtual assistant might say, "It looks like you are feeling a little quiet today; would you like to talk to me about it?" can encourage participation or help a child with a relaxation or mindfulness session.

Through AI, children might disclose their feelings to virtual objects more often than adults, especially if the system is considered non-treatening and empathic by them. Automated feedback systems encourage desirable behavior, such as praising the child for performing well after using the coping tools or reminding them that they have missed their break. Such "micro-interventions" emotionally prepare and build children's resilience.

Data-Driven Insights for Educators and Parents: AI tools aim to support adults in making evidence-based, comprehensive decisions through transparent analysis. Contrasting dashboards that communicate patterns, such as sleep cycles, stress triggers, and peer interactions, AI for children can help teachers and parents track emotions. For instance, a teacher dashboard may reveal that a student demonstrates a higher level of frustration during math-related activities, thus, activities should be targeted for emotional co-management during this subject. These data-driven mechanisms to enhance mental health care mean it can be proactive. That is, rather than waiting for a child to misbehave, the teacher can anticipate the behavior based on observations and recommendations from the AI summaries and personalize classroom interventions accordingly or refer the student for counseling.

Scalability: The capacity of AI to provide scalable interventions is commendable in a world where the shortage of psychologists' and counselors' capacity in a school system worsens. AI-powered devices can interface with 100 or 1,000 learners at once, and the staff would not be overwhelmed (Kumar et al., 2022).

Therefore, chatbots and a programmed journal or exercises combined with a gamified wellness system will provide seamless, high-grade, and continuous services to nurses while leaving patients to focus on learners who need intensive human interventions. However, quality must not be compromised by scale.

The goal should be not substitute of the therapist's services so that every student in the school will still get human intervention

Ethical Considerations and Limitations of AI in Child Mental Health

AI introduction into children's mental wellbeing arouses ethical and practical challenges despite the positivity it shows. Primarily, the main issue is data privacy. Children's emotional and behavioral information is the most confidential kind of data, and mismanagement of this issue by AI service providers can bring stigma and financial exploitation to children. Educational settings' and mobile applications' creators must ensure that they use tough encryption, privacy policies, and transparent protocols on storage and disposal.

The problem of algorithm bias is also an issue. While AI systems are trained on biased minorities' data (based on race, language, or social class), it can bring further inequality. For instance, the language used may not parse or assess the sounds or facial expressions of children from a wide range of communities and would eventually give inaccurate results.

Moreover, the other concern is an enormous reliance on the technology itself. Using AI in medicine has many benefits, but it is devoid of feelings, which is an essential element of care and flourishing management. To develop the ability to converse with someone, children need an actual person, or that would prevent them from learning loyalty or sympathy. As a result, the use of AI may be limited to just giving assistance to human counselors or educators.

The last factor is clarity and accountability in AI development. The technology's functioning must be explicit for teachers, parents, and children, who should also be offered ways to question and recast the technology's results. Ethical integration relies not only on technology but also on building trust through transparency and shared responsibility.

SYNTHESIZING THE STRENGTHS: GAMIFICATION AND AI FOR ELEMENTARY MENTAL HEALTH

Gamification, the application of game mechanics and design principles to non-gaming situations, is based on motivation, curiosity, and reward systems that make the process of learning more enjoyable. The incorporation of gamification and AI turns it into not just fun but a smart, adaptive, and mentored platform for mental health research and support.

AI-Powered Individualization within Gamified Tools. AI makes games responsive and adaptive, monitoring the child's intellectual and emotional state. Suppose a student experiences anxiety; the AI-integrated game would recognize avoidant actions and offer a step-by-step plan of small exercises to regain confidence. At the same time, the tailored sites might praise failures rather than accomplishments, gaining persistence through gamification. It ensures that gamified interventions are not discriminative and adapted to developmental restrictions.

Gamified Collection of Information. Among the strongest testaments to the power of gamification and AI is high data engagement. Games typically track and store response time, decision-making skills, and resilience. AI processes this data to uncover mood shifts, frustration limits, or social capabilities. Since the setting is happy, games are cooperative, and the psychological exam is more natural than a school test.

It is a noninvasive and considers the game as a core diagnostic tool, which is ethical and child friendly. AI is the "Smart" Solicitor or Companion. In the hybrid environment, AI integration enables the machine to act as a supportive and empathic character. Further refinements in AI technology can help achieve this goal. AI can also be considered as a subject-matter expert. With more advances in AI, hopefully, it can convey more emotions.

Short stories with virtual characters can also be made. For example, Ita, a virtual character, carries a child through the overwhelming period, can take deep breaths when needed. The child can press a key that starts inhaling and exhaling while following the virtual character. Prompts can also be given ("Let's breathe—two, three, four"). Social praises can be done to celebrate the child's achievements ("You remained calm even when the situation was tough—well done!").

Since assistance is personified, AI acquires emotional engagement. The children can imitate these statements for self-control and self-talk after the gamified process as independent practice.

DISCUSSION

Immersive and Dynamic Educational Developments

By implementing gamified AI features, a teacher can teach interpersonal skills such as empathy, perspective-taking, and cooperation. Virtual reality(VR) can take it a step further. In VR-based role-playing games, the potential peer conflicts can be reduced to encourage players to seek more acceptable social solutions. A high degree of immersion can result to emotional flexibility: they may experiment with feelings and activities within the protected zone, which can have real-world consequences for actual interactions.

Specific Applications and Scenarios

Gamified Apps for Emotional Regulation. Using narration, games like the "mood monsters" or "emotion quests" offer children an opportunity to identify and manage their feelings. Challenges may be customized using AI to suit a child's rising skill level. For instance, if a student often replies with "sad" in a mood book, the output would be related to hope or gratitude. Exercises such as deep breathing or guided imagery may be presented as short stories or games to learn to cope with anxiety or defeat.

AI-Powered Virtual Companions for Social Skills. In such avatars and social scenarios may be introduced that children can engage with, such as greeting, listening, or conflict resolution (Dell 'Aquilla et al., 2022). Lessening anxiety or shyness can be done in a non-threatening way. The AI can also insert prompts in real time, such as reflection on eye contact, the child's character growth, or an alternative line of response. The child may become socially confident with successive interactions and apply the learned skills in unfamiliar social settings.

Interactive Stories and Quests Teaching Empathy. A certain genre of interactive narratives created through AI depends on children's ethical and emotional decisions. For instance, one could choose to help a character who is bullied by the other players in the game. The AI entity would decode one's selection and insert subsequent questions such as "How do you think your character felt after your intervention?" Thus, gamified teaching helps develop empathy.

Early Warning Systems in Educational Games. Using AI, one can observe signs of distress or disengagement and track immediate mood and performance alterations during the online games. For example, if the child immediately drops the game after one round due to disappointment, the teacher will receive a notification with evidence and helpful feedback offering the student time or suggestion to continue or stop the activity. The transition from observing gameplay to monitoring mood within the game capitalizes on children's surroundings at the time of the game and may convert the entire gaming ecosystem into early detection tools.

Parent and Teacher Dashboards. AI tools could collect data to determine whether the child experienced a steady rise in mood-related resilience or frustrations The outcomes act as guides for an empathic and careful attitude at home and in the school setting.

Implementation Considerations and Best Practices

User-Centered Design. The universal design process can be used as a guide by the successful AI-gamified tool. Children, their teachers, and adults should equally be heard during the creation of such tools. Cultural expectations must also be practiced. The child's developmental stage and emotional safety must be considered. The developers should be cautious about the child's frustration or overstimulation.

Ethical Guidelines and Data Security. All apps must integrate encryption, de-identification, and consent criteria. Schools and programmers should have a clear policy that describes what data is gathered, how it's used, and when it's deleted. Good communication fosters trust and decrease tension with respect to monitoring requirements. The ethics policy must direct the written instructions in such a way that the targeted children are not jeopardized with the risk of being excluded or judged by their classmates.

Teacher Training and Supporting. As students develop their understanding of the involvement of AI in human services that aim to improve their well-being, they would likely require guidance on how to effectively and properly use AI data to apply such interventions in classrooms. Teacher training should also enable educators to appreciate the use of AI-generated reports, handle discourse around psychosocial supports, and maintain the distinction between mechanical assistance and human interest. Teachers should be equipped with more than just an understanding of how AI software operates; they must also appreciate its psychosocial impacts.

Parental Engagement. The role of harmonizing any digital culture cannot be underestimated. Sessions, talks, or feedback can assist parents in gaining insights into how their child used the platform, interpreting AI comments, and enhancing their control techniques in a domestic setting. Inviting parents to bring culture to the conversation strengthens the association between instruction in classrooms and settings at home. This is instrumental for social maturation.

Hybrid Models: Technology as a Supplement, Not a Substitute

The partnership between AI and gamification should maximally serve as support for human compassion and connection instead of a replacement. Balanced hybrid models that integrate technology to provide data, order, and incentives, teachers and counselors to supply people-to-people care are the most efficient methods. While technology can predict struggle and create bridges, humans will still be available to offer sanctuary in the very communities that protect us.

Accessibility and Equity. The last element of incorporating technology should be intentional equity and accessibility. Children from all groups or from all socioeconomic status should gain from mental health AI and gamified tools. Multilingual options, low-speed applications, and text-to-speech should be made available to address the needs of marginalized populations by promoting equity. Regulations for equity, such as government funding or easy-to-access open-source strategies, will ensure no child will be excluded from digital mental health resources.

AI provides many benefits; it has shortcomings as well. However, it can be noted that . AI provides accuracy, flexibility, and personalization, whereas gamification delivers motivation, appeal, and delight. The two unite to build empathetic and educative learning environments, creating links between humanity and technology.

Nevertheless, the accomplishment lies in balance. Collective efforts that bring educators, technologists, parents, and guardians together, working with children's best interests in mind, can help shift from clinical or crisis mental health responses to fun, therapeutic settings.

CHALLENGES AND FUTURE DIRECTIONS

The rise of AI and gamification in providing mental health support for children in education settings presents both outstanding benefits and severe challenges as part of their integration. Although these solutions guarantee inclusiveness, personalization, and scalability, they also force a rigorous evaluation of the socioeconomic, moral, and infrastructural conditions that determine their effectiveness. To that end, providing the future lacks indulgence for innovation and responsible implementation.

Challenges

Cost and Infrastructure. One of the immediate roadblocks to blended AI and gamification for children's mental health is infrastructure and cost. Advanced AI platforms, cloud storage, and cybersecurity services are costly to acquire, especially for resource-constrained schools in less-developed nations or underfunded public-school systems, creating inequalities. Schools have tight resource lists that cover fundamental needs such as teacher resources, classrooms, and employee wages; mental health technology may not be prioritized. In addition, the successful execution of AI operations requires sufficient online capacity, current hardware, and maintenance as the old model should remain relevant. Pressing schools in rural communities or far areas lack sufficient conditions that maintain a digital divide, creating poor children nameless access to mental health-related platforms.

The infrastructure extends beyond hardware to human investment: experts and teachers to interpret and ethically use digital tools. Without funding to support computer acquisition or capacity-building, AI innovations risk creating a divide instead of serving as relief or bridging the gap in education.

However, the government, technology programmers, and educational systems should collaborate to shrink the gap. Partnerships, grants, and open-access frameworks ensure that mental health technologies do not become luxuries afforded to the select few but function as public goods.

Resistance to Technology and the Digital Divide. Fear, doubt, and lack of understanding are the major sources of technological resistance. Educators may resist the use of AI applications for fear of losing their jobs and independence in the workplace. Parents may be wary of children participating in online programs for privacy fears or believing that too much exposure to digital tools will harm their child. Communities may feel uncomfortable sharing emotional or psychological health in a digital medium, depending on cultural values or norms throughout their lives that still make mental health taboo.

The digital divide exacerbates the problem. Unequal access to new technology due to poverty, geographic settings, or a disability causes some children to have better access to AI-based mental health support, while others do not. Children in well-resourced, urban settings will benefit from AI-based immersive mental health programs, while children in far and impoverished rural settings will receive less education on mental health. A divide risks further inequalities in mental health, engagement, and education achievement.

Focusing on digital literacy and equity is paramount to overcoming the challenge and inequality. Educators and parents should watch how AI tools function, why they are used, and how developers protect users' privacy. Transparency regarding data use, training, and the reframing of new content should build trust. A similar approach should ensure that technologies extend care rather than replace it, mitigating teachers' fears that tech advances will be their rival, rather than a trusted accomplice, in the classroom and profession.

Ensuring Evidence-Based Efficacy and Evaluation. The market for mental health apps that use AI and gamification is comparatively new, rapidly growing, and unproven using empirical studies. Most services promise stress and better emotional regulation but lack clear evidence or screening by scientific scholars. The lack of empirical evidence further compounds issues that the impact of technology can be overstated or produces side effects that are unfavorable.

A lack of several approaches for evaluation is preceding the effectiveness of interventions capable of helping or even inactivating harm. Schools and platforms should collaborate with researchers to finalize pilot tests and long-term follow-up to evaluate the short-term and long-term emotional, behavioral, and academic outcomes. Beyond metrics such as engagement or user satisfaction, such evaluation should consider clinically meaningful outcomes, such as the number of days experiencing acute anxiety symptoms, the number of days in which a person engaged in coping strategies, or the number of social interactions made.

Moreover, the use of AI must be evaluated as appropriate age. Children and adolescents have different forms, levels, and awareness of their emotional experiences, with age, temperament, and cultural context (Yeh, 2025). An algorithm trained on adult data or a small demographic sample can misinterpret a child's behavioral patterns, leading to inaccuracies and misinformation. Creating explainable digital infrastructure should lead to teachers, psychologists, and several other professionals receiving outputs that are explainable to them, ensuring the reliability of results.

Legal and Ethical Frameworks. The ethical and legal implications of AI-assisted mental health are both multilayered and rapidly evolving. The legislation of privacy and child protection is rarely explicitly tailored to AI-enabled interventions or the nuances of emotional information. The lack of legal and ethical protection makes children vulnerable to data misuse, algorithmic bias, and mental health risks due to inappropriate interventions.

The fields of consent, ownership, and accountability are at the forefront of concerns. Whose data is added to the emotional archive of an AI that a child interacts with: school, developers, or child dependents and family? How must guardians' consent be managed, and what steps can be taken to ensure that a child's digital privacy is protected? Without adequate ethical and legal governance, schools risk hesitation and complexity in navigating policy issues with their AI initiatives.

Building on this, there is a need for governments and intergovernmental organizations to fortify policies toward children's welfare, regulate transparency and accountability of the algorithm, and expand partnerships for digital mental health with educational and child protection initiatives.

Balancing Technology and Human Connection. While AI can provide real-time emotional responses and logistical assistance, it does not have the ability to provide warmth, veracity, and respect that Humans provide. Resilience and emotional development are largely human processes, with children depending on external support—in the classroom, a teacher who notices a behavioral change, a classmate who provides empathy, or a counselor who has a listening ear. Too reliant on AI platforms, children's brains are risk-decreasing from tangible bonds to near or complete loneliness or reliance on an artificial entity. For children-in-progress, constant monitoring should include facilitating discussion and intervention by an adult around mental health issues (Tariq, 2026).

In such a case, a healthy mixing of the two—human and technological support—needs to be made, not a culture of depending on machines for care. AI seeks to supplement teachers and psychologists with given information and research about the data while allowing interventions to be related to human emotion. Getting children to decipher AI data with adult support creates a balance between the digital and the physical.

Essentially, technical contributions to mental health are not the replacement of inter-human relationships, but rather the growth of relational consciousness through giving children and caregivers spaces to talk about emotions, conduct, and coping behaviors.

Future Directions

Even though there are risks with AI and gamification in child mental health, there is a surprising, good future for it. With cutting-edge technological research and developed capacity to understand children's development and neuropsychology, teachers can expect to see more relevant, pleasant, and effective interventions in the future.

In the future, AI will likely introduce further improvements to its ability systems to analyze emotions. Systems that decipher human feelings using heterogeneous inputs such as voice tone, facial expressions, posture, and physiological data fall into this category. This will further the emotional calibration of the children, making them accurate and capable of picking up the context. Take low engagement, for instance. Instead of alarmingly flagging all boredom, fatigue, and temporarily distracted children, AI would learn to differentiate among these activities (Tariq, 2026).

This accuracy can turn mental health care from broad strategies into customized ones. Nevertheless, such systems should be designed to be easy to understand and explain and developed with proper respect for users' privacy. Emotional data is private; therefore, ethical design should ensure it is never used to collect people's data or control their behavior.

> **Immersive Therapy.** With ways such as VR and AR, these technological tools give remarkable new territory for emotional learning and therapy. These realistic surroundings seek to replicate real situations to enable children to refine their abilities, for instance, self-control and empathy, and acquire practical strategies, like coping mechanisms in expressions that are safe and controlled.

Take for example a VR experience of anxiety-provoking situations (e.g., public speaking, a peer dispute) demonstrating physiological patterns through AI to provide precise adaptive feedback. In class, AR overlays could transform mindfulness into a fun, interactive, and therapeutic experience. These hybrids couple skills training with emotional coaching, engaging both the mind and the senses to strengthen resilience and self-knowledge.

With device prices falling, the chance to use VR and AR for emotional learning could be a reality. With this regard, it would help in destigmatizing it and make the processes of therapy captivating and enjoyable.

If educators improve existing AI and gamification interventions, there is a need to conduct long-term evaluations. Yes, short-term assessments focus mainly on the engagement and satisfaction. Efficacy studies are yet to be done on the benefits of these AI tools. By using longitudinal studies, we can see if the programs were created can indeed contribute to emotional regulation, social competence, and achievement.

Free Resources. The free access systems that foster certification, clear rules, and a drive for transparency are the key to the democratization of mental health technology. The creation of databases, the construction of ethical design templates, and the platforms that will be integrated will help schools and researchers build on what already exists.

Policy Advocacy for Greater Coverage and Budgets. To ensure forward movement in the context of AI-promoted mental health treatments, governments must commit the effort to the policy decisions. Digital mental health should be recognized by governments as a public good and made a part of entire education and child protection strategy. The source of funding should shy away from pilot programs, teachers' preparedness, and equal facilities. Policymakers can allow the involvement of academic and private sectors, as well as civil society, to help this field expand and for ethical use. It is possible to include the teaching of digital well-being and emotional literacy in our daily curriculum to tackle technology- and mental health-related issues from an early age. It is worth noting that adopting AI and gamified strategies in the mental health education of high-potential students is a form of investment and intends to equip these learners' with self-awareness, resilience, and compassion. By making children identify feelings, be empathic, as well as seeking help. these effective interactive equipment enables children to retain emotional health and security. Addressing the mental health needs of children cannot be exclusively done by machines. There is a need for a human touch of warmth. In the future, technology might be able to convey more human compassion. Nonetheless, schools can be caring ecosystems, employing technology as a compassion amplifier, providing a guide map for educators, and allowing every student to travel their march by the road to their vibrant well-being.

REFERENCES

Baig-Ward, K. M., Jha, M. K., & Trivedi, M. H. (2023). The individual and societal burden of treatment-resistant depression: An overview. *Psychiatria Clinica, 46*(2), 211–226. PMID: 37149341

Bulut, M. B., Kurtaran, D., Bostancı, V., Sarı, Y., & Çil, K. N. (2024). Self-esteem, hopelessness, quality of life, and psychological symptoms in individuals diagnosed with periodontal disease. *Current Psychology, 43*(8), 7071–7083. DOI: 10.1007/s12144-023-04924-3

Cefai, C., Simões, C., & Caravita, S. (2021). A systemic, whole-school approach to mental health and well-being in schools in the EU.

Coyle, S., Malecki, C. K., & Emmons, J. (2021). Keep your friends close: Exploring the associations of bullying, peer social support, and social anxiety. *Contemporary School Psychology, 25*(2), 230–242. DOI: 10.1007/s40688-019-00250-3

Del Casale, A., Zocchi, C., Kotzalidis, G. D., Fiaschè, F., & Girardi, P. (2021). Prevention of depression in children, adolescents, and young adults: The role of teachers and parents. *Psychiatry International, 2*(3), 353–364. DOI: 10.3390/psychiatryint2030027

Fazel, M., & Soneson, E. (2023). Current evidence and opportunities in child and adolescent public mental health: A research review. *Journal of Child Psychology and Psychiatry, and Allied Disciplines, 64*(12), 1699–1719. DOI: 10.1111/jcpp.13889 PMID: 37771261

Gajalakshmi, G., & Meenakshi, S. (2023). Understanding the psycho-social problems of vulnerable adolescent girls and effect of intervention through life skill training. *Journal of Education and Health Promotion, 12*(1), 429. DOI: 10.4103/jehp.jehp_612_23 PMID: 38464658

Gkintoni, E., Vantaraki, F., Skoulidi, C., Anastassopoulos, P., & Vantarakis, A. (2024). Promoting physical and mental health among children and adolescents via gamification—A conceptual systematic review. *Behavioral Sciences (Basel, Switzerland), 14*(2), 102. DOI: 10.3390/bs14020102 PMID: 38392455

Handayani, P. W., Raharjo, S. R., & Putra, P. H. (2021). Active student learning through gamification in a learning management system. *Electronic Journal of e-Learning, 19*(6), 601–613. DOI: 10.34190/ejel.19.6.2089

Hill, D. L., Christakis, D. A., & Feudtner, C. (2022). Illness in the family and shared stress, work, and struggle. *JAMA Pediatrics*, *176*(6), 549–550. DOI: 10.1001/jamapediatrics.2022.0491 PMID: 35404432

Ho, L. L. K., Li, W. H. C., Cheung, A. T., Luo, Y., Xia, W., & Chung, J. O. K. (2022). Impact of poverty on parent–child relationships, parental stress, and parenting practices. *Frontiers in Public Health*, *10*, 849408. DOI: 10.3389/fpubh.2022.849408 PMID: 35548071

Hutt, S. J., Tyler, S., Hutt, C., & Christopherson, H. (2022). *Play, exploration and learning: a natural history of the pre-school*. Routledge. DOI: 10.4324/9781003324751

Indah, S. (2025). Gamification in Early Childhood Education: Improving Students' Learning Motivation through Game-Based Learning Strategies. *Journal of Education Technology and Inovation*, *8*(1), 50–64. DOI: 10.31537/jeti.v8i1.2333

Indrio, F., Pettoello-Mantovani, M., Giardino, I., & Masciari, E. (2024). The role of artificial intelligence in pediatrics from treating illnesses to managing children's overall well-being. *The Journal of Pediatrics*, *275*, 275. DOI: 10.1016/j.jpeds.2024.114291 PMID: 39242077

Kasaudhan, K. (2025). AI-Driven Tools for Detecting and Monitoring Mental Health Conditions Though Behaviour Patterns. [IJPMH]. *International Journal of Preventive Medicine and Health*, *5*(3), 14–19. DOI: 10.54105/ijpmh.B1054.05030325

Kumar, P., Baliyan, A., Prasad, K. R., Sreekanth, N., Jawarkar, P., Roy, V., & Amoatey, E. T. (2022). Machine learning enabled techniques for protecting wireless sensor networks by estimating attack prevalence and device deployment strategy for 5G networks. *Wireless Communications and Mobile Computing*, *2022*(1), 5713092. DOI: 10.1155/2022/5713092

Kusec, A., Methley, A., Murphy, F. C., Peers, P. V., Carmona, E., & Manly, T. (2023). Developing behavioural activation for people with acquired brain injury: A qualitative interpretive description study of barriers and facilitators to activity engagement. *BMC Psychology*, *11*(1), 207. DOI: 10.1186/s40359-023-01230-2 PMID: 37443147

Maroju, P. K., & Bhattacharya, P. (2025). Understanding emotional intelligence: The heart of human-centered technology. In *Humanizing Technology With Emotional Intelligence* (pp. 1–18). IGI Global Scientific Publishing.

Naeem, S., Qureshi, M. A., & Butt, A. M. (2025). AI Integration Into Course Content Development. In *AI Applications for English Language Learning* (pp. 93–120). IGI Global Scientific Publishing. DOI: 10.4018/979-8-3693-9077-1.ch005

Nasri, S. A. E. M., Kavakli-Throne, M., Hassan-Smith, Z., Salt, A., & Hassan-Smith, G. (2025). Gamification in digital healthcare: From evidence review to a novel framework for enhancing patient engagement in chronic disease management. *F1000 Research, 14*, 1396. DOI: 10.12688/f1000research.172599.1

Pasa, S. M. B., & Moleño, J. N. (2023). Behavior Modification Strategies for Learners' Disruptive Behavior. *Best Practices in Disability-Inclusive Education, 2*(2).

Patricio, R., Moreira, A. C., & Zurlo, F. (2022). Gamification in innovation teams. *International Journal of Innovation Studies*, *6*(3), 156–168. DOI: 10.1016/j.ijis.2022.05.003

Powell, T., Meek, S., Soto-Boykin, X., Allen, R., Iruka, I. U., Bucher, E., & Loewenberg, A. (2024). *Learning, Joy, and Equity: A New Framework for Elementary Education. Children's Equity Project*. New America.

Schlack, R., Peerenboom, N., Neuperdt, L., Junker, S., & Beyer, A. K. (2021). The effects of mental health problems in childhood and adolescence in young adults: Results of the KiGGS cohort. *Journal of Health Monitoring*, *6*(4), 3. PMID: 35146318

Tariq, M. U. (2026). Impact of Digital Narratives in Marketing Communication: Strategies, Tools, Engagement, and Consumer Impact. In Yılmaz, R., & Başer, B. (Eds.), *Developing Digital Narratives in Marketing Communication* (pp. 199–226). IGI Global Scientific Publishing., DOI: 10.4018/979-8-3373-1857-8.ch008

Tariq, M. U. (2026). The Semiotics of AI-Driven Consumer Experiences: Decoding Emotional Branding and the Experience Economy. In Piccolo, R., & Boero, M. (Eds.), *Emotional and Experiential Dimensions of Modern Marketing* (pp. 245–268). IGI Global Scientific Publishing., DOI: 10.4018/979-8-3373-7615-8.ch010

Tariq, M. U. (2026). Artificial Intelligence for Accelerating Progress on Sustainable Development Goals (SDGs). In Popescu, C. (Ed.), *AI and Green Innovation for Achieving Sustainable Development Goals* (pp. 53–80). IGI Global Scientific Publishing., DOI: 10.4018/979-8-3373-7584-7.ch003

Van Lissa, C. J. (2023). Developmental data science: How machine learning can advance theory formation in developmental psychology. *Infant and Child Development, 32*(6), e2370. DOI: 10.1002/icd.2370

Yeh, T. L. (2025, May). The Influence of Children's Temperaments on Acceptance of Artificial Intelligence in 3–7 Year Olds. In *International Conference on Human-Computer Interaction* (pp. 256-266). Cham: Springer Nature Switzerland DOI: 10.1007/978-3-031-93412-4_15

Zhang, R. E., Ringland, K., Paan, M. C., Mohr, D., & Reddy, M. (2021, May). Designing for emotional well-being: integrating persuasion and customization into mental health technologies. In *Proceedings of the 2021 CHI Conference on Human Factors in Computing Systems* (pp. 1-13). DOI: 10.1145/3411764.3445771

Chapter 6
Gamified AI Tools and Simulation Platforms for Transforming Entrepreneurial Education in South Africa

Sthokozile Mamba
http://orcid.org/0009-0005-3789-4030
University of KwaZulu-Natal, South Africa

Andrisha Beharry Ramraj
http://orcid.org/0000-0001-5674-885X
University of KwaZulu-Natal, South Africa

ABSTRACT

Entrepreneurial education in South Africa has become a vital mechanism for addressing unemployment and inequality by nurturing innovation and self-reliance among youth. However, the current pedagogical landscape remains dominated by theory-based instruction that fails to translate knowledge into entrepreneurial competence, particularly within the Curriculum and Assessment Policy Statement (CAPS)-aligned curriculum. A qualitative desk-based research design was employed, drawing on systematic content analysis of secondary data published between 2019 and 2025 from peer-reviewed journals, policy documents, and institutional reports. The findings revealed that AI and gamified simulations enhance learner motivation, decision-making, and creativity by bridging theoretical knowledge and experiential practice. However, challenges such as limited infrastructure, teacher readiness, and

DOI: 10.4018/979-8-2600-2438-6.ch006

ethical governance constrain effective implementation. The study recommended capacity-building for educators, equitable digital access, and ethical localisation of AI tools to ensure inclusion and sustainability.

INTRODUCTION

Entrepreneurial education has become a vital pillar for equipping learners with the skills to navigate South Africa's complex socioeconomic landscape. According to Singh (2024), entrepreneurship is central to achieving the country's inclusive growth goals; however, education systems remain constrained by traditional pedagogies that fail to connect theory with practice. Waghid (2019) asserts that the current CAPS-aligned curriculum in Economic and Management Sciences (EMS) and Business Studies is heavily theoretical, limiting learners' ability to develop innovative and problem-solving competencies. However, as Anderson-Coto (2024) explains, the rapid advancement of AI presents an unprecedented opportunity to reimagine entrepreneurship education through intelligent, data-driven, and adaptive learning environments.

Raimi, Bamiro, and Lim (2024) emphasize that gamified AI tools combine motivational learning design with adaptive feedback systems, transforming learning from a static process into an interactive and engaging experience. Furthermore, Devi, Raghunath, Patil, and Shanti (2025) state that AI-driven simulations allow learners to experiment, make decisions, and learn from failure in safe digital spaces that mirror real-world business contexts. This aligns with Kim, Ding and Cho's (2025) view that experiential learning promotes deeper understanding by enabling learners to move beyond memorisation to active application. According to Van der Berg, Gustafsson and Malindi (2023), this experiential shift is essential in bridging South Africa's persistent gap between education and employability.

However, as Khavasi (2025) argues, the localization of AI-based entrepreneurial learning must go beyond technological adoption to ensure cultural and ethical relevance in diverse learning environments. Hossain (2024) concurs that equitable access, inclusivity, and sustainability must underpin digital innovation to prevent the reinforcement of existing inequalities. Therefore, this study explores how gamified AI tools and simulation platforms can transform entrepreneurial education by offering immersive, adaptive, and localized learning experiences that empower South African learners to participate meaningfully in an evolving digital economy.

BACKGROUND OF THE STUDY

Entrepreneurship education has emerged as a strategic response to South Africa's persistent challenges of unemployment, inequality, and slow economic transformation. According to Bux and Van Vuuren (2019), entrepreneurship education holds the potential to build self-efficacy and entrepreneurial intention among learners; however, it remains largely theoretical and disconnected from practice. Iwu, Opute, Nchu, Eresia-Eke, Tengeh, Jaiyeoba and Aliyu (2021) explain that while many higher education institutions have introduced entrepreneurship programmes, these initiatives often replicate traditional academic models rather than fostering creativity, innovation, and problem-solving abilities. This pedagogical stagnation limits students' preparedness to engage productively with a rapidly changing digital economy.

Van der Berg et al. (2023) emphasise that South Africa's education system continues to produce graduates whose skills do not align with labour market demands, resulting in a mismatch between policy aspirations and practical outcomes. Similarly, Singh (2024) highlights that despite progressive policy frameworks such as the National Development Plan (NDP) 2030, the translation of entrepreneurship policy into effective, context-responsive pedagogy has been inconsistent. This disconnect between policy and practice reflects broader systemic gaps in integrating technology, experiential learning, and digital literacy in entrepreneurship education.

Garg and Sharma (2025) note that recent global shifts towards digital and remote learning have intensified the need for adaptive pedagogies that merge innovation with accessibility. However, as Gala, Namit, and Kidwai (2025) caution, African youth remain digitally marginalized, lacking equitable access to digital infrastructure and the skills necessary to participate in technology-driven learning environments. In this context, the introduction of AI and gamified learning systems represents a transformative opportunity to reimagine entrepreneurship education as interactive, personalized, and adaptive. Anderson-Coto (2024) asserts that AI-driven learning tools can enhance inclusivity through computational equity, while Raimi et al. (2024) argue that gamified simulations strengthen learner engagement by blending motivation with cognitive development.

Drawing from these insights, this study positions AI-enabled gamified simulations as a potential bridge between abstract entrepreneurial theory and real-world applications. By embedding experiential, localized, and adaptive technologies within entrepreneurship education, learners can move beyond rote memorization to active participation in decision-making and innovation. As Hossain (2024) explains, aligning smart educational technologies with sustainability and equity is crucial for long-term human capital development. Therefore, this study explores how integrating gamified AI and simulation-based tools can transform entrepreneurship education into an immersive, contextually relevant, and future-oriented system capable of driving inclusive economic growth in South Africa.

PROBLEM STATEMENT

Despite growing recognition of entrepreneurship education as a catalyst for socioeconomic transformation, South African classrooms remain dominated by outdated pedagogical practices that fail to translate entrepreneurial theory into practical competence. According to Iwu et al. (2021), most entrepreneurship programmes continue to prioritize cognitive learning over experiential engagement, resulting in limited creativity, problem-solving, and opportunity recognition among learners. Van der Berg et al. (2023) assert that this theoretical bias has perpetuated a misalignment between education and the labour market, where graduates are insufficiently equipped to respond to the demands of a digital and innovation-driven economy. However, as Garg and Sharma (2025) explain, structural barriers, such as underdeveloped digital infrastructure and limited teacher capacity, prevent the adoption of more interactive, technology-enhanced pedagogies in schools.

Furthermore, Waghid (2019) notes that entrepreneurship, as embedded within the CAPS curriculum through EMS and business studies, is taught in a fragmented and assessment-driven manner that restricts learners' exposure to real-world decision-making or entrepreneurial experimentation. Singh (2024) adds that while national policy frameworks (such as the NDP 2030) emphasize entrepreneurship as a vehicle for inclusive growth, the absence of pedagogical innovation continues to limit their realization. Consequently, entrepreneurship education remains disconnected from South Africa's socioeconomic realities, particularly in rural and township contexts, where learners face digital marginalization (Gala et al., 2025).

According to Raimi et al. (2024), AI and gamified simulations have the potential to transform learning environments by enhancing motivation, feedback, and adaptability. However, their application in South Africa remains minimal, largely due to concerns about localization, ethics, and equitable access. Khavasi (2025) argued that global AI education models often fail to reflect African cultural and linguistic contexts, leading to exclusion and pedagogical irrelevance. Similarly, Anderson-Coto (2024) cautions that without computational equity and ethical governance, AI-driven systems risk reinforcing rather than reducing educational inequality.

Therefore, the central problem lies in the persistent gap between policy ambitions and pedagogical transformation. South Africa's entrepreneurship education system remains ill-equipped to cultivate the digital, adaptive, and innovative capacities necessary in the 21st century. The challenge is not merely access to technology, but reimagining teaching and learning through gamified AI and simulation-based models that are immersive, localized, and ethically grounded, capable of transforming entrepreneurship education into a practical, inclusive, and future-oriented process of human development.

PURPOSE OF THE STUDY

This study examined how gamified AI tools and simulation-based learning platforms can transform entrepreneurship education in South Africa by creating immersive, adaptive, and localized learning experiences that bridge the gap between theory and practice. It uncovered how these technologies can enhance learner engagement, creativity, and problem-solving while aligning entrepreneurial education with the demands of a digital economy. Stakeholders who stand to benefit include educators, who will gain innovative pedagogical strategies and digital competencies for teaching entrepreneurship more effectively; students, who will develop practical, future-ready entrepreneurial skills through experiential and interactive learning; and policymakers, who will acquire evidence-based insights to reform curriculum and policy frameworks towards inclusive, technology-enabled education. Additionally, higher education institutions and educational technology developers may use the findings to design context-sensitive, ethically grounded digital tools that promote sustainable entrepreneurship and equitable access to learning across diverse South African contexts.

OBJECTIVE OF THE STUDY

This study explores how gamified AI tools and simulation platforms can transform entrepreneurial education by offering immersive, adaptive, and localized learning experiences.

LITERATURE REVIEW

This literature review explores the transformation of entrepreneurial education in South Africa, using gamified AI tools and simulation-based learning platforms. It examines how current entrepreneurship curricula, particularly within the CAPS framework, remain theoretical and disconnected from real-world practices. The review was structured into four interrelated themes. The first reconsiders the current state of entrepreneurial education in South Africa, exposing its limitations in terms of experiential engagement and digital integration. The second investigates how AI and gamification act as pedagogical co-facilitators, reshaping teaching and learning into adaptive participatory processes. The third explores simulation-based learning and dual-user platform design as mechanisms for bridging theory and practice, focusing on how such models enable co-learning between teachers and students. The fourth addresses localization, ethics, and sustainability in AI-enhanced learning, emphasizing equity, cultural contextualization, and ethical governance in technology adoption. Collectively, these sections provide a coherent theoretical foundation for embedding gamified AI and simulation tools into entrepreneurship education, offering a roadmap for context-responsive innovation in under-resourced South African learning environments.

Rethinking Entrepreneurial Education in South Africa

Entrepreneurial education in South Africa has long been recognized as a key mechanism for addressing unemployment, inequality, and slow economic transformation; however, its pedagogical effectiveness remains contested. According to Bux and Van Vuuren (2019), entrepreneurship education has been largely confined to theoretical instruction that prioritizes cognitive knowledge over practical competence, thereby limiting its ability to nurture entrepreneurial mindsets. Similarly, Iwu et al. (2021) explain that while universities and schools have introduced entrepreneurship modules, these often mirror traditional academic learning rather than promoting creativity, innovation, and opportunity recognition. Consequently, there is a disjuncture between policy aspirations and actual learner outcomes, in which students complete formal education without developing the resilience or problem-solving skills necessary to participate effectively in dynamic economic environments (Mankgele, Ratsoma & Ramasobana, 2023).

Entrepreneurship within South African schools is primarily embedded in the CAPS through subjects such as EMS and business studies; however, these subjects are often delivered as static, content-heavy modules with limited experiential engagement. Waghid (2019) asserts that the design of business education curricula in South Africa tends to reproduce linear learning sequences that fail to link theory with practice or the realities of informal economies. McDonald et al. (2022) concur that these limitations persist despite policymakers' widespread recognition that entrepreneurial learning should prepare youth for the digital, innovation-driven economy. However, the pedagogical structure of CAPS continues to favor assessment memorization over entrepreneurial experimentation. Consequently, students rarely encounter problem-based or project-based learning activities that mirror real-world business scenarios (Iwu et al., 2021).

This disconnection between curriculum design and entrepreneurial praxis reflects a broader issue within the education system. Van der Berg et al. (2023)

argue that the South African education system remains inadequately aligned with labour market realities, producing skills that do not translate into employability or enterprise creation. Dzomonda and Fatoki (2019) note that institutions of higher learning have yet to bridge the gap between academic training and practical entrepreneurship development, largely because entrepreneurship education lacks systemic coordination across schooling levels. Consequently, learners are socialized into viewing entrepreneurship as a theoretical concept rather than a lived experience of problem-solving and innovation (Tariq, 2025).

Policy frameworks such as NDP 2030, the Department of Basic Education (DBE), and the Department of Higher Education and Training (DHET) have consistently underscored the need for entrepreneurship to drive inclusive growth and sustainable job creation. Singh (2024) emphasizes that the NDP envisions an education system capable of producing adaptable, skilled youth who can generate employment through innovation. However, as Courtney (2024) points out, the translation of such policy rhetoric into classroom practice remains slow and uneven, primarily due to resource inequalities, undertrained educators, and a lack of integration between educational objectives and the digital transformation agenda. Street and Sikaka (2025) further reveal that despite the Education, Training, and Development (ETD) Sector Skills Plan's focus on digital literacy and entrepreneurial competence, implementation in schools remains fragmented. Therefore, although policy frameworks are conceptually progressive, the absence of contextualized pedagogical strategies has hindered meaningful transformation within classrooms.

One of the central challenges underpinning this stagnation is the dominance of traditional pedagogies that privilege rote learning over critical inquiry and experiential engagement. Garg and Sharma (2025) explain that South African educators often face structural and technological constraints that prevent them from adopting participatory, technology-enhanced approaches to teaching entrepreneurship. Bittner, Mirbabaie, and Morana (2021) add that without digital facilitation tools, learners are deprived of interactive and collaborative learning opportunities that could mirror authentic entrepreneurial problem-solving. These findings support Olutuase, Brijlal, and Yan's (2023) assertion that to cultivate entrepreneurial skills in African contexts, education systems must prioritize experiential, context-relevant learning models that emphasize experimentation and iterative feedback.

However, attempts to modernize entrepreneurship education have often remained superficial. Rudhumbu, Du Plessis, and Maphosa (2020) highlight that while gender-inclusive and locally relevant entrepreneurship programs have emerged in parts of southern Africa, they continue to lack digital integration and sustained mentorship mechanisms. Mankgele et al. (2023) similarly found that even when learners demonstrate interest in entrepreneurship, the lack of experiential exposure (such as simulations, mentorship, and digital engagement) dampens their self-efficacy and entrepreneurial intention. This observation aligns with Iwu et al. (2021), who assert that lecturer competence and digital literacy are essential determinants of how effectively entrepreneurship is taught. Therefore, the educational ecosystem requires a shift from passive knowledge transfer to interactive, technology-enabled learning that situates learners as value creators.

Additionally, existing entrepreneurial curricula fail to reflect South Africa's socioeconomic and technological realities. According to Nxesi and Hindle (2019), entrepreneurship policies have yet to reconcile rural-urban disparities in resource access and infrastructure, resulting in unequal exposure to innovation-driven learning. Gala et al. (2025) argue that African youth remain digitally marginalised, limiting their ability to acquire future-oriented skills that drive entrepreneurial adaptability. In under-resourced schools, the absence of affordable digital tools and teacher readiness further entrenches the divide between privileged and marginalized learners (Garg & Sharma, 2025). Consequently, entrepreneurial education risks reinforcing inequality rather than dismantling it.

Moreover, pedagogical frameworks underpinning entrepreneurship education often neglect to integrate emerging technological paradigms, such as AI and gamified simulations, which have proven effective in enhancing engagement and adaptive learning (Devi et al., 2025). Raimi et al. (2024) assert that AI-driven educational tools offer transformative potential for entrepreneurship by enabling personalised, data-informed feedback loops and immersive learning experiences. However, South African educational institutions have been slow to adopt these innovations, reflecting a persistent hesitancy to reimagine teaching as a dynamic, learner-centred process (Anderson-Coto, 2024).

Therefore, the current state of entrepreneurial education in South Africa is characterized by a paradox: a proliferation of progressive policy frameworks alongside pedagogical stagnation. The literature reveals a consensus that entrepreneurship education must move beyond content delivery towards developing adaptable, opportunity-oriented learners (Olutuase et al., 2023). However, systemic barriers, ranging from inadequate teacher preparation to limited technological integration, continue to inhibit this evolution. Consequently, this study responds to the identified gap by exploring how gamified AI tools and simulation platforms can bridge the divide between theory and practice. By offering immersive, adaptive, and localized learning experiences, such technologies have the potential to transform entrepreneurship education from a theoretical exercise into a lived, experiential journey that equips learners with the skills and mindsets necessary to thrive in South Africa's evolving digital economy.

Gamification and Artificial Intelligence as Pedagogical Co-Facilitators

The integration of AI and gamification into educational contexts represents a paradigm shift from teacher-centred instruction towards participatory, adaptive, and experiential learning environments. According to Anderson-Coto (2024), AI's growing role in education marks a transition from traditional pedagogical design to data-driven, personalized learning systems that dynamically respond to learners' needs. As noted by Raimi et al. (2024), gamification complements this transformation by embedding motivational design, feedback loops, and experiential engagement into learning processes. Together, these innovations have the potential to redefine how entrepreneurship education is delivered, particularly in contexts where learners require adaptive, context-sensitive, and immersive approaches to acquire complex problem-solving and innovation skills.

AI's central pedagogical contribution lies in its ability to generate adaptive feedback and personalize learning trajectories through intelligent tutoring systems. Devi et al. (2025) explain that AI-driven classroom management systems enhance learning by analysing student performance data and providing timely, tailored support. Similarly, Hossain (2024) emphasizes that AI's predictive analytics allow educators to identify learning gaps early, fostering differentiated instruction that enhances inclusivity and equity. However, as Anderson, Nguyen, and Ucok Hughes (2025) caution, the pedagogical power of AI depends on educators' ability to contextualize algorithmic insights within human-centered teaching strategies. This underscores the view that AI should not replace teachers but rather act as a co-facilitator that amplifies their instructional capacity through intelligent adaptation and learner analytics.

In parallel, gamification has gained attention for its ability to transform abstract concepts into tangible, motivational learning experiences. Dubay and Richards (2024) argue that game-based elements, such as progress tracking, levels, and challenges, stimulate learner engagement and persistence by aligning educational content with psychological motivators, such as competition and achievement. Raimi et al. (2024) concur that these elements foster a sense of autonomy and competence, which is particularly vital in entrepreneurship education where intrinsic motivation drives creativity and innovation. However, Bittner et al. (2021) warn that gamification without a cognitive purpose risks superficial engagement; therefore, effective implementation must ensure that game mechanics align with learning outcomes. Consequently, when AI is integrated into gamified systems, it strengthens the pedagogical link between motivation and cognitive engagement by adjusting the difficulty and relevance of tasks in real time (Yang, Liu, Liu, & Huang, 2024).

Experiential learning theory provides a useful lens for understanding how AI and gamification jointly enhance entrepreneurship education. Kim et al. (2025) explain that experiential learning transforms passive knowledge absorption into active knowledge construction through cycles of experience, reflection, conceptualisation, and experimentation. Gamified AI environments operationalize these principles by allowing learners to simulate entrepreneurial decision-making, receive feedback from virtual agents, and iterate strategies in safe, risk-free environments. Pasmala, Nilsook, Wannapiroon, and Jantakoon (2025) add that such models foster digital competency and problem-solving skills because learners are required to apply knowledge within dynamic, technology-mediated contexts. Therefore, the integration of AI and gamification aligns with the epistemological shift towards constructivist and experiential paradigms that prioritize authentic, learner-centred engagement.

Furthermore, the technological pedagogical and content knowledge (TPACK) framework advances the understanding of how teachers can effectively merge technology, pedagogy, and content knowledge in AI-supported gamified learning. Thongkum and Buaraphan (2024) contend that TPACK underscores the necessity for teachers to possess not only subject expertise but also pedagogical dexterity to meaningfully integrate technology. Peñaojas and Palomar (2025) similarly highlight that effective AI-enhanced teaching requires reflective practice and ongoing adaptation to learners' feedback patterns. However, Tadjibayeva (2025) argues that without sufficient professional development, educators struggle to balance these domains, leading to surface-level technology adoption. Hence, teacher digital literacy and pedagogical adaptability have emerged as crucial enablers in implementing AI-gamified ecosystems that enhance learner agency and entrepreneurial thinking (Tariq, 2025).

Globally, AI and gamification have demonstrated complementary strengths in fostering deeper learning. Anderson et al. (2025) assert that AI-enhanced environments cultivate diversity of thought by exposing learners to multiple problem-solving perspectives. Dubay and Richards (2024) emphasize that gamified tasks create emotionally engaging contexts that sustain attention and perseverance. This synthesis reflects a shared pedagogical orientation towards learner autonomy and collaboration, supported by AI's ability to individualize experiences while maintaining collective interaction. However, these benefits are often mediated by contextual factors, such as resource availability, infrastructure, and digital readiness, particularly in developing countries (Gala et al., 2025). In the African context, Garg and Sharma (2025) note that while online and technology-enhanced learning gained traction during the pandemic, inadequate teacher preparedness and unstable digital infrastructure remain major barriers to sustaining innovation.

A critical tension in the literature concerns the ethical and practical challenges of embedding AI in gamified learning. Raimi et al. (2024) caution that while AI-driven systems can expand creative and entrepreneurial capacities, they may also reproduce algorithmic bias and digital inequality. Khavasi (2025) highlights that educators must navigate ethical dilemmas surrounding data privacy, learner autonomy, and the unintended reinforcement of socioeconomic disparities. These concerns are particularly pressing in low-resource educational systems, where AI tools developed in the Global North may inadequately represent diverse learner contexts. Anderson-Coto (2024) therefore calls for a computational equity approach that localises AI algorithms to ensure fairness, transparency, and inclusivity in pedagogical design.

Despite these challenges, there is growing consensus that when implemented responsibly, AI and gamification can co-create transformative educational ecosystems. Yang et al. (2024) demonstrated that AI-enhanced gamified training increases engagement regulation and collaborative learning through deep reinforcement learning models that adapt to each learner's cognitive state. Similarly, Devi et al. (2025) showed that intelligent tutoring systems facilitate personalized progress tracking, fostering sustained motivation and self-regulation. These findings resonate with Hossain's (2024) observation that AI-powered tools in entrepreneurship education promote sustainability by linking digital innovation to real-world problem-solving. However, as Pasmala et al. (2025) argued, achieving such integration requires systemic alignment between technological design, curriculum objectives, and pedagogical practice, an alignment that remains uneven in many developing education systems.

Therefore, the literature collectively underscores that AI and gamification function most effectively not as isolated technologies but as pedagogical co-facilitators that reconfigure learning into an interactive, personalized, and motivational process. When embedded within experiential and TPACK frameworks, these tools reposition teachers as facilitators of inquiry rather than transmitters of knowledge and enable learners to become active agents in constructing entrepreneurial understanding. Nevertheless, persistent issues such as digital inequality, teacher readiness, and ethical complexity continue to challenge equitable implementation. By engaging critically with these intersections, the present study seeks to embed AI as a co-facilitator in entrepreneurial pedagogy, thereby transforming entrepreneurship education into an adaptive, immersive, and contextually relevant experience that reflects the realities of South Africa's evolving digital economy.

Simulation-Based Learning and Dual-User Platform Design

Simulation-based learning has emerged as a transformative pedagogical approach that bridges the persistent gap between theoretical instruction and real-world application in entrepreneurship education. Kim et al. (2025) assert that simulations create authentic learning environments where students actively engage in problem-solving, experimentation, and reflection. Through this experiential process, learners are exposed to entrepreneurial uncertainty and complexity, gaining practical insights that conventional lecture-based instruction cannot replicate. According to Pasmala et al. (2025), simulation-based learning enhances digital competency by immersing learners in technology-enabled scenarios that mirror real business ecosystems. This approach closely aligns with the objective of developing entrepreneurial readiness and resilience by allowing students to make decisions, experience risk, and learn from simulated failure in safe environments.

The pedagogical foundation of simulation-based learning is deeply rooted in experiential learning theory, which positions experience as the central component of cognitive development. Thongkum and Buaraphan (2024) explain that simulations extend Kolb's experiential learning cycle by enabling learners to move from abstract conceptualisation to concrete experimentation. This allows them to apply theoretical knowledge in contextualised, iterative ways that reinforce understanding. Similarly, Peñaojas and Palomar (2025) highlight that when simulations are integrated with reflective activities, they enhance learners' self-efficacy and readiness for blended or hybrid learning contexts. In entrepreneurship education, this means that students can test strategies, assess consequences, and iterate business models, developing both confidence and critical thinking skills. Therefore, simulation-based learning provides a dynamic mechanism through which entrepreneurial competencies can be cultivated beyond the traditional classroom.

A defining feature of modern simulation learning environments is the dual-user platform design, in which teachers and learners actively interact within a shared digital ecosystem. Yang et al. (2024) describe dual-user systems as interactive frameworks based on deep reinforcement learning that regulate engagement between instructors and learners in real-time. In such models, teachers act as facilitators who provide adaptive guidance, while students engage autonomously with simulation tasks that evolve based on their performance. This interactive co-regulation of learning embodies a participatory pedagogy in which feedback, reflection, and experimentation occur simultaneously. Anderson et al. (2025) concur that such technology-mediated environments empower educators to shift from transmitters of information to learning partners who guide exploration and decision-making. The dual-user model therefore promotes reciprocal agency, in which teachers and learners co-create value through shared learning experiences.

The concept of co-creation resonates strongly with service-dominant logic (SDL), which redefines education as a value co-creation process rather than a one-directional transfer of knowledge. Vargo, Koskela-Huotari, and Vink (2020) state that SDL positions learners as active participants who contribute to the construction of knowledge through interaction, engagement, and exchange. Jaakkola, Kaartemo, Siltaloppi and Vargo (2024) further explain that this framework underscores systemic interdependence between educators, learners, and digital tools, each acting as a resource integrator in the educational value network. In the context of simulation-based entrepreneurship education, SDL emphasizes that teachers and students jointly shape the learning experience through iterative dialogue and feedback. Hartwig, von Saldern, and Jacob (2021) add that this co-creative process transforms educational spaces into service ecosystems, where digital platforms facilitate the continual exchange of ideas and experiences. Consequently, dual-user simulation platforms align seamlessly with the SDL perspective by transforming entrepreneurship education into an interactive service experience driven by collaboration and mutual learning.

Simulation-based platforms have been employed internationally to develop entrepreneurial decision making, financial literacy, and strategic thinking. Dubay and Richards (2024) discussed project-based simulations in marketing education that integrate AI analytics to provide real-time feedback on learner performance. These systems enable students to visualize the consequences of their decisions, fostering reflective practice and innovation. Similarly, Devi et al. (2025) noted that intelligent tutoring systems enhance personalized learning by adapting simulation complexity according to learner progress. These tools promote self-regulation and persistence by offering adaptive challenges and feedback. However, Raimi et al. (2024) caution that while AI-driven simulations can stimulate creativity and problem-solving, they also risk over-standardising learning if algorithmic design fails to account for contextual diversity. Hence, while global examples highlight the pedagogical power of simulations, their transfer to the South African context requires sensitivity to local realities, including infrastructure constraints and cultural nuances.

Within the South African classroom, simulation-based entrepreneurship learning faces both opportunity and constraint. Garg and Sharma (2025) explain that while digital learning adoption accelerated during the pandemic, persistent gaps in teacher training and technological access hinder equitable participation. Gala et al. (2025) highlight that many African learners, particularly in rural and township areas, remain digitally marginalised, reducing their exposure to experiential and technology-enabled learning. These limitations underscore the importance of context-sensitive localisation in the design of dual-user platforms. According to Nxesi and Hindle (2019), policy instruments such as the ETD Sector Skills Plan emphasise the development of digital skills and entrepreneurial capacity, yet implementation remains uneven across schools. Street and Sikaka (2025) add that structural inequalities continue to impede access to devices, connectivity, and teacher support, making it essential for simulation technologies to operate effectively under low-resource conditions.

Aligning simulation-based learning with the CAPS framework is therefore crucial. Waghid (2019) observes that while CAPS integrates entrepreneurship in subjects such as EMS and Business Studies, its linear assessment structure constrains experiential exploration. Simulation platforms, however, can extend CAPS outcomes by translating theoretical content into practice-oriented modules. Van der Berg et al. (2023) argue that entrepreneurship education must align with labour market demands by equipping learners with problem-solving and decision-making competencies. Simulation-based models directly address this need by replicating authentic entrepreneurial environments that allow learners to test hypotheses, manage risk, and experience the consequences of their actions without real-world penalties.

The adaptability of international simulation platforms to South Africa's socio-educational context depends on their scalability, inclusivity, and localisation. Hossain (2024) suggests that smart educational technologies can drive sustainability in entrepreneurship when aligned with local development goals. Khavasi (2025) agrees, noting that contextualizing simulation design within regional educational cultures enhances ethical and pedagogical relevance. However, as Anderson-Coto (2024) argues, achieving computational equity in AI-enhanced simulations requires algorithms to be trained on diverse data representative of African learner contexts. Therefore, simulation-based and dual-user platforms hold immense promise for transforming entrepreneurship education by integrating experiential, digital, and localized pedagogies. When grounded in SDL, these technologies reimagine teaching as a shared journey of value co-creation, bridging the enduring gap between entrepreneurial theory and practice in South Africa's evolving digital landscape.

Localisation, Ethics, and Sustainability of AI-Enhanced Entrepreneurial Learning

The growing integration of AI and gamified simulations in education presents both opportunities and ethical dilemmas, particularly in the context of entrepreneurial learning in the Global South. Anderson-Coto (2024) explains that the ethical implementation of AI in education must consider computational equity, ensuring that digital systems are designed and deployed in ways that promote inclusivity, fairness, and contextual relevance. However, in many developing countries, such as South Africa, digital inequality, infrastructural constraints, and linguistic diversity complicate efforts to localize AI-enhanced learning. As Hossain (2024) asserts, sustainable entrepreneurship education through technology requires a balance between innovation and equitable access, ensuring that digital tools enhance rather than entrench existing socioeconomic disparities.

The localization of AI in education involves adapting content to local cultural, linguistic, and infrastructural realities. Khavasi (2025) contends that adopting generative AI in entrepreneurship education requires a deep understanding of the socio-educational environment in which it operates, as algorithms trained on Western data may inadvertently reproduce bias or ignore regional learning styles. Raimi et al. (2024) further caution that AI-based learning systems can exacerbate inequity if they are not aligned with local pedagogical norms and resource capacities. Therefore, localization goes beyond translation or superficial customization; it demands an ethical design that reflects indigenous knowledge systems, local business practices, and the lived experiences of learners. According to Dubay and Richards (2024), aligning AI technologies with sustainable development frameworks helps ensure that their application in entrepreneurship education contributes to both social inclusion and long-term human capital development.

Data privacy is a critical ethical issue in AI-enhanced education. Anderson et al. (2025) argue that AI systems used in learning environments often depend on extensive data collection for adaptive feedback and performance analytics, raising questions about consent, transparency, and ownership. When these technologies are deployed in under-regulated or resource-limited contexts, learners may be exposed to exploitation through unprotected data usage. Similarly, Raimi et al. (2024) highlight the tension between using AI to personalize learning and protecting the autonomy and privacy of users in data-driven ecosystems. This concern is heightened in low-income regions, where digital literacy and regulatory safeguards are weak, making ethical governance essential for sustainable educational innovation.

Sustainability in AI-enhanced entrepreneurship learning is not merely environmental but also social and economic. Appio, Platania, and Hernandez (2024) emphasize that AI technologies should promote virtuous pathways that link digital innovation to long-term human development goals. In the South African context, this means leveraging AI to expand youth and marginalized communities' participation in entrepreneurship while mitigating exclusionary effects. Hossain (2024) concurs that sustainable AI systems must integrate environmental awareness, social equity, and economic empowerment as interrelated goals. However, as Garg and Sharma (2025) note, achieving sustainability through digital pedagogy remains challenging in contexts marked by unequal access to infrastructure, unstable connectivity, and low teacher readiness. Consequently, localization becomes a mechanism for achieving sustainability by tailoring AI tools to local needs and resource realities rather than adopting one-size-fits-all global models.

The digital divide remains one of the most significant barriers to equitable AI-enhanced learning. Gala et al. (2025) reveal that African youth, particularly those classified as "NEET" (not in education, employment, or training), lack the digital skills and access needed to participate in technology-driven learning ecosystems. This inequality restricts the scalability of AI-enhanced entrepreneurship training, especially in rural and township schools. Nxesi and Hindle (2019) and Street and Sikaka (2025) similarly indicate that South Africa's education and training policies recognize digital literacy as a national priority; nevertheless, implementation is often hindered by systemic disparities in infrastructure and teacher capacity. Thus, while AI offers opportunities for adaptive and personalized learning, without deliberate localization and ethical integration, it risks reinforcing social stratification rather than alleviating it.

Cultural relevance is another ethical dimension that shapes the sustainability of AI-driven educational systems. Khavasi (2025) explains that the pedagogical success of generative AI depends on how well it reflects local cultural narratives and learning values. In the South African context, entrepreneurship is deeply intertwined with community-based knowledge systems and informal economies, which globalized AI platforms rarely capture. Anderson-Coto (2024) notes that ethical localisation requires reconfiguring AI models to reflect linguistic diversity, cultural norms, and socio-economic realities. Similarly, Raimi et al. (2024) stress that sustainable digital learning must value creativity, indigenous entrepreneurship, and participatory learning, principles that resonate strongly with African educational philosophies. Therefore, ethical localization in AI-enhanced entrepreneurial learning must ensure that digital tools are both culturally resonant and pedagogically responsive.

From a policy perspective, the sustainable implementation of AI in entrepreneurship education requires integration with national frameworks, such as the NDP 2030 and the ETD Sector Skills Plan. Singh (2024) asserts that these frameworks aim to align education with inclusive growth and digital transformation, positioning entrepreneurship as a vehicle for achieving the Sustainable Development Goals. However, van der Berg et al. (2023) point out that South Africa's current education system remains misaligned with labor market needs, producing theoretical rather than applied entrepreneurial skills. Ethical AI integration therefore has the potential to operationalize these policy goals by creating experiential, adaptive learning systems that prepare students for real-world economic participation. Courtney (2024) further argues that inclusive growth requires a reconfiguration of fiscal and educational strategies to ensure that technology adoption promotes equity rather than exacerbating inequality.

SDL provides an important theoretical lens for understanding sustainability and ethics in AI-enhanced learning. Jaakkola et al. (2024) explain that SDL frames learning as a co-created process in which value emerges through interactions among teachers, learners, and technologies. This perspective aligns with the notion of computational equity advanced by Anderson-Coto (2024), which views technology as a facilitator of collaborative knowledge production rather than a substitute for human agency. Hartwig et al. (2021) emphasise that service ecosystems thrive on shared responsibility, where ethical and sustainable outcomes depend on how well stakeholders align goals and values. Applying SDL to AI-driven entrepreneurial education thus highlights the need for mutual accountability between designers, educators, and learners to ensure inclusivity and sustainability.

Therefore, the literature reveals that ethical and localized deployment of AI-enhanced entrepreneurial learning requires balancing innovation with inclusion, technological sophistication with contextual relevance, and data-driven efficiency with human-centered values. As Raimi et al. (2024) and Hossain (2024) collectively argue, sustainable education systems must integrate digital equity, privacy protection, and cultural resonance into their design frameworks. In South Africa, where structural inequalities and cultural diversity intersect, these dimensions are fundamental to transforming entrepreneurial education. The success of AI-driven, gamified simulations ultimately depends on their ability to operate ethically within diverse learning environments, supporting equitable access, long-term competence development, and the creation of adaptive, localized pathways for entrepreneurial growth.

Overall, the reviewed literature establishes that while entrepreneurship education in South Africa is policy-rich, it remains pedagogically stagnant and technologically underdeveloped. Across the four themes, scholars agree that integrating AI, gamification, and simulation-based learning offers an opportunity to move from content-driven instruction to experiential, adaptive, and learner-centred practice. AI facilitates personalized feedback and cognitive engagement, gamification enhances motivation and creativity, and simulation-based learning enables learners to apply theory through experimentation and decision-making in safe environments. The dual-user platform model and SDL further position teachers and learners as co-creators of entrepreneurial knowledge, reflecting the need for collaboration and mutual learning. However, the sustainability of such innovations depends on ethical localization, ensuring fairness, inclusivity, and data protection while addressing infrastructural inequalities. The literature concludes that the transformative potential of gamified AI and simulations lies in their ability to combine technological sophistication with contextual sensitivity, creating equitable and future-ready entrepreneurial learning ecosystems in South Africa.

METHODOLOGY

This study adopted a qualitative desk-based research design to examine how gamified AI tools and simulation platforms can transform entrepreneurship education by promoting immersive, adaptive, and localized learning experiences. A qualitative approach was selected because it enables an interpretive and contextual exploration of complex educational phenomena, particularly those related to technology integration, pedagogical transformation, and learner engagement within diverse socioeconomic contexts. According to Aspers and Corte (2021), qualitative research allows for a deep conceptual understanding of meaning-making processes, whereas Bassot (2022) explains that desk-based research is particularly suitable for synthesizing extensive secondary data to address broad and evolving topics in education. Therefore, this design was appropriate for systematically interrogating the existing literature on AI, gamification, and simulation-based pedagogy, especially given the rapid pace of technological development and limited empirical research in the South African entrepreneurial education context.

Data were collected through a structured review of secondary sources published between 2019 and 2025. This timeframe captures the most recent advances in AI-driven educational technologies, gamified learning environments, and experiential teaching models, while reflecting shifts in post-pandemic digital pedagogy. As Kulibanova, Teor, and Ilyina (2025) note, desk-based methods are effective for mapping technological transformations within emerging disciplines as they integrate data from diverse sources to reveal conceptual and contextual trends. The reviewed materials included peer-reviewed journal articles, policy documents, institutional reports, and academic books obtained from recognized databases such as Google Scholar, UKZN library, ScienceDirect, Taylor & Francis, and SpringerLink. Inclusion criteria focused on studies that examined (i) the pedagogical use of AI and gamification in education, (ii) simulation-based learning models, (iii) localization and ethical dimensions of educational technologies, and (iv) implications for entrepreneurship or skills development in developing countries. Sources that lacked methodological transparency or empirical grounding were excluded to preserve analytical rigour and credibility.

This study employed qualitative content analysis as its primary analytical technique. As Gn, Hleza, Shonhiwa, and Mathonsi (2021) explain, qualitative content analysis is a systematic method for identifying recurring patterns, meanings, and relationships within textual data while maintaining flexibility for interpretive depth. This process involved multiple stages: first, data familiarization was conducted by reading and summarizing all relevant documents to extract key insights relating to AI-enhanced entrepreneurship education; second, open and axial coding were used to organize findings into thematic categories that aligned with the study's focus areas, including experiential learning, technological adaptation, ethical localization, and pedagogical innovation; third, the emergent themes were compared, synthesized, and interpreted to uncover conceptual linkages, contradictions, and theoretical implications. This approach allowed for an integrated understanding of how gamified AI and simulation platforms are conceptualized globally and how they might be applied effectively within South Africa's educational landscape.

To ensure the reliability and validity of the findings, data were triangulated across multiple academic and institutional sources to confirm thematic consistency. Rawdon, Sampson, Gilleece, and Cosgrove (2020) highlight that triangulation strengthens interpretive credibility by corroborating insights derived from diverse materials and contexts. Additionally, an iterative analysis was used to refine the thematic framework, enabling the researcher to critically assess not only what the existing literature reveals but also what it omits, particularly regarding the localization and sustainability of AI-enhanced entrepreneurial education. This reflexive process ensured that interpretations were grounded in both empirical evidence and theoretical reasoning (Aspers & Corte, 2019).

The synthesis of data followed an inductive logic, allowing patterns to emerge naturally from the reviewed literature rather than being constrained by predefined theoretical assumptions. This open-ended analysis was critical for identifying nuanced insights into how AI and gamified simulations contribute to learner engagement, adaptive feedback, and entrepreneurial skill formation. As Muasya and Mulwa (2023) observed, flexibility in qualitative research facilitates a deeper understanding of dynamic and multifaceted educational processes. Thus, the study prioritized contextual interpretation over generalization, focusing on how digital pedagogies can be ethically and sustainably adapted within South Africa's specific cultural, infrastructural, and policy environments.

As this study relied solely on publicly available secondary data, ethical clearance was not required. However, all sources were acknowledged to uphold academic integrity and intellectual transparency. By systematically analyzing and synthesizing global and regional literature, this methodological framework provides a robust foundation for understanding how gamified AI and simulation-based learning can reimagine entrepreneurship education as an immersive, inclusive, and context-sensitive process of innovation and empowerment in South Africa.

FINDINGS AND DISCUSSION

The findings from this desktop analysis reveal that the transformation of entrepreneurial education in South Africa through gamified AI and simulation platforms is both a pedagogical necessity and a systemic challenge. The reviewed secondary data consistently demonstrate that while policy frameworks such as the NDP 2030 and the ETD Sector Skills Plan emphasize entrepreneurship as a key driver of inclusive growth, implementation remains hindered by outdated teaching methods, digital inequality, and underdeveloped pedagogical frameworks (Singh, 2024; Street & Sikaka, 2025). This suggests that, despite the policy momentum, entrepreneurial education continues to prioritize theoretical knowledge over experiential competence. The absence of immersive, adaptive, and localized pedagogical models limits learners' ability to translate entrepreneurial concepts into practical innovation. Therefore, the findings indicate a structural mismatch between policy aspirations and classroom realities, particularly within the CAPS, which still favors memorization over simulation or project-based learning (Waghid, 2019).

Drawing from these insights, this study identifies that gamified AI tools can bridge this pedagogical gap by integrating experiential learning into entrepreneurship education. Anderson-Coto (2024) and Raimi et al. (2024) have demonstrated that AI-based gamification enhances motivation and engagement through adaptive feedback, personalized progression, and real-time learner analytics. In contrast to the rigidity of traditional pedagogy, gamified AI environments are dynamic, enabling learners to experience entrepreneurial processes through simulation, risk assessment, and failure recovery. This form of interactive learning aligns with Kim et al.'s (2025) assertion that experiential learning theory transforms passive information reception into active knowledge construction. Therefore, integrating AI-driven gamification repositions entrepreneurship education from an information-based exercise to an experiential, learner-centred process that encourages creativity, problem-solving, and innovation. However, this transformation requires the simultaneous empowerment of educators, as AI cannot substitute human facilitation but rather coexists as a pedagogical co-facilitator that amplifies teaching effectiveness (Anderson et al., 2025).

The findings also reveal that simulation-based learning constitutes a practical and scalable solution for contextualizing entrepreneurship education. Simulation models promote decision-making, risk-taking, and iterative learning by allowing learners to operate within virtual business ecosystems (Kim et al., 2025). This pedagogical method supports the principle that entrepreneurial competence emerges through practice and reflection rather than theoretical abstraction. Furthermore, the introduction of dual-user platforms, where educators guide while students interact, creates a balance between autonomy and mentorship. Yang et al. (2024) explain that such systems use reinforcement learning to adapt difficulty levels, ensuring continuous engagement and personalized challenges. This co-regulated structure mirrors SDL, which views education as a process of value co-creation between teachers and learners (Vargo et al., 2020). Therefore, both educators and learners act as collaborators within a digital ecosystem that fosters reflection, experimentation, and innovation. These findings underscore that effective simulation design relies not only on technological sophistication but also on pedagogical intentionality, ensuring that simulated experiences align with curricular objectives and the realities of entrepreneurship within the South African context (Van der Berg et al., 2023).

However, several divergences in the findings illustrate the complex interplay between technology, equity, and context. While international studies highlight the transformative potential of AI and gamified simulations in enhancing creativity and learner autonomy (Devi et al., 2025; Dubay & Richards, 2024), evidence from South Africa suggests persistent barriers, such as poor digital infrastructure, limited teacher readiness, and socioeconomic inequality (Gala et al., 2025; Garg & Sharma, 2025). These constraints demonstrate that the success of technological innovation is contingent on contextual adaptation rather than wholesale adoption of global models. In under-resourced schools, particularly in rural and township areas, simulation platforms must be designed for accessibility and low data usage, while AI algorithms must reflect local languages and business realities (Nxesi & Hindle,

2019). Therefore, localization emerges as a critical determinant of sustainability in AI-enhanced entrepreneurship learning. This aligns with Khavasi's (2025) view that generative AI must be contextualized within cultural and linguistic frameworks to avoid reproducing Western pedagogical norms.

Ethical considerations are also a key finding. AI-enhanced educational tools rely on data-driven analytics to tailor feedback and monitor performance; however, such data collection raises issues of privacy, consent, and ownership. Anderson et al. (2025) note that in contexts with limited data governance, learners' personal information may be at risk of misuse, raising questions about the moral accountability of technology providers. This challenge is compounded by the fact that algorithms trained on homogenous datasets risk perpetuating bias against underrepresented learner populations (Raimi et al., 2024). Therefore, ethical AI integration requires clear governance structures that prioritize data protection, transparency, and equity. Anderson-Coto (2024) supports this by advocating for a computational equity framework that ensures AI models are inclusive and locally representative. In entrepreneurship education, this ethical grounding is particularly vital, as learners' digital footprints can reflect socioeconomic vulnerabilities. Hence, sustainability in AI-enhanced entrepreneurial learning cannot be disentangled from ethical responsibility and local governance.

Another key observation emerging from the findings is that teacher competence and institutional readiness play decisive roles in mediating the impact of AI and simulation technologies. Thongkum and Buaraphan (2024) emphasize that teachers must possess TPACK to integrate these tools effectively. However, the South African system continues to suffer from limited professional development in digital pedagogy (Street & Sikaka, 2025). This results in uneven implementation, where technologically advanced schools adopt interactive learning, while others remain confined to static instruction. Such discrepancies undermine the egalitarian purpose of education and highlight the importance of capacity-building initiatives that empower educators to use AI not as a substitute, but as an extension of their pedagogical creativity. Drawing from this, it becomes evident that sustainable transformation demands both infrastructural support and epistemic change; educators must view technology not as external to pedagogy, but as intrinsic to knowledge construction and learner engagement.

The findings also affirm that sustainability in AI-driven entrepreneurship education is multidimensional, encompassing technological, social, and economic aspects. Appio et al. (2024) argue that AI can drive sustainable entrepreneurial ecosystems by linking digital innovation to long-term human development. In South Africa, this translates into enabling youth from marginalized communities to develop entrepreneurial mindsets that contribute to local economic resilience. However, this potential remains unrealized unless digital tools are aligned with inclusive policy strategies and community-driven educational models. Hossain (2024) further contends that sustainability must involve equitable access and environmental consciousness, suggesting that the ethical use of technology extends beyond education into broader societal transformation. Therefore, achieving sustainable AI integration requires balancing efficiency with empathy, ensuring that technological sophistication enhances, rather than replaces, human connection and community learning.

Drawing from the totality of these findings, this study demonstrates that gamified AI tools and simulation-based learning platforms can transform entrepreneurship education by creating immersive, adaptive, and localized learning environments that align with South Africa's socio-educational realities. These innovations offer a pathway for bridging the gap between theory and practice, revitalizing learner motivation, and promoting co-created value through teacher–learner collaboration. However, the evidence also highlights that the transformative potential of these technologies depends on ethical governance, contextual design, and sustained teacher development. Thus, the discussion confirms that the future of entrepreneurial education in South Africa lies not in adopting technology for its own sake but in embedding AI and simulations within culturally resonant, ethically grounded, and pedagogically purposeful frameworks that advance equity, creativity, and sustainable learning outcomes.

RECOMMENDATIONS

Entrepreneurship education in South Africa should be redesigned to integrate gamified AI and simulation platforms into the CAPS curriculum, shifting from theory-based teaching to experiential and project-driven learning. Policymakers, educators, and curriculum developers should collaborate to ensure that these technologies are contextually relevant and aligned with national educational priorities. Teacher development is critical. Structured professional training in digital pedagogy and TPACK should equip educators to use AI and simulations effectively. Establishing professional learning communities can further promote innovation, peer support, and consistent implementation across schools.

Improving digital infrastructure is equally essential. Targeted investments should expand affordable access to devices, connectivity, and AI learning systems, particularly in rural and township schools. Locally developed software should reflect South Africa's languages, cultures, and entrepreneurial contexts to enhance relevance and inclusivity. Clear ethical frameworks must guide AI deployment. Data privacy, algorithmic fairness, and accountability standards should be institutionalized to protect learners and promote equity. Dedicated oversight mechanisms can ensure the transparent and responsible use of educational technologies. Finally, sustainability should underpin all innovations. Partnerships between the government, academia, and industry should support scalable, energy-efficient, and culturally responsive AI systems that prepare learners for real-world entrepreneurship. Embedding dual-user simulation platforms can further foster co-creation between teachers and learners, cultivating creativity, critical thinking, and lifelong entrepreneurial competence.

FUTURE RESEARCH

Future research should empirically examine how gamified AI tools and simulation-based platforms influence entrepreneurial learning outcomes across diverse South African educational settings. Longitudinal studies could explore how these technologies impact students' entrepreneurial intention, creativity, and problem-solving over time. Further investigation is also needed to evaluate the pedagogical adaptability of dual-user simulation models in different contexts, particularly in rural and township schools where infrastructural limitations persist. Comparative studies between AI-enhanced and traditional entrepreneurship teaching methods could provide evidence of effectiveness and scalability, whereas qualitative research involving teachers and learners could offer deeper insights into user experiences, motivation, and digital readiness. Future research should also focus on developing frameworks for ethical AI integration that prioritize data privacy, equity, and contextual localization. Additionally, interdisciplinary studies linking education, technology, and local economic development could assess how AI-driven entrepreneurial learning contributes to broader socioeconomic transformation. Exploring partnerships between universities, governments, and the private sector may further illuminate how collaborative innovation can sustain AI-enabled entrepreneurship education in South Africa and other Global South contexts.

CONCLUSION

This study demonstrates that the transformation of entrepreneurial education in South Africa requires a decisive shift from traditional, theory-heavy instruction to a dynamic, technology-enhanced pedagogy. The integration of gamified AI and simulation-based learning platforms offers a practical and sustainable pathway for achieving this transformation. By creating immersive and adaptive learning environments, these tools bridge the divide between abstract knowledge and real-world entrepreneurial practice, enabling learners to develop the creativity, critical thinking, and problem-solving skills essential in today's digital economy.

The evidence reveals that while South Africa's policy frameworks recognize the importance of entrepreneurship and digital competence, implementation remains limited by outdated pedagogies, inadequate infrastructure, and insufficient teacher readiness. Gamified AI and simulation technologies address these shortcomings by fostering experiential learning, real-time feedback, and collaborative engagement between teachers and learners. When embedded within frameworks such as experiential learning theory, TPACK, and SDL, these innovations transform classrooms into participatory ecosystems of co-created knowledge and entrepreneurial exploration.

However, the success of this transformation depends on ethical localization, sustainable investment, and professional capacity building. Technologies must reflect South Africa's diverse cultural, linguistic, and socioeconomic contexts while safeguarding learner data and ensuring equitable access. The future of entrepreneurial education therefore lies not merely in adopting new technologies but in embedding them within human-centered, ethically grounded pedagogical frameworks that prioritize inclusion, adaptability, and lifelong learning. In doing so, gamified AI and simulation-based platforms can redefine entrepreneurship education as a catalyst for empowerment, innovation, and sustainable economic development across South Africa.

REFERENCES

Anderson, J., Nguyen, C. A., & Ucok Hughes, M. (2025). Mapping theory to practice: AI-enhanced teaching theories for fostering diverse perspectives in business education. *Journal of International Education in Business*.

Anderson-Coto, M. J. (2024). *Advancing AI Education: The Computational Equity Approach* (Doctoral dissertation, University of California, Irvine).

Appio, F. P., Platania, F., & Hernandez, C. T. (2024). Pairing AI and sustainability: Envisioning entrepreneurial initiatives for virtuous twin paths. *IEEE Transactions on Engineering Management*, *71*, 11669–11686. DOI: 10.1109/TEM.2024.3428913

Aspers, P., & Corte, U. (2019). What is qualitative in qualitative research. *Qualitative Sociology*, *42*(2), 139–160. DOI: 10.1007/s11133-019-9413-7 PMID: 31105362

Aspers, P., & Corte, U. (2021). What is qualitative in research. *Qualitative Sociology*, *44*(4), 599–608. DOI: 10.1007/s11133-021-09497-w PMID: 31105362

Bassot, B. (2022). *Doing qualitative desk-based research: A practical guide to writing an excellent dissertation*. Policy Press.

Bittner, E., Mirbabaie, M., & Morana, S. (2021). Digital facilitation assistance for collaborative, creative design processes.

Bux, S., & Van Vuuren, J. (2019). The effect of entrepreneurship education programmes on the development of self-efficacy, entrepreneurial intention and predictions for entrepreneurial. *Acta Commercii*, *19*(2), 1–13. DOI: 10.4102/ac.v19i2.615

Courtney, P. (2024). Education, inclusive growth, and fiscal consolidation.

Devi, K. S., Raghunath, S., Patil, J. S., & Shanti, M. (2025). AI-Driven Classroom Management With Intelligent Tutoring Systems. In *Driving Quality Education Through AI and Data Science* (pp. 259–282). IGI Global Scientific Publishing.

Dubay, C. M., & Richards, M. B. (2024). Leveraging artificial intelligence in project-based service learning to advance sustainable development: A pedagogical approach for marketing education. *Marketing Education Review*, *34*(4), 307–323. DOI: 10.1080/10528008.2024.2411975

Dzomonda, O., & Fatoki, O. (2019). The role of institutions of higher learning towards youth entrepreneurship development in South Africa. *Academy of Entrepreneurship Journal*, *25*(1), 1–11.

Gala, P. M., Namit, K., & Kidwai, H. (2025). *Strategies for Enhancing Digital Skills among Africa's NEET Youth* (No. 203090). The World Bank.

Garg, S., & Sharma, R. C. (2025). Pedagogical Challenges of Online Teaching-Learning: Lessons Learned, Measures Adopted, and Suggestions for Way Forward. In *Education and Pedagogical Experiences* (pp. 7-24). Routledge India.

Gn, S., Hleza, S., Shonhiwa, S., & Mathonsi, E. (2021). Qualitative content analysis, utility, usability and processes in educational research. *International Journal of Research and Innovation in Social Science*, *5*(07), 553–558.

Hartwig, K., von Saldern, L., & Jacob, F. (2021). The journey from goods-dominant logic to service-dominant logic: A case study with a global technology manufacturer. *Industrial Marketing Management*, *95*, 85–98. DOI: 10.1016/j.indmarman.2021.04.006

Hossain, S. F. A. (Ed.). (2024). *Utilizing AI and Smart Technology to Improve Sustainability in Entrepreneurship*. IGI Global. DOI: 10.4018/979-8-3693-1842-3

Iwu, C. G., Opute, P. A., Nchu, R., Eresia-Eke, C., Tengeh, R. K., Jaiyeoba, O., & Aliyu, O. A. (2021). Entrepreneurship education, curriculum and lecturer-competency as antecedents of student entrepreneurial intention. *International Journal of Management Education*, *19*(1), 100295. DOI: 10.1016/j.ijme.2019.03.007

Jaakkola, E., Kaartemo, V., Siltaloppi, J., & Vargo, S. L. (2024). Advancing service-dominant logic with systems thinking. *Journal of Business Research*, *177*, 114592. DOI: 10.1016/j.jbusres.2024.114592

Khavasi, A. (2025). *Exploring the Integration of Generative AI in Entrepreneurship Education Pedagogical and Ethical Dimensions*. Case Study in a Finnish University of Applied Sciences.

Kim, D., Ding, L., & Cho, T. (2025). Bridging theory and practice: The effects of experiential learning-based simulation training on technology integration competency among pre-service teachers. *Journal of Research on Technology in Education*, •••, 1–19. DOI: 10.1080/15391523.2025.2456057

Kulibanova, V. V., Teor, T. R., & Ilyina, I. A. (2025). Desk Research Methods for Place Reputation Monitoring and Evaluation in the Digital Economy: Place Reputation Monitoring of the Region. In *Multidisciplinary Analysis of Digital Transformation and Global Market Dynamics* (pp. 43-64). IGI Global.

Mankgele, K. P., Ratsoma, J. M., & Ramasobana, M. (2023). The effect of entrepreneurship education on entrepreneurial intention of high school students in Sekhukhune District, South Africa. *Journal of Entrepreneurship Education*, *26*(1), 1–6.

Mcdonald, Z., Xaba, N., Molokwane, P., Neville, R., Baloyi, N., & De Kock, T. A. R. R. Y. N. (2022). Bridging the Gap: Levers of Change scoping report.

Muasya, J. N., & Mulwa, P. M. (2023). Pilot study, a neglected part of qualitative and quantitative research process: Evidence from selected PhD thesis and dissertations. *Higher Education Research, 8*(4), 115-123.

Nxesi, N., & Hindle, M. D. (2019). Submission Of the Final 2020–2025 ETD Sector Skills Plan.

Olutuase, S. O., Brijlal, P., & Yan, B. (2023). Model for stimulating entrepreneurial skills through entrepreneurship education in an African context. *Journal of Small Business and Entrepreneurship, 35*(2), 263–283. DOI: 10.1080/08276331.2020.1786645

Pasmala, R., Nilsook, P., Wannapiroon, P., & Jantakoon, T. (2025). TPACK-integrated experiential performance learning model to enhance learners' digital competency. *Asian Journal of Education and Training, 11*(4), 130–143. DOI: 10.20448/edu.v11i4.7502

Peñaojas, J. I., & Palomar, B. C. (2025). A multiple regression analysis on pre-service science teachers' TPACK, efficacy belief, experiential learning and blended teaching readiness. *Discover Education, 4*(1), 1–14. DOI: 10.1007/s44217-025-00846-3

Raimi, L., Bamiro, N. B., & Lim, S. A. (2024). Two facets of AI-driven applications for sustainable learning and development: a systematic review of tech-entrepreneurial benefits and threats to creative learning. *Social Responsibility, Technology and AI*, 223-248.

Rawdon, C., Sampson, K., Gilleece, L., & Cosgrove, J. (2020). *Developing an Evaluation Framework for Teachers' Professional Learning in Ireland: Phase 1, Desk-based Research*. Educational Research Centre.

Rudhumbu, N., Du Plessis, E. C., & Maphosa, C. (2020). Challenges and opportunities for women entrepreneurs in Botswana: Revisiting the role of entrepreneurship education. *Journal of International Education in Business, 13*(2), 183–201. DOI: 10.1108/JIEB-12-2019-0058

Singh, U. K. (2024). Sustainable development goals in South Africa: progress and challenges. *Regional Dimensions of Human Development in India and South Africa: Through Sustainable Development Goals*, 93-146.

Street, F. B., & Sikaka, P. D. M. (2025). Final Submission of the 2026/27 ETD Sector Skills Plan.

Tadjibayeva, A. (2025). TPACK and reflective practice: A pathway to student centered learning. *Zamonaviy filologiya muammolari, 2*(3), 23-28.

Tariq, M. (Ed.). (2025). *Merging Artificial Intelligence With the Internet of Things*. IGI Global., DOI: 10.4018/979-8-3693-8547-0

Tariq, M. (Ed.). (2025). *Emerging Multisector Applications of AI and IoT*. IGI Global., DOI: 10.4018/979-8-3373-4332-7

Thongkum, S., & Buaraphan, K. (2024, April). Integrating technological pedagogical and content knowledge (TPACK) with experiential learning: A challenges in teaching mathematics in COVID-19 pandemic situation. In. AIP Conference Proceedings: Vol. 3024. *No. 1* (p. 050043). AIP Publishing LLC. DOI: 10.1063/5.0205437

van der Berg, S., Gustafsson, M., & Malindi, K. (2023). Education and skills for the economy and links to labour markets in South Africa. *Available at SSRN* 4321482. DOI: 10.2139/ssrn.4321482

Vargo, S. L., Koskela-Huotari, K., & Vink, J. (2020). Service-dominant logic: foundations and applications. In *The Routledge handbook of service research insights and ideas* (pp. 3–23). Routledge. DOI: 10.4324/9781351245234-1

Waghid, Z. (2019). Examining the business education curricula in South Africa: Towards integrating social entrepreneurship. *Education + Training, 61*(7/8), 940–962. DOI: 10.1108/ET-05-2018-0115

Yang, Y., Liu, X., Liu, Z., & Huang, P. (2024). Learner engagement regulation of dual-user training based on deep reinforcement learning. *Robotica, 42*(1), 179–202. DOI: 10.1017/S0263574723001418

KEY TERMS AND DEFINITIONS

Computational equity: Computational equity is an ethical framework that ensures that AI-driven educational technologies are fair, culturally relevant, and contextually adapted to diverse learning environments (Anderson-Coto, 2024; Khavasi, 2025).

Dual-user platform design: Dual-user platform design refers to interactive digital systems that allow teachers and students to participate simultaneously within the same simulation environment (Yang et al., 2024; Anderson et al., 2025).

Experiential Learning Theory (ELT): Experiential learning theory is a pedagogical model that asserts that knowledge is constructed through cycles of experiencing, reflecting, conceptualizing, and experimenting (Kim et al., 2025; Pasmala et al., 2025).

Gamified artificial intelligence tools: Gamified AI tools refer to digital learning systems that combine artificial intelligence with game-based mechanics (such as levels, rewards, feedback loops, and adaptive challenges) to enhance learner motivation and engagement (Raimi et al., 2024; Devi et al., 2025).

Simulation-based learning: Simulation-based learning is an experiential pedagogical approach that immerses learners in virtual environments where they can practise entrepreneurial decision-making, experiment with strategies, and learn from simulated outcomes without real-world consequences. (Pasmala et al., 2025).

Chapter 7
Preparing Cambodian Students for Integration Into AI-Driven Societies:
Future Trends Toward 2050 and Beyond

Ry Hour
http://orcid.org/0009-0002-6488-4370
National University of Battambang, Battambang, Cambodia

Channthoeurn Ny
http://orcid.org/0009-0006-9077-6719
Royal Academy of Cambodia, Cambodia

Virak Voan Ratha
Securities and Exchange Regulator of Cambodia, Phnom Penh, Cambodia

Chhun Hong
Svay Rieng University, Svay Rieng, Cambodia

Worn Prak
Svay Rieng University, Svay Rieng, Cambodia

Ramet Kim
Svay Rieng University, Svay Rieng, Cambodia

Mardy Serey
http://orcid.org/0009-0002-1049-7324
Svay Rieng University, Svay Rieng, Cambodia

Sereyrath Em
http://orcid.org/0000-0002-6803-195X
National University of Cheasim Kamchaymear, Kampong Cham, Cambodia

ABSTRACT

This chapter discusses ways to prepare Cambodian students for an AI-driven society by 2050 and beyond. Cambodia struggles with infrastructure, educator preparation, and socio-cultural factors affecting technology integration. A comprehensive

DOI: 10.4018/979-8-2600-2438-6.ch007

strategy must include curriculum development, educator training, technological accessibility, community involvement, and policy endorsement. AI, ICT literacy, STEM, and coding in Cambodian-specific curricula will improve critical thinking, creativity, and practical problem-solving. Effective AI instruction requires teacher preparation through gradual professional development. Technology availability through public-private partnerships will reduce digital gaps and promote equal education. Parents, communities, and NGOs may raise awareness, encourage innovation, and motivate students to learn AI. Finally, a comprehensive national AI education strategy, along with monitoring and evaluation tools, will ensure Cambodia's success in an AI-driven society.

INTRODUCTION

Preparing Cambodian students for AI-driven societies in 2050 is a challenging yet vital task. Currently, many Cambodian education experts and teachers have not fully understood how artificial intelligence (AI) will shape future professions and careers (McKinsey & Company, 2023). By examining global trends, they can begin to appreciate the need to adapt to this new landscape (Simplilearn, 2025). Cambodia's current educational system faces longstanding challenges, notably a shortage of skilled teachers, particularly in subjects supporting STEM (science, technology, engineering, and mathematics) education and the development of computational thinking skills (Cambodian Education Forum, 2023; UNESCO, 2025). Insights from specialists in AI, robotics, and related fields further clarify the knowledge and competencies students should acquire (On, 2025). Ultimately, the country must leverage all available resources and capacities to prepare a diverse and inclusive young population for AI-based jobs in 2050 (Kiri Post, 2025).

UNDERSTANDING AI AND ITS IMPACT

Artificial intelligence (AI) refers to a branch of computer science devoted to creating computer systems capable of performing tasks that traditionally require human intelligence. Such tasks include decision-making, object recognition (in images or sounds), and speech recognition and production (Russell & Norvig, 2021). The term AI dates back to the 1950s but began to draw widespread public attention in the 1980s (Haenlein & Kaplan, 2019). Advances in machine learning, deep learning, neural networks, and natural language processing over the past decade have led to a rapid expansion in the application of AI technology (Goodfellow, Bengio, & Courville, 2016). Popular tools, such as ChatGPT, have further elevated the prominence of AI.

Despite the economic and social advantages it brings to developed countries, the lack of AI infrastructure in developing nations threatens to widen the gap between the rich and the poor (UNESCO, 2021). Education, deemed essential for human development, plays a pivotal role in enabling countries to keep pace with AI advancements (OECD, 2023). Cambodian students require adequate preparation to navigate future AI-driven societies. Without such preparation, students will be at risk of facing many challenges as AI reshapes the nation and the world (On, 2025). The fundamental question is: How should Cambodia prepare its students to become AI-ready by 2050 and beyond?

Definition of AI

Artificial intelligence (AI) is a branch of computer science that aims to develop systems or machines capable of performing tasks or activities that normally require human intelligence (Russell & Norvig, 2021). More specifically, AI involves designing systems with human-like cognitive abilities, such as reasoning, learning, and problem-solving (Haenlein & Kaplan, 2019). Such systems should also perceive their environment and make decisions or perform actions to achieve both short-term and long-term goals (Goodfellow, Bengio, & Courville, 2016).

In the past, the role of AI software was often to simply follow rules—for example, recognizing images or filtering online spam (Nilsson, 2010). In these early stages, AI systems exhibited very limited intelligence. However, in the 1990s, AI researchers began developing algorithms that enabled AI software to learn by analyzing large amounts of data (Domingos, 2015). Through this data-driven approach, AI applications such as Google Search and Google Translate quickly improved and began to deliver useful performance levels (Em, 2025; Koehn, 2017). The second wave of AI systems is now capable of performing considerably more complex and diverse functions (Brynjolfsson & McAfee, 2017).

Historical Context of AI Development

In the late 1950s, after the creation of computers, interest grew in developing software to replicate human behavior and decision-making processes. The term "artificial intelligence" was first coined in 1955 (McCarthy, Minsky, Rochester, & Shannon, 1955). Despite the field's potential and increasing research funding, researchers could not deliver on the early promises during the first 20 years, leading to two decades of diminished interest, commonly referred to as AI winters (Crevier, 1993). The fourth AI winter occurred around 2001, due to challenges in convolutional neural networks, market deflation, and the failure of Turkman's Asian market strategy (Nilsson, 2010). Public interest resurged with IBM's Watson victory in 2011, the inception of Apple's Siri in 2011, and Google's development of DeepMind in 2010 (Russell & Norvig, 2021).

AI development can be partitioned into four generations: artificial intelligence agent (AIE), intelligent machine (IM), artificial brain (AB), and autonomous machine (AM) (Haenlein & Kaplan, 2019). AIEs, such as chatbots developed in the 1960s (e.g., ELIZA, PARRY), are symbolic-based systems designed to simulate human behavior and serve as artificial humans interacting with users (Weizenbaum, 1966; Colby, 1975). In the 1970s, the IM stage focused on AI software functioning as a machine with independent intelligence. The 1980s saw the emergence of AB models capable of learning and adaptation (Goodfellow, Bengio, & Courville, 2016). The 1990s initiated the aiming machine phase, which aimed to create self-aware, autonomous machines. The following stage, identified as AM, envisions robots operating independently without human control (Brynjolfsson & McAfee, 2017). By 2020, Apollo 11 was noted as the first driverless rover to land on the Moon (NASA, 2020).

Current Trends in AI Technology

AI, robotics, connected devices, and quantum computers offer possibilities that will transform society (Brynjolfsson & McAfee, 2017; Arute et al., 2019). In addition to improving technological methods, these technologies stimulate imagination regarding future applications. These technologies are developing rapidly, exemplified by the development of quantum computing, which reduces problem-solving times from thousands of years to minutes or seconds (Arute et al., 2019). Other technologies, such as 5G, will enormously increase automation and the transfer of information between devices (Shafi et al., 2017).

Faced with such possibilities within 30 years, it is estimated that 70% of the jobs of the future do not yet exist (World Economic Forum, 2020). Education must keep pace to ensure that students acquire new skills and ways of thinking that will allow them to create and build new services for future society (OECD, 2023). Along with the nature and content of current and future jobs, AI is profoundly shaping our societies and revolutionizing the professional environment (Chui et al., 2018). The wide deployment of data collection technologies, such as video surveillance, connected sensors, and drones, combined with the development of processing and analysis capacities, is paving the way for new tools, processes, and novel professional applications (Manyika et al., 2017).

Table 1. Definition, Development, Trends, and Educational Implications of AI

Theme	Key Points
Definition of AI	Artificial intelligence (AI) is a branch of computer science that enables machines to perform tasks requiring human-like intelligence, including reasoning, learning, decision-making, and problem-solving. Early AI followed strict rules, whereas modern AI uses data-driven approaches and machine learning.
Historical Context	The term AI was coined in 1955. AI development has faced periods of low progress, known as AI winters. The modern AI resurgence began in the 2010s with Watson, Siri, and DeepMind. AI development has four generations: artificial intelligence agent (1960s), intelligent machine (1970s), artificial brain (1980s), and autonomous machine (1990s–present).
Current Trends	Rapid growth in AI, robotics, quantum computing, and connected devices. Quantum computing drastically reduces problem-solving times. 5G enhances automation and data transfer. Future jobs do not yet exist, requiring education to adapt. AI reshapes society, work, and professional skills.
Impact on Education	Education is critical to preparing students for AI-driven societies. Developing countries without AI infrastructure risk falling behind. Cambodian students need to develop AI readiness by 2050.
Significance	Although AI offers economic and social advantages, it poses challenges in equity, employment, and skill requirements. It is a transformative force in technology, society, and professional life.

THE CAMBODIAN EDUCATIONAL LANDSCAPE

Cambodia's education system has experienced significant growth in both quantity and quality since the conclusion of the Vietnamese occupation in 1989 (Em et al., 2023; UNESCO, 2021). However, major challenges remain, particularly when measured against the standards of the Organisation for Economic Co-operation and Development and other emerging neighboring countries (OECD, 2023). The Cambodia Development Centre, in its *Next Generation Cambodia* report, proposed a long-term education vision designed to align with the demands of Industry 4.0 and the broader global labor market (CDC, 2022; Tariq, 2025).

The existing curriculum is overly academic, lacking practical skills development and co-curricular activities that actively engage and spark the curiosity of contemporary students (On, 2025). It is also highly theoretical, failing to provide the necessary abilities for active engagement in dynamic work environments. Academia currently places limited emphasis on AI and soft skill training. The shortage of qualified teachers and lecturers further exacerbates the gap in required competence (MoEYS, 2020). Moreover, the absence of a formal AI curriculum has resulted in inadequate teacher preparedness. The development of infrastructure and technology related to AI education remains weak, as does the partnership between the government and the private sector (OECD, 2023). Social attitudes and culture have yet to encourage and raise awareness of the advantages of AI (World Bank, 2021). Ultimately, schools are not adequately preparing students for entry into an AI-driven society.

Overview of the Current Education System

The present Cambodian educational system, shaped by a tumultuous past, has indisputably made significant advances (UNESCO, 2021). The signing of the Paris Peace Agreement in 1991 paved the way for new beginnings. However, the replacement of the political legacy and the reforms undertaken at the Ministry of Education, Youth, and Sport revealed only partial achievements. Highlighting a few informative facts generates a clearer perspective. For example, education covers 15% of the national budget, the twin enrollment ratio indicates female student domination, and the Ministry's deployment on national Internet access indicates that more than 60% of the registered population cannot access the website, thus revealing an Internet penetration ratio of less than 40% (MoEYS, 2020; World Bank, 2021). These considerations expose clear weaknesses in both the quantity and quality aspects.

However, despite these weaknesses, technological applications are always seeking solutions and mitigating adverse effects. The Ministry's responsive attitude to COVID-19 resulted in a non-stop teaching process. Teachers, students, and staff joined together in applying advanced adaptive models by employing Zoom platforms, e-learning, Google Classroom, Telegram, Facebook, and so forth. The functions of the Internet and modern channels enabled teachers and students to resume studies remotely and remotely, with the ideal being connected (On, 2025). The accumulating working process, irrespective of the developing country, is obviously performed widely. Although the process has not produced expected achievements, it has paved the way for the application of the latest technology in the future to follow and to be prepared at its best.

Challenges Facing Cambodian Education

Several factors jeopardize the current Cambodian educational system. First, although education is a tripartite shared responsibility between the government, private sector, and society, implementation primarily rests with the government. As a lower-middle-income country, Cambodia struggles to adequately fund education. The Ministry of Education, Youth, and Sport (MoEYS) receives approximately 16% of the annual national budget; however, less than 10% of that is allocated directly to education (World Bank, 2021). The quality of teachers and schools varies considerably, affecting learning outcomes. Moreover, enrollment and retention rates remain below expectations, leading to high levels of illiteracy and reduced access across all levels of higher education. Poor human and educational development outcomes further impede Cambodia's socioeconomic progress.

Second, a significant policy implementation gap exists throughout many levels of educational institutions. These institutions operate largely independently of the Ministry and often pursue their own strategies, leading to a lack of coordination (OECD, 2023). Third, technological disparities between rural and urban areas exacerbate educational inequalities. The government and NGOs closely monitor urban–rural and rural–rural disparities, which directly influence access to quality education and limit socioeconomic development (CDC, 2022). Finally, attitudinal and cultural considerations are undervalued; however, their inclusion could enhance education and planning initiatives for AI development. Education is crucial for societal development; without proper education, communities struggle to understand and adopt technological innovations (On, 2025). Therefore, a comprehensive educational strategy is essential.

Opportunities for Reform

The implementation of the national policy on Education Development 2019–2023, in conjunction with the Rectangular Strategy Phase IV and the Fifth Mandate of the Royal Government of Cambodia, aims to transform Cambodia into an upper-middle-income nation by 2030 and a high-income nation by 2050 (RGC, 2019). An essential component of these targets involves cultivating a new generation that can realize an AI-oriented nation, beginning with an education system aligned with the demands of technology-driven daily life and society (Em et al., 2025). Education is the cornerstone of national human resource development. Sustaining economic growth and development, enhancing people's livelihoods, and reversing poverty trends depend on producing a skilled workforce for the labor market and society (OECD, 2023; World Bank, 2021).

The growth of the digital economy offers rising incomes and enhanced social welfare. Cambodia must strengthen education and lifelong learning to prepare the workforce and society to respond to digital economy trends. Such preparation includes developing core skills and the ability to actively engage in the labor market and contribute socially. Digital skills are crucial for accessing and utilizing digital technologies; information skills allow access to data for national development; communication skills enable effective interaction and governance participation; and problem-solving skills prepare individuals to adapt to digital economy changes (On, 2025; UNESCO, 2021).

SKILLS REQUIRED FOR AI-DRIVEN SOCIETIES

Once students are prepared for a society driven by AI, what skills will they require? Many researchers have forecast the skills students will need in future societies; however, the skills listed here are necessary, based on an analysis of the Cambodian secondary educational system, an assessment of student learning capacities on AI, and current trends in AI (World Economic Forum, 2020; OECD, 2023).

It is never too early for students to learn about AI and the careers and activities it enables. Educators should create foundations in primary and secondary education and provide continuing development as technology advances (On, 2025). This focus must include formal curriculum requirements and build a culture of learning in students, teachers, parents, and the wider community (UNESCO, 2021).

Technical Skills

Technical skills are required for people living in AI-driven societies (Brynjolfsson and McAfee, 2017). Cambodia's existing educational system mainly focuses on the hard skills required to gain qualifications and succeed in working life. However, this is not sufficient (MoEYS, 2020).

Students' technical skills in areas such as AI and big data should be developed during their education (Goodfellow, Bengio, & Courville, 2016). They should learn about how related technologies function, how to apply those technologies to different types of work, and, of course, how to create their own AI technology systems (Chui et al., 2018). Such an educational approach will be necessary for people living in Cambodia in AI-driven societies of the future to successfully find employment and develop their lifestyles and society. AI is not just the future of technology but is indeed a trend for the future of humanity. Current official and private-sector university, college, and even secondary school-level curricula in Cambodia do not sufficiently promote AI-related learning (On, 2025).

Soft Skills and Emotional Intelligence

Education remains crucial in AI societies (World Economic Forum, 2020). First, humans are creative and innovative, capable of conceiving ideas or projects and reflecting on the quality of their work through lessons learned and experience transfer. Second, tasks involving human-to-human interaction require emotional intelligence, which is difficult to replace by robots or AI (Goleman, 1995). For example, a travel operator with an attractive personality can provide better services and earn more money than a robot serving airline customers; a customer support operator satisfied with the work conditions can improve the customer experience much better than a robot; and a high school teacher who regularly and positively interacts with students can best prepare them for their professional lives.

However, Cambodian society is currently disadvantaged in this area. When comparing Cambodian people's attitudes with those from developed countries, Cambodian people pay much less attention to providing the best customer experience, showing positive attitudes toward work, or living in harmony with others in their society (On, 2025). These are deeply rooted factors that are difficult to change in the short term. However, starting with the next generation, good education can help change these attitudes, thereby benefiting the whole society in the long term.

Lifelong Learning and Adaptability

Despite still being sometimes over-prescriptive, Cambodian curricula nevertheless include activities that encourage analysis, brainstorming, curiosity, and open conversations around student ideas (MoEYS, 2020; Tariq, 2025). In addition to English and Chinese, other foreign languages reflecting inward or outward expansion can be envisioned. Nevertheless, Cambodia's new reality toward 2050 and beyond could suggest a stronger and earlier focus on training for enterprises within or supportive of the high-tech industry (World Economic Forum, 2020). Such an approach could build a larger proportion of the country's economic engine and create what would otherwise be considered "higher-wage" jobs, akin to those in more traditional supply chains already referred to in this report.

The new reality views high-tech industries not only as ready to adopt AI technologies and systems but also as becoming partners in the development of new technologies and platforms (Brynjolfsson & McAfee, 2017). The training model will not simply focus on creating students capable of "the work of AI robots" but also on training those who can help create the next generation of AI tools, algorithms, and processes (Chui et al., 2018). These capabilities and the underlying construction of an AI-powered environment will still require badges, diplomas, and degrees for recognition and validation; equally crucial will be the drive and feeling for "continuous learning" and "always being ready to change" (OECD, 2023). These capabilities are directly related to the personal characteristics and developmental environment of each person and all students, workers, and professionals, regardless of age (On, 2025).

CURRICULUM DEVELOPMENT FOR AI INTEGRATION

Globally, educational systems are undergoing reforms to prepare students for AI-driven societies, including matters relating to fundamental character and AI awareness. Integrating AI and machine-learning concepts within curricula is a high priority (OECD, 2023; UNESCO, 2021). Designing educational programs to instill relevant knowledge and attitudes is equally important (World Economic Forum, 2020). As AI technologies continue to evolve, lifelong learning for students in an AI-driven society must be emphasized. Continuing education is increasingly important for adults who wish to upskill in a rapidly evolving AI landscape (Brynjolfsson & McAfee, 2017).

Building Cambodian students' AI awareness is not simply "all about the robot," but rather about delivering quality basic education. The government does not want Cambodia to fall behind others in the machine age (RGC, 2019). Research reveals that starting too early within the educational system may be counterproductive. Instead, the government seeks to first achieve a solid foundation with quality basic education, after which targeted efforts in AI can be undertaken (On, 2025). While Cambodia currently suffers from poor infrastructure and a shortage of qualified teachers, its people are skilled in navigating limitations. This quality can be harnessed via the promotion of innovation during digital transformation (Em et al., 2024; Heng, 2023), which is already well underway (Innovation Disclosure Report, 2021). The 2021 Innovation Disclosure Report (IDR) reveals that 70 percent of Cambodians consider themselves innovators. Moreover, 50 percent are proud to be identified as Cambodian, despite their informal existence. These cultural norms provide a foundation for developing AI skills and capabilities, thereby enabling a more rapid response to future trends and challenges (World Bank, 2021).

Integrating AI into Existing Curricula

The use of AI to improve existing courses can benefit teaching and learning (Luckin et al., 2016). Monitoring students' progress, providing personalized learning materials and advice, facilitating special group activities, assessing students' level of material understanding, and assigning appropriate reading homework and test tasks are just some examples of AI in education today. However, in Cambodia, which is on the para-industrial stage, these teaching–learning primitives are far from common. They rely on TPACK (technological, pedagogical, and content knowledge) skills by local teachers and the availability of a set of supporting technology facilities (e.g., high-performance computing and a large number of electronic devices) for student support (Mishra & Koehler, 2006).

Cambodia's current implementation of a new curriculum is more human-centric than AI-centric. This is especially clear for the new standards of teaching skills that are currently required of the country's new teachers, with an emphasis on new content and pedagogical knowledge but no requirement for knowledge in the field of AI (MoEYS, 2020). Such a human-centric curriculum can be a strong foundation for building the Cambodian style of human–machine cooperation in the future. However, within a decade, AI will be a foundational skill and form the basis of the government's offerings in the education sector (OECD, 2023).

Developing New Educational Programs

AI learning can be introduced as part of a general education program (Chui et al., 2018). When AI learning becomes a specialized major, it should be introduced as a regular program at the higher education level. Teachers ready to teach can do this immediately, especially for programs in applied fields such as engineering, computer science, business, and economics (Brynjolfsson & McAfee, 2017). For the control group, the topic of AI can be incorporated into the teaching of related subjects. The development of this curriculum or major can be jointly undertaken by educational institutions and those working in the AI sector. It is important to note that there are few people working in the AI sector in Cambodia. At the same time, a multi-dynamic and multicultural approach should be promoted (World Economic Forum, 2020).

Collaborations with the Tech Industry

Collaborating with the technology industry is vital to ensuring that Cambodian students are adequately prepared for AI-driven societies (OECD, 2023). Emerging industries specializing in AI will offer apprenticeship opportunities, enabling students to work directly with cutting-edge technologies. Such experiences cultivate practical skills and expose students to real-world AI applications (Luckin et al., 2016). Furthermore, forging partnerships between educational institutions and technology firms helps align curricula with industry requirements, ensuring that graduates possess the competencies necessary to adapt to rapidly evolving AI landscapes. These collaborations also allow for the sharing of resources, including the latest software and hardware, which can enrich the educational environment (Chui et al., 2018).

The Cambodian government and non-governmental organizations also play a crucial role by facilitating connections between schools and external partners (World Bank, 2021). By networking with pioneering companies worldwide, they can bring inspirational guides and mentors into Cambodian educational settings. These relationship-building efforts ignite students' passion for technology and AI, motivating them to pursue careers in these fields. Ultimately, such cooperative frameworks foster an ecosystem in which talent development keeps pace with AI innovations, thereby accelerating Cambodia's progress toward an AI-enriched economy and society by 2050 (RGC, 2019).

TEACHER TRAINING AND PROFESSIONAL DEVELOPMENT

Educators are agents of change in preparing Cambodian students for integration into AI-driven societies toward 2050 and beyond (On, 2025; World Economic Forum, 2020; Tariq, 2025). In-service teachers and secondary students require knowledge of AI, related technologies, future trends, and the skills needed to excel in an AI-driven society and future workplace (OECD, 2023). Teacher training in Khmer and English should cover AI and ICT literacy, STEM and coding, online teaching, AI-powered personalized learning, AI in education, and student preparation for integration into an AI-driven society and future workplace (Luckin et al., 2016; UNESCO, 2021). Partnerships with Cambodian STEM centers and the tech industry can support institutions in implementing new curricula and training (Chui et al., 2018).

Only 10% of Cambodian public schools have computer rooms, often without sufficient computers or reliable Internet access, and most teachers have never used ICT for instruction (MoEYS, 2020). Developing technology infrastructure for Cambodian teachers at all levels of education is crucial. Preparedness directly influences students; in a recent survey, only 38% of secondary students said their teachers were ready to teach with ICT (MoEYS, 2020). Advocating for teachers' use of AI in instruction and demonstrating its benefits will encourage more widespread adoption. Positive attitudes toward AI among parents and the broader community are also important for fostering student engagement and interest in AI-related topics (World Bank, 2021).

Importance of Teacher Preparedness

Teacher Preparedness: The successful preparation of students for integration into AI-driven societies critically depends on the preparedness of Cambodian teachers (Brynjolfsson & McAfee, 2017). Teachers must possess AI literacy not only to facilitate essential discussions in the classroom but also to understand and leverage the influence of AI in their own lives and work (Guszcza et al., 2018). Ensuring teacher preparedness presents a significant and complex challenge. As officials from the Ministry of Education, Youth, and Sport have acknowledged, teacher training should be prioritized in future teacher education projects, recognizing the fundamental role of well-prepared educators in equipping students for AI-driven societies (MoEYS, 2020).

Preparing Students for AI-Driven Societies: This chapter addresses the preparation of Cambodian students for future AI-driven societies through a detailed examination of essential knowledge and skills. It explores the present state of education in Cambodia, identifies necessary skills and attitudes, and outlines the broader requirements for students confronted with profound changes (On, 2025); World Economic Forum, 2020). Student preparation involves training in AI-related knowledge and skills, the development of new curricula, ongoing reform of the educational system, collaboration with the IT sector, and the provision of AI-related teacher training (OECD, 2023). The analysis concludes with a study of recent key concepts and trends shaping future societies over the next 30 years and beyond (Brynjolfsson & McAfee, 2017).

Training Programs for Educators

To prepare Cambodian students for AI-driven societies of 2050 and beyond, teachers must be prepared for future teaching and learning by undertaking professional development and training programs (Luckin et al., 2016). Teachers may be exposed to the potential applications of AI in education and its ethical considerations (UNESCO, 2021). Their development should be formulated by experts in AI and specialists in teacher training (On, 2025). They may be delivered face-to-face or online and should consider the development needs of primary, secondary, and university teachers (OECD, 2023). Finally, pre-service training may be offered for computing teacher educators at universities (MoEYS, 2020).

The pre-service training of computer teacher educators can be separated into three phases: Phase I) computing fundamentals; Phase II) AI fundamentals; and Phase III) AI applications to teaching and learning relevant to Cambodia (Brynjolfsson & McAfee, 2017). Classes for Phase I may cover mathematics for computing, programming in Python, object-oriented programming, English for science and technology, and management information systems, whereas classes for Phase II may include the basics of Python programming, probability and statistics, data structures and algorithms, database management systems, computer architecture, operating systems, AI, and machine learning (Goodfellow et al., 2016).

Building a Supportive Teaching Community

To prepare students for societies supported by AI, Cambodia's education system must nurture a highly motivated teaching community willing to excel in AI-related topics and capable of assisting students in their learning (Luckin et al., 2016). Teachers require profound AI knowledge that can be shared and propagated. However, due to resource limitations, especially in terms of information technology and support infrastructures, only a few teachers may initially accept the challenge (MoEYS, 2020). Motivation within the teaching community will be applied differently according to the four outlined levels of AI education (OECD, 2023).

At the foundational levels—AI awareness and general AI studies—teachers without formal AI education can still participate and support students in their basic learning (On, 2025). However, to efficiently prepare students in the latter two levels, which involve AI-focused curricula and AI specialization, comprehensive training for qualified teachers becomes indispensable (World Economic Forum, 2020). Consequently, collaboration among the government, institutions, organizations, and universities is vital to design and provide training programmes that achieve these objectives (Chui et al., 2018; World Bank, 2021).

INFRASTRUCTURE AND TECHNOLOGY ACCESS

Understanding the current state of Cambodia's infrastructure and technology access is crucial (World Bank, 2021; UNESCO, 2021). Despite well-documented economic growth, progress in information and communication technology has been slower (MoEYS, 2020). Government efforts include deploying logistic and service infrastructure, expanding transmission capacity, and welcoming a multitude of visitors (RGC, 2023). Although these initiatives enhance the quality of life, they cannot be the sole contributors. Cambodia ranks low in terms of services insufficient to meet demand. Maintaining the quality of education requires comprehensive solutions that also consider practical support (OECD, 2023).

Cambodia is identified as a developing country with a low-to-moderate level of digital application (UNESCO, 2021). The improper teaching-application-method approach further contributes to the low level of educational outcomes. The government is urged to ensure that all students can access appropriate infrastructure and technology (World Bank, 2021). Related organizations should provide support to students without resources to avoid a digital divide (On, 2025). Community involvement may cultivate motivation and a habit of using technology in daily life. Evaluating current projects and implementations will help identify practical ways of preparing students for future challenges and help reduce negative impacts during the transition to an AI society (Brynjolfsson & McAfee, 2017).

Current State of Technology in Cambodia

One of the issues that the Cambodian government must consider to prepare students for the 2050 era is technology (MoEYS, 2020). Present-day technologies are critical for the development of learning activities to help students achieve the proficiency necessary for a future career. Cambodia has a plentiful supply of human resources and is focusing more on digital economy development in national plans, as can be seen in the Government's Rectangular Strategy, Phase IV, the National Strategic Development Plan update, and the Rectangular Strategy Outlook 2023–2030 (RGC, 2023). The Rotary Club Phnom Penh Midtown also states that Cambodia's future depends on AI, stating, "It will be necessary for everyone to understand and be adept in the use of AI if they want to remain relevant as the economy changes" (Rotary Club Phnom Penh Midtown, 2022). A 2022 report from the Ministry of Education, Youth, and Sport reveals that while digital computers are no longer a luxury in Cambodia, there are still many schools without access to computers or the Internet (MoEYS, 2022).

Improving Access to Technology

Greater access to technology and improved education are crucial for preparing Cambodian students for AI-based societies in 2050 and beyond (World Economic Forum, 2020; UNESCO, 2021). Various initiatives, funded by governments, NGOs, and other organizations, target Cambodia's educational needs.

Although not a traditional part of education, modern technology is highly relevant. Cambodia's fast-growing economy, abundant natural resources, and increasing trade with neighboring countries necessitate large-scale infrastructure development (World Bank, 2021). Adapting emerging technology for infrastructural use must fit local conditions; however, most Cambodian educational institutions have limited access to new technology, constrained by cost, infrastructure, and other issues (MoEYS, 2020). Government and NGO initiatives are promoting broader access to technology (OECD, 2023).

Role of Government and NGOs

Role of the Government and NGOs Government Sponsorship: Given that AI is accelerating across all sectors of life in all countries, governments must carefully consider its effects on their citizens (Brynjolfsson & McAfee, 2017). To provide the best social conditions for citizens in the future, governments will have to create policies that address accelerating AI and its impact on humans. For example, government policies will need to consider how AI threatens people's jobs, how it enables people's jobs, and what skills are needed to take advantage of the new AI world (Chui et al., 2018). Moreover, governments will have to cooperate with AI-based companies and NGOs that tackle AI impacts on humans and communities (Luckin et al., 2016).

Role of NGOs: The rapid development of AI has brought considerable potential benefits and risks to society (World Economic Forum, 2020). However, the ability to shape the development and use of AI for the benefit of society is disproportionately dominated by a few large corporations and a limited number of countries (UNESCO, 2021). To address this, a significant number of groups from academia, civil society, philanthropy, government, and related sectors are examining the AI ecosystem (Guszcza et al., 2018). Through collaboration and inclusive dialogue, these groups aim to identify the distinct roles that governments, developers, and users can play in shaping a world where AI benefits all people. Efforts include funding initiatives focused on assessing progress in AI development, researching its impact on social cohesion, supporting AI for social good, providing a global and multilingual perspective on AI ethics, considering AI implications on human rights, evaluating the relationship between AI and democracy, developing frameworks for responsible technology through citizen engagement, facilitating global consultations on future AI development, supporting female leadership in AI development, advancing AI-integrated disaster risk management, initiating citizen science projects related to AI, and conducting research on public perceptions of AI that inform AI policy development (Brynjolfsson & McAfee, 2017; Chui et al., 2018; World Economic Forum, 2020).

CULTURAL CONSIDERATIONS IN EDUCATION

The integration of AI into Cambodia's education system represents a pivotal challenge in the 21st century (Luckin et al., 2016; UNESCO, 2021). Although the potential of AI technologies is widely lauded, integrating AI education within Cambodia's unique cultural context is necessary to ensure acceptance by students and parents (Brynjolfsson & McAfee, 2017). Cultures are not static; educational practices and knowledge are continually shaped by them because of the political, social, and economic forces that influence both the development of knowledge and its transmission (On, 2025).

Cambodian attitudes toward using and learning about AI may be complex and resistant to change (OECD, 2023). Cultural learning factors can impede students' ability to appreciate the interrelatedness of information and communicate complex ideas effectively, and may cause them to display little interest in AI. Parents and other stakeholders may also be reluctant to allow their children and grandchildren to explore AI innovations that could influence how they work and live in the future (Chui et al., 2018). The government, schools, and non-governmental organizations must work with local communities to generate a greater understanding of AI and encourage AI educational innovations (World Economic Forum, 2020). Teachers might organize informative activities and initiate dialogues among the broader community, enabling the public to question how AI, together with related technologies, could benefit society (Luckin et al., 2016).

Cultural Attitudes Towards Technology

Cambodian culture shows a positive attitude toward technology. Ninety-four percent of the respondents wanted to receive training on new technology; 95% agreed that when machine workers gradually replaced manual workers, Cambodia would become a smart society; 90% agreed that the government should support people in need who have difficulty affording access to technology; and 88% of respondents wanted better internet access (MoEYS, 2022).

Although Cambodians view technology positively, in practice, some use it for convenience or entertainment rather than for job creation or solving practical problems (OECD, 2023). This attitude influences a country's potential for technological development. Increased government policies and support could enhance access to technology for all people, potentially encouraging the use of technical knowledge and skills beyond personal convenience (World Bank, 2021).

Incorporating Local Contexts into Learning

Many low-income and developing countries often stress the theoretical and practical support related to AI education implementation, establishing AI pilot schools, and training educators; however, they rarely consider the cultural backgrounds and attitudes of local learners or how to nurture a culture aimed at using AI and creating new technologies (Luckin et al., 2016; UNESCO, 2021). Consequently, learners in these schools may comprehend AI concepts and skills but lack the motivation to apply AI in their communities and countries. Ideally, student skills and knowledge should be acquired within a cultural context that combines AI ideas and local culture to address national challenges (On, 2025). AI education should stimulate, prepare, and motivate students to be good and devoted citizens of their community and country while serving as a driving force for innovation and technology creation (Brynjolfsson & McAfee, 2017).

The Cambodian Ministry of Education, Youth, and Sports (MoEYS) approved an AI curriculum designed to prepare Cambodian students for AI-driven societies in 2050 and beyond (MoEYS, 2022). The government plans to commence AI teaching and learning from lower secondary education. Implementing the curriculum across all middle secondary schools necessitates assistance from various supporting stakeholders. The study of AI applications in the Cambodian context involved interviewing the executive directors, processing unit heads, and chief operating officers of eight non-governmental organizations (NGOs) engaged in the education and technology sectors (On, 2025).

Promoting Inclusivity in Education

Inclusivity is a critical consideration for transformative education, especially in preparing students to live and work in an AI-driven society of the future (World Economic Forum, 2020; Luckin et al., 2016). However, attitudes towards the formal education system remain mixed: while there is growing acceptance of the need for change and modernization, many people in the country still value traditional Cambodian education, in which young people learn to read and write Khmer, attend temples, receive instructions on karma and good citizenship, and so forth (OECD, 2023). This presents opportunities for all concerned to broaden their understanding of what constitutes good education for young Cambodians and how the education system should be (On, 2025).

Table 2. Cultural Considerations for Integrating AI in Cambodian Education

Theme	Key Points
Integration of AI in Education	AI education in Cambodia must consider the cultural context to ensure acceptance among students, parents, and communities. Political, social, and economic forces shape the development and transmission of knowledge.
Cultural Attitudes Towards Technology	Positive attitudes toward technology: high interest in training, belief in a smart society, support for government aid, and desire for better Internet access. However, technology is often used for convenience or entertainment rather than for practical or economic purposes.
Cultural Barriers	Resistance to change can impede learning, and cultural factors may limit students' ability to understand complex AI concepts or communicate ideas. Stakeholders (parents and communities) may be hesitant to embrace AI innovations.
Incorporating Local Contexts	AI education should combine AI concepts with local culture to motivate students to apply knowledge in communities. Pilot schools often neglect cultural adaptation, thereby reducing students' motivation to innovate.
Government Initiatives	The MoEYS approved an AI curriculum starting from lower secondary schools, aiming to prepare students for AI-driven societies by 2050. Implementation requires collaboration with NGOs and other stakeholders.
Promoting Inclusivity	Education must be inclusive to prepare students for a future AI-driven society. Traditional Cambodian education values coexist with modernization, requiring a balance in curriculum design.

CASE STUDIES OF SUCCESSFUL INTEGRATION

AI integration in education has advanced successfully in many countries (Luckin et al., 2016; UNESCO, 2021). Australia has conducted research on AI, machine learning, and deep learning. It is rated as having the best higher education system;

however, children also gain programming skills in primary schools (Brynjolfsson & McAfee, 2017). Singapore is an example of a country that has gradually incorporated AI into its education system. It started by teaching AI knowledge in schools and colleges and establishing various AI programs in universities (World Economic Forum, 2020). With a suitable infrastructure and trained educators, Singapore's system enables students to learn AI theory and apply it to real-life projects.

In Cambodia, numerous government and private institutions have introduced AI courses and programs in higher education (On, 2025). These efforts suggest that embedding AI learning activities into curricula and subject learning programs is necessary to prepare Cambodian students for AI-driven societies by 2050 and beyond. Formulating a suitable curriculum for nurturing future AI professionals and implementing efficient professional development for educators across all levels can be achieved through partnerships with technology-oriented organizations (MoEYS, 2022).

Global Examples of AI in Education

AI has reshaped humanity's organization in all key aspects of life, appearing in education, agriculture, food, medicine, health, living, social services, industries, trading, finance-banking, the military, crime investigation and prevention, as well as in areas of personal satisfaction and recreation (OECD, 2023). In addition, a new generation of AI machines has revealed the AI or advanced intelligence system, in which robots can already behave and will behave like human beings, executing millions of jobs at an amazing speed and processing all tasks at a super-high level (Chui et al., 2018). Our children will soon live and work with, and alongside, AI-powered machines as their work assistants and partners. Understanding and implementing AI in Cambodia's education system will ensure that our children's education is adequate and relevant to prepare them to adapt and integrate into societies driven by AI, not only by the year 2050 but right now at present, and into the future (Luckin et al., 2016).

The Global Trends Study by Fusuyama (2021) examines how nations across the globe are preparing themselves for an AI future in education. Fusuyama (2021) examined how nations across the globe are preparing for an AI future in education through a series of 13 case studies encompassing a range of different contexts, such as developed and developing countries, centralized and decentralized education systems, and societies from five continents. The variety of examples, from wholly dedicated centers in Canada, non-profit organizations in Kenya and Germany, to high-school cybersecurity competitions in the USA, and whole-school reforms in Singapore, illustrates the many strands of education that need to be understood with respect to AI. Likewise, the range of AI competencies is broad and varies depending on the local situation: while some countries introduce the foundations of programming at the primary school level, others invest in teacher training to promote AI thinking in their country or bring in new initiatives to retrain workers. The examination included how the AI industry stimulates education and how education interacts with the AI industry, for example, to meet its demand for talent. Four key areas emerged as critical for the successful preparation of societies and their future generations: curriculum and learning, teacher development, infrastructure and resources, and students' capacity (Fusuyama, 2021).

Lessons from Other Southeast Asian Nations

Vietnam, a neighbor of Cambodia, has attained a comparable share of shape-paid jobs in the formal sector. In Vietnam, the informal economy represented 51% of employment and 38% of GDP in 2018 (World Bank, 2021). A considerable share of Cambodia's current informal employment is in subsectors such as construction and manufacturing, where permanent jobs are being built rapidly. Within the Asian region, Malaysia and Thailand have well-developed financial markets and extensive credit guarantee mechanisms; consequently, they enjoy lower SME credit gaps. Malaysia and Thailand also lead in electronic business-to-business (B2B) trading platforms to bridge SMEs with domestic and international supply chains and to support SMEs in obtaining credit and enabling trade finance (OECD, 2023).

Cambodia's SME relative size and productivity lag far behind the progress noted in many nearby countries (World Bank, 2021). On a per-worker basis, Cambodian manufacturing firms were among the least productive in ASEAN and across Asia and the Pacific in 2016. As in many other developing economies, productivity growth is heavily concentrated in formal firms engaged in export activities. In Cambodia, the informal sector remains substantial, although some recent estimates suggest that a significant share of the informal sector may also contribute to economic growth (albeit to a lesser degree than larger firms). Credit in Cambodia remains heavily concentrated in the hands of larger firms. SME financing has generally focused on working capital financing, with little effort to fund capital investments. Malaysia, Thailand, to a certain extent Vietnam, and Indonesia have recently made the most progress in SME financing in domestic and export markets through credit guarantee mechanisms and SME-specific financial market instruments (OECD, 2023).

Local Success Stories in Cambodia

In Cambodia, there are exemplary cases of integrating AI and robotics into education (On, 2025). At the upper secondary level, Sisowath High School, situated in the capital, has applied AI and robotics to its teaching and learning activities.

These innovations have greatly enhanced students' experiences in STEM (science, technology, engineering, and mathematics) subjects. Students deploy emerging technologies, including AI and robotics, in their curriculum through the organization of a robotics competition, activities involving AI robots, and drones. Key supporting factors include the involvement and support of local authorities in education and a strong connection with the local technology and telecommunications company Smart Axiata.

At the post-secondary level, the Build Bright University's Department of Computing has introduced an operational AI program since 2020/2021 (MoEYS, 2022). The university acknowledges the growing demand for AI specialists to address challenges in agriculture, health, education, and commerce. The program offers students an integrated AI and machine learning course and plans to collaborate with the technology industry. These initiatives have been instrumental in preparing Cambodian students for employment in Cambodian and international corporations, as well as in the international community (On, 2025).

FUTURE TRENDS IN AI AND EDUCATION

Preparing Cambodian students for integration into "AI-Driven Societies": Future trends toward 2050 and beyond. The AI impetus is the most important factor for Cambodian students' knowledge capacity that should be addressed after the COVID-19 crisis (UNESCO, 2021). This tremendous challenge will bring exciting developments and threats. Depending on the educational procedures, Cambodian students can be digitally excluded or become active drivers for AI integration in Cambodia by 2050 and beyond. After a definition of AI and a discussion on the possibilities of a better understanding, the educational requirements to face the threat and be prepared for AI-driven societies in 2050 are examined (Luckin et al., 2016).

The future trends of technology must first be analyzed in the development of this challenging topic. In particular, AI aspects must be analyzed and understood to prepare new curricula and skills for Cambodia. The preparation of Cambodian students for AI-accompanying societies requires more prospects in explaining and describing AI terminology and the concept of intelligence. The methodology considers the existing Cambodian educational system, possible existing reforms, and, last but not least, students' requirements for AI-driven societies in 2050. Other important analyses deal with teachers, educators, and families, who could play a decisive role in sensitizing students, parents, communities, and Cambodia in general on AI (Brynjolfsson & McAfee, 2017).

Predictions for AI Development

Artificial intelligence (AI) is a part of computer science that focuses on developing machines and computers that can imitate the intelligence processes of human beings and animals (Russell & Norvig, 2021). Rapid advancements in AI have driven significant changes across numerous sectors of society, such as work, the economy, and social interaction. Given the crucial role of AI in national development, Cambodian students must learn about AI to prepare for AI-driven societies (OECD, 2023). The integration of AI tools in education will significantly impact virtually every aspect of society in the near future.

During the development of AI, its definitions have often been modified amid successes and failures. The time scale for prediction was approximately 10–15 years. In the long term, changes in the educational system tend to occur gradually (Chui et al., 2018). The landscape of AI research has recently undergone a significant transformation with the emergence of large language models, such as GPT-4, Bing Chat, Google Bard, and LLaMa. Worldwide predictions related to AI development can serve as a reference point for outlining trends that will continue toward 2050.

Emerging Educational Technologies

Modern technologies that have been adopted and distributed in schools around the world continually support education. These technologies are often categorized into educational technology, such as e-learning, mobile learning, online learning, learning management systems, multimedia, Zoom meetings, Microsoft Teams, Google Classroom, and Udemy; and cutting-edge technology, such as the Internet of Things, virtual reality, augmented reality, mixed reality, blockchain, and artificial intelligence (Luckin et al., 2016). Furthermore, virtual assistants will guide many activities for students and assist teachers, parents, and students alike.

Consequently, future education in Cambodia will be immersed in new technologies used globally, and Cambodia cannot avoid AI-connected technologies in the future. Developed countries have developed e-learning and have teamed up with AI companies to prepare their students for AI roles. Although Cambodia has revised some courses, such as STEM or STEM robotics, that are relevant to AI, the country remains in the initial stages of establishing connections with AI companies (On, 2025).

Preparing for Future Job Markets

Preparing Cambodian students for future jobs is one of society's main aims, as students will comprise the future workforce. Various aspects, such as culture, education, society, the economy, and politics, influence these jobs (World Bank, 2021).

The roles and needs in the job market will change because historical factors are time-specific. Cambodia's current education system forces students into static, rigid thought modes and roles, uniquely conceived for the peace and stability of a country emerging from a destructive war. Such conceptualization does not prepare students for future labor markets shaped by AI and other new technologies (Brynjolfsson & McAfee, 2017). Students graduating from Cambodia's current educational system will neither survive in nor contribute to an AI society, which is not only a technical invention but an entirely new conception of being.

Cambodia is transforming its education system across all aspects to meet the requirements of an emerging AI society by 2050 and beyond. In addition to being equipped with knowledge and skills, students must be taught appropriate attitudes and culture as good citizens of an AI society. The technological environment in Cambodia, which is far behind that of other countries, has received considerable attention. All stakeholders, across public and private sectors, have joined forces to communicate, support, and enhance AI education in Cambodian society (MoEYS, 2022).

POLICY RECOMMENDATIONS

Cambodia's vision for integration into an AI-driven future by 2050 requires supportive policies and laws across various sectors. Legal frameworks encompassing intellectual property rights, data, privacy, and cyberspace must be devised (OECD, 2023). Partnerships across government bodies, the private sector, and civil society are essential for creating a cohesive, holistic strategy covering policy formulation, implementation, and evaluation (UNESCO, 2021).

Economic policies are needed to facilitate business development and growth within the AI ecosystem. A culture conducive to technology innovation can be nurtured through community engagement, which involves students, parents, and the broader public (World Bank, 2021). Ensuring access to education and digital resources for disadvantaged groups is also a priority. Open forums and dialogues with citizens will help gather viewpoints and raise awareness about the importance of AI education (UNESCO, 2021).

Government Initiatives for AI Education

Government actions to prepare future generations for life in an AI-driven world are essential to ensuring stability and progress in Cambodian society by 2050. One first step is to establish a clear strategic vision for AI education that integrates the main policy directions for Cambodia's national development plans for the coming decades and is in line with other international development goals (Em & Khampirat, 2025b; MoEYS, 2022). This ambition must extend beyond the Ministry of Education. The Ministries of Finance and Posts, Telecommunications, and Technology also have a stake in ensuring that students are equipped with the right set of AI-related skills for the future. Private sector involvement in this process is essential, as is agreement on the financial resources allocated to this endeavor (OECD, 2023).

Public and private organizations can already contribute to improving students' access to AI-related knowledge and skills. For example, public and private banks can develop interest-free lending programs for disadvantaged students to allow them to study key sciences; both groups can also finance teacher training and purchase the necessary computers and peripherals. Nongovernmental and not-for-profit groups can help set up AI centers of excellence in universities and make them accessible to all students, even those from poorer backgrounds (UNESCO, 2021). Many foundations offer grants for the acquisition of equipment and the provision of computer training to vulnerable students.

Partnerships Between Public and Private Sectors

Cambodian students should prepare to integrate into AI-driven societies; otherwise, they may struggle to succeed in future jobs, not only by 2050 but also beyond (Brynjolfsson & McAfee, 2017). Partners must therefore work together to develop such preparations for students. Educational institutions can partner with public and private organizations to provide training programs and other learning opportunities that equip students with the skills needed to succeed in future careers (OECD, 2023).

Cambodia faces many challenges in providing relevant education for AI-driven societies. To prepare students for such jobs, it is necessary to integrate AI into curricula, provide teacher training, equip schools with resources such as computers and software, and foster a lifelong learning mindset. Strengthening connections between universities and relevant industries can also help bridge the skills gap (MoEYS, 2022). Several business leaders, policymakers, educators, and stakeholders have therefore advocated partnerships between the public and private sectors.

Creating a National AI Education Strategy

In the digital era, information and communication technologies have permeated every corner of society. However, disparities in access, technical skills, and cultural attitudes hinder the full realization of the benefits these developments can bring (World Bank, 2021). Governments in developing countries often bear an undeniable responsibility to ensure that their societies possess the capabilities to generate technology themselves; otherwise, transformative growth remains an unattainable goal.

For Cambodia, it is crucial to create the right conditions to realize the ambitions and visions outlined in the nation's TVET development plan and related policies (MoEYS, 2022). Cambodia, like most countries, has a nationwide education system that ostensibly facilitates knowledge acquisition for all citizens. However, the fact that advanced nations have developed technologies that others import illustrates that unequal access to education translates into unequal opportunities, making the generation of new knowledge and technology difficult in some countries, with Cambodia being a case in point (Brynjolfsson & McAfee, 2017).

Table 3. Policy Recommendations for Advancing AI Education in Cambodia

Theme	Key Points
Legal and Policy Frameworks	Cambodia requires laws on intellectual property, data privacy, and cyberspace to support AI integration. Policy formulation, implementation, and evaluation must involve partnerships between the government, private sector, and civil society.
Economic and Community Policies	Economic policies should foster AI business development and an innovative culture. Community engagement, citizen dialogue, and inclusive access to education and digital resources are critical.
Government Initiatives	A strategic national vision for AI education should align with Cambodia's development plans and international goals. Ministries beyond those of education (Finance, Posts & Technology) must be involved, along with the private sector, for resource mobilization and skills development.
Public-Private Partnerships	Collaboration between educational institutions, businesses, NGOs, and foundations can provide training, equipment, AI centers, grants, and scholarships to support equitable AI education.
Curriculum and Teacher Preparation	Integrating AI into curricula, providing teacher training, equipping schools, fostering lifelong learning, and linking universities with industry are essential for preparing students for AI-driven careers.
National AI Education Strategy	Governments must address disparities in access, skills, and culture to enable transformative growth. Cambodia needs conditions to generate technology locally and bridge the gap between knowledge acquisition and innovation capacity.

COMMUNITY ENGAGEMENT AND AWARENESS

To prepare students to live and work in an AI community, engagement between schools and families is critical. Other forms of community engagement by all stakeholders also assist in raising awareness of and understanding of AI adoption and the challenges faced by educational reform in general (UNESCO, 2021). Historically, Cambodians have been concerned with working hard to be prosperous, which was made difficult by genocide and the ensuing efforts to rebuild the country (Chandler,

2008). The introduction of new technologies, such as AI, now makes working hard less necessary if one has the skills needed to function in such a society (OECD, 2023).

Local attitudes toward AI within educational institutions should also be considered through the application of a cultural lens to ensure that AI education can be understood and learned by everyone. Indeed, the cultural context of Cambodia must determine the direction and methodology of implementing future AI education. Community engagement, including with parents, is necessary to raise understanding and reduce resistance to required changes. Such engagement can transform the present focus on working hard into an interest in learning the skills required to prosper in Asian and global AI-driven societies (World Bank, 2021).

Involving Parents and Communities

Parents and communities play important roles in the education of children and young people. With AI education, they should be involved to nurture and encourage children and students in their AI pursuits (UNESCO, 2021).

Parents should be encouraged to learn alongside their children. In the future, a smartphone, which is a type of mobile robot endowed with artificial intelligence functions, should be able to translate any language it receives. With this tool, parents could remain actively involved in their children's AI education. Although machine translation may contain inaccuracies, parents with deeper knowledge can help children identify linguistic or conceptual errors, allowing learning to become a more interactive and challenging process (OECD, 2023).

Awareness Campaigns on AI Benefits

Cambodians generally have positive attitudes toward companies that invest in AI development, not only in Phnom Penh but also in the provinces. However, some people are concerned that AI may destroy jobs in the future (Brynjolfsson & McAfee, 2017). The younger generation, parents, teachers, leaders, and organizations, both private and public, must be aware of AI's societal benefits and recognize that AI also creates new jobs (World Bank, 2021).

Awareness campaigns highlighting the benefits of AI and job creation can help Cambodia develop in step with other countries with advanced technology. Participants can gain a clearer understanding of AI, its limitations, and how it can improve their lives. Additionally, they can learn to prepare for future roles in which humans and AI collaborate or for tasks that require human cognitive skills (OECD, 2023).

Creating a Culture of Innovation

Cambodian society requires a cultural shift to support AI education. Innovation and forward-thinking projects are essential for AI education, and students must develop creative and critical thinking skills to pursue new ideas (UNESCO, 2021). Cambodian cultural, religious, and customary beliefs may influence learning approaches; therefore, educational programs and technological awareness events should be designed to reach individuals from all walks of life (Chandler, 2008).

Support from parents, teachers, administrators, and policymakers is critical. This support fosters a culture that reduces fear and deprivation, encouraging active engagement with an AI society. As more people collaborate in this way, Cambodia's AI culture will evolve toward a more inclusive and innovation-driven society, amplifying the demand and support for AI education (World Bank, 2021).

MONITORING AND EVALUATION

AI education is a new field without established methods to measure whether Cambodian educational reforms are on the right track or require adjustment (UNESCO, 2021). Thus, a system to monitor and evaluate the development of AI at universities and across the education system is needed. AI education in Cambodia is a long-term endeavor that includes primary school, secondary school, universities, teacher training, and lifelong learning (Em & Khampirat, 2025a). The system must also consider cultural factors and relationships with human experts in the relevant disciplines (OECD, 2023).

Monitoring and evaluation are important for several reasons. First, the government must determine whether the current AI educational strategy is appropriate or requires revision. Second, the government and private sectors can identify areas that demand more resources. Finally, parents of students should be informed about the importance of AI and new technologies in the education system. An appropriate framework for monitoring and evaluation provides indicators and measurement methods to assess future progress (World Bank, 2021).

Assessing Educational Outcomes

Assessing educational outcomes plays a critical role in preparing Cambodian students for full integration into AI-driven societies by 2050 and beyond. Formal and informal education systems must encourage the adoption of a "learning-to-learn" attitude, enabling lifelong learning in support of talent development (Brynjolfsson & McAfee, 2017). A nationwide framework for monitoring and evaluating the effectiveness of education will require the partnership and support of all stakeholders, including the government, the education sector, parents, communities, and development partners.

As the world gradually recovers from the third and fourth waves of COVID-19, Cambodia is also recovering. Cambodian people, students, and youth must be prepared for the post-pandemic world with all its opportunities and challenges (Em et al., 2022). Many Cambodians still lack a deep understanding of Fourth Industrial Revolution (4IR) technologies and artificial intelligence (AI), including how these technologies will influence their lives, studies, and future work (OECD, 2023). However, 4IR technologies and AI are already here, and their real-life applications continue to expand globally.

Feedback Mechanisms for Continuous Improvement

To ensure the successful preparation of Cambodian students for AI-driven societies, periodic assessment of long-term impacts is essential. Determining the realization of this objective requires large-scale, long-term studies employing robust scientific methods (UNESCO, 2021). Evaluating the influence of AI on Cambodian students' daily lives, including entertainment, social relationships, and education, can serve as an initial approach.

Positive attitudes toward AI are crucial. Students' readiness to embrace AI will encourage their active involvement in creating novel applications that can improve community life. Continuous advancements in AI tools are expected to shape how entertainment, social interaction, and education are experienced in Cambodia (Brynjolfsson & McAfee, 2017).

Measuring Success in AI Integration

The world is changing rapidly; however, adaptation occurs at different speeds. To ensure that Cambodian students are prepared for life in an AI-driven society, the education system must integrate AI now. A coherent national strategy should cover AI integration into existing curricula, development of new AI programs, teacher preparation, technology infrastructure, and engagement with the high-tech industry. Parental and community involvement are also essential to foster innovation and leadership in Cambodia (World Bank, 2021).

Historical and emerging technological trends provide insights into the society in which Cambodians may live by 2050 and beyond. While these trends offer valuable guidance, they may require adaptation to local culture and conditions. Continuous exploration of such trends will enhance understanding and preparedness. Education remains the foundation for the quality of life; students without the proper skills to use new technologies risk marginalization. Three critical components must be addressed in Cambodia's education system: curricula, skills, and teacher support. These interconnected elements collectively ensure that Cambodian students are fully prepared to succeed in AI-driven societies (OECD, 2023).

CONCLUSION

To prepare Cambodian students for integration into AI-driven societies in 2050 and beyond, curricula must include education about AI and related technologies. Rapid technological advances necessitate entrepreneurial instruction in AI to foster innovation in the AI industry, particularly in Cambodia. Teacher–student engagement is crucial; educators must receive training to develop appropriate curricula, programs, and subjects, ideally in partnership with the technology industry. Tailoring the educational approach to local contexts enhances relevance and effectiveness.

High-tech tools, equipment, and upgraded Internet access are needed in Cambodian schools, requiring governmental support. These initiatives, already underway with assistance from organizations such as the German government, must continue and be expanded. Addressing cultural aspects is equally important, promoting interest in learning, a positive attitude toward AI and innovation, and tolerance for failure. Community and parental support constitute vital resources in this empowerment process. Cambodia can look to worldwide, regional, and local case studies in which AI and related technological subjects have been successfully integrated into curricula for further guidance.

RECOMMENDATION

A comprehensive and multi-stakeholder approach is required to guarantee that Cambodian students will be adequately equipped to incorporate AI-driven societies by 2050. Curricula at all levels of education–primary, secondary, and tertiary–must incorporate AI, information and communication technology (ICT) literacy, STEM, coding, and AI ethics. These curricula should be contextualized to Cambodian culture and local needs, with an emphasis on hands-on projects, digital storytelling, and real-world applications, with the goal of cultivating abilities in critical thinking, creativity, and problem-solving. When students are prepared in this manner, they will be equipped to navigate and effectively contribute to future workplaces and societies driven by AI.

To be successful in this endeavor, teacher training and professional development are essential. Cambodian educators should be trained in computing principles, AI concepts, and the practical application of AI in teaching and learning. This training should be phased and competency-based. Teachers will be able to function as facilitators of AI knowledge through ongoing professional development programs supported by collaborations with universities, STEM centers, and the technology industry. These programs will enable teachers to guide students to better comprehend AI principles and creatively apply these concepts.

Access to technology and infrastructure must be expanded across the country, particularly in neglected places. For schools to cultivate successful learning environments, they need a sufficient number of computers, a dependable Internet connection, and tools that are enabled with AI. Public-private partnerships can provide funds for these resources, thereby narrowing the digital gap and guaranteeing that all students have equal access to opportunities. Additionally, it is essential to have active interactions with parents, communities, and local groups to promote awareness of the benefits of AI, establish a culture of innovation, and motivate students to investigate and acquire knowledge and skills related to AI.

Finally, the government of Cambodia ought to implement a comprehensive national AI education policy that is in line with broader development objectives. The implementation of this plan ought to involve the implementation of supportive legislation, economic incentives, frameworks for teacher training, and partnerships with the commercial sector. To track progress, evaluate educational outcomes, and continuously improve AI programs, robust monitoring and assessment mechanisms are also required. Cambodia has the potential to enable students, teachers, and communities to embrace AI as a driver of learning, creativity, and sustainable national development by adopting this strategically coordinated, culturally sensitive, and future-focused strategy. This will ensure that Cambodia is prepared for AI-driven societies by 2050.

REFERENCES

Arute, F., Arya, K., Babbush, R., Bacon, D., Bardin, J. C., Barends, R., Biswas, R., Boixo, S., Brandao, F. G. S. L., Buell, D. A., Burkett, B., Chen, Y., Chen, Z., Chiaro, B., Collins, R., Courtney, W., Dunsworth, A., Farhi, E., Foxen, B., & Martinis, J. M. (2019). Quantum supremacy using a programmable superconducting processor. *Nature, 574*(7779), 505–510. DOI: 10.1038/s41586-019-1666-5 PMID: 31645734

Axiata, S. (2021). *Technology partnerships in Cambodian education.* Smart Axiata Corporate Report.

Brynjolfsson, E., & McAfee, A. (2017). *Machine, platform, crowd: Harnessing our digital future.* W. W. Norton & Company. https://cir.nii.ac.jp/crid/1971993809789801089

. Cambodia Development Centre (CDC). (2022). *Next generation Cambodia: Education and workforce development.*

Cambodian Education Forum. (2023, September 18). *STEM education in Cambodia: Progress and challenges.* https://cefcambodia.com/2023/09/18/stem-education-in-cambodia-progress-and-challenges/

Chandler, D. P. (2008). *A history of Cambodia.* Westview Press. https://cir.nii.ac.jp/crid/1971149384846462136

Chui, M., Manyika, J., Bughin, J., Dobbs, R., Roxburgh, C., & Sarrazin, H. (2018). *The impact of AI on the future of work.* McKinsey Global Institute.

Colby, K. M. (1975). *Artificial paranoia: A computer simulation of paranoid processes.* Pergamon Press.

Crevier, D. (1993). *AI: The tumultuous history of the search for artificial intelligence.* Basic Books. https://cir.nii.ac.jp/crid/1970586434887638420

Domingos, P. (2015). *The master algorithm: How the quest for the ultimate learning machine will remake our world.* Basic Books. https://www.redalyc.org/pdf/6380/638067264018.pdf

Em, S. (2025). *Effectiveness of school directors' transformational leadership on teachers' self-efficacy and job performance in Cambodia* [Doctoral dissertation, The University of Cambodia]. CJESS Online Library. https://ejournal.educationalfields.com/index.php/CJESSOL/article/view/63

Em, S., Chin, P., & Pen, D. (2024). COVID-19 and school closures: Transformation of shadow education in the Cambodian context. In Md. B. Alam (Ed.), *Shadow education in Asia: Policies and practices* (pp. 136-159). IGI Global Scientific Publishing. DOI: 10.4018/979-8-3693-2952-8.ch009

Em, S., & Khampirat, B. (2025a). Facilitating scholarly pursuits in higher education: Cambodia's endeavors toward research advancement. In Mdikana, A. A. (Ed.), *Enhancing research output in higher education: Research proposals, profiles, and publishing* (pp. 39–66). IGI Global Scientific Publishing., DOI: 10.4018/979-8-3373-0806-7.ch002

Em, S., & Khampirat, B. (2025b). Cooperative education for sustainability: AI in learning opportunities, challenges, and future directions. In Tariq, M. U., & Sergio, R. P. (Eds.), *Convergence of AI, education, and business for sustainability* (pp. 75–92). IGI Global Scientific Publishing., DOI: 10.4018/979-8-3373-1917-9.ch004

Em, S., Khan, S., & Nun, N. (2023). Education system in Cambodia: A brief review from the prehistoric period to the present, and an education strategic plan for the future. *FIRE: Forum for International Research in Education*, *7*(3), 141–164. DOI: 10.32865/fire202273320

Em, S., Mok, S., Sam, R., Kurniawan, G. F., & Pen, D. (2025). History of education in Cambodia: A review of literature from past to present. *Paramita: Historical Studies Journal*, *35*(1), 32–47. DOI: 10.15294/paramita.v35i1.9207

Em, S., Phann, S., & Khan, S. (2022). Cambodian EFL university students' perceptions of online learning effectiveness during the COVID-19 pandemic: A survey study. *Cambodian Journal of Educational Research*, *2*(2), 15–34. DOI: 10.62037/cjer.2022.02.02.02

Fusuyama, N. (2021). *Global trends in AI and education: Case studies across five continents*. International AI in Education Research Group.

Goleman, D. (1995). *Emotional intelligence: Why it can matter more than IQ*. Bantam Books. https://cir.nii.ac.jp/crid/1970023484866461959

Goodfellow, I., Bengio, Y., & Courville, A. (2016). *Deep learning*. MIT Press. https://cir.nii.ac.jp/crid/1971149384893273390

Guszcza, J., Mahoney, S., & Mahoney, J. (2018). Preparing for AI in the workforce. *Deloitte Review, 22*, 6–15. https://arxiv.org/vc/arxiv/papers/2105/2105.05424v1.pdf

Haenlein, M., & Kaplan, A. (2019). A brief history of artificial intelligence: On the past, present, and future of artificial intelligence. *California Management Review*, *61*(4), 5–14. DOI: 10.1177/0008125619864925

Heng, K., Sol, K., & Em, S. (2023). COVID-19 and digital transformation of Cambodian higher education: Opportunities, challenges, and the way forward. In de Pablos, P. O., Zhang, X., & Almunawar, M. N. (Eds.), *Handbook of research on education institutions, skills, and jobs in the digital era* (pp. 307–327). IGI Global Scientific Publishing., DOI: 10.4018/978-1-6684-5914-0.ch018

Koehn, P. (2017). *Neural machine translation.* Cambridge University Press., https://www.cambridge.org/qa/universitypress/subjects/computer-science/artificial-intelligence-and-natural-language-processing/neural-machine-translation

Luckin, R., Holmes, W., Griffiths, M., & Forcier, L. B. (2016). *Intelligence unleashed: An argument for AI in education.* Pearson. https://discovery.ucl.ac.uk/id/eprint/1475756/

Manyika, J., Chui, M., Miremadi, M., Bughin, J., George, K., Willmott, P., & Dewhurst, M. (2017). *A future that works: Automation, employment, and productivity.* McKinsey Global Institute. https://www.jbs.cam.ac.uk/wp-content/uploads/2020/08/170622-slides-manyika.pdf

McCarthy, J., Minsky, M., Rochester, N., & Shannon, C. E. (1955). *A proposal for the Dartmouth summer research project on artificial intelligence.* Dartmouth College. http://aigraph.cslt.org/courses/06/Dartmouth_workshop.pdf

McKinsey & Company. (2023). *Generative AI and the future of work in America.* McKinsey Global Institute. https://www.mckinsey.com/mgi/our-research/generative-ai-and-the-future-of-work-in-america

. Ministry of Education, Youth and Sport (MoEYS). (2022). *Digital education report 2022.*

. Ministry of Education, Youth and Sport (MoEYS). (2022). *Strategic plan for AI integration in Cambodian education.*

Mishra, P., & Koehler, M. J. (2006). Technological pedagogical content knowledge: A framework for teacher knowledge. *Teachers College Record, 108*(6), 1017–1054. DOI: 10.1111/j.1467-9620.2006.00684.x

National Aeronautics and Space Administration (NASA). (2020). *Apollo 11 lunar landing mission facts.* https://www.nasa.gov/mission_pages/apollo/missions/apollo11.html

Nilsson, N. J. (2010). *The quest for artificial intelligence: A history of ideas and achievements.* Cambridge University Press., DOI: 10.1017/CBO9780511819346

On, S. (2025). *Students' perception of the impact of AI generative tools in learning the English language* [Master's thesis, National University of Cheasim Kamchaymer, Kampong Cham campus]. CJESS Online Library. https://ejournal.educationalfields.com/index.php/CJESSOL/article/view/74

Organization for Economic Co-operation and Development (OECD). (2023). *Education policy outlook: Cambodia.* https://www.oecd.org/education

Post, K. (2025, February 10). *Is Cambodia ready to integrate AI in education?* https://kiripost.com/stories/is-cambodia-ready-to-integrate-ai-in-education

Innovation Disclosure Report (IDR). (2021). *Innovation and entrepreneurship in Cambodia: National trends.*

Rotary Club Phnom Penh Mid-town. (2022). *Annual report on community development.* Rotary Club.

Royal Government of Cambodia (RGC). (2019). *Education development policy 2019–2023.*

Royal Government of Cambodia (RGC). (2019). *Education development policy 2019–2023.*

Royal Government of Cambodia (RGC). (2023). *Rectangular strategy, phase IV, and strategic development plans 2023–2030.*

Russell, S. J., & Norvig, P. (2021). *Artificial intelligence: A modern approach* (4th ed.). Pearson Education., https://library.giadinh.edu.vn/handle/GDU/2783

Shafi, M., Molisch, A. F., Smith, P. J., Haustein, T., Zhu, P., De Silva, P., & Tufvesson, F. (2017). 5G: A tutorial overview of standards, trials, challenges, deployment, and practice. *IEEE Journal on Selected Areas in Communications*, *35*(6), 1201–1221. DOI: 10.1109/JSAC.2017.2692307

Simplilearn. (2025). *The rise of AI and machine learning job trends.* https://www.simplilearn.com/rise-of-ai-and-machine-learning-job-trends-article

Tariq, M. (Ed.). (2025). *Merging Artificial Intelligence With the Internet of Things.* IGI Global., DOI: 10.4018/979-8-3693-8547-0

Tariq, M. (Ed.). (2025). *Emerging Multisector Applications of AI and IoT.* IGI Global., DOI: 10.4018/979-8-3373-4332-7

United Nations Educational, Scientific, and Cultural Organization. (UNESCO). (2021). *Artificial intelligence and education: Guidance for policy-makers.* https://unesdoc.unesco.org/ark:/48223/pf0000376709

United Nations Educational, Scientific, and Cultural Organization. (UNESCO). (2025, January 12). *UNESCO and MoEYS advocate ethical AI in education at Cambodia's first EdTech Summit.* https://www.unesco.org/en/articles/unesco-and-moeys-advocate-ethical-ai-education-cambodias-first-edtech-summit

Weizenbaum, J. (1966). ELIZA—A computer program for the study of natural language communication between man and machine. *Communications of the ACM*, *9*(1), 36–45. DOI: 10.1145/365153.365168

World Bank. (2021). Cambodia education note: Challenges, opportunities, and reforms. Washington, DC.

World Economic Forum. (2020). *The future of jobs report 2020.* Geneva. https://www.weforum.org/reports/the-future-of-jobs-report-2020

KEYWORDS AND DEFINITIONS

Artificial Intelligence Education: The application of artificial intelligence (AI) in the field of education refers to the utilization of computer systems that are capable of carrying out tasks that need human intellect in order to enhance teaching and learning, personalize student experiences, and automate administrative assignments.

Community Engagement and Policy: Community Engagement and Policy is a term that describes the process of actively and inclusively involving members of a community in the process of formulating, implementing, and evaluating policies and choices that have an impact on their lives within the community.

Curriculum Development: The process of establishing, developing, and refining educational programs in order to accomplish particular learning outcomes is referred to as curriculum development.

Teacher Training and Professional Development: The term "teacher training and professional development" refers to the continual education that teaching professionals get in order to improve their knowledge, abilities, and teaching practices, with the ultimate goal of enhancing the outcomes for their students.

Technology Access and Infrastructure: Technology access and infrastructure refer to the combination of physical hardware, software, networks, and facilities that support the creation, operation, and delivery of technology services and innovations. participate in and benefit from the digital economy and services.

Chapter 8
Raising Future Innovators: AI Education for Children

Chikesh Ranjan
http://orcid.org/0000-0003-1197-601X
National Institute of Technology, Rourkela, India

Bikash Panja
http://orcid.org/0000-0002-4673-7169
Swami Vivekananda University, India

Sanjiv Kumar Tiwari
http://orcid.org/0000-0003-0272-0805
Birla Institute of Technology, Mesra, India

Kaushik Kumar
http://orcid.org/0000-0002-4237-2836
Birla Institute of Technology, Mesra, India

ABSTRACT

In an increasingly digital world, Artificial Intelligence (AI) is reshaping how we live, work, and learn. Introducing AI education at an early age is crucial to prepare children not just as technology users, but as future innovators and responsible creators. This chapter highlights the importance of integrating AI into school curricula using age-appropriate methods, interactive strategies, and tools that make complex ideas accessible. It reviews global trends and successful initiatives in AI education for children, including notable case studies and curriculum models. Emphasis is placed on hands-on, no-code platforms that encourage creativity, critical thinking, and ethical understanding. The chapter also explores key implementation challenges

DOI: 10.4018/979-8-2600-2438-6.ch008

such as teacher training, curriculum design, and equitable access, while offering practical solutions for educators, policymakers, and institutions. Building foundational AI literacy in children helps nurture a future-ready generation capable of responsible innovation in an AI-driven world.

INTRODUCTION

The concept of AI education for children emerged as part of broader efforts to introduce computational thinking and coding in early education. In the 1960s and 1970s, Seymour Papert's Logo programming language was one of the first tools designed to teach children coding and problem-solving in an interactive manner. This laid the foundation for visual programming platforms that would later support AI learning (Grigenti, 2022). During the 1990s and early 2000s, platforms such as Scratch (2007) and Blockly made coding more accessible to children through drag-and-drop interfaces. While these tools initially focused on programming, they later incorporated AI-related extensions to introduce concepts such as decision-making and data handling (Kahn et al., 2021). The 2010s marked a significant shift, with the rise of AI-powered tools such as Teachable Machine, Machine Learning for Kids, and Cognimates, which allowed children to train simple AI models without advanced coding. Simultaneously, robotics kits such as LEGO Mindstorms and Arduino-based tools became popular for teaching AI and automation concepts through hands-on learning. In recent years, initiatives such as the AI4K12 framework have provided structured guidelines for integrating AI literacy into school curricula. Educational organizations, governments, and tech companies are increasingly collaborating to create resources, courses, and workshops to make AI education more inclusive and accessible to children worldwide (McCalla, 2023). Today, AI education has evolved beyond coding to include ethical discussions, real-world applications, and interdisciplinary learning, preparing children to be responsible users and creators of AI technologies. Figure 1 illustrates the chronological evolution of artificial intelligence (AI) education for children from the 1960s to the projected future of the 2030s. The infographic presents six color-coded arrows, each representing a distinct developmental phase in the history of AI-integrated learning. The timeline begins in the 1960s and 1970s with early AI-inspired learning, marked by the introduction of the LOGO programming language and constructivist teaching approaches. The 1980s highlight the emergence of intelligent tutoring systems (ITS), introducing adaptive and personalized instruction. Moving into the 1990s, computer-assisted learning and robotics (e.g., LEGO Mindstorms) encouraged hands-on experiential education. The 2000s show the rise of AI literacy initiatives such as Scratch, focusing on visual programming and automation. The 2010s emphasize generative AI and immersive technologies, such as adaptive chatbots and augmented reality/virtual reality (AR/VR) educational systems, promoting interactive and personalized learning. Finally, the 2030s (Future Direction) project the integration of emotional and neuroadaptive AI, highlighting the role of empathetic and brain–computer interface systems in fostering cognitive–emotional intelligence and lifelong adaptability in learners.

Figure 1. Evolution of AI Education for Children

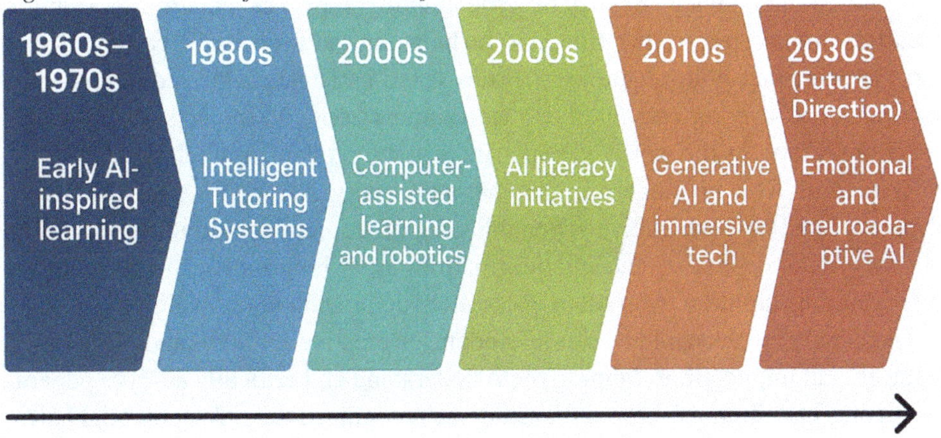

Artificial intelligence (AI) has rapidly evolved from a specialized field of computer science into a transformative force shaping every dimension of modern life, including education. In recent years, the focus has expanded beyond using AI as a tool for instruction to teaching children about AI itself, its principles, capabilities, and ethical implications. This paradigm, known as AI education for children, aims to cultivate an early understanding of intelligent systems, preparing young learners not only to use AI technologies responsibly but also to innovate and shape their development.

The foundation of AI education lies in computational thinking, data literacy, and ethical reasoning. By introducing these concepts in age-appropriate formats, children learn to analyze problems, recognize patterns, and understand how algorithms make decisions. Early exposure to AI fosters creativity, critical thinking, and adaptive learning, encouraging students to view technology not as a mystery but as a co-creative partner in problem-solving.

Globally, initiatives such as AI4K12 (USA), AI for Kids (Europe), and Teachable Machine (Google) have promoted structured frameworks for integrating AI into K–12 education. These programs emphasize hands-on experimentation, such as training simple models or interacting with intelligent robots, making abstract AI concepts tangible and engaging. Educational platforms are increasingly employing AI-driven personalization, allowing learners to progress at their own pace and receive real-time feedback tailored to their abilities.

In today's digital society, where children interact daily with AI-powered tools—from recommendation systems to conversational agents–developing AI literacy is as fundamental as reading or numeracy. Moreover, with the rise of generative and emotional AI, the emphasis is shifting from technical understanding to ethical awareness, empathy, and collaboration between humans and machines.

Artificial intelligence (AI) has become an integral part of modern life, shaping industries, transforming education, and influencing the way people communicate, work, and interact with technology. From voice assistants and recommendation systems to self-driving cars and healthcare innovations, AI impacts almost every aspect of society. As the world becomes increasingly reliant on intelligent systems, understanding AI is no longer a choice but a necessity. Ali and his team (Ali et al., 2021) explored how generative AI enables digital content creation but also raises concerns about deepfakes and misinformation. They highlighted the need for AI literacy among children, who often encounter such media unknowingly.

Their study involved middle school students in creative activities and discussions on the ethical implications, helping them understand and critically analyze generative media. The findings showed that students recognized the risks, potential harm, and the need for policies to regulate AI-generated content on social media. Reimers (Reimers, 2020) highlighted five principles that guide the development of curriculum resources to foster student empowerment and civic participation: starting with the end in mind when designing the curriculum, leveraging improvement networks for curriculum design, learning by doing, utilizing the power of problem-based education, and promoting collaboration within diverse teams. Berson and his group (Berson et al., 2025) reviewed 42 studies on AI in early childhood education, highlighting major ethical concerns around data privacy, child development, algorithmic bias, and weak regulatory frameworks. They found gaps in protecting children's data, risks from emotional AI tools, and a lack of developmentally appropriate design, which can worsen inequities. The study stressed the need for global frameworks focusing on transparency, fairness, and participatory governance to ensure ethical and equitable AI use in early learning. Golden et al. (Golden et al., 2025) explained that rapid advancements in artificial intelligence (AI) are profoundly transforming education. AI enables personalized learning, streamlines administrative tasks, and reshapes the roles of teachers and students, with future possibilities including AI research agents, learning companions, and generative AI tools. However, these opportunities also bring challenges related to equity, ethics, large-scale implementation, and the need for updated governance and policies to ensure that education benefits all learners. Thakur (Thakur, 2024) discussed how artificial intelligence (AI) has become a transformative technology that enhances business efficiency and competitiveness.

The chapter outlines the origin, evolution, types, applications, benefits, challenges, and future of AI in business management. It emphasizes the need for ethical global governance, including government-led ethical auditing and guidelines, to ensure the responsible use of AI in organizations. With proper regulation and strategy, AI can serve as a powerful tool for business growth and innovation in a competitive environment.

IMPORTANCE OF AI IN THE MODERN WORLD

The rapid proliferation of artificial intelligence across industries, communication, and everyday life underscores the urgent need to introduce AI education at the school level. As digital technologies increasingly mediate human experiences, children must not only learn with AI but also understand how intelligent systems function, make decisions, and influence society. Early AI education equips learners with the cognitive, ethical, and creative skills necessary to thrive in a future driven by automation and data intelligence. One of the primary needs for AI education is future workforce readiness. Studies indicate that over 60% of today's schoolchildren will work in jobs that do not yet exist, many of which will require AI-related competencies. Introducing AI concepts early, such as algorithms, pattern recognition, and data ethics, helps bridge the gap between current curricula and the skills demanded by Industry 4.0 and beyond. This early exposure nurtures computational thinking, logical reasoning, and problem-solving, which are transferable across disciplines. The ethical and social dimensions of AI education are equally significant. As children engage daily with AI through voice assistants, recommendation systems, and adaptive learning platforms, it is essential to foster AI literacy and digital responsibility. Educating children about algorithmic bias, data privacy, and the moral implications of automation ensures that they become conscious users and ethical creators of technology, capable of questioning and improving the systems they use. Moreover, AI education promotes inclusivity and accessibility in learning. AI-powered adaptive tools can identify individual learning patterns, adjust content difficulty, and support students with diverse abilities, ensuring equitable learning opportunities. This fosters personalized learning pathways that enhance motivation and engagement. From a developmental perspective, engaging with AI through hands-on experiments, coding platforms, or educational robotics encourages creativity, collaboration, and design thinking skills essential for innovation in science, engineering, and the arts. It transforms learners from passive consumers of technology into active co-creators of intelligent solutions.

AI powers many technologies that make everyday tasks easier and more efficient. It enables personalized recommendations on streaming platforms, provides instant answers through voice assistants, improves medical diagnoses, and supports innovations, such as autonomous vehicles and smart devices. In industries such as finance, agriculture, manufacturing, and education, AI has transformed processes, increased productivity, and created new opportunities. As AI continues to evolve, it is expected to play a major role in solving global challenges, including climate change, healthcare accessibility, and sustainable development. Therefore, understanding AI is essential for participating in and contributing to a technology-driven world. AI also plays a vital role in tackling large-scale issues such as climate change modeling, disaster management, and resource optimization. It enables faster scientific research, contributing to advancements in clean energy, environmental sustainability, and global health. By automating repetitive tasks, AI increases productivity and creates new opportunities for innovation. However, it also reshapes the job market by changing the nature of work and creating demand for new skill sets. Countries investing in AI are experiencing significant growth in competitiveness and technological leadership. As AI becomes more integrated into everyday life, understanding its principles, applications, and implications is crucial. AI literacy ensures that individuals are not only passive users but informed participants who can adapt to future developments, use AI responsibly, and make ethical decisions in a rapidly evolving digital world (Patel et al., 2024).

WHY AI LITERACY IS ESSENTIAL FOR CHILDREN

In the 21st century, artificial intelligence (AI) literacy has become a fundamental skill, comparable in importance to reading, writing, and numeracy. As AI increasingly shapes the way we learn, communicate, and make decisions, children must develop an informed understanding of how these systems operate, their capabilities, and their limitations. AI literacy empowers young learners not only to use AI tools but also to think critically, act ethically, and innovate responsibly in a world where intelligent systems are ever-present.

AI literacy is essential for several key reasons.

- **Early Understanding of the Digital World:** Children interact with AI daily, whether through voice assistants, recommendation algorithms, or adaptive learning apps, often without realizing it. Teaching children about AI demystifies these technologies and helps them understand the logic behind machine decisions and the influence of data in shaping outcomes.
- **Foundation for Future Careers:** As AI and automation transform industries, tomorrow's workforce will demand strong skills in data analysis, algorithmic thinking, and problem-solving. Introducing AI concepts at an early

age ensures that children are prepared for emerging fields such as robotics, data science, healthcare technology, and smart manufacturing.

- **Fostering Critical Thinking and Creativity:** AI education encourages children to question how machines learn, recognize patterns, and make choices. By experimenting with coding, robotics, and model training, learners can enhance their creative reasoning and analytical abilities by blending scientific curiosity with innovation.
- **Building Ethical Awareness:** Understanding AI's societal implications, such as bias, privacy, and fairness, helps children become ethically aware digital citizens. Teaching children to recognize bias in algorithms or the misuse of data builds moral responsibility and empathy in the age of automation.
- **Empowering Informed Decision-Making:** As AI systems influence opinions, purchases, and even education pathways, AI-literate children can evaluate information critically rather than passively accepting automated outcomes. This promotes independence, discernment, and accountability in digital interactions.
- **Promoting Inclusive and Personalized Learning:** AI-powered educational tools adapt to individual learning speeds and styles, allowing children to experience personalized and equitable education. Understanding how these systems function enables students to take ownership of their learning processes and advocate for fairness in AI-driven education.

Children are growing up in a digital era in which AI-powered tools are a part of their daily lives. Early AI education ensures that they are not merely passive consumers of technology but active creators and informed users. By understanding how AI works, children can develop problem-solving, creativity, and computational thinking skills that are vital for future careers. Moreover, AI literacy empowers children to recognize the ethical implications of technology, such as data privacy, bias, and fairness. It helps them become responsible digital citizens who can use AI for positive change rather than misuse it. Presently, artificial intelligence is becoming a part of children's everyday lives through smart toys, voice assistants, educational applications, and social media platforms. As they grow up in a world shaped by AI, understanding its basic principles and implications is crucial for their personal development and future opportunities (Sheikh, 2021).

PREPARING FOR A TECHNOLOGY-DRIVEN FUTURE

The world is rapidly evolving with advancements in artificial intelligence (AI), automation, and digital technologies. Future careers across almost every industry, including healthcare, education, business, agriculture, transportation, and entertainment, will require knowledge of AI and related technologies (Holmes, 2020). Early AI literacy helps children develop computational thinking, problem-solving, creativity, and adaptability, which are essential skills for the jobs of tomorrow. By learning how AI works and how it is applied, children gain the ability to design solutions, analyze data, and use technology to innovate.

As AI continues to reshape industries, many existing jobs will be automated, while new job roles will emerge that require expertise in AI, machine learning, robotics, and data science. Teaching AI concepts at an early age ensures that children are not merely technology users but future-ready creators, innovators, and leaders who can thrive in a competitive, technology-driven world (Knox et al., 2019).

Encouraging Creativity and Innovation

AI literacy fosters creativity by helping children shift from passive consumers of technology to active creators. When children understand how AI works, they can explore its potential to solve real-world problems, design interactive projects, and invent new applications using AI tools (Kamalov et al., 2023).

Through hands-on experiences, such as building chatbots, training simple machine learning models, or using AI-powered platforms like Scratch with AI extensions, children learn to combine logic with imagination. This integration of technical skills and creative thinking enables them to develop original ideas, enhance storytelling, and experiment with innovative solutions. Moreover, AI-based learning environments often promote curiosity, exploration, and iterative learning, which are key drivers of innovation. Encouraging children to create with AI not only nurtures inventive thinking but also builds confidence in using technology as a powerful tool for expression, problem-solving, and future entrepreneurship (Lytvynova et al., 2024).

Promoting Critical Thinking

AI literacy helps children develop critical thinking by encouraging them to question how intelligent systems work, where information comes from, and whether the outputs are reliable. As AI tools generate text, images, and recommendations, it becomes essential for children to analyze and evaluate such content rather than accept it at face value (Carella et al., 2024). By engaging in activities such as identifying deepfakes, understanding algorithmic bias, or exploring how AI makes decisions, children learn to think logically and assess the credibility of AI-generated information. They begin to recognize that AI systems can be limited, biased, or even misleading, fostering skepticism and informed judgment (Goralski et al., 2020). This critical perspective equips children to use technology responsibly, make better decisions, and navigate the digital world with the awareness skills that are vital for becoming informed citizens in a society increasingly influenced by AI.

Developing Ethical Awareness

AI literacy involves not only understanding how technology works but also recognizing the ethical issues associated with its use. As AI becomes more integrated into daily life, children must learn about privacy, fairness, transparency, and accountability in AI systems. Teaching ethical awareness helps children understand that AI can be biased, invade privacy, or be misused to spread misinformation. Through discussions and examples, children can explore questions such as: Is it fair for an AI system to make decisions about people? How should personal data be protected? Who is responsible when AI makes a mistake? By addressing these concerns early, children develop a sense of responsibility in using and creating AI tools. This understanding ensures that they grow up as responsible digital citizens who value fairness, respect privacy, and support the ethical use of technology to benefit society.

Building Digital Citizenship

Building digital citizenship through AI literacy ensures that children become responsible, informed, and ethical users of technology. As AI influences social media, communication, and information sharing, children must understand how to interact safely and respectfully in digital environments. Digital citizenship involves teaching children about online privacy, data protection, responsible sharing, and the impact of AI-generated content on society. It also encourages them to critically evaluate online information, avoid misinformation, and respect others' rights in digital spaces. By learning these principles early, children gain the ability to use AI tools thoughtfully, make informed decisions online, and contribute positively to digital communities. This foundation prepares them to be active, responsible participants in a technology-driven society while using AI for constructive and ethical purposes.

GOALS OF AI EDUCATION AT AN EARLY AGE

AI education for children aims to build the knowledge, skills, and values necessary to navigate and contribute to an AI-driven world responsibly. The main goals include:

Building Foundational Skills

Building foundational skills is the first step in AI education for children, as it equips them with the basic knowledge required to understand how intelligent systems work. These skills include computational thinking, logical reasoning, pattern recognition, and problem-solving, which form the basis for learning AI concepts. Through interactive activities such as coding games, puzzles, and block-based programming tools (e.g., Scratch or Blockly), children learn how algorithms process information and how data can be used to make decisions. These early experiences help them understand concepts such as inputs, outputs, and step-by-step instructions, which are essential for AI systems. By developing these fundamental skills, children gain the confidence to explore advanced technologies in the future. It also encourages curiosity and prepares them to transition from being passive technology users to active creators and innovators.

Encouraging Creativity and Innovation

Encouraging creativity and innovation is a key goal of AI education at an early age. When children understand the basics of AI, they can use it as a tool to express ideas, design unique projects, and solve real-world problems. AI-based activities, such as creating chatbots, training simple models to recognize images or sounds, or designing AI-powered games, help children combine imagination with technical knowledge. Hands-on learning experiences stimulate curiosity and allow children to experiment, make mistakes, and improve their ideas. This process builds resilience, problem-solving ability, and confidence in using technology for innovation. By nurturing creativity through AI education, children develop an inventive mindset that prepares them for future opportunities in which designing and improving technology will be as important as using it.

Promoting Critical Thinking

Promoting critical thinking in AI education helps children question, analyze, and evaluate the information and decisions made by AI systems. As AI-generated content becomes more common, it is essential for children to understand that not all AI outputs are accurate, fair, or unbiased. Through practical activities such as identifying deepfakes, exploring how algorithms make recommendations, or discussing examples of biased AI, children learn to think logically and make informed judgments. They begin to understand the limitations of AI and recognize when it may produce misleading or harmful results. By developing these skills early, children become cautious and thoughtful users of technology, able to analyze information critically, solve problems effectively, and make responsible decisions in a digital world shaped by AI.

Developing Ethical Awareness

Developing ethical awareness is a vital part of AI education, as it teaches children to understand the moral responsibilities that come with using and creating AI technologies. AI systems can be biased, invade privacy, or be misused to spread misinformation, making it important for children to learn about fairness, transparency, accountability, and data protection. Through discussions, real-life examples, and simple case studies, children can explore questions such as: Who is responsible for an AI's decision? Is it fair if an AI system is biased? How should personal data be protected? These conversations help them recognize the social impact of AI and the importance of using it responsibly.

By fostering ethical awareness early, children grow up as responsible digital citizens who value fairness, respect privacy, and support ethical development and the use of technology to benefit society.

PREPARING FOR THE FUTURE

Preparing children for the future is one of the key goals of AI education. As AI continues to transform industries such as healthcare, education, transportation, and business, future careers will require strong digital literacy and problem-solving abilities. Introducing AI concepts at an early age equips children with computational thinking, creativity, adaptability, and logical reasoning, which are essential for succeeding in a technology-driven world. By learning how AI works and exploring its applications, children gain confidence to move beyond being just technology users to becoming creators, innovators, and leaders. This early exposure ensures that they are ready to face the challenges and opportunities of an AI-powered future, enabling them to contribute meaningfully to society and thrive in a rapidly evolving global economy (Joseph et al., 2024).

Building Digital Citizenship

Building digital citizenship through AI education ensures that children learn to use technology safely, responsibly, and ethically. As they interact with AI-powered tools on social media, educational platforms, and entertainment apps, it is crucial that they understand their rights and responsibilities in the digital world. AI education helps children grasp key aspects of digital citizenship, including data privacy, respectful online behavior, recognition of misinformation, and understanding the influence of AI algorithms on the content they see. It encourages them to think critically about how they share information, engage with others, and use digital tools. By instilling these values early, children grow into thoughtful and informed digital citizens who contribute positively to online communities and use AI in fair, safe, and socially responsible ways.

IMPORTANCE OF AI EDUCATION FOR CHILDREN

AI education for children is essential because it prepares them to live and work in a world where artificial intelligence is deeply integrated into everyday life. Early exposure to AI concepts helps children understand how intelligent systems work, develop problem-solving and logical reasoning skills, and become active creators of technology rather than mere users. By learning AI, children gain creativity, innovation, and critical thinking abilities, enabling them to design projects, explore new ideas, and evaluate AI-generated information responsibly. It also helps them recognize ethical issues, such as privacy, bias, and fairness, fostering responsible and informed digital citizenship. As AI continues to transform industries and careers, early AI literacy ensures that children are future-ready, equipped with the skills required to adapt to emerging technologies, pursue new opportunities, and contribute positively to society.

Technological Literacy

Technological literacy refers to the ability to use, understand, and evaluate technology effectively in everyday life. For children, developing technological literacy means gaining knowledge about how digital devices and systems work, understanding their applications, and being able to interact confidently and responsibly. In the context of AI education, technological literacy involves basic coding skills, understanding algorithms, recognizing how AI makes decisions, and understanding the benefits and limitations of technology. It also includes awareness of ethical issues, such as privacy, security, and digital responsibility. By building technological literacy at an early age, children become better equipped to adapt to new technologies, solve real-world problems, and actively participate in a rapidly changing digital society rather than being passive consumers of technology (Chen et al., 2020).

Critical Thinking

Critical thinking is the ability to analyze information, evaluate evidence, and make reasoned decisions. In AI education, it helps children question how AI systems work, understand their limitations, and assess the accuracy and fairness of AI-generated outcomes. By engaging in activities such as identifying biased outputs, exploring how AI makes predictions, or comparing human and AI decision-making, children learn to think logically and independently. They begin to understand that AI is not always correct or neutral and that its outputs must be carefully examined. Developing critical thinking skills ensures that children become informed and responsible technology users capable of making thoughtful decisions in a world where AI influences many aspects of life.

Creativity and Innovation

Creativity and innovation are key skills fostered through AI education, enabling children to move from using technology to designing and improving it. By learning how AI works, children can combine logical thinking with imagination to create new solutions, applications, or projects. Hands-on activities, such as building chatbots, designing AI-powered games, or training simple models, encourage experimentation and problem-solving. These experiences help children see technology as a tool for expressing ideas and addressing real-world challenges. Nurturing creativity and innovation at an early age prepares children to become future innovators and leaders, capable of developing original ideas and contributing to technological advancements in a rapidly changing world.

Future Career Opportunities

AI is transforming industries such as healthcare, education, finance, agriculture, transportation, and manufacturing, creating new roles that require advanced digital and analytical skills. Many future careers will involve working with AI systems, data analysis, machine learning, and automation technologies. Introducing AI education at an early age prepares children with computational thinking, problem-solving, creativity, and adaptability, which are essential for these emerging job markets. By understanding how AI works and applying it to real-world problems, children can explore potential career paths as developers, researchers, engineers, data scientists, or AI ethicists. Early AI literacy ensures that children are future-ready, capable of seizing opportunities in a technology-driven economy, and contributing meaningfully to innovation and societal growth.

AGE-APPROPRIATE AI LEARNING

Age-appropriate AI learning ensures that concepts of AI are introduced to children in ways suitable for their cognitive abilities and developmental stages. It focuses on gradually building understanding, from simple ideas about patterns and decision-making to more advanced concepts, such as algorithms and machine learning (Lim et al., 2023).

Early Childhood (Ages 4–7)

At this stage, children learn best through play, exploration, and visual experiences. AI education for early childhood should focus on the basic concepts of patterns, sequencing, and cause-and-effect relationships rather than technical details.

- **Learning Approach:** Storytelling, games, and hands-on activities that demonstrate how instructions lead to specific outcomes.
- **Tools:** Interactive toys, unplugged coding games, and simple apps that teach logic through drag-and-drop actions.
- **Key skills developed:** pattern recognition, logical thinking, problem-solving, and curiosity about how technology works.

This early exposure builds a foundation for computational thinking, helping children gradually understand that machines follow instructions and can "learn" from data in very simple ways.

Primary Level (Ages 8–10)

At this stage, children can begin to understand basic computing and problem-solving concepts in a more structured way. AI education should focus on introducing simple coding, algorithms, and decision-making processes through interactive and visual tools.

Learning Approach: Hands-on activities, coding games, and guided projects that demonstrate how instructions create outcomes.

Tools: Platforms such as Scratch, Blockly, Code.org, and AI-enabled educational apps that allow children to create simple stories, animations, or games.

Key skills developed: logical reasoning, step-by-step thinking, creativity, and an initial understanding of how data and instructions guide AI behavior.

These experiences help children connect technology with real-world problem solving, preparing them for more advanced AI concepts in later stages.

Middle School (Ages 11–13)

At this stage, children are ready to explore the practical applications of AI and understand how machines can learn from data. They can work on simple projects that demonstrate real-world AI concepts.

- **Learning Approach:** Project-based learning, including building chatbots, image- or voice-recognition models, and exploring AI tools for creative purposes.
- **Tools:** Teachable Machine, Scratch with AI extensions, basic Python coding for AI, and beginner-friendly robotics kits.
- **Key skills developed:** problem-solving, basic programming, understanding how data is used for predictions, and developing critical thinking about AI-generated outputs.

This stage emphasizes hands-on experiences and ethical discussions to help children become aware of both the potential and limitations of AI technologies.

High School (Ages 14+)

At this stage, students can engage with advanced AI concepts and real-world applications, preparing them for future studies or technological careers. They are capable of understanding the fundamentals of machine learning, data analysis, and ethical issues related to AI use.

- **Learning Approach:** Project-based learning, coding in Python or other languages, experimenting with datasets, and exploring AI applications in fields such as healthcare, robotics, and business.
- **Tools:** Python with libraries such as TensorFlow or scikit-learn, AI-based platforms, Arduino/robotics kits, and online AI courses.
- **Key skills developed:** programming, data handling, algorithmic thinking, ethical reasoning, and innovation through AI-based projects.

This stage emphasizes both technical proficiency and ethical responsibility, helping students become informed users and potential creators of AI technology.

TOOLS AND RESOURCES FOR AI LEARNING

Effective AI education requires age-appropriate tools and resources to make learning interactive, engaging, and practical. These tools help children understand AI concepts through hands-on experiences, coding activities, and creative projects.

Unplugged Activities

Unplugged activities are hands-on learning methods that teach AI and coding concepts without the use of computers or digital devices. They include coding games, puzzles, sequence cards, and pattern recognition tasks that help children understand logic and step-by-step instructions. Storytelling and role-playing can also be used to demonstrate how algorithms and decision-making work in real-life situations. These activities make abstract concepts simple and engaging, allowing children to develop problem-solving, logical thinking, and creativity in a fun, interactive way (Sousa et al., 2024).

Visual Coding Platforms

Visual coding platforms allow children to learn programming using drag-and-drop blocks instead of text-based code. Tools such as Scratch, Blockly, and Code.org enable children to create animations, games, and stories interactively. MIT App Inventor helps beginners design simple mobile applications through a visual interface. These platforms make coding easy, engaging, and accessible for young learners while building logical thinking and creativity (Soo-Siang & Sonia, 2019).

AI-Specific Tools

AI-specific tools help children understand and experiment with AI concepts in a practical way. The Teachable Machine (by Google) allows children to train simple models for image, sound, and pose recognition. Cognimates introduces children to creating chatbots and training AI models, whereas Machine Learning for Kids combines basic coding with machine learning projects. These tools make learning about AI interactive and fun, encouraging creativity and hands-on exploration (Zhang & Aslan, 2021).

Robotics Kits

Robotics kits provide hands-on experience in building and programming robots, helping children understand coding and AI concepts in a practical way. LEGO Mindstorms, LEGO Spike Prime, and Arduino kits allow students to create and program customizable robots. Sphero and Dash & Dot are interactive robots designed for younger learners to explore coding through fun activities. These kits make learning engaging while fostering problem-solving, creativity, and interest in technology.

Online Resources and Courses

Online resources and courses provide accessible ways for children to learn AI and coding concepts from anywhere. Code.org 'sAI & Machine Learning courses offer beginner-friendly lessons on AI basics through interactive activities. The AI4K12 Initiative provides guidelines and curricula to help educators teach AI literacy effectively at different grade levels. These resources support self-paced learning and help children build a strong foundation in AI concepts (Nurhayati et al., 2025).

TEACHING STRATEGIES

Effective AI education for children requires strategies that make learning interactive, engaging, and age-appropriate, while promoting creativity and critical thinking. Some key teaching strategies include the following:

Hands-On Learning

Hands-on learning involves teaching AI concepts through practical activities, experiments, and real-world projects. Instead of simply reading or listening, children actively participate in tasks such as building simple models, coding games, or training AI tools. This approach makes learning engaging and interactive, helping students understand how AI works by applying concepts in practice. It encourages problem-solving, creativity, and critical thinking, allowing children to explore technology in a meaningful and fun way while building confidence in their skills (Guan et al., 2020).

Gamified Learning

Gamified learning uses game-like elements, such as points, badges, levels, and challenges, to make AI education engaging and motivating for children. By turning lessons into interactive games or competitions, students stay interested while learning important concepts such as coding, algorithms, and problem-solving. Platforms such as Code.org, Scratch, and Blockly often include gamified tasks in which children complete missions or unlock rewards as they progress. This approach makes learning fun, improves participation, and encourages students to experiment, explore, and achieve goals while gaining essential AI and programming skills.

Project-Based Approach

Project-based learning focuses on teaching AI concepts through real-world projects in which children create solutions using technology. Instead of studying theory alone, students work on tasks such as building chatbots, training simple AI models, and designing AI-powered games.

This approach encourages problem-solving, creativity, teamwork, and critical thinking as children learn by applying their knowledge to meaningful activities. By observing the results of their work, they gain confidence and better understand how AI can be used to address real-life challenges.

Storytelling and Role-Play

Storytelling and role-playing make AI concepts easier for children to understand by explaining them through relatable stories or interactive scenarios. For example, a story can show how a robot follows instructions, whereas role-playing can allow students to act as "AI, " making decisions based on given rules. This approach helps children grasp abstract ideas, such as algorithms, decision-making, and data usage, in a fun and engaging way. It also builds communication, creativity, and empathy, making AI learning more interactive and memorable.

Collaborative Learning

Collaborative learning involves students working together in pairs or groups to explore AI concepts, solve problems, and create projects. By sharing ideas and dividing tasks, children develop teamwork, communication, and problem-solving skills while learning from one another. Activities such as group coding challenges, AI-based projects, and discussions on ethical issues encourage students to think critically and respect different perspectives. This approach not only makes learning more engaging but also helps students build confidence and a sense of responsibility while working as a team.

ETHICAL AND RESPONSIBLE AI USE

Ethical and responsible AI use entails understanding that while AI can simplify and enhance life, it also raises concerns related to privacy, bias, fairness, and accountability. Teaching children these aspects ensures that they recognize both the benefits and risks of AI technologies. AI systems can sometimes make biased decisions if they are trained on unfair or incomplete data. For example, a face recognition system may not work equally well for all people if the dataset lacks diversity. Similarly, AI tools can collect personal data, raising privacy concerns if the data are misused.

Children should be taught to ask important questions, such as the following:

- Is an AI decision fair to everyone?
- What data are being collected, and is it safe to share?
- Who is responsible if an AI makes a mistake?

By using real-life examples, such as deepfakes, AI in social media, and recommendation algorithms, students can understand the social impact of AI decisions. Including ethical discussions in AI education helps them learn the importance of transparency, accountability, and respect for privacy. Developing this awareness early ensures that children grow up to be responsible digital citizens, using AI thoughtfully, making ethical choices, and supporting the development of technologies that are inclusive, fair, and beneficial to society. It is essential to educate children about fairness, transparency, and the social impact of AI. Discuss real-world examples of AI bias and promote responsible technology use.

ROLE OF PARENTS AND EDUCATORS

Parents and educators play a crucial role in helping children understand and use AI responsibly. They act as guides to ensure that children not only learn technical skills but also develop the right values, ethics, and critical thinking about AI technologies.

Creating Awareness

Raising awareness is the first step in helping children understand AI and its impact on daily life. Parents and educators should introduce AI concepts in simple, relatable ways using examples such as voice assistants, chatbots, and recommendation systems on streaming platforms.

Using stories, games, and real-life examples, adults can explain how AI helps in various tasks and why it is important to learn about it. Awareness also includes discussing both the benefits and risks of AI, such as privacy concerns, misinformation, and bias in decision-making.

By making children aware of how AI works and where it is used, they develop curiosity, interest, and a basic understanding of technology, preparing them to explore it more deeply in later stages.

Encouraging Curiosity and Exploration

Encouraging curiosity and exploration helps children actively engage with AI concepts instead of simply learning theory. Parents and educators can create an environment in which children ask questions, try new tools, and experiment with technology to understand how AI works.

Hands-on activities such as coding games, building simple robots, or training AI models using beginner-friendly tools like Teachable Machine make learning interactive and exciting. Project-based tasks, in which children create stories, games, or chatbots, further promote problem-solving and creative thinking. Allowing children to explore AI applications in everyday life, such as voice assistants or recommendation systems, sparks interest and helps them relate technology to real-world uses. Providing guidance while giving them the freedom to experiment builds confidence, innovation, and a deeper understanding of AI concepts. This approach ensures that children see AI as a tool for creation and innovation, motivating them to learn more and develop skills for future opportunities.

Teaching Ethics and Responsibility

Teaching ethics and responsibility ensures that children understand the moral aspects of using AI. Parents and educators should help children recognize that while AI offers many benefits, it can also raise issues, such as privacy violations, misinformation, and unfair bias, if not used carefully. Through real-life examples, such as biased AI decisions or the misuse of deepfakes, children can learn why fairness, transparency, and accountability are important in technology. Discussions should include questions such as" Who is responsible if AI makes a wrong decision? and Is it safe to share personal data with AI systems? Educators can include simple activities where students analyze AI outputs, discuss whether they are fair, and think about ways to improve them. Parents can guide children in making safe and thoughtful choices online, such as protecting personal information and questioning the reliability of AI-generated content. By teaching these values early, children become responsible digital citizens who use AI in ways that are ethical, safe, and beneficial for society.

Monitoring and Guiding AI Use

Monitoring and guiding AI use is essential to ensure that children interact with technology safely and responsibly. Parents and educators should supervise the AI-powered tools, apps, and platforms that children use, ensuring that the content is age-appropriate and secure. Parents can set boundaries on screen time, check privacy settings, and explain the importance of not sharing personal information with AI-based applications. Educators can guide students on how to critically evaluate AI-generated information and avoid misinformation. By providing proper guidance while allowing exploration, adults help children develop healthy digital habits, understand the benefits and risks of AI, and use technology as a tool for learning and creativity rather than just entertainment. This combined approach ensures that children gain confidence in using AI responsibly while staying safe and informed in the digital world.

Supporting Future Skills Development

Supporting future skills development ensures that children are prepared for a world in which AI and technology will play a central role in careers and daily life. Parents and educators should focus on building problem-solving, creativity, critical thinking, collaboration, and computational skills from an early age. Providing access to coding platforms, robotics kits, and AI-based tools helps children gain hands-on experience with technology. Encouraging participation in projects, competitions, and group activities fosters teamwork, innovation, and confidence in applying AI concepts. Guidance should also include discussions about real-world applications of AI in industries such as healthcare, education, and business, helping children connect learning to future opportunities. By nurturing these skills, children are better equipped to adapt to technological changes, explore new career paths, and become active contributors to innovation in the future workforce. Both parents and teachers should encourage children to develop skills such as problem-solving, creativity, teamwork, and computational thinking, which are essential for future careers in a technology-driven world. By working together, parents and educators can create a balanced environment in which children not only learn about AI but also understand its ethical implications, becoming responsible and informed digital citizens (Pedro et al., 2019).

CHALLENGES AND SOLUTIONS

Teaching AI to children presents several challenges; however, each can be addressed with practical solutions.

Limited Access to Resources

Challenge:

Many schools and families, especially those in rural or underprivileged areas, may lack access to devices, Internet connectivity, or AI learning tools. This creates a barrier to providing quality AI education to all children.

Solution:

Teachers and parents can use free or low-cost platforms such as Scratch, Code.org, and Teachable Machine that work on basic devices. Unplugged activities, such as coding games, puzzles, and role-playing, can also teach AI and coding concepts without advanced technology. Community programs, libraries, and shared resources can further help bridge this gap.

Lack of Trained Educators

Challenge:

Many teachers may not have the necessary skills, knowledge, or confidence to teach AI concepts because AI is a relatively new subject in most school curricula.

Solution:

Providing professional development programs, online training courses, workshops, and AI teaching toolkits can help educators gain the required knowledge. Collaboration with experts, use of pre-designed lesson plans, and continuous learning opportunities ensure that teachers can confidently introduce AI concepts to students in an engaging and age-appropriate manner.

Complexity of AI Concepts

Challenge:

AI concepts, such as algorithms, machine learning, and data processing, can be too abstract or technical for young learners to easily understand.

Solution:

Introduce AI through age-appropriate, hands-on, and visual methods such as games, stories, coding puzzles, and drag-and-drop platforms like Scratch or Blockly. Using real-life examples, such as how a voice assistant answers questions or how a chatbot works, makes AI concepts more relatable and easier for children to grasp.

Ethical Concerns and Misinformation

Challenge:

Children may use AI tools without understanding their ethical implications, leading to issues such as privacy violations, the spread of misinformation, and exposure to biased AI outputs.

Solution:

Teachers and parents should include discussions on ethics, online safety, and responsible AI use as part of AI education. Real-life examples, such as deepfakes, biased recommendations, and the misuse of personal data, can help children understand fairness, accountability, and the importance of verifying information before sharing it.

Unequal Opportunities and Digital Divide

Challenge:

Students in rural or underprivileged areas often have limited access to devices, the Internet, and AI learning programs, resulting in fewer opportunities to gain AI literacy compared to urban students.

Solution:

Governments, NGOs, and educational institutions can organize community learning programs, provide shared digital resources, and conduct low-cost AI literacy workshops. Initiatives such as mobile tech labs, free online courses, and public-private partnerships can help bridge the gap and ensure that AI education is accessible and inclusive for all children.

CASE STUDIES

Case Study 1: Introducing AI through Teachable Machine in Middle School

With the growing emphasis on AI literacy, middle schools have begun to integrate interactive platforms that simplify AI concepts for young learners. Google's Teachable Machine offers an accessible way for students to understand how machines can learn from data. This web-based tool allows children to train simple image, sound, or pose recognition models without any prior coding experience, making it ideal for introducing the fundamentals of machine learning (ML) and pattern recognition.

Objective

The goal of this case study was to introduce basic AI principles data collection, training, testing, and prediction to middle school students (ages 12–14) using Teachable Machine. The activity aimed to:

- Build curiosity about how AI systems "learn" from examples.
- Understand how data quality affects model accuracy.
- Promote teamwork, critical thinking, and ethical reflection on AI applications.

Methodology

A total of **60 students** from a middle school were divided into small groups and guided through a three-day AI learning module.

- **Day 1:** Introduction to artificial intelligence and machine learning using interactive discussions and visual examples.
- **Day 2:** Hands-on training using Teachable Machine. Each group selected a project theme (e.g., recognizing facial expressions, differentiating objects,

or classifying sounds). The students captured the datasets using webcams or microphones and then trained and tested their models.

- **Day 3:** Reflection and presentation. The students analyzed their model accuracy, discussed errors, and explored ethical considerations, such as data bias and privacy.

Results and Observations

- **Engagement:** Over **90% of the students** reported a high level of interest and motivation throughout the project.
- **Conceptual Understanding:** Students successfully articulated core AI concepts like "training data," "prediction," and "bias."
- **Creativity:** Projects ranged from *emotion recognition games* to *sound-based command models*, demonstrating strong innovation and contextual relevance.
- **Ethical Awareness:** Discussions revealed increased awareness of how data selection can influence model behavior and fairness.

Challenges Identified

- Limited access to high-quality devices affected the consistency of data collection.
- Some students initially struggled to understand why the model made incorrect predictions, indicating the need for guided conceptual reinforcement.

Outcome

This hands-on approach demonstrated that AI can be effectively introduced at the middle school level through experiential learning. Students not only learned the mechanics of training AI models but also developed ethical awareness and data literacy. The activity bridged the gap between theoretical learning and real-world application, making abstract AI concepts tangible and engaging.

Case Study 2: Coding and AI Integration with Scratch

As artificial intelligence (AI) becomes integral to modern education, introducing children to coding platforms that integrate AI principles provides a foundation for logical reasoning and creative exploration. Scratch, developed by the MIT Media Lab, is a block-based visual programming language designed for children aged 8–16 years. It allows learners to create stories, games, and animations through a drag-and-drop interface. Recent extensions such as Scratch X and AI-enhanced plugins (e.g., "Machine Learning for Kids") have made it possible to blend coding with basic AI learning, enabling students to design projects that interact with data, recognize patterns, or respond to user input intelligently.

Objective

This case study aimed to introduce students to the fundamental link between coding and Artificial Intelligence using Scratch. The objectives were to:

- Foster computational thinking and creativity through visual programming
- Demonstrate how AI concepts (e.g., classification, prediction, and response) can be implemented using simple code blocks.
- Encourage students to design AI-inspired projects that reflect real-world problems

Methodology

A cohort of 75 students (grades 6–8) participated in a six-day AI-integrated coding workshop.

- **Days 1–2:** Introduction to Scratch and core programming concepts, such as loops, conditionals, and events.
- **Days 3–4:** Integration of AI components using Machine Learning for Kids, where students trained simple image and text models (e.g., recognizing hand gestures, classifying emojis, or sorting positive/negative phrases).
- **Days 5–6:** Students developed and presented AI-powered projects combining Scratch logic with machine learning models; examples included *emotion-based games*, *voice command storyboards*, and *AI quiz bots*.

Results and Observations

- **Skill Development:** Over 85% of the students demonstrated improved problem-solving and algorithmic reasoning skills.
- **Conceptual Clarity:** Students successfully related coding functions to AI concepts, such as input–output learning, training data, and response prediction.
- **Creativity and Ownership:** The learners showcased strong creativity by designing original, context-driven AI projects, linking technology with personal interests.

- **Ethical Awareness:** Class discussions led to meaningful reflections on data fairness, privacy, and the responsibility of coding for good.

Challenges Identified

- Some students found connecting external machine learning tools (e.g., Teachable Machine or ML for Kids) technically challenging because of device compatibility issues.
- The concept of "model accuracy" requires simplified analogies for full comprehension.

Outcome

The integration of AI and coding via Scratch proved to be an effective, age-appropriate entry point for understanding intelligent systems. Students learned not only to code but also to train and apply simple AI models, bridging abstract AI concepts with tangible, interactive experiences. Teachers reported enhanced engagement and deeper learning retention compared to traditional coding sessions.

Case Study 3: Robotics and AI for Hands-On Learning

The integration of robotics and artificial intelligence (AI) in early education has revolutionized how students engage with science, technology, engineering, and mathematics (STEM). Robotics platforms such as LEGO Mindstorms, VEX Robotics, Cozmo, and Makeblock mBot combine physical interaction with AI-driven programming, providing children with tangible experiences that illustrate abstract computational principles. These tools enable students to build, code, and interact with intelligent systems, fostering an early understanding of automation, sensors, perception, and decision-making, which are core to AI.

Objective

The objective of this case study was to explore how hands-on robotics projects could enhance children's comprehension of AI concepts while promoting creativity, teamwork, and problem-solving skills. The specific aims were as follows:

- The role of AI in real-world problem-solving through robotics
- Promote experiential learning and design thinking.
- Develop communication, collaboration, and ethical reasoning among students.

Methodology

A four-week robotics and AI workshop was conducted for 50 students (grades 7–9) at a STEM-focused middle school. The program followed a project-based learning (PBL) model:

- **Week 1:** Introduction to robotics, components, and AI fundamentals; students learned about sensors, actuators, and data-based decision-making.
- **Week 2:** Hands-on assembly and coding of robots using LEGO Mindstorms EV3 and VEX IQ kits.
- **Week 3:** The students integrated AI behavior and programmed robots to follow lines, recognize colors, avoid obstacles, and respond to voice commands using AI modules.
- **Week 4:** The students designed AI-driven robots for specific applications (e.g., waste-sorting bots, smart traffic vehicles, and robotic pets) in group projects.

Results and Observations

- **Engagement and Motivation:** Ninety-five percent of the participants reported increased enthusiasm for science and engineering activities.
- **Conceptual Understanding:** Students demonstrated an improved understanding of AI principles, such as *sensor data processing, feedback loops,* and *machine learning-based behavior modification.*
- **Collaboration and Communication:** Group projects encourage teamwork and interdisciplinary thinking, integrating physics, mathematics, and computer science concepts.
- **Creativity and Innovation:** Students designed unique AI-enabled robots, some capable of detecting light intensity, following paths autonomously, or responding to human gestures.
- **Ethical Reflection:** Classroom discussions on robot responsibility and human–AI interaction nurtured ethical awareness regarding automation's societal impact.

Challenges Identified

- Technical issues, such as software calibration and hardware limitations, occasionally slowed progress.
- Some younger students required additional support in connecting coding logic to the behavior of physical robots.

Outcome

The robotics-based approach to AI education proved highly effective in transforming abstract AI concepts into tangible, experiential learning. Students developed both technical proficiency and soft skills, such as problem-solving, collaboration, and innovation. Teachers observed that robotics fostered long-term interest in STEM fields, with students showing sustained curiosity beyond the classroom.

Case Study 4: AI Ethics Workshop for Teenagers

As artificial intelligence becomes increasingly embedded in daily life, powering social media, digital assistants, and decision-making systems, it is critical for young people to understand not only how AI works but also its ethical and societal implications. Teenagers, in particular, are frequent users of AI-driven platforms that influence their opinions, choices, and privacy. The AI Ethics Workshop was designed to equip students with the skills to think critically about issues such as algorithmic bias, data privacy, misinformation, and responsible AI use.

Objective

The main goal of the workshop was to develop AI literacy with an ethical focus, enabling teenagers to reflect on the moral, social, and environmental impact of AI technologies. The specific objectives were as follows:

- Promote critical discussions on fairness, accountability, transparency, and privacy in AI.
- Cultivating empathy and ethical reasoning in technology use and design
- Enable students to identify real-world ethical dilemmas involving AI and propose solutions.

Methodology

A three-day AI Ethics Workshop was conducted for 80 students (ages 14–17) from different schools as part of an interdisciplinary summer program. The workshop blended interactive learning, debates, and creative problem-solving activities.

- **Day 1: Understanding AI and Its Influence**
    - o Interactive lecture on AI systems in daily life (social media algorithms, facial recognition, and chatbots).

- Group activity: "Spot the AI" – students identified examples of AI in everyday technologies.
- **Day 2: Exploring Ethical Challenges**
  - Case discussions on algorithmic bias (e.g., biased hiring systems and facial recognition errors).
  - Role-playing activity: "Who is Responsible?" – groups debated accountability in AI-driven decisions.
  - Reflection on privacy, misinformation, and data misuse on digital platforms.
- **Day 3: Designing Ethical AI Solutions**
  - The students formed teams to design an "Ethical AI Charter" for a fictional company developing a new application.
  - The presentations included ideas related to transparency, consent, data protection, and inclusivity.
  - Concluding seminar on UNESCO and IEEE AI ethics principles

Results and Observations

- **Awareness and Understanding:** Over 90% of the participants demonstrated improved understanding of ethical principles, such as fairness, transparency, and accountability in AI.
- **Critical Thinking:** Students actively questioned real-world AI practices, from deepfakes to targeted advertising.
- **Empathy and Responsibility:** Discussions revealed an enhanced sensitivity toward the social consequences of biased or opaque algorithms.
- **Active Engagement:** Role-playing and group design activities increased participation and peer learning.

Challenges Identified

- Students initially found abstract ethical concepts (such as algorithmic accountability) difficult to grasp without concrete examples.
- Limited prior exposure to AI terminology requires educators to simplify discussions without losing conceptual depth.

Outcome

The workshop demonstrated that AI ethics education is both feasible and impactful for teenagers. By integrating dialogue, creativity, and real-world examples, students developed a balanced understanding of the technical and moral dimensions of AI. Teachers noted that participants became more reflective about their digital behavior, showing increased awareness of privacy, consent, and responsible AI use.

Case Study 5: Community AI Learning Program in Rural Areas

Access to artificial intelligence (AI) education in rural and underprivileged regions remains limited due to inadequate infrastructure, a lack of trained educators, and minimal exposure to emerging technologies. However, the global movement toward AI for all has encouraged initiatives focused on inclusive and equitable learning. The Community AI Learning Program was developed to empower students in rural areas by introducing foundational AI concepts through low-cost, activity-based, and context-driven learning methods. The program combined digital literacy, computational thinking, and hands-on AI demonstrations tailored to local contexts, such as agriculture, healthcare, and environmental sustainability.

Objective

The primary objective of this initiative was to reduce the rural–urban AI education gap by providing accessible, localized AI learning experiences. The specific goals were as follows:

- Introducing the basics of AI, data, and automation to students in an engaging and practical manner.
- Enhancing curiosity, creativity, and problem-solving through community-relevant challenges.
- Building local teacher capacity to sustain AI education through low-cost teaching modules
- Promote digital inclusion and awareness of ethical AI use in rural societies

Methodology

The program was implemented across five rural schools involving 120 students (ages 11–15) and 10 local teachers in a three-month cycle. The methodology followed a community-centered participatory model:

- **Phase 1: Teacher Training and Resource Development**
    - Teachers underwent a week-long workshop on AI fundamentals using unplugged (non-computer-based) teaching methods and open-source tools, such as Google Teachable Machine and AI4K12 resources.

- Locally relevant examples, such as predicting crop yield patterns, classifying waste, and providing weather-based farming alerts, were integrated into the curriculum.

- **Phase 2: Student Engagement and Learning Activities**
  - Weekly sessions included demonstrations of AI applications, storytelling about intelligent systems, and hands-on group activities (e.g., sorting images and recognizing objects using mobile AI applications).
  - Students participated in an "Design Thinking Challenge" to propose AI-based community solutions, such as *smart irrigation alerts* or *AI-driven animal health check* concepts.
- **Phase 3: Community Exhibition and Reflection**
  - The students presented their projects in a local exhibition attended by parents, teachers, and village representatives.
  - Feedback sessions were conducted to discuss the social acceptance, feasibility, and ethical implications of AI technologies.

Results and Observations

- **Increased Awareness:** Over **88% of students** demonstrated an improved understanding of AI and its relevance to daily life.
- **Practical Application:** Students linked AI concepts to local challenges, demonstrating contextual creativity in areas such as agriculture and sanitation.
- **Teacher Empowerment:** Educators gained confidence in teaching AI using low-cost tools and community examples.
- **Social Impact:** The exhibition fostered community pride and increased awareness of AI's role in sustainable development.
- **Gender Inclusion:** Participation of girls (45%) indicated that inclusive community-based models can bridge gender gaps in STEM learning.

Challenges Identified

- Limited internet connectivity and availability of digital devices
- The need for continuous mentorship and refresher sessions for teachers was evident.
- Difficulty in sustaining engagement beyond the initial program period without policy-level support.

Outcome

The Community AI Learning Program successfully demonstrated that AI literacy can be introduced effectively in rural environments through creativity, collaboration, and contextual learning. By adapting AI concepts to familiar community issues and utilizing affordable resources, the program built local capacity, curiosity, and confidence among students and teachers.

CONCLUSION

AI education for children is essential for preparing them to thrive in a technology-driven world and fostering creativity, critical thinking, problem-solving, and ethical awareness from an early age. AI education for children is not just about coding; it is about nurturing curiosity, ethics, and innovation. By providing the right tools, guidance, and opportunities, educators and parents can equip children with the skills needed to become informed digital citizens and future innovators. Overcoming challenges such as limited resources, lack of trained educators, and unequal access requires collaborative efforts between governments, schools, and communities. With the right approach, AI education can empower children to use technology responsibly, pursue future career opportunities, and contribute to building innovative solutions for global challenges, ultimately raising future innovators ready to shape a better world.

FUTURE DIRECTIONS

The future of AI education for children holds immense potential to prepare the next generation as innovators, problem-solvers, and responsible digital citizens. In the coming years, AI literacy is likely to become a core part of school curricula, supported by interactive tools such as augmented reality/virtual reality-based AI labs, personalized learning platforms, and robotics kits. Governments and organizations will focus on bridging the digital divide and ensuring equal access to AI learning resources for students in underserved areas. Greater emphasis will be placed on teaching ethical and responsible AI use, helping children understand fairness, privacy, and bias. Collaborative programs between schools, industries, and research institutions will provide opportunities for real-world projects and innovation. By integrating AI education early, children will gain the skills needed for future careers, entrepreneurship, and meaningful contributions to solving global challenges through technology.

REFERENCES

Ali, S., DiPaola, D., Lee, I., Sindato, V., Kim, G., Blumofe, R., & Breazeal, C. (2021). Children as creators, thinkers and citizens in an AI-driven future. *Computers and Education: Artificial Intelligence*, *2*, 100040. DOI: 10.1016/j.caeai.2021.100040

Berson, I. R., Berson, M. J., & Luo, W. (2025). Innovating responsibly: Ethical considerations for AI in early childhood education. *AI. Brain and Child*, *1*(1), 2. DOI: 10.1007/s44436-025-00003-5

Carella, G., Colombo, F., Migliozzi, S., & Arquilla, V. (2024). Design Thinking as an enabler of change in the technological market. A practical case study of company's innovation and differentiation. *INTED Proceedings*, •••, 3025–3033. DOI: 10.21125/inted.2024.0817

Chen, L., Chen, P., & Lin, Z. (2020). Artificial intelligence in education: A review. *IEEE Access : Practical Innovations, Open Solutions*, *8*, 75264–75278. DOI: 10.1109/ACCESS.2020.2988510

Golden, L. M., & Struloeff, K. (2025). The Future of AI in Education: Innovations and Insights. *Social Innovations Journal, 30*.

Goralski, M. A., & Tan, T. K. (2020). Artificial intelligence and sustainable development. *International Journal of Management Education*, *18*(1), 100330. DOI: 10.1016/j.ijme.2019.100330

Grigenti, F. (2022). The child program and the history of AI. *Orbis Idearum, 10* (2), 41-63. https://www.doi.org/10.26106/gb8e-p413

Guan, C., Mou, J., & Jiang, Z. (2020). Artificial intelligence innovation in education: A twenty-year data-driven historical analysis. *International Journal of Innovation Studies*, *4*(4), 134–147. DOI: 10.1016/j.ijis.2020.09.001

Holmes, W. (2020). Artificial intelligence in education. In *Encyclopedia of education and information technologies* (pp. 88–103). Springer International Publishing. DOI: 10.1007/978-3-030-10576-1_107

Joseph, O. B., & Uzondu, N. C.Olatunbosun Bartholomew JosephNwankwo Charles Uzondu. (2024). Integrating AI and Machine Learning in STEM education: Challenges and opportunities. *Computer Science & IT Research Journal*, *5*(8), 1732–1750. DOI: 10.51594/csitrj.v5i8.1379

Kahn, K., & Winters, N. (2021). Constructionism and AI: A history and possible futures. *British Journal of Educational Technology, 52*(3), 1130–1142. DOI: 10.1111/bjet.13088

Kamalov, F., Santandreu Calonge, D., & Gurrib, I. (2023). New era of artificial intelligence in education: Towards a sustainable multifaceted revolution. *Sustainability (Basel), 15*(16), 12451. DOI: 10.3390/su151612451

Knox, J., Wang, Y., & Gallagher, M. (2019). Introduction: AI, Inclusion, and 'Everyone Learning Everything. In Knox, J., Wang, Y., & Gallagher, M. (Eds.), *Artificial Intelligence and Inclusive Education. Perspectives on Rethinking and Reforming Education*. Springer., DOI: 10.1007/978-981-13-8161-4_1

Lim, W. M., Gunasekara, A., Pallant, J. L., Pallant, J. I., & Pechenkina, E. (2023). Generative AI and the future of education: Ragnarök or reformation? A paradoxical perspective from management educators. *International Journal of Management Education, 21*(2), 100790. DOI: 10.1016/j.ijme.2023.100790

Lytvynova, S., Vodopian, N., & Sysoeva, O. (2024). Artificial Intelligence in Secondary Education: An Innovative Teacher's Tool to Ensure Individualised Learning for Students. In: Tomczyk, Ł. (eds) *New Media Pedagogy: Research Trends, Methodological Challenges, and Successful Implementations*. NMP 2023. Communications in Computer and Information Science, vol 2130. Springer, Cham. https://doi.org/ DOI: 10.1007/978-3-031-63235-8_26

McCalla, G. (2023). The history of artificial intelligence in education–the first quarter century. In *Handbook of artificial intelligence in education* (pp. 10–29). Edward Elgar Publishing UK. DOI: 10.4337/9781800375413.00010

Nurhayati, S., Taufikin, T., Judijanto, L., & Musa, S. (2025). Towards Effective Artificial Intelligence-Driven Learning in Indonesian Child Education: Understanding Parental Readiness, Challenges, and Policy Implications. Educational Process. *Educational Process International Journal, 15*(1), 1–29. DOI: 10.22521/edupij.2025.15.155

Patel, N. S., Puah, S., & Kok, X. F. K. (2024). Shaping future-ready graduates with mindset shifts: Studying the impact of integrating critical and design thinking in design innovation education. *Frontiers in Education, 9*, 1358431. DOI: 10.3389/feduc.2024.1358431

Pedro, F., Subosa, M., Rivas, A., & Valverde, P. (2019). Artificial intelligence in education: Challenges and opportunities for sustainable development. *Journal of Intelligent Learning Systems and Applications, 15*(4). https://unesdoc.unesco.org/ark:/48223/pf0000366994

Reimers, F. M. (2020). Transforming education to prepare students to invent the future. *PSU Research Review*, *4*(2), 81–91. DOI: 10.1108/PRR-03-2020-0010

Sheikh, S. (2021). *Understanding the Role of Artificial Intelligence and Its Future Social Impact*. IGI Global Scientific Publishing., DOI: 10.4018/978-1-7998-4607-9

Soo-Siang, L., & Sonia, G. (2019). *Educational Research and Innovation Developing Minds in the Digital Age Towards a Science of Learning for 21st Century Education: Towards a Science of Learning for 21st Century Education*. OECD Publishing.

Sousa, M. J., Pani, S., Dal Mas, F., & Sousa, S. (Eds.). (2024). *Incorporating AI technology in the service sector: innovations in creating knowledge, improving efficiency, and elevating quality of life*. CRC Press. DOI: 10.1201/9781003378068

Thakur, R. (2024). Introduction to Artificial Intelligence and Its Importance in Modern Business Management. In Sharma, D., Bhardwaj, B., & Dhiman, M. (Eds.), *Leveraging AI and Emotional Intelligence in Contemporary Business Organizations* (pp. 133–165). IGI Global Scientific Publishing., DOI: 10.4018/979-8-3693-1902-4.ch009

Zhang, K., & Aslan, A. B. (2021). AI technologies for education: Recent research & future directions. *Computers and education. Artificial Intelligence*, *2*, 100025. DOI: 10.1016/j.caeai.2021.100025

Zimmerman, M. (2018). *Teaching AI: Exploring new frontiers for learning*. International society for technology in education.

KEY TERMS AND DEFINITIONS

Age-Appropriate AI Learning: The process of introducing AI concepts to children according to their developmental stage—from basic pattern recognition in early childhood to algorithmic and ethical understanding in adolescence.

AI Literacy: The ability to understand, use, and critically evaluate artificial intelligence technologies. For children, AI literacy includes recognizing how AI systems make decisions, understanding data ethics, and using AI responsibly in everyday contexts.

AI4K12 Initiative: A structured framework that provides guidelines for integrating artificial intelligence into K–12 education, emphasizing conceptual understanding, ethical awareness, and hands-on engagement with AI technologies.

Artificial Intelligence (AI): The simulation of human intelligence processes by machines, especially computer systems, which can perform tasks such as learning, reasoning, problem-solving, perception, and language understanding. In education, AI supports personalized learning, assessment, and automation.

Computational Thinking: A problem-solving approach that involves breaking down complex tasks into smaller steps, recognizing patterns, and designing algorithms. It is the foundation for understanding programming and AI behavior.

Digital Citizenship: The responsible and ethical use of technology, including understanding online safety, privacy, and digital rights. AI education encourages children to become thoughtful digital citizens who use AI tools constructively.

Ethical AI: The responsible development and use of AI systems that ensure fairness, transparency, accountability, and respect for privacy. In AI education, this concept teaches children to understand moral implications such as bias and data protection.

Hands-On Learning: An experiential teaching strategy where children actively participate in building, coding, or experimenting with AI tools and robotics to understand abstract concepts through practice.

Machine Learning: A subset of AI that allows computers to learn from data and improve performance over time without explicit programming. Tools like Teachable Machine enable children to experience machine learning concepts hands-on.

Visual Coding Platforms: Programming environments like Scratch and Blockly that use drag-and-drop blocks instead of text-based code, making coding and AI learning more accessible and engaging for children.

Chapter 9
Future Trends:
Preparing Children for AI-Driven Societies of 2040 and Beyond

Froilan Delute Mobo
http://orcid.org/0000-0002-4531-8106
Philippine Merchant Marine Academy, Philippines

Katarzyna Miłek
http://orcid.org/0000-0003-4603-4604
Akademia Nauk Stosowanych in Wrocław, Poland

ABSTRACT

The rapid advancement of artificial intelligence (AI) is transforming societies, economies, and the global workforce, presenting both unprecedented opportunities and complex challenges. As AI becomes increasingly embedded in daily life, there is an urgent need to redesign educational systems to prepare children for AI-driven societies of 2040 and beyond. This paper explores the intersection of AI, education, and child development, offering a comprehensive analysis of future skills requirements, curriculum innovations, the evolving role of teachers, and the psychological, ethical, and social implications for children. It highlights how nations such as Finland, Singapore, Estonia, and China are leading education reforms that integrate AI literacy, ethical considerations, and equitable access to technology. The manuscript provides policy recommendations and a global framework for ensuring that AI-driven education fosters human-centered growth, ethical awareness, and lifelong adaptability

DOI: 10.4018/979-8-2600-2438-6.ch009

INTRODUCTION

The rapid adaptation of artificial intelligence (AI) in recent decades remains one of the most astonishing phenomena of the new millennium. It has completely transformed the world's industries and guilds, automated the most menial and tedious chores, and evolved into more sophisticated soft systems that learn, rationalize, and ultimately synthesize highly complex systems (Russell & Norvig, 2020). In the more integrated societies of 2040 and beyond, interactions with Artificial Intelligence will be much different compared to earlier epochs. Today's education systems will have to radically alter the ways in which they train the current generation, for the coming societies will function in a widely integrated AI environment (Luckin, 2018). This is more than an educational problem; it is a moral and developmental responsibility and a policy problem (OECD, 2020; UNESCO, 2021).

AI has found applications in almost every industry. For instance, driverless cars are changing traditional methods of transportation, and self-predicting machines are changing the way healthcare diagnostics are performed (Bohr & Memarzadeh, 2020). AI systems that provide intelligent guidance are customized for everyone. Advanced AI systems that operate on algorithms are changing the way policies are created and resources are allocated (Topol, 2019; Floridi, 2020). According to the 2020 World Economic Forum, approximately 85 million positions will be lost due to an imbalance in the distribution of work between machines and humans. This has been highlighted as a shift in the way people work with machines. On the other hand, 97 million new jobs will be introduced in the more technology-driven workplaces of tomorrow. These jobs will require a blended expertise of emotional intelligence, technical proficiency, ethical reasoning, and flexibility (Acemoglu & Restrepo, 2020). The rigid approach of traditional systems of education ignores the predominant factors of the modern economy. As noted by the OECD (2020), learners of the new age should have more than basic concepts. They should have developed soft skills such as systems thinking and problem-solving and be proficient in digital citizenship. Compared to dull memorization, the appreciation of more human-centered, innovative, and lifelong practices is much preferred. Children today will probably take on careers still not invented and will deal with challenges we haven't thought of yet. Such children would need to be protected from paternalistic, dominant approaches and instead provided with training to utilize technology ethically. According to a 2020 report from UNICEF, children preparing for the age of AI need these skills. AI systems that implant systems of social care, health systems, and education in children must be developed in a way that enables them to critique and engage with these technologies responsibly. This chapter presents a thorough examination of potential strategies and new techniques for helping children prosper in an AI society. From global policies, interdisciplinary studies, and technological pathways, it delineates the shifts in cognition, feelings, ethics, and digital adeptness needed for the forthcoming society. It analyzes the changing functions of teachers, the use of AI-assisted educational technology, and the internal and external consequences of being raised in a digitally streamlined environment. Overall, the chapter offers a practical framework for teachers, decision-makers, and parents who want to nurture inclusive, equitable, and people-centered AI teaching.

THE RISE OF AI AND ITS IMPACT ON SOCIETY

The acceleration of artificial intelligence (AI), which has always been a hypothetical subject, has become a major transformative element in society and is being applied in daily tasks, such as autonomous driving vehicles, virtual agents, healthcare prediction systems, and automated finance services (OECD, 2020). SPAI systems are able to analyze and act on huge volumes of data, identify unique factors in different data, create different data, and make decisions at a much higher efficiency than human beings.

The World Economic Forum (2020) claims that this is the fourth industrial revolution, which is being driven at the moment by the integration of different AI, machine learning, and other robotics, blockchain, and quantum computing technologies. This is not only a technological revolution but also a change to the ways of producing, making decisions, and creating new forms of economic value, which has, in turn, changed the very basis of defining and handling knowledge, a so-called revolution in the knowledge system. By the year 2040, it is estimated that AI will be able to outmatch humans in the execution of a multitude of cognitive tasks while being effectively integrated into healthcare systems, educational systems, and the creative industry. This raises many questions regarding the ways in which governments and ethics can maintain a balance with human freedom. This is the reason why it is essential to actively make changes in the educational structure.

The impact of AI on employment: Work and the labor market are experiencing profound changes because of AI. The World Economic Forum (2020) has underscored the fact that while 43% of the surveyed businesses expect downsizing because of automation, 34% predict expansion of activities that will be boosted through AI. This is paradoxical because it shows a reconfiguration of labor, in which monotonous and boring tasks are automated, and new tasks created require human and AI collaboration.

The traditional employment spheres of the cashier, driver, and clerk are increasingly automated, whereas the new employment spheres of AI ethicist, human-AI interaction designer, data curator, and algorithm trainer are being created. These are not merely technical jobs and require a high degree of ethical, creative, and emotional intelligence. The future is precarious and requires innovative thinking, weeding out traditional paradigms of education, and developing new systems that will hybridize skills in children. The effects of AI on social structures. In addition to employment, AI is changing the construction of social institutions. AI diagnostic systems in medicine are more proficient than human specialists at recognizing illnesses, such as cancer (Topol, 2019). In education, adaptive intelligent tutoring systems construct personalized learning routes and adjust content to suit children's numerous requirements. Artificial intelligence is increasingly important in policy formulation, public resource management, and public service delivery optimization in public sector institutions. However, the advances in question elicit moral and societal concerns. There are numerous potential consequences connected to the relational triad diversity, equity, and inclusion in the context of artificial intelligence.

The Brookings Institution states that algorithmic discrimination is discrimination embedded and perpetuated in training data (Brookings Institution, 2021). As such, it is equally important that students are taught the theory of computer ethics and algorithmic and data-driven environment accountability, as well as their associated rights. To help our future learners grow to become active and engaged citizens, it is important that they are taught the critical importance of the impact of AI on society. Impact on social interaction and communication: AI is affecting the ways people communicate and interact with each other, particularly children. AI social media reinforces cultural, political, and personal identity changes. Children are dealing with AI friends, digital avatars, and the virtual world; therefore, their social and emotional growth is changing in new ways (Floridi, 2020).

Students in such radically changed environments need to build empathy, critical media literacy, and the ability to distinguish between human and computer influences. Children need to learn how to use the Internet ethically and how to manage their feelings as the AI world becomes the best representative of human interaction and as social interaction is mediated by AI. Socio-emotional learning must be at the center of educational policy to offer the greatest chance of ensuring that technology is used to enrich human relationships.

Social and Global Concerns Artificial intelligence (AI) has the capability to transform the approach to key issues on the planet, such as climate change, pandemics, and disaster resilience. Machine learning assists with forecasting extreme weather, optimizing energy usage, and accelerating biomedical research, including vaccine research and development (UNESCO, 2021). These examples illustrate the promise of AI with respect to the attainment of United Nations Sustainable Development Goals (SDGs) as well as the health of the planet.

To prepare children for the above, education needs to incorporate systems thinking and sustainability literacy. The integration of AI with environmental stewardship and global problem solving empowers learners to be responsible innovators and ethical participants in a common destiny. The next generation of thinkers will be required at the interface of AI and sustainability for the responsible use of technology for environmental and social good.

FUTURE SKILLS REQUIRED IN AI-DRIVEN SOCIETIES

The developments in artificial intelligence (AI) technology and its influence on the job market and society predict a shift in the skills required in the year 2040 and beyond. These shifts in skills and knowledge required will be different from the skills that were needed in the 20th century. As the World Economic Forum (2022) states, while knowledge-based skills will be required, there will be a more pronounced need for skills in the realms of thought production, emotional intelligence, and reasoning skills. This resonates with the OECD (2020), as there is a need in the world for more than the passive receiving and memorizing of information to acquire skills that will foster the ability to work in synergy with intelligent systems and address complicated issues to offer solutions.

In the coming years, critical cognitive abilities will be indispensable. Brookings (2021) indicated that critical thinking, along with problem-solving skills, will be imperative aspects in the future. In that future, humans will have to analyze results, scrutinize outputs of AI, and create new approaches as AI technology handles mundane, repetitive, and data-driven tasks. Additionally, as UNESCO (20221) discusses, one of the most important aspects of an AI world will be systems thinking—understanding the relationships of complex ecological, technological, and social systems. This is crucial, as an AI-based problem will involve a number of complex, interrelated systems. In addition, digital 'literacy' will be understood in the world of complex thinking as computational thinking—understanding the dynamics of algorithms, appreciating boundaries, and recognizing biases. Hence, coding is in a new age, positioned as a critical adaptive skill and a new form of literacy, enabling its possessor to approximate technologies, as Wing (2006) posited.

Above and beyond cognitive capabilities and socio-emotional and ethical competences will sharpen the uniquely human advantage in the age of AI. Emotional intelligence, in the form of empathy, caring, and emotional attunement, will continue to be a human trait in which AI will fall short (World Economic Forum, 2020). Similarly, ethical AI and 'AI literacy,' as future members of society will contend with the issues of AI and algorithmic bias, data privacy and AI, and the responsible use of AI. UNICEF (2020) states that AI literacy entails the AI's impact on human rights, freedoms, and social equity. Finally, among others, in an AI-permeated world, intercultural competence and global citizenship will be mandatory as collaboration will span beyond borders, and so will the requirements to appreciate differences and deal with ethical issues in pluralistic settings (OECD, 2020).

Technological and Data Skills

Like any other workplace skill, data literacy has become an important asset both professionally and personally. As the world continues to expand and data becomes the core of systems such as AI, it becomes increasingly more important to understand how decisions are made and based on what data. Information and data are the basis of advanced modern civilization. To successfully handle and process data, an individual must be trained to identify the source, determine the gaps or biases, and identify the pattern. Managing AI ethically, along with other big data technologies, is a moral obligation today, and not merely a technical issue. Owing to the increasing pollution, big data, and AI, along with the mechanical context from collected big data, it is important to form adaptable and ethically data-literate individuals. Education is the main point where AI and democracy meet. The primary concern is to build systems that cater to the rising concern about the social responsibilities of technology.

Equity and inclusion issues exist; however, the effects of the biased data context concerning artificial intelligence and machine learning should be elaborated. Any form of artificial intelligence that works with unbalanced or uncorrected data may worsen existing social structures. For instance, some recruitment and even predictive policing systems, winning systems, are biased in favor of or against different population groups. Therefore, it would be unwise for schooling systems of the future not to center their ambitions on teaching data ethics and how to construct frameworks free from such biases. Countries that emphasize data literacy for their citizens are confident in generating highly ethical data citizens who deploy effective data-driven thinking, moving from basic data consumption to actively analyzing and reasoning data.

AI collaboration skills are equally critical. While leaders such as Brynjolfsson and McAfee (2017) have proposed fears of full automation with humans being replaced, they argue that AI will act as a collaborator, rather than a replacement. In this scenario, humans and machines will complement each other, reinforcing each other's advantages. AI's strengths lie in computation, data analytical work, and other monotonous activities, whereas humans contribute originality, ethical considerations, and emotional intelligence. For children and future professionals, this means there is a need to learn how to communicate with AI systems, issue clear commands, AI command over the units of analysis, and identify the domains of machine intelligence.

The development of collaboration skills with respect to AI goes beyond mere technique proficiency; it also requires a certain type of cognitive flexibility. It requires, for the sake of this example, one of them to understand the synergy of machine intelligence and human evaluation. In medicine, for instance, an AI assistant can support physicians with the image-based evaluation of a disease, although the final judgment would still require some level of human expertise, empathy, and ethical consideration. In education, AI will also assist in the personalization of education and instruction suited to the needs and abilities of individual students, although teachers' roles in providing emotional support and moral guidance will still be essential. The emphasis here is on the development of a new pedagogical model that positions AI as an equal partner in the process of learning and creative collaboration, a co-pilot in the augmentation of human skills, not a reduction.

The advancement of technology will require the global workforce to embrace greater levels of flexibility, a culture of lifelong learning, and skills development. "The 21st-century illiterate will not be someone who does not know how to read and write, but someone who cannot learn, unlearn, and relearn," remarked Toffler (1970). Toffler's words are particularly true in the context of AI-driven automation. In the contemporary climate of rapidly advancing technology, the ability to learn new information, replace obsolete information, and replace outdated methods with new, innovative methods will be exceedingly valuable. Educational institutions should make the necessary changes by moving away from rote memorization and shifting towards the cultivation of a growth mindset.

RETHINKING EDUCATION SYSTEMS: CURRICULAR INNOVATIONS

As each year goes by, define the Integrative, Interdisciplinary, and Interdisciplinary recesses and how they would relate learning to an Interdisciplinary context. Outline the different Integrative and Transdisciplinary Interdisciplinary models, their outcomes, and their research attributes. Explain the different models of Interdisciplinary Learning and Teaching.

To be future-ready, curriculums must include cognitive, technological, emotional, ethical, and environmental domains. More importantly, AI and computational thinking should be among the foundational learning areas. Students need to comprehend algorithms, machine learning models, and the ethics of data and technology. This is important for the proper understanding of AI and responsible technology use. Such literacy must begin in early education, in the form of UNICEF recommended gamified coding, robotics, and initial AI exposure. Schools should use a playful and experimental approach as a requirement to construct a culture of comfort and curiosity around AI, instead of fear and misunderstanding.

The Performance Assessment System (PAS) plays a significant role in intellectual socialization, highlighting the need for a robust framework for other functions within specific contextual requirements. The implementation and institutionalization of policies and systems (IIPS) is a multidimensional strategy that requires coordinated social functioning across diverse groups and other stakeholders. Zeithaml (2001) suggests the need for a paradigm shift; social functioning across other systems needs holistic integration. In the case of OM, we need to utilize feedback, especially negative feedback, from the wider Integrated Outcome Assessment (IOA) more efficiently. Unlearning and reframing negative feedback differently is the new system and feedback thinking approach that we need to employ. The World Economic Forum (2020) and other roles for emotional and social learning help children manage the mental and emotional difficulties of an AI-driven world. Ambedkar (2019) has posted the need for more emotional and social learning in the complex world driven by AI. Technology, new knowledge, and other such are shapeshifting structures. Options are to shift personally and socially into private systems of other. Added value is emotional and social learning for an AI world.

Sustainability and global citizenship remain vital pillars of education in the era of AI. Learners must acquire knowledge regarding climate literacy, the Sustainable Development Goals (SDGs), and the moral responsibilities of global citizenship (UNESCO, 2021). Education must enable learners to pivot and focus their talents on addressing the world's challenges through innovative and service-oriented avenues. The principles of ethical AI and responsible technology frameworks must be introduced to familiarize learners with the intricacies of the ethics of algorithmic bias, algorithmic data privacy, and human-absentee decision-making systems. According to UNICEF (2020), youth must be trained to examine the moral dilemmas within AI systems and the underlying human rights issues, equity, and social justice implications of the technology.

To deliver these competencies, it is necessary to develop new pedagogical frameworks. Within these supported frameworks, there is the opportunity for learners to tackle real world challenges. The days of rote memorization, in which learners are passive recipients of knowledge, are over. Active learners are now expected to ideate, innovate, and troubleshoot, including the use of AI. For instance, learners have built AI applications to manage waste, examine climate data trends, and develop disaster response simulations to control and map disaster response systems. Such initiatives, which span the realms of science, technology, and social responsibility, are being promoted worldwide (OECD, 2020). Another breakthrough development is interdisciplinary learning. It is the ability to avoid traditional learning boundaries, which enables learners to appreciate the interconnectedness of the disciplines and the problems in the real world. The integration of mathematics and ethics, computer science and social studies are the real world in which learners are prepared to work in the world of work and are AI supported (Brookings, 2021). Such learning enables learners to appreciate the world of systems, appreciate complexity, and solve highly integrated problems.

The impact of personalized and adaptive learning is much deeper than that of the previously discussed elements. Unlike traditional education systems, which follow one teaching methodology, customized learning is far more effective because AI-powered learning systems calibrate each student's pace, shifts in interest, and learning strengths. These systems function by assessing students' performance data and analyzing them, which in turn helps the students gain a better understanding of knowledge, even on complex topics, through customized gaps of knowledge and tailored assistance interventions (World Economic Forum, 2020). In addition, technologies for gamification and immersion learning, especially virtual (VR) and augmented reality (AR) learning systems, have changed the engagement paradigms for students learning abstract concepts. Active learning and sustained attention are crucial for mastering topics such as neural networks, machine learning, and data visualization. These studies are emphasized by UNESCO (2021) as central topics. Learners are physically transported by immersive simulations into virtual laboratories, historical epochs, or even into the systems of artificial intelligence, thus enabling experiential and interactive learning.

The era of artificial intelligence thinking should extend beyond the limits of the classroom. Establishing external theory–community and industry linkages is essential for participating in the bridging of theory and practice. Schools can partner with AI firms and NGOs, as well as research institutes, for mentorships and internships, and students can tackle real-world problems, which is the application of classroom concepts (Brookings, 2021). Such exposure also introduces learners to professional ethics, technical workplace communication, and the innovation and entrepreneurship ecosystem. Furthermore, the idea of global classrooms considers learning as an experience beyond the borders of a given geographical region. For example, students can interact with colleagues in other countries through virtual exchanges and other forms of online cooperative learning (OECD, 2020). This global reach also improves students' intercultural communication and digital collaboration skills, which they can apply in international and remote workplaces. In the era of AI and globalization, the ability to work across borders and appreciate cultural diversity will rank as important as other skills in the industry.

Shifting teaching techniques related to the implementation of the AI era is equally important. Traditional examinations set forth to gauge students' abilities of retention, formulating answers, and memorization are unable to assess the extent to which future challenges and complexities can be handled. There is a need to incorporate real-world projects, AI simulations, and research presentations into the curriculum to assess creativity, problem-solving, and collaboration skills. Portfolios help assess a student's development and achieve step goals over a duration of time, aiding in the process of achieving positive feedback and sustainable growth. Self- and peer assessments are valuable in guiding students to self-reflect and evaluate their learning gaps. These shifts in philosophy aim to achieve a culture of learning and engagement. Despite the promises of increased innovative work, there remain some barriers. Inequitable access to AI-based learning, especially in developing regions, continues to be hindered by the digital divide. Students with no reliable Internet access or Internet-enabled devices are excluded from AI-based educational systems. In addition, there is the challenge of teacher preparedness. To integrate new technologies and new ways of teaching, many educators are AI illiterate, making it redundant to propose new systems. Changes in policy and the slow bureaucratic tendency to 'change' remain the biggest barriers to education systems integrating with technological advancements. UNICEF (2020) cautions that, if unaddressed, these challenges will form the basis upon which the AI revolution grows and develops gaps that other technologies could bridge. Therefore, policymakers have no other option than to invest in infrastructure, teacher education, and curriculum changes that will allow every learner to benefit from digital transformation.

Nations such as Finland, Singapore, and Estonia have begun pioneering AI-integrated curricula, serving as exemplars to follow; Finland has started to teach primary school students about AI through "Elements of AI," Singapore has incorporated modules on teaching responsible AI ethics at the secondary school level, and Estonia has taught coding and digital literacy as early as kindergarten. Finland lags behind the other two countries in terms of AI curriculum integration, as Singapore and Estonia are already teaching learners about responsible machine learning as well as coding and digital literacy, particularly in the age of ethics. These archetypes, along with others in the aforementioned countries, exemplify that with adequate national policies, teacher resources, and community framework support, systemic policies and useful changes can be effectively and strategically instituted.

THE ROLE OF TEACHERS IN AI-AUGMENTED CLASSROOMS

While changing the educational system, the roles of educators and the need for improvisation are tremendous. Teachers are no longer focused exclusively on transferring and transmitting information and are now integrating human and technological components as facilitators, mentors, and experience designers (OECD, 2020). Knowledge in the 21st-century classroom is no longer static; instead, it is abundant and constantly evolving. Educators, in this case, are tasked with the cultivation of critical thinking, emotional intelligence, and increasing the ability to navigate complexity. Instead of competing with AI, educators are using technology to personalize learning experiences, provide adaptive feedback, and focus more on the socio-emotional aspects of every student—dimensions of teaching that AI systems, no matter how complex, would scrap. The World Economic Forum (2020) states that future educators will be "learning engineers" – people who integrate pedagogy and technological skills and nurture empathy, ethics, and global awareness.

Owing to the significant impact of artificial intelligence and other digital tools on many sectors, including education, the expectations placed on professionals have increased to include multiskilled, innovative, and management roles. Digital pedagogy is one such area that has gained importance, and it involves the use of tools based on digital technologies and artificial intelligence to enhance the ease and effectiveness of teaching and learning. Teachers ought to be adept at learning management systems, adaptive learning systems, and algorithm-driven virtual laboratories that analyze learners and ascertain tiered curriculum suggestions (UNESCO, 2021). Both teachers and learners need to understand the structure of these systems—how they examine, analyze, and adapt content–so that technology is used to enhance the teaching and learning processes rather than control them. This also includes the ability to comprehensively scrutinize artificial intelligence systems to establish bias, inaccuracy, and exclusion.

Another critical competency is AI literacy for educators, which includes basic-level concepts, possible usages, and ethical considerations related to AI. Without considering AI holistically through the lens of established concepts, educators will not be able to properly navigate or teach students critical concepts surrounding AI-enhanced ecosystems. As outlined by UNICEF (2020), AI literacy for teachers should encompass an understanding and justification of algorithmic and other biased data issues, data ethics, and the societal consequences of automation. This helps educators situate AI in relation to larger societal issues and prepares students not only as consumers of AI but also as responsible, ethical citizens who have the ability to shape AI development.

Emerging at the same level of importance is the competence to implement data-driven instructions. Vast amounts of learner data are generated by AI systems, ranging from student engagement data to real-time performance data. It is critical that teachers learn to construct their instructions based on such data. Reports and data dashboards have been developed to assist educators in identifying students who have not mastered the content, personalizing their instruction, and mapping their growth over time (OECD, 2020). Educators need to remember that the ethical issues surrounding the data that students have generated and the possible privacy violations need to be balanced with the positive side of the analytical data. Teachers need to be data literate and increase their capability in working with data in a way that shifts the educational and student outcome performance positively to garner the best results from actionable data.

In classrooms supported by AI, teachers' roles as socio-emotional mentors become even more important. Conversational empathy, compassion, and ethical reasoning are absent from AI. It is the function of the teacher to develop the emotional and social intelligence of the student. This includes guiding students on responsible and ethical decision-making and anticipating and managing emotional states in themselves and others (Brookings, 2021). The more technology used in classrooms, the more important the human factor becomes. Teachers are responsible for creating an environment that fosters self-expression, social resilience, and interpersonal skills needed to function in an automated environment.

AI uses large language models to respond to numerous requests and questions from educators and students with the same efficiency and speed that humans can process. It can carry out the mundane and time-consuming tasks of grading, maintaining attendance, and summarizing documents. This allows educators to spend more time on the social and creative aspects of their professions. AI can also automate lesson planning. Once the learning objectives have been set and student data have been uploaded, AI can generate resources and text with the right level of differentiation, recommending them at the right times. Intelligent tutoring systems focus on self-paced learning of math, language, or other tuition subjects. Predictive analytics can even inform teachers of students likely to need intervention (World Economic Forum, 2020). Teachers and AI do more than just collaborate with each other. It is a symbiotic relationship. Each does their part, with AI handling efficiency and human empathy and motivation.

Although the deployment of AI can enhance productivity, there are human aspects that it cannot replicate. Caring is essential because it helps educators appreciate students' mental and emotional struggles. AI lacks the ability to rationalize and make the correct decisions on ethical questions. Teachers inspire students through motivation, which AI is incapable of (Floridi, 2020). AI falls short of the reality needed to establish the functional dynamics that a perfect teacher should possess.

Equipping educators with the skills to adapt to new realities in teaching and learning will necessitate that PD undergo transformational changes and incorporate AI-related instruction and ongoing learning. Specialist teacher education programs should include AI-related ethical issues, digital teaching, and data education to ensure that teachers are prepared for AI-dominated environments. For practicing educators, the need for sustained PD is imperative. Workshops, webinars, and certification programs are essential for enabling teachers to cope with the latest technologies and adaptive learning facilitators (UNESCO, 2021). Professional learning communities (PLCs) are excellent platforms for collaborative self-directed peer learning, enabling teachers to share their successes and challenges and design AI-infused teaching activities together (OECD, 2020).

Despite the usefulness of AI in the classroom, it is traumatizing to think of the daunting tasks it requires from teachers every day. Through their pedagogical training, teachers are taught the ethical standards acceptable for their positions. Socially, the trauma of AI-driven pedagogy takes root the fastest. Teachers all over the world have reported withdrawing from social anxiety as part of the stress patterns. The apprehension of being socially overpowered by their own AI arises from having to adapt to the new methodologies that AI offers. Teachers should not have to stress about such things. It must herd the thoughts of eager teachers, that training should be devoid of stress from such things. should not have since it muddies their enthusiasm. Capping is not what the most eager should think about. The shortage of technological infrastructure that is vital to classrooms, AI classrooms, thoroughly impedes pedagogy. With little to no technology, what is taught becomes irrelevant. Furthermore, teachers must learn to accept the paradox that AI presents to their students. As a powerful educational tool, it helps them learn in a new dimension; however, the boundaries of privacy and personal data become a sophisticated quagmire. While young students have been considered data-free, AI tends to shun that care. The data students feed is their own, as processed by the AI, which presents a sophisticated ethical quagmire. Teachers must be bound by policy. With zero funding, the most exclusionary digital framework bends over to the ethical quagmire.

In the age of AI, the role of the teacher is currently undergoing a transformation. Teachers are no longer simply the givers of knowledge but instead are curators who must select, interpret, and contextualize the content generated by AI to suit pedagogical aims. They are guides for digital citizenship, helping students learn the ethics of using different technologies, how to recognize misinformation, and the etiquette of technology use. Teachers, in particular, are facilitators of human flourishing and guides to purpose, creativity, and moral character in a world filled with algorithms (Brookings, 2021). The focus of the future of education should be on how to help teachers reshape their work in collaboration with technology, not on AI substituting teachers. By combining human compassion with the reasoning capabilities of AI, educators will be able to develop learning environments that are not only intellectually advanced but also empathetic, just, and profoundly humane.

IMPACT OF IMPLEMENTING AI ON CHILDREN'S PSYCHOSOCIAL ACTIVITIES

Children living in an AI-infused society will inevitably experience considerable psychosocial changes that will transform their social interactions, learning processes, and worldview. AI technology will begin to shape a child's learning, play, communication, and self-concept during their formative years. Although AI has some positive psychosocial applications, including adaptive educational technologies, disability support, and interactive virtual environments, there are negative psychological costs. The psychosocial risks of AI technologies and society, including attention deficit disorders, digital addictions, poor mental health, and identity problems/disorders, are already documented (UNICEF, 2020).

The balance between children's tendency to develop and their immersion in AI technology must be meticulously monitored and controlled to facilitate growth rather than impede it.

From a monetary perspective, learning systems focused on the use of AI technology allow for learner skill development and acquisition to advance at a supersonic speed, and contributors instantly adjust specific elements to their learning curves. Take the illustrative instance of adaptive learning systems designed to help children learn. These systems are programmed to detect and pinpoint gaps in a learner's understanding of a topic and, in real time, reteach and restructure the topic to the learner's level, thereby optimizing the learner's understanding of the topic. However, a downside of such systems is that AI feedback, if not balanced with human interaction, will result in the learner's lack of critical thinking and reasoning. The OECD (2020) white paper points out that the overuse of AI tools leads to passive learning, in which students are simply told to complete steps without engaging in the necessary questioning and analysis of the proposed steps. This is a problem because students do not gain understanding through the process. Teaching therefore, should embrace the idea that AI technology should be an external enhancer, as opposed to the core of the thinking used in problem solving and creative actions.

In addition to changes in cognition, AI technology affects attention and behavior. Many AI applications, particularly those in games and social media, have user engagement maximization recommendation algorithms. These algorithms improve user experience; however, they often cause excessive screen time, attention fragmentation, and even addictive behaviors. Permanent presence in reward-based online environments diminishes children's capability to focus and engage meaningfully in activities in the analog world (Floridi, 2020). The lack of real-world social interactions that follows social media use can undermine the development of interpersonal skills, such as empathy and emotional control. Therefore, in the AI era, real-world socialization, in addition to screen time and online activities, has become an essential part of child development.

Another component of life affected negatively by AI is the emotional aspect. AI chatbots, companions, and virtual assistants can provide children with emotional support, comfort, and even educational help. However, such relationships could replace real human interactions that children need. Children might 'fall in love' emotionally with devices that are incapable of feeling, having a conscience, and lacking any moral values (UNICEF, 2020). Such emotional development can be counterproductive, as the child will lack interpersonal empathy. Parents and educators should be the most active in this regard, using AI in a manner that promotes human relationships.

For AI systems to function properly, they constantly collect and analyze various personal, biometric, behavioral, academic, and contextual data. The absence of privacy protections for the collection of children's autonomy and right to consent is concerning. UNICEF notes how children and younger individuals are frequently unaware of the surveillance systems, how their data are collected, and how data are tracked and stored, which is instrumental in their exploitation. The ethical problem of developing biased algorithms is an additional concern. As AI systems are trained on historical data, they may include biased information, such as gender, racial inequality, or socioeconomic status. Discrimination within education, social scoring, gatekeeping of opportunities, and other spheres is still discrimination (Floridi, 2020; Brookings, 2021).

Analyzing the rights of children and the ethical implications of artificial intelligence (AI) applications is highly complex. Young children use AI-powered technology without understanding the terms of use, the workings of AI, or how the technology is cashing out. Children who cannot understand and process their digital personas should be supported by adults who provide and teach respectful parenting and meaningful consent (UNICEF, 2020). In addition, children who are unable to identify what is real or fabricated can be an outcome of AI-generated content, such as misinformation and deepfakes. Given the content, the distortion of digital media can manipulate children's understanding of the world and create cognitive distrust in the social and political order (OECD, 2020).

AI technology is redefining children's understanding, relationships, and interactions with the concept of community. Increased reliance on digital technology can, paradoxically, lead to social isolation and a reduced ability to practice empathy, active listening, and collaborative problem-solving. Children's relationships become superficial, and their ability to navigate complex social ecosystems is impaired (Brookings, 2021).

From another perspective, the UNICEF (2020) report, AI and Children's Rights, outlines the need to harmonize the governance of AI technologies with the legal frameworks established by the United Nations Convention on the Rights of the Child (CRC). Central to this are the principles of protecting children from AI systems that exploit them for profit, ensuring privacy through data protection and children's advocacy, active participation in the right to non-discrimination, and the promotion of equity and inclusion. AI systems should be designed and implemented using a collaborative approach that involves children affected directly, allowing children to advocate for their interests and raise their concerns constructively.

In order to prepare children to engage with AI in an ethical manner, such engagement should integration into the school syllabus and taught as part of core subjects.

Every student, beyond all of this, also needs to cross certain thresholds, such as the ability to counter and remove digital suppression, counter disinformation core skills, deepfakes, Brookings (2021) – digital violence, and information suppression out of the AI world. In light of Brookings (2021) and referring to hopping systems, critical and ethical technology thinkers aim to produce digital citizens that harness the power of AI to achieve social equity.

Ultimately, fostering psychological resilience along with taught skills is a core element that children need to meet the emotional and cognitive demands of an AI-centered world. Schools and parents need to find a balance that promotes mental health while lessening digital absorption. Approaches that foster healthy self-regulation and technology habits, coupled with mindfulness and emotional balance, can contribute to lessening the challenges of digital saturation. Above all, children need to learn to become critical media that encourages the questioning of all information presented to resist and counter the misinformation swamp (OECD, 2020).

Cultivating psychological resilience, self-regulation, and digital wisdom together promises to foster children's growth beyond the expectations of society – emotionally, ethically, and technologically.

POLICY RECOMMENDATIONS AND GLOBAL FRAMEWORKS

Governments, educational institutions, and global entities should formulate policies that prepare children for the future without delay. Unmanaged and un-strategized AI will deepen existing social inequities, violate children's rights, and compromise educational equity. The intelligent tutoring systems and automated assessments that AI is currently capable of implementing in brick-and-mortar and virtual classrooms are the reason for the global policy concern. It is astonishing to see the potential claim within the ethical and educational policy discourse that a generation will be prepared to face the world without AI. According to documents from UNICEF (2020) and the OECD (2020), the importance of policy responses to AI is not limited to the teaching and learning context but extends to the preservation of equity, justice, and inclusion principles.

Regarding governance, any country is expected to follow educational policies based on international guidelines. One fundamental step is the integration of AI into the school curriculum. AI instruction should begin at the primary school level and focus on key elements such as ethics, coding, algorithmic thinking, and data.

The OECD (2020) states that, even at the earliest stages of schooling, instruction on fundamental AI concepts helps foster computational thinking and broader critical thinking about the digital environment. In addition to these proposals for curriculum modernization, the professional development of teachers should also be reframed to include programmes targeting school AI integration. Professional educators require ongoing support to use AI efficiently for instruction and for students to use the tools ethically and productively. According to UNESCO (2021), frontline educators of AI are directly responsible for the use of AI in education; therefore, their professional development is crucial to successful AI integration by pupils.

Ensuring that no one is left behind in the AI revolution is of utmost importance. Governments must focus on the construction of digital infrastructures so that all learners, especially those in remote and neglected areas, can enjoy AI-supported education. These AI-supported education frameworks must include the provision of digital devices, internet connectivity, and the development of AI resources aligned with the plurality of learners' cultures and languages. The digital divide, as pointed out by the World Economic Forum (2020), is one of the most challenging hurdles in providing equitable and inclusive AI education. Students who do not have access to reliable technology are becoming increasingly disadvantaged in a growing number of digital learning opportunities.

Alongside the above, safeguarding the privacy and data of children and young people is an important focus. The development of data legislation for children that goes beyond one-size-fits-all policies, such as the GDPR and COPPA, is imperative. Necessary policies must include AI educational applications that explain the processes of data collection, analysis, and storage.

The rational integration of sustainability in operations is centered on the right funding strategies and resource allocation and deployment. Integrating the teaching of AI and its related technologies as one of the primary research educational budget line items should be mandatory in the national budgets of every country. Furthermore, subsidized and grant-aided funding of community digital literacy programs in resource-poor areas is necessary to address the most severe disparities in digital com.

Investments in human capital, particularly those based on digital ways and means, will undoubtedly, as the OECD (2020) argues, help improve a nation's global competitiveness and enhance social cohesion. Bridging the digital divide is one of the major obstacles to the implementation of education AI. Every learner has a right to basic education, and a vital aspect of this is the ability to gain access to the Internet to help them with their digital learning. AI programs that focus on device donation and programmatic content development can help reduce this gap. UNESCO (2021) argues that AI teaching materials should be adapted to local and appropriate local contexts to recognize differences in languages, cultures, and other social values.

Finally, any policy on AI education should include clear monitoring and evaluation of the impact of AI tools.

Technology will no longer replace the teacher but rather work as a seamless collaboration tool to strengthen teaching, inclusive learning, and adaptive environments. AI-integrated educational technologies serve different yet interconnected purposes and functions at various phases of the learning journey. For example, intelligent tutoring systems (ITS) offer personalized instruction designed to be respectful of students' individual learning styles, pace, and levels of understanding. These systems sustain automated (formative) assessments and provide feedback so that instructional adjustments can be made dynamically to promote seamless learning. Notable examples of ITSs include Carnegie Learning and Squirrel AI (adaptive learning systems provided in China), and Duolingo (World Economic Forum, 2020). In addition to ITS, there are adaptive learning systems driven by AI and machine learning. DreamBox, Century Tech, and Knewton are examples of adaptive learning systems that use real-time data and machine learning to dynamically adjust learning materials so that every student follows a personalized educational pathway (UNESCO, 2021). These systems provide automated instructional feedback, replace tedious instructional adjustments, and help balance the instructional workload.

Another substantial advancement is AI assessment systems. These systems reduce the instructional workload generated by student assessments by automating the scoring of student essays and other open-ended tasks and even provide some objective scoring. They include Gradescope and Turnitin's AI writing detection system, which assesses outputs for originality, coherence, and structure. In addition, these systems provide diagnostic insights that help teachers track learning trends and pinpoint where students might need more support (OECD, 2020). Automating functions in educational assessments improves fairness and efficiency.

Including robotics and physical computing in the curriculum closes the gap between theory and practice. Students learn automation, coding, and the foundational principles of machine learning using robotics kits such as LEGO Mindstorms VEX Robotics and MIT Scratch-integrated robots (UNICEF, 2020). Students gain soft and hard skills through interactive and responsive communication features and feedback in applications such as Grammarly and Google Assistant, Socratic by Google, and other natural language processing (NLP) tools. These applications serve as virtual tutors, assisting learners in writing, problem-solving, and comprehension. All these tools encourage learners to develop the necessary analytical skills. Emerging technologies, including virtual reality (VR) and augmented reality (AR), continue to augment learning and embedded artificial intelligence (AI) technologies. Students are able to delve deep and understand the intricate details of various disciplines, scientific and historical, through these immersive and interactive technologies. Google Expeditions and Labster are other tools that learners use in the classroom.

The former provides AR/VR experiences of remote places and historical events, and the latter offers safe virtual laboratories.

Learning tools have been created to teach AI concepts to children and make the process easier and more fun. For example, the course Machine Learning for Kids helps students learn how to build and train simple machine learning models and builds a foundation for understanding the core concepts of AI. In addition, the AI + Ethics Curriculum created by MIT Media Lab helps students learn the technical and ethical dimensions of AI, fostering thoughtful and responsible use of such technology. Similarly, Google's Teachable Machine allows students to construct fundamental AI models with no advanced coding required, helping them become creators and not just consumers of technology.

Artificial intelligence helps more than learning; that is, AI technology helps manage lessons and school administration more efficiently. Self-service automated attendance systems scan the pupils' faces and make a good first pass at collection, but the ethical and privacy issues remain to

AI-integrated educational technologies serve different yet interconnected purposes and functions at various phases of the learning journey. For example, intelligent tutoring systems (ITS) offer personalized instruction designed to be respectful of students' individual learning styles, pace, and levels of understanding. These systems sustain automated (formative) assessments and provide feedback so that instructional adjustments can be made dynamically to promote seamless learning. Notable examples of ITSs include Carnegie Learning and Squirrel AI (adaptive learning systems provided in China), and Duolingo (World Economic Forum, 2020). In addition to ITS, there are adaptive learning systems driven by AI and machine learning. DreamBox, Century Tech, and Knewton are examples of adaptive learning systems that use real-time data and machine learning to dynamically adjust learning materials so that every student follows a personalized educational pathway (UNESCO, 2021). These systems provide automated instructional feedback, replace tedious instructional adjustments, and help balance the instructional workload.

Another substantial advancement is AI assessment systems. These systems reduce the instructional workload generated by student assessments by automating the scoring of student essays and other open-ended tasks and even provide some objective scoring. They include Gradescope and Turnitin's AI writing detection system, which assesses outputs for originality, coherence, and structure. In addition, these systems provide diagnostic insights that help teachers track learning trends and pinpoint where students might need more support (OECD, 2020). Automating functions in educational assessments improves fairness and efficiency. Including robotics and physical computing in the curriculum closes the gap between theory and practice. Students learn automation, coding, and the foundational principles of machine learning using robotics kits such as LEGO Mindstorms VEX Robotics and MIT Scratch-integrated robots (UNICEF, 2020). Students gain soft and hard skills through interactive and responsive communication features and feedback in applications such as Grammarly and Google Assistant, Socratic by Google, and other natural language processing (NLP) tools. These applications serve as virtual tutors, assisting learners in writing, problem-solving, and comprehension. All these tools encourage learners to develop the necessary analytical skills. Emerging technologies, including virtual reality (VR) and augmented reality (AR), continue to augment learning and embedded artificial intelligence (AI) technologies. Students are able to delve deep and understand the intricate details of various disciplines, scientific and historical, through these immersive and interactive technologies. Google Expeditions and Labster are other tools that learners use in the classroom. The former provides AR/VR experiences of remote places and historical events, and the latter offers safe virtual laboratories.

Learning tools have been created to teach AI concepts to children and make the process easier and more fun. For example, the course Machine Learning for Kids helps students learn how to build and train simple machine learning models and builds a foundation for understanding the core concepts of AI. In addition, the AI + Ethics Curriculum created by MIT Media Lab helps students learn the technical and ethical dimensions of AI, fostering thoughtful and responsible use of such technology. Similarly, Google's Teachable Machine allows students to construct fundamental AI models with no advanced coding required, helping them become creators and not just consumers of technology.

Artificial intelligence helps more than learning; that is, AI technology helps manage lessons and school administration more efficiently. Although self-service automated attendance systems can scan pupils' faces and make a good first pass at collection, ethical and privacy issues remain to be solved. Predictive analytics AI tools can recognize pupils at risk of academic disengagement or failure to employ appropriate interventions. AI also helps school managers with resource allocation, scheduling, and budgeting to improve equity and the efficiency of educational administration. AI-enhanced learning tools provide numerous and highly beneficial transformations. One of the greatest advantages of these tools is AI-enabled personalization. AI systems design individualized learning pathways that account for the varying paces and preferred styles of learners. Another benefit is accessibility. AI-driven assistive technologies, including speech recognition software, captioning tools, and screen readers, provide essential support to learners with disabilities. Such innovations facilitate and foster the inclusiveness of education. Additionally, the automation of monotonous, repetitive tasks enables educators to redirect their efforts to more meaningful student-centered teaching. Learner engagement is also increased through AI tools that incorporate gamification and other immersive technologies to make the learning experience interactive and enjoyable.

The integration of AI in educational systems poses identifiable difficulties. For instance, the collection of personal information related to minors raises important concerns regarding the violation of legal and ethical standards (UNICEF, 2020). Furthermore, biases inherent in the data used to train AI models can exacerbate existing problems of cultural, racial, and gender biases in the educational materials recommended to students. Excessive reliance on AI technology can also reduce interpersonal relationships, human imagination, and collective problem-solving. Lastly, the digital divide means that students in AI-enhanced, poorly connected, and digitally provided regions of the world will always lack the necessary innovation (UNESCO, 2021). The issues that AI poses to the educational systems of the world need strategic ethical digital infrastructure, design for civil investment, and comprehensive governance to the new problems artificial intelligence posits.

Future development of AI in education focuses on systems that ensure total transparency and ethical considerations. Work on explainable AI (XAI) is designed to develop educational technologies that make autonomous decisions and subsequently articulate the reasoning behind those decisions and the causal pathways that produced those decisions. This enhances trust and rapport with the user and understanding of the processes involved. The initiative, “AI Ethics by Design, ” aims at one of the newly identified goals of incorporating the principles of equity, accountability, and transparency into the design of AI systems. The predicted development of new hybrid learning ecosystems combining AI, virtual reality, traditional classrooms, and digital networks is likely to become the educational systems of the future. These systems will provide flexible, inclusive, and adaptive learning opportunities to equip students for the world of constant change.

AI-enabled education presents a paradox of great opportunity and responsibility. Advanced education technologies, with great ethical and moral responsibility, will make learning opportunities more flexible, inclusive, and empowering. The implementation of technology in education still requires the cooperation of educators, technologists, policymakers, and the community to ensure that new educational technologies promote and strengthen educational equity and human development rather than division and exclusion.

CONCLUSION AND FUTURE DIRECTIONS

The integration of artificial intelligence (AI) into children’s personal, educational, and vocational spheres by 2040 appears to be a realistic projection of the current technological advancement rate. Not to mention the incorporation of AI into education, which will extend beyond teaching (hard) facts and technical skills, education to prepare children for living, learning, and working in an AI-dominant environment will incorporate teaching more complex systems such as ethics and problem-solving both critically and creatively, as well as emotionally, to equip children with the multifaceted competencies to tackle the anticipated challenges of the future.

The influence of artificial intelligence (AI) has spread beyond the realm of science fiction and begun to shape industries, governance, and personal relationships worldwide. Future citizens will need to be flexible, ethical, and technologically savvy. The Organisation for Economic Co-operation and Development (OECD, 2020) and the World Economic Forum (2020) agree that AI will be pivotal in transformations in the world of work, citizenship, and social relations. Hence, the education system must adapt to equip learners with an understanding of the functioning of AI and the societal implications, potential ramifications, including, but not limited to, privacy concerns, the consequences of automation on employment, and the ethical challenges surrounding data collection, machine learning, automation, and other applications of artificial intelligence.

The competencies necessary for children to navigate the future implications of AI include critical thinking, emotional intelligence, AI literacy, data ethics, and the willingness to learn throughout life. UNESCO (2021) emphasizes the value of these competencies by stating that they enable learners to respond to fast-changing technologies while exercising ethical judgment in the digital space. Automation will replace repetitive tasks, and uniquely human attributes, such as empathy, creativity, and ethical reasoning, will become highly sought after. Thus, cultivating technical knowledge and socio-emotional competencies to help children become balanced and responsible global citizens is paramount.

Educational reform is at the center of this change. Curricula must evolve toward interdisciplinary learning that spans the sciences, technology, humanities, and ethics. It is essential to integrate ethically focused AI education and AI-driven adaptive learning tools in classrooms to meet the cognitive personalization of inclusive adaptive educational environments. As UNICEF (2020) describes, AI-driven adaptive learning tools have the potential to transform education by providing real-time feedback, personalizing learning pathways, and leveraging predictive analytics to close learning inequity gaps. Most importantly, however, is the reminder that technology in education will, and must, always be a means to an end, not the end itself.

It is unavoidable that AI will alter the role of teachers. When educators no longer transmit knowledge and instead become facilitators, all the while mentors and ethical guides, the role of teaching will shift. Teachers will help students navigate and make sense of the convoluted and ever-evolving digital realm, including understanding what it means to act upon an algorithm. They will help shape and refine the concept of responsible digital citizenship. According to Brookings (2021), AI and other emerging technologies will serve as tools to support human-centered pedagogical approaches. Therefore, teachers will have to learn to integrate other-centered empathy, compassion, and moral reasoning into the learning experience. To preserve the integrity of the discipline taught, teachers will need to engage in continuous professional development in AI-enabled tools and digital technologies. Teachers instructional human connection is irreplaceable and integral in the formation of character and instilling values, and nothing will ever change that.

Considering the implications for ethics and psychology, particularly the protection of children, the use of AI raises important concerns. Defending children against potential threats requires urgent action regarding mental health, the privacy of personal data, biased algorithms, and the digital divide. UNICEF statements call for regulation and warn that unregulated AI may deepen inequities and discrimination and expose children to predatory and biased digital content. Thus, education at all levels should include ethics and AI awareness components. Students need to assess digital instruments, comprehend the responsible use of technology, data rights, and consent, and learn about responsible technology use. Differential access to the Internet in developing countries and the associated lack of educational resources reinforce existing economic disparities and challenges in accessing education.

In Finland, Singapore, and Estonia, the promotion of digital citizenship and the integration of AI in the education system have been declared government priorities. These nations are viewed as role models worldwide because they have built ethics into the curriculum and developed strategic government initiatives and programs for comprehensive digital access to the entire population. Their practices have underscored the need for government action and cross-sector collaboration regarding digital citizenship. The purposeful integration of AI into educational practices enhances equity, innovation, and inclusiveness.

Preparing for the future shaped by artificial intelligence entails focusing on much more than the current state of the world. Quantum computing, artificial general intelligence, and bio–digital convergence are expected to offer unprecedented tools and technologies by the year 2040. Education must therefore equip children with the skills needed not only to work with AI technologies but also to prepare for future innovations that are beyond the current realm of imagination. Adaptability, resilience, ethical reasoning, and the ability to learn continuously will be fundamental meta-skills (Toffler, 1970; UNESCO, 2021). Students will be required to develop a growth mindset, while resilience will allow them to approach uncertainty with imagination and resourcefulness.

To fulfill these objectives in the next decade, several core foundations must be established. First, AI literacy should be treated like any other literacy, and all learners should be taught the fundamentals of AI and data literacy. In addition, responsible and ethical digital citizenship necessitates the teaching of ethics as a foundational subject. Therefore, ethics education must be provided alongside the other fundamentals of mathematics, science, and language. Moreover, to ensure that teachers can utilize

AI in an effective and ethical manner, investment in teacher AI training is required. In the interest of equity, the right of all people, especially learners, to access the internet and other digital technologies should be guaranteed by governments. The global exchange of AI educational practices, sharing of open-source curricula, and collaborative research on AI in education should also be encouraged. Finally, any AI tools designed for and used by children should be safe, equitable, and inclusive, devoid of opaque principles, and guided by the best interests of the child.

Ultimately, AI adaptation for children goes beyond pure education. This call for action is directed at governments, tech developers, parents, children, and civil society. Our present-day decisions will either cement the potential of AI to assist and integrate or isolate and undermine democratic processes. Education remains the most powerful tool for promoting positive change and sustainable development, but it must be imbued with heart, motivation, and community. Only a combination of character and intellect will enable children to adapt to the AI revolution and build a more human, creative, and compassionate world.

REFERENCES

Acemoglu, D., & Restrepo, P. (2020). Robots and jobs: Evidence from US labor markets. *Journal of Political Economy*, *128*(6), 2188–2244. DOI: 10.1086/705716

Bohr, A., & Memarzadeh, K. (2020). *Artificial Intelligence in Healthcare*. Academic Press.

. Brookings Institution. (2021). *Preparing children for the AI era: Ethical, educational, and social considerations*. Brookings.edu.

Brynjolfsson, E., & McAfee, A. (2017). *The Second Machine Age: Work, Progress, and Prosperity in a Time of Brilliant Technologies*. W. W. Norton & Company.

Floridi, L. (2020). *The Ethics of Artificial Intelligence*. Oxford University Press.

Floridi, L. (2020). *The Fight for the Future of AI: How We Can Shape It*. Oxford University Press.

Luckin, R. (2018). *Machine Learning and Human Intelligence: The Future of Education in the 21st Century*. UCL Institute of Education Press.

OECD. (2019). *OECD AI Principles: Recommendation of the Council on Artificial Intelligence*. https://legalinstruments.oecd.org/en/instruments/OECD-LEGAL-0449

OECD. (2020). *OECD Digital Economy Outlook 2020*. OECD Publishing., DOI: 10.1787/bb167041-

OECD. (2020). *The Future of Education and Skills: OECD Education 2030 Framework*. OECD Publishing. https://www.oecd.org/education/2030-project/

Russell, S. J., & Norvig, P. (2020). *Artificial Intelligence: A Modern Approach* (4th ed.). Pearson.

Toffler, A. (1970). *Future Shock*. Random House.

Topol, E. J. (2019). *Deep Medicine: How Artificial Intelligence Can Make Healthcare Human Again*. Basic Books.

UNESCO. (2021). *AI and Education: Guidance for Policy-Makers*. United Nations Educational, Scientific and Cultural Organization.

UNESCO. (2021). *Recommendation on the Ethics of Artificial Intelligence*. https://unesdoc.unesco.org/ark:/48223/pf0000381137

UNICEF. (2020). *Policy Guidance on AI for Children*. https://www.unicef.org/globalinsight/reports/policy-guidance-ai-children

University of Helsinki. (2020). *Elements of AI*. https://www.elementsofai.com/

World Economic Forum. (2020). *The Future of Jobs Report 2020*. https://www.weforum.org/reports/the-future-of-jobs-report-2020/

KEY TERM AND DEFINITIONS

Artificial Intelligence (AI): The simulation of human intelligence processes by machines. In this paper, it refers specifically to systems capable of learning, reasoning, and adjusting inputs to achieve specific goals in education and the labor market.

Generative AI: A subset of AI (e.g., LLMs like ChatGPT) capable of creating new content—text, images, or code—based on patterns learned from existing data. In 2040, this is viewed as a primary tool for creative collaboration.

Computational Thinking: A problem-solving process that involves breaking down complex challenges into smaller, manageable parts (decomposition), identifying patterns, and designing algorithmic solutions.

Machine Learning (ML): The process by which AI improves its performance through exposure to data rather than explicit programming. This is the "engine" behind personalized learning paths.

Compilation of References

Acemoglu, D., & Restrepo, P. (2020). Robots and jobs: Evidence from US labor markets. *Journal of Political Economy*, *128*(6), 2188–2244. DOI: 10.1086/705716

Ali, S., DiPaola, D., Lee, I., Sindato, V., Kim, G., Blumofe, R., & Breazeal, C. (2021). Children as creators, thinkers and citizens in an AI-driven future. *Computers and Education: Artificial Intelligence*, *2*, 100040. DOI: 10.1016/j.caeai.2021.100040

Aljemely, Y. (2024). Challenges and best practices in training teachers to utilize artificial intelligence: A systematic review. *Frontiers in Education*, *9*, 1–19. DOI: 10.3389/feduc.2024.1470853

Al-Zahrani, A. M., & Alasmari, T. M. (2024). Exploring the impact of artificial intelligence on higher education: The dynamics of ethical, social, and educational implications. *Humanities & Social Sciences Communications*, *11*(1), 912. DOI: 10.1057/s41599-024-03432-4

Amankwah-Amoah, J., Abdalla, S., Mogaji, E., Elbanna, A., & Dwivedi, Y. K. (2024). The impending disruption of creative industries by generative AI: Opportunities, challenges, and research agenda. International Journal of Information Management. https://linkinghub.elsevier.com/retrieve/pii/S0268401224000070

Anantrasirichai, N., & Bull, D. (2022). Artificial intelligence in the creative industries: A review. *Artificial Intelligence Review*, *55*(1), 589–656. https://link.springer.com/article/10.1007/s10462-021-10039-7. DOI: 10.1007/s10462-021-10039-7 PMID: 41625196

Anderson, J., Nguyen, C. A., & Ucok Hughes, M. (2025). Mapping theory to practice: AI-enhanced teaching theories for fostering diverse perspectives in business education. *Journal of International Education in Business*.

Anderson-Coto, M. J. (2024). *Advancing AI Education: The Computational Equity Approach* (Doctoral dissertation, University of California, Irvine).

Appio, F. P., Platania, F., & Hernandez, C. T. (2024). Pairing AI and sustainability: Envisioning entrepreneurial initiatives for virtuous twin paths. *IEEE Transactions on Engineering Management*, *71*, 11669–11686. DOI: 10.1109/TEM.2024.3428913

Artificial-intelligence-ai-in-product-design-and-development-market. (2025). https://www.marketsandmarkets.com/Market-Reports/artificial-intelligence-ai-in-product-design-and-development-market-123456789.html

Arute, F., Arya, K., Babbush, R., Bacon, D., Bardin, J. C., Barends, R., Biswas, R., Boixo, S., Brandao, F. G. S. L., Buell, D. A., Burkett, B., Chen, Y., Chen, Z., Chiaro, B., Collins, R., Courtney, W., Dunsworth, A., Farhi, E., Foxen, B., & Martinis, J. M. (2019). Quantum supremacy using a programmable superconducting processor. *Nature*, *574*(7779), 505–510. DOI: 10.1038/s41586-019-1666-5 PMID: 31645734

Aspers, P., & Corte, U. (2019). What is qualitative in qualitative research. *Qualitative Sociology*, *42*(2), 139–160. DOI: 10.1007/s11133-019-9413-7 PMID: 31105362

Aspers, P., & Corte, U. (2021). What is qualitative in research. *Qualitative Sociology*, *44*(4), 599–608. DOI: 10.1007/s11133-021-09497-w PMID: 31105362

Attaluri, V., & Mudunuri, L. N. R. (2025). Generative AI for Creative Learning Content Creation: Project-Based Learning and Art Generation. In Smart Education and Sustainable Learning Environments in Smart Cities (pp. 239-252). IGI Global Scientific Publishing. https://philarchive.org/rec/VIVGAF-2

Axiata, S. (2021). *Technology partnerships in Cambodian education*. Smart Axiata Corporate Report.

Babanoğlu, M. P., Karataş, T. Ö., & Dündar, E. (2025). Envisioning the Future of AI-Assisted EFL Teaching and Learning: Conceptual Representations of Prospective Teachers. *SAGE Open*, *15*(2), 21582440251341590. DOI: 10.1177/21582440251341590

Baig-Ward, K. M., Jha, M. K., & Trivedi, M. H. (2023). The individual and societal burden of treatment-resistant depression: An overview. *Psychiatria Clinica*, *46*(2), 211–226. PMID: 37149341

Baker, R. S., & Hawn, A. (2022). Algorithmic Bias in Education. *International Journal of Artificial Intelligence in Education*, *32*(4), 1052–1092. DOI: 10.1007/s40593-021-00285-9

Bassot, B. (2022). *Doing qualitative desk-based research: A practical guide to writing an excellent dissertation*. Policy Press.

Bautista, N., Femiani, J., & Inclezan, D. (2025). *Understanding K-12 teachers' needs for AI education: A survey-based study. Proceedings of the AAAI Conference on Artificial Intelligence.* https://ojs.aaai.org/index.php/AAAI/article/view/35183

Belpaeme, T., Kennedy, J., Ramachandran, A., Scassellati, B., & Tanaka, F. (2018). Social robots for education: A review. *Science Robotics*, *3*(21), eaat5954. Advance online publication. DOI: 10.1126/scirobotics.aat5954 PMID: 33141719

Bers, M. U. (2020). *Coding as a Playground.* Routledge., DOI: 10.4324/9781003022602

Berson, I. R., Berson, M. J., & Luo, W. (2025). Innovating responsibly: Ethical considerations for AI in early childhood education. *AI. Brain and Child*, *1*(1), 2. DOI: 10.1007/s44436-025-00003-5

Bhuvaneshwaran, A., Kavya, P., Dhaksana, N., Amuthaguka, D., Eraianbu, R., & Agilan, S. (2024, October). Artistic Fusion: AI Powered Artistry for Story Boarding. In 2024 4th International Conference on Sustainable Expert Systems (ICSES) (pp. 795-800). IEEE. https://www.semanticscholar.org/paper/Artistic-Fusion%3A-AI-Powered-Artistry-for-Story-Bhuvaneshwaran-K./a51a4bf5234e7d4b0520d62724fc5381bfd48d30

Bittner, E., Mirbabaie, M., & Morana, S. (2021). Digital facilitation assistance for collaborative, creative design processes.

Bodrova, E., & Leong, D. J. (2015). Vygotskian and Post-Vygotskian Views on Children's Play. *American Journal of Play*, *7*(3), 371–388.

Bohr, A., & Memarzadeh, K. (2020). *Artificial Intelligence in Healthcare.* Academic Press.

Bon, S., & Charubusp, S. (2024). Teachers' attitudes toward English as Lingua Franca (ELF), World Englishes (WEs), and Teachers' Professional Identities (TPIs). *Athens Journal of Philology*, *11*, 311–326. DOI: 10.30958/ajp.11-4-3

Bon, S., & Inpin, B. (2024). Roles of two PD modes in technology integration for EFL classes: Training and professional learning communities. *Issues in Educational Research*, *34*(1), 1–18. https://www.iier.org.au/iier34/bon-abs.html

Bon, S., & Koem, V. (2025). STEM Education: Pre-Service Teachers' Knowledge, Attitude, Practice Intention, and Possible Challenges. *International Journal of Technology in Education and Science*, *9*(2), 270–284. DOI: 10.46328/ijtes.617

Bowen, J. P. (2024). Alan Turing: Breaking the Code, Computing, and Machine Intelligence. In The Arts and Computational Culture: Real and Virtual Worlds (pp. 75-94). Cham: Springer Nature Switzerland. https://www.researchgate.net/publication/381789532_Alan_Turing_Breaking_the_Code_Computing_and_Machine_Intelligence

Brynjolfsson, E., & McAfee, A. (2017). *Machine, platform, crowd: Harnessing our digital future.* W. W. Norton & Company. https://cir.nii.ac.jp/crid/1971993809789801089

Brynjolfsson, E., & McAfee, A. (2017). *The Second Machine Age: Work, Progress, and Prosperity in a Time of Brilliant Technologies.* W. W. Norton & Company.

Bulut, M. B., Kurtaran, D., Bostancı, V., Sarı, Y., & Çil, K. N. (2024). Self-esteem, hopelessness, quality of life, and psychological symptoms in individuals diagnosed with periodontal disease. *Current Psychology*, *43*(8), 7071–7083. DOI: 10.1007/s12144-023-04924-3

Buolamwini, J., & Gebru, T. (2018). Gender Shades: Intersectional Accuracy Disparities in Commercial Gender Classification. *Proceedings of the 1st Conference on Fairness, Accountability and Transparency*, 77–91. https://proceedings.mlr.press/v81/buolamwini18a.html.

Bux, S., & Van Vuuren, J. (2019). The effect of entrepreneurship education programmes on the development of self-efficacy, entrepreneurial intention and predictions for entrepreneurial. *Acta Commercii*, *19*(2), 1–13. DOI: 10.4102/ac.v19i2.615

Calvo, R. A., & Peters, D. (2014). *Positive computing: technology for wellbeing and human potential.* MIT press. DOI: 10.7551/mitpress/9764.001.0001

Cambodian Education Forum. (2023, September 18). *STEM education in Cambodia: Progress and challenges.* https://cefcambodia.com/2023/09/18/stem-education-in-cambodia-progress-and-challenges/

Cambridge-MIT Institute. (n.d.). *Knowledge transfer*. Retrieved from https://www.cambridge.org/engage/api-gateway/mit/assets/orp/resource/item/63e2b3b8c6b8a4f4a4f4b4b4/original/knowledge-transfer.pdf

Carella, G., Colombo, F., Migliozzi, S., & Arquilla, V. (2024). Design Thinking as an enabler of change in the technological market. A practical case study of company's innovation and differentiation. *INTED Proceedings*, •••, 3025–3033. DOI: 10.21125/inted.2024.0817

Cefai, C., Simões, C., & Caravita, S. (2021). A systemic, whole-school approach to mental health and well-being in schools in the EU.

Chandler, D. P. (2008). *A history of Cambodia.* Westview Press. https://cir.nii.ac.jp/crid/1971149384846462136

Chen, L., Chen, P., & Lin, Z. (2020). Artificial intelligence in education: A review. *IEEE Access : Practical Innovations, Open Solutions*, *8*, 75264–75278. DOI: 10.1109/ACCESS.2020.2988510

Chiu, T. K. F., Ahmad, Z., & Çoban, M. (2025). Development and Validation of Teacher Artificial Intelligence (AI) Competence Self-Efficacy (TAICS) Scale. *Education and Information Technologies*, *30*(5), 6667–6685. DOI: 10.1007/s10639-024-13094-z

Choe, N. S., & Hinz, L. D. (2024). The Role of the Expressive Therapies Continuum in Human Creativity in the Age of AI. *Art Therapy: Journal of the American Art Therapy Association*, •••, 1–9. https://eric.ed.gov/?id=EJ1475514

Chubb, J., Missaoui, S., Concannon, S., Maloney, L., & Walker, J. A. (2022). Interactive storytelling for children: A case-study of design and development considerations for ethical conversational AI. *International Journal of Child-Computer Interaction*, *32*, 100403. https://www.sciencedirect.com/science/article/abs/pii/S2212868921000921. DOI: 10.1016/j.ijcci.2021.100403

Chui, M., Manyika, J., Bughin, J., Dobbs, R., Roxburgh, C., & Sarrazin, H. (2018). *The impact of AI on the future of work*. McKinsey Global Institute.

Cohen, A., & Miller, M. (2022). Conducting focus groups in multicultural educational settings. *International Journal of Qualitative Methods*, *21*, 1–12. DOI: 10.1177/16094069221076928

Colby, K. M. (1975). *Artificial paranoia: A computer simulation of paranoid processes*. Pergamon Press.

Courtney, P. (2024). Education, inclusive growth, and fiscal consolidation.

Cowls, J., Tsamados, A., Taddeo, M., & Floridi, L. (2023). The AI gambit: Leveraging artificial intelligence to combat climate change—opportunities, challenges, and recommendations. *AI & Society*, *38*(1), 283–307. DOI: 10.1007/s00146-021-01294-x PMID: 34690449

Coyle, S., Malecki, C. K., & Emmons, J. (2021). Keep your friends close: Exploring the associations of bullying, peer social support, and social anxiety. *Contemporary School Psychology*, *25*(2), 230–242. DOI: 10.1007/s40688-019-00250-3

Craig, C., & Kerr, I. (2025). The death of the AI author. In *Robot Law* (Vol. II, pp. 250–285). Edward Elgar Publishing., https://robots.law.miami.edu/2019/wp-content/uploads/2019/03/Kerr_Death-of-AI-Author.pdf

Crawford, K. (2021). *The atlas of AI: Power, politics, and the planetary costs of artificial intelligence.* Yale University Press.

Crescenzi-Lanna, L., Araya, R., & Kafai, Y. B. (2021). Designing developmentally appropriate AI learning experiences for young children. *IDC '21: Interaction Design and Children Conference*, 269–274. https://doi.org/DOI: 10.1145/3459990.3465184

Crevier, D. (1993). *AI: The tumultuous history of the search for artificial intelligence.* Basic Books. https://cir.nii.ac.jp/crid/1970586434887638420

Daniele, A., Di Bernardi Luft, C., & Bryan-Kinns, N. (2021). "What Is Human?" A Turing Test for Artistic Creativity. In Artificial Intelligence in Music, Sound, Art and Design: 10th International Conference, EvoMUSART 2021, Held as Part of EvoStar 2021, Virtual Event, April 7–9, 2021, Proceedings 10 (pp. 396-411). Springer International Publishing. https://dl.acm.org/doi/abs/10.1007/978-3-030-72914-1_26

Del Casale, A., Zocchi, C., Kotzalidis, G. D., Fiaschè, F., & Girardi, P. (2021). Prevention of depression in children, adolescents, and young adults: The role of teachers and parents. *Psychiatry International*, *2*(3), 353–364. DOI: 10.3390/psychiatryint2030027

Devi, K. S., Raghunath, S., Patil, J. S., & Shanti, M. (2025). AI-Driven Classroom Management With Intelligent Tutoring Systems. In *Driving Quality Education Through AI and Data Science* (pp. 259–282). IGI Global Scientific Publishing.

Domingos, P. (2015). *The master algorithm: How the quest for the ultimate learning machine will remake our world.* Basic Books. https://www.redalyc.org/pdf/6380/638067264018.pdf

Druga, S., Williams, R., Breazeal, C., & Resnick, M. (2017). "Hey Google, is it OK if I eat you?": Initial explorations in child–AI interaction. *Proceedings of the 2017 Conference on Interaction Design and Children*, 595–600. https://doi.org/DOI: 10.1145/3078072.3084330

Dubay, C. M., & Richards, M. B. (2024). Leveraging artificial intelligence in project-based service learning to advance sustainable development: A pedagogical approach for marketing education. *Marketing Education Review*, *34*(4), 307–323. DOI: 10.1080/10528008.2024.2411975

Dzomonda, O., & Fatoki, O. (2019). The role of institutions of higher learning towards youth entrepreneurship development in South Africa. *Academy of Entrepreneurship Journal*, *25*(1), 1–11.

Echave, J. A. (2024). Exploring teachers' perceptions, practices, and potential impact of AI technologies in education. *Journal of Educational Technology*, *10*(1), 78–92. DOI: 10.1016/j.jedutech.2024.02.004

Egon, K., Potter, K., & Lord, M. L. (2023). Ai in art and creativity: Exploring the boundaries of human-machine collaboration. *OSF Preprints*, 20, 1-11. https://osf.io/preprints/osf/g4nd5_v1

Eisenberg, N., Spinrad, T. L., & Valiente, C. (2016). Emotion-related self-regulation, and children's social, psychological, and academic functioning. In Balter, L., & Tamis-LeMonda, C. S. (Eds.), *Child Psychology* (pp. 219–244). Psychology Press., DOI: 10.4324/9781315764931

Elfar, M., & Dawood, M. E. T. (2024). Artificial Intelligence Ethics: A Discussion of Potential Risks and Associated Ethical Dilemmas in Art and Design. *Journal of Heritage and Design*, *4*(23), 370–385. https://jsos.journals.ekb.eg/article_308526.html?lang=en

Em, S. (2025). *Effectiveness of school directors' transformational leadership on teachers' self-efficacy and job performance in Cambodia* [Doctoral dissertation, The University of Cambodia]. CJESS Online Library. https://ejournal.educationalfields.com/index.php/CJESSOL/article/view/63

Em, S. (2021). Challenges of online learning during the COVID-19 pandemic: A survey of Cambodian high school students. *Cambodian Journal of Educational Research*, *1*(2), 96–108. DOI: 10.62037/cjer.2021.01.02.09

Em, S. (2023). Cambodian students' online learning challenges during the COVID-19 pandemic: A vision for future measures. *International Journal of Cambodian Education*, *1*(1), 1–5. https://sereyrathlearning.wordpress.com/2023/01/05/cambodian-students-online-learning-challenges-during-the-covid-19-pandemic-a-vision-for-future-measures/

Em, S., Chin, P., & Pen, D. (2024). COVID-19 and school closures: Transformation of shadow education in the Cambodian context. In Alam, M. B. (Ed.), *Shadow education in Asia: Policies and practices* (pp. 136–159). IGI Global., DOI: 10.4018/979-8-3693-2952-8.ch009

Em, S., & Khampirat, B. (2025a). Facilitating scholarly pursuits in higher education: Cambodia's endeavors toward research advancement. In Mdikana, A. A. (Ed.), *Enhancing research output in higher education: Research proposals, profiles, and publishing* (pp. 39–66). IGI Global Scientific Publishing., DOI: 10.4018/979-8-3373-0806-7.ch002

Em, S., & Khampirat, B. (2025b). Cooperative education for sustainability: AI in learning opportunities, challenges, and future directions. In Tariq, M. U., & Sergio, R. P. (Eds.), *Convergence of AI, education, and business for sustainability* (pp. 75–92). IGI Global Scientific Publishing., DOI: 10.4018/979-8-3373-1917-9.ch004

Em, S., Khan, S., & Nun, N. (2023). Education system in Cambodia: A brief review from the prehistoric period to the present, and an education strategic plan for the future. *FIRE: Forum for International Research in Education*, *7*(3), 141–164. DOI: 10.32865/fire202273320

Em, S., Mok, S., Sam, R., Kurniawan, G. F., & Pen, D. (2025). History of education in Cambodia: A review of literature from past to present. *Paramita: Historical Studies Journal*, *35*(1), 32–47. DOI: 10.15294/paramita.v35i1.9207

Em, S., Phann, S., & Khan, S. (2022). Cambodian EFL university students' perceptions of online learning effectiveness during the COVID-19 pandemic: A survey study. *Cambodian Journal of Educational Research*, *2*(2), 15–34. DOI: 10.62037/cjer.2022.02.02.02

Epstein, Z., Hertzmann, A., Herman, L., Mahari, R., Frank, M., Groh, M., Schroeder, H., Smith, A., Akten, M., Fjeld, J., Farid, H., Leach, N., Pentland, A., & Russakovsky, O. (2023). Art and the science of generative AI. Science. https://arxiv.org/abs/2306.04141

Eubanks, V. (2025). *Automating inequality: How high-tech tools profile, police, and punish the poor*. Macmillan+ ORM.

Eyal, L., & Gil, E. (2022). *Hybrid Learning Spaces — A Three-Fold Evolving Perspective* (pp. 11–23). DOI: 10.1007/978-3-030-88520-5_2

Fazel, M., & Soneson, E. (2023). Current evidence and opportunities in child and adolescent public mental health: A research review. *Journal of Child Psychology and Psychiatry, and Allied Disciplines*, *64*(12), 1699–1719. DOI: 10.1111/jcpp.13889 PMID: 37771261

Fernandes, T., Nisi, V., Nunes, N., & James, S. (2024, September). ArtAI4DS: AI Art and Its Empowering Role in Digital Storytelling. In International Conference on Entertainment Computing (pp. 78-93). Cham: Springer Nature Switzerland. https://www.stuart-james.com/publications/2024ICEC/FernandesICEC24.pdf

Flick, C., & Worrall, K. (2022). The ethics of creative AI. In *The language of creative AI: Practices, aesthetics and structures* (pp. 73–91). Springer International Publishing., https://liedra.net/misc/Flick_Worrall-Ethics_of_Creative_AI.pdf DOI: 10.1007/978-3-031-10960-7_5

Floridi, L. (2020). *The Ethics of Artificial Intelligence.* Oxford University Press.

Floridi, L. (2020). *The Fight for the Future of AI: How We Can Shape It.* Oxford University Press.

Floridi, L., & Cowls, J. (2022). A Unified Framework of Five Principles for AI in Society. In *Machine Learning and the City* (pp. 535–545). Wiley., DOI: 10.1002/9781119815075.ch45

Fusuyama, N. (2021). *Global trends in AI and education: Case studies across five continents.* International AI in Education Research Group.

Gaggioli, A., Bartolotta, S., Ubaldi, A., Gerardini, K., Sarcinella, E. D., & Chirico, A. (2025). Extended Creativity: A Conceptual Framework for Understanding Human-AI Creative Relations. https://arxiv.org/abs/2506.10249

Gajalakshmi, G., & Meenakshi, S. (2023). Understanding the psycho-social problems of vulnerable adolescent girls and effect of intervention through life skill training. *Journal of Education and Health Promotion, 12*(1), 429. DOI: 10.4103/jehp.jehp_612_23 PMID: 38464658

Gala, P. M., Namit, K., & Kidwai, H. (2025). *Strategies for Enhancing Digital Skills among Africa's NEET Youth* (No. 203090). The World Bank.

Gao, R., Merzdorf, H. E., Anwar, S., Hipwell, M. C., & Srinivasa, A. (2023). Automatic assessment of text-based responses in post-secondary education: A systematic review. *arXiv*. https://doi.org//arXiv.2308.16151DOI: 10.48550

Gao, H., Li, Y., & Chen, J. (2023). *AI-enhanced collaborative learning: Applications and pedagogical strategies.* Springer.

Garcia Ramos, J., & Wilson-Kennedy, Z. (2024). Promoting equity and addressing concerns in teaching and learning with artificial intelligence. *Frontiers in Education, 9*, 1487882. Advance online publication. DOI: 10.3389/feduc.2024.1487882

Garcia, M. B. (2024). The paradox of artificial creativity: Challenges and opportunities of generative AI artistry. *Creativity Research Journal*, •••, 1–14. https://manuelgarcia.info/publication/artificial-creativity#:~:text=The%20distinction%20between%20generative%20AI,sole%20purview%20of%20sentient%20beings

Garg, S., & Sharma, R. C. (2025). Pedagogical Challenges of Online Teaching-Learning: Lessons Learned, Measures Adopted, and Suggestions for Way Forward. In *Education and Pedagogical Experiences* (pp. 7-24). Routledge India.

Gasser, U., & Almeida, V. A. F. (2017). A Layered Model for AI Governance. *IEEE Internet Computing*, *21*(6), 58–62. DOI: 10.1109/MIC.2017.4180835

Generative, A. I. 2024 Report | Bloomberg Professional Services. (2025). https://www.bloomberg.com/professional/products/bloomberg-terminal/research/bloomberg-intelligence/download/generative-ai-2024-report/

Gizir, S. (2007). Focus groups in educational studies. *Mersin Üniversitesi Eğitim Fakültesi Dergisi, 3*(1), 1–9. https://www.researchgate.net/publication/265106271

Gjorgjieski, V. (2024). Art Redefined: AI's Influence on Traditional Artistic Expression. *Journal of Art and Design*, *1*(1), 49–60. https://www.researchgate.net/publication/382104061_Art_Redefined_AI's_Influence_on_Traditional_Artistic_Expression

Gkintoni, E., Vantaraki, F., Skoulidi, C., Anastassopoulos, P., & Vantarakis, A. (2024). Promoting physical and mental health among children and adolescents via gamification—A conceptual systematic review. *Behavioral Sciences (Basel, Switzerland)*, *14*(2), 102. DOI: 10.3390/bs14020102 PMID: 38392455

Gn, S., Hleza, S., Shonhiwa, S., & Mathonsi, E. (2021). Qualitative content analysis, utility, usability and processes in educational research. *International Journal of Research and Innovation in Social Science*, *5*(07), 553–558.

Golden, L. M., & Struloeff, K. (2025). The Future of AI in Education: Innovations and Insights. *Social Innovations Journal, 30*.

Goleman, D. (1995). *Emotional intelligence: Why it can matter more than IQ*. Bantam Books. https://cir.nii.ac.jp/crid/1970023484866461959

Goodfellow, I., Bengio, Y., & Courville, A. (2016). *Deep learning*. MIT Press. https://cir.nii.ac.jp/crid/1971149384893273390

Goralski, M. A., & Tan, T. K. (2020). Artificial intelligence and sustainable development. *International Journal of Management Education*, *18*(1), 100330. DOI: 10.1016/j.ijme.2019.100330

Grigenti, F. (2022). The child program and the history of AI. *Orbis Idearum, 10* (2), 41-63. https://www.doi.org/10.26106/gb8e-p413

Guan, C., Mou, J., & Jiang, Z. (2020). Artificial intelligence innovation in education: A twenty-year data-driven historical analysis. *International Journal of Innovation Studies*, *4*(4), 134–147. DOI: 10.1016/j.ijis.2020.09.001

Guszcza, J., Mahoney, S., & Mahoney, J. (2018). Preparing for AI in the workforce. *Deloitte Review, 22*, 6–15. https://arxiv.org/vc/arxiv/papers/2105/2105.05424v1.pdf

Haase, J., & Pokutta, S. (2024). Human-AI Co-Creativity: Exploring Synergies Across Levels of Creative Collaboration. https://arXiv preprint arXiv:2411.12527.

Haenlein, M., & Kaplan, A. (2019). A brief history of artificial intelligence: On the past, present, and future of artificial intelligence. *California Management Review*, *61*(4), 5–14. DOI: 10.1177/0008125619864925

Handayani, P. W., Raharjo, S. R., & Putra, P. H. (2021). Active student learning through gamification in a learning management system. *Electronic Journal of e-Learning*, *19*(6), 601–613. DOI: 10.34190/ejel.19.6.2089

Hartwig, K., von Saldern, L., & Jacob, F. (2021). The journey from goods-dominant logic to service-dominant logic: A case study with a global technology manufacturer. *Industrial Marketing Management*, *95*, 85–98. DOI: 10.1016/j.indmarman.2021.04.006

Heng, K., & Sol, K. (2024). The use of AI and ChatGPT for education and research in Cambodia: Current state and future directions. *Cambodian Journal of Educational Research*, *4*(2), 1–11. DOI: 10.62037/cjer.2024.04.02.01

Heng, K., Sol, K., & Em, S. (2023). COVID-19 and digital transformation of Cambodian higher education: Opportunities, challenges, and the way forward. In Ordóñez de Pablos, P., Zhang, X., & Almunawar, M. N. (Eds.), *Handbook of research on education institutions, skills, and jobs in the digital era* (pp. 307–327). IGI Global., DOI: 10.4018/978-1-6684-5914-0.ch018

Hennekeuser, D., Vaziri, D. D., Golchinfar, D., Schreiber, D., & Stevens, G. (2025). Enlarged Education – Exploring the Use of Generative AI to Support Lecturing in Higher Education. *International Journal of Artificial Intelligence in Education*, *35*(3), 1096–1128. DOI: 10.1007/s40593-024-00424-y

Hill, D. L., Christakis, D. A., & Feudtner, C. (2022). Illness in the family and shared stress, work, and struggle. *JAMA Pediatrics*, *176*(6), 549–550. DOI: 10.1001/jamapediatrics.2022.0491 PMID: 35404432

Ho, L. L. K., Li, W. H. C., Cheung, A. T., Luo, Y., Xia, W., & Chung, J. O. K. (2022). Impact of poverty on parent–child relationships, parental stress, and parenting practices. *Frontiers in Public Health, 10,* 849408. DOI: 10.3389/fpubh.2022.849408 PMID: 35548071

Holmes, W. (2020). Artificial intelligence in education. In *Encyclopedia of education and information technologies* (pp. 88–103). Springer International Publishing. DOI: 10.1007/978-3-030-10576-1_107

Holmes, W., Bialik, M., & Fadel, C. (2019). *Artificial intelligence in education promises and implications for teaching and learning*. Center for Curriculum Redesign.

Holmes, W., Bialik, M., & Fadel, C. (2022). *Artificial Intelligence in Education: Promises and Implications for Teaching and Learning*. Centre for Curriculum Redesign.

Hossain, S. F. A. (Ed.). (2024). *Utilizing AI and Smart Technology to Improve Sustainability in Entrepreneurship*. IGI Global. DOI: 10.4018/979-8-3693-1842-3

How Netflix Content Recommendation System Works – HelloPM. (2025). https://hellopm.co/netflix-content-recommendation-system-product-analytics-case-study/

How Respeecher's Voice Cloning Brought Young Luke Skywalker to. … (2024). https://www.respeecher.com/case-studies/respeecher-synthesized-younger-luke-skywalkers-voice-disneys-mandalorian

Hughes, R. T., Zhu, L., & Bednarz, T. (2021). Generative adversarial networks–enabled human–artificial intelligence collaborative applications for creative and design industries: A systematic review of current approaches and trends. *Frontiers in Artificial Intelligence*, *4*, 604234. https://www.frontiersin.org/journals/artificial-intelligence/articles/10.3389/frai.2021.604234/full. DOI: 10.3389/frai.2021.604234 PMID: 33997773

Hussen, N., Samir, A., Adel, A., Gaber, A., Attaia, M., & Mohamed, A. (2025). Advancing Creativity: A Comprehensive Review of AI-Driven Text-to-Image Generation and Its Applications. Advanced Sciences and Technology Journal, 2(2), 1-17. https://astj.journals.ekb.eg/article_420273_b616acfb6bbfaaf59d6001872828d067.pdf

Hutt, S. J., Tyler, S., Hutt, C., & Christopherson, H. (2022). *Play, exploration and learning: a natural history of the pre-school*. Routledge. DOI: 10.4324/9781003324751

IBM. (2023). *AI Education Series for Educators*. https://www.ibm.com/skills/ai-education

Iddrisu, H. M., & Iddrisu, S. A. (2025). Teacher Readiness to Use AI Tools in the Classroom. *International Journal of Research in Education and Science, 11*(3), 494–510. https://eric.ed.gov/?id=EJ1480991. DOI: 10.46328/ijres.1314

Indah, S. (2025). Gamification in Early Childhood Education: Improving Students' Learning Motivation through Game-Based Learning Strategies. *Journal of Education Technology and Inovation, 8*(1), 50–64. DOI: 10.31537/jeti.v8i1.2333

Indrio, F., Pettoello-Mantovani, M., Giardino, I., & Masciari, E. (2024). The role of artificial intelligence in pediatrics from treating illnesses to managing children's overall well-being. *The Journal of Pediatrics, 275*, 275. DOI: 10.1016/j.jpeds.2024.114291 PMID: 39242077

Innovation Disclosure Report (IDR). (2021). *Innovation and entrepreneurship in Cambodia: National trends.*

Iwu, C. G., Opute, P. A., Nchu, R., Eresia-Eke, C., Tengeh, R. K., Jaiyeoba, O., & Aliyu, O. A. (2021). Entrepreneurship education, curriculum and lecturer-competency as antecedents of student entrepreneurial intention. *International Journal of Management Education, 19*(1), 100295. DOI: 10.1016/j.ijme.2019.03.007

Jaakkola, E., Kaartemo, V., Siltaloppi, J., & Vargo, S. L. (2024). Advancing service-dominant logic with systems thinking. *Journal of Business Research, 177*, 114592. DOI: 10.1016/j.jbusres.2024.114592

Japan International Cooperation Agency (JICA). (2024). *Preparatory survey report for the project for the construction of teacher education colleges in the Kingdom of Cambodia*. Retrieved from https://openjicareport.jica.go.jp/pdf/12301396_01.pdf

Jobin, A., Ienca, M., & Vayena, E. (2019). The global landscape of AI ethics guidelines. *Nature Machine Intelligence, 1*(9), 389–399. DOI: 10.1038/s42256-019-0088-2

Joel, A. (2024). The Impact Of Generative Ai On Creative Industries: Revolutionizing Art, Writing, And Music. https://www.researchgate.net/publication/391489737_THE_IMPACT_OF_GENERATIVE_AI_ON_CREATIVE_INDUSTRIES_REVOLUTIONIZING_ART_WRITING_AND_MUSIC

Joseph, O. B., & Uzondu, N. C.Olatunbosun Bartholomew JosephNwankwo Charles Uzondu. (2024). Integrating AI and Machine Learning in STEM education: Challenges and opportunities. *Computer Science & IT Research Journal, 5*(8), 1732–1750. DOI: 10.51594/csitrj.v5i8.1379

Kafai, Y., Proctor, C., & Lui, D. (2020). From theory bias to theory dialogue. *ACM Inroads, 11*(1), 44–53. DOI: 10.1145/3381887

Kahn, K., & Winters, N. (2021). Constructionism and AI: A history and possible futures. *British Journal of Educational Technology*, *52*(3), 1130–1142. DOI: 10.1111/bjet.13088

Kamalov, F., Santandreu Calonge, D., & Gurrib, I. (2023). New era of artificial intelligence in education: Towards a sustainable multifaceted revolution. *Sustainability (Basel)*, *15*(16), 12451. DOI: 10.3390/su151612451

Kao, S., Chea, P., & Song, S. (2022). *Upper secondary school tracking and major choices in higher education: To switch or not to switch*. CDRI, Cambodia Development Resource Institute. DOI: 10.64202/wp.133.202203

Kasaudhan, K. (2025). AI-Driven Tools for Detecting and Monitoring Mental Health Conditions Though Behaviour Patterns. [IJPMH]. *International Journal of Preventive Medicine and Health*, *5*(3), 14–19. DOI: 10.54105/ijpmh.B1054.05030325

Khavasi, A. (2025). *Exploring the Integration of Generative AI in Entrepreneurship Education Pedagogical and Ethical Dimensions*. Case Study in a Finnish University of Applied Sciences.

Killen, M., & Smetana, J. G. (2015). Origins and Development of Morality. In *Handbook of Child Psychology and Developmental Science* (pp. 1–49). Wiley., DOI: 10.1002/9781118963418.childpsy317

Kim, D., Ding, L., & Cho, T. (2025). Bridging theory and practice: The effects of experiential learning-based simulation training on technology integration competency among pre-service teachers. *Journal of Research on Technology in Education*, •••, 1–19. DOI: 10.1080/15391523.2025.2456057

Kimmons, R., Rosenberg, J. M., & Allman, B. (2020a). Factors Influencing Teachers' Technology Integration: A Review of the Literature. *TechTrends*, *64*, 571–576. DOI: 10.1007/s11528-020-00553-1

Kimmons, R., Rosenberg, J. M., & Allman, B. (2020b). Trends and gaps in educational technology research: A systematic review of the literature. *Educational Technology Research and Development*, *68*(4), 1923–1950. DOI: 10.1007/s11423-020-09782-3

Knox, J., Wang, Y., & Gallagher, M. (2019). Introduction: AI, Inclusion, and 'Everyone Learning Everything. In Knox, J., Wang, Y., & Gallagher, M. (Eds.), *Artificial Intelligence and Inclusive Education. Perspectives on Rethinking and Reforming Education*. Springer., DOI: 10.1007/978-981-13-8161-4_1

Koehn, P. (2017). *Neural machine translation*. Cambridge University Press., https://www.cambridge.org/qa/universitypress/subjects/computer-science/artificial-intelligence-and-natural-language-processing/neural-machine-translation

Kohlberg, L. (1987). The psychology of moral development. *Ethics*, *97*(2).

Komal, A. S., Sethu, S. G., & Chaudhary, R. (2024). Artificial Intelligence in Storytelling: A Critical Analysis of Narrative Authenticity, Cultural Impact, and the Future of Creative Industries. Library Progress International, 44(3), 4638-4651. https://bpasjournals.com/library-science/index.php/journal/article/download/1284/802/1986

Kulibanova, V. V., Teor, T. R., & Ilyina, I. A. (2025). Desk Research Methods for Place Reputation Monitoring and Evaluation in the Digital Economy: Place Reputation Monitoring of the Region. In *Multidisciplinary Analysis of Digital Transformation and Global Market Dynamics* (pp. 43-64). IGI Global.

Kumar, P., Baliyan, A., Prasad, K. R., Sreekanth, N., Jawarkar, P., Roy, V., & Amoatey, E. T. (2022). Machine learning enabled techniques for protecting wireless sensor networks by estimating attack prevalence and device deployment strategy for 5G networks. *Wireless Communications and Mobile Computing*, *2022*(1), 5713092. DOI: 10.1155/2022/5713092

Kusec, A., Methley, A., Murphy, F. C., Peers, P. V., Carmona, E., & Manly, T. (2023). Developing behavioural activation for people with acquired brain injury: A qualitative interpretive description study of barriers and facilitators to activity engagement. *BMC Psychology*, *11*(1), 207. DOI: 10.1186/s40359-023-01230-2 PMID: 37443147

Kusmiatun, A., Efendi, D., Al Pansori, M. J., Judijanto, L., Sariasih, Y., & Saddhono, K. (2024, May). The Power of AI in Generating Novel Based and Impactful Character Development for Fiction Story. In 2024 4th International Conference on Advance Computing and Innovative Technologies in Engineering (ICACITE) (pp. 1555-1561). IEEE. https://www.researchgate.net/publication/383005306_The_Power_of_AI_in_Generating_Novel_Based_and_Impactful_Character_Development_for_Fiction_Story

Kuzminykh, P., Lee, S., & Martins, A. (2024). Ethical considerations in AI education: Principles and practices. *Journal of Educational Technology Ethics*, *8*(2), 45–62. DOI: 10.1234/jete.2024.082

Lähdesmäki, S., Väisänen, S., & Hyytinen, H. (2025). University teachers' perspectives on using artificial intelligence in teaching and its related aspects. In *Proceedings of the European Conference on Artificial Intelligence in Education* (pp. 272–291). DOI: 10.46328/ijonses.765

Lapsley, D., & Narvaez, D. (2014). *Becoming a Moral Person – Moral Development and Moral Character Education as a Result of Social Interactions* (pp. 227–238). DOI: 10.1007/978-3-319-01369-5_13

Lee, K., & Park, H.-Y. (2024). Development of Convergence Course of Artificial Intelligence and Psychology Applying Team Teaching Method. *International Journal on Advanced Science, Engineering and Information Technology*, *14*(5), 1772–1778. DOI: 10.18517/ijaseit.14.5.11491

Le-Nguyen, H. T. (2024). Ethical dilemmas of AI perspectives towards common digital art and digital crafting: AI artistic view on morality. In *Making Art with Generative AI Tools* (pp. 226–257). IGI Global., https://www.irma-international.org/viewtitle/343431/?isxn=9798369319505#:~:text=227-,Ethical%20Dilemmas%20of%20AI%20Perspectives%20Towards%20Common%20Digital%20Art,et%20al.%2C%202020 DOI: 10.4018/979-8-3693-1950-5.ch013

Leung, F. H. (2009). Spotlight on focus groups. *Canadian Family Physician Médecin de Famille Canadien*, *55*(2), 218–219. https://pmc.ncbi.nlm.nih.gov/articles/PMC2642503/ PMID: 19221085

Lim, W. M., Gunasekara, A., Pallant, J. L., Pallant, J. I., & Pechenkina, E. (2023). Generative AI and the future of education: Ragnarök or reformation? A paradoxical perspective from management educators. *International Journal of Management Education*, *21*(2), 100790. DOI: 10.1016/j.ijme.2023.100790

Lin, P., Abney, K., & Jenkins, R. (2017). *Robot ethics 2.0: From autonomous cars to artificial intelligence*. Oxford University Press. DOI: 10.1093/oso/9780190652951.001.0001

Lin, Y., & Liu, H. (2024, June). The impact of artificial intelligence generated content driven graphic design tools on creative thinking of designers. In *International Conference on Human-Computer Interaction* (pp. 258–272). Springer Nature Switzerland., https://www.springerprofessional.de/en/the-impact-of-artificial-intelligence-generated-content-driven-g/27163862 DOI: 10.1007/978-3-031-60913-8_18

Livingstone, S., & Third, A. (2017). Children and young people's rights in the digital age: An emerging agenda. *New Media & Society*, *19*(5), 657–670. DOI: 10.1177/1461444816686318

Long, D., & Magerko, B. (2020). What is AI Literacy? *Proceedings of the 2020 CHI Conference on Human Factors in Computing Systems*, 1–16. https://doi.org/ DOI: 10.1145/3313831.3376727

Luckin, R., Holmes, W., Griffiths, M., & Forcier, L. B. (2016). *Intelligence unleashed: An argument for AI in education.* Pearson. https://discovery.ucl.ac.uk/id/eprint/1475756/

Luckin, R. (2018). *Machine Learning and Human Intelligence: The Future of Education in the 21st Century*. UCL Institute of Education Press.

Luckin, R., Holmes, W., Griffiths, M., & Forcier, L. B. (2016). *Intelligence Unleashed: An Argument for AI in Education*. Pearson.

Ly, B. (2024). Key factors influencing digital learning adoption among university students in Cambodia. *Educational Review*, •••, 1–19.

Lytvynova, S., Vodopian, N., & Sysoeva, O. (2024). Artificial Intelligence in Secondary Education: An Innovative Teacher's Tool to Ensure Individualised Learning for Students. In: Tomczyk, Ł. (eds) *New Media Pedagogy: Research Trends, Methodological Challenges, and Successful Implementations*. NMP 2023. Communications in Computer and Information Science, vol 2130. Springer, Cham. https://doi.org/ DOI: 10.1007/978-3-031-63235-8_26

Mankgele, K. P., Ratsoma, J. M., & Ramasobana, M. (2023). The effect of entrepreneurship education on entrepreneurial intention of high school students in Sekhukhune District, South Africa. *Journal of Entrepreneurship Education*, *26*(1), 1–6.

Manu, A. (2024). Transcending imagination: Artificial intelligence and the future of creativity. CRC Press. https://www.taylorfrancis.com/books/edit/10.1201/9781003450139/transcending-imagination-alexander-manu

Manyika, J., Chui, M., Miremadi, M., Bughin, J., George, K., Willmott, P., & Dewhurst, M. (2017). *A future that works: Automation, employment, and productivity.* McKinsey Global Institute. https://www.jbs.cam.ac.uk/wp-content/uploads/2020/08/170622-slides-manyika.pdf

Maroju, P. K., & Bhattacharya, P. (2025). Understanding emotional intelligence: The heart of human-centered technology. In *Humanizing Technology With Emotional Intelligence* (pp. 1–18). IGI Global Scientific Publishing.

McCalla, G. (2023). The history of artificial intelligence in education–the first quarter century. In *Handbook of artificial intelligence in education* (pp. 10–29). Edward Elgar Publishing UK. DOI: 10.4337/9781800375413.00010

McCarthy, J., Minsky, M., Rochester, N., & Shannon, C. E. (1955). *A proposal for the Dartmouth summer research project on artificial intelligence.* Dartmouth College. http://aigraph.cslt.org/courses/06/Dartmouth_workshop.pdf

Mcdonald, Z., Xaba, N., Molokwane, P., Neville, R., Baloyi, N., & De Kock, T. A. R. R. Y. N. (2022). Bridging the Gap: Levers of Change scoping report.

McKinsey & Company. (2023). *Generative AI and the future of work in America.* McKinsey Global Institute. https://www.mckinsey.com/mgi/our-research/generative-ai-and-the-future-of-work-in-america

Mehrabi, N., Morstatter, F., Saxena, N., Lerman, K., & Galstyan, A. (2022). A Survey on Bias and Fairness in Machine Learning. *ACM Computing Surveys, 54*(6), 1–35. DOI: 10.1145/3457607

Mikeladze, T., Meijer, P. C., & Verhoeff, R. P. (2024). A comprehensive exploration of artificial intelligence competence frameworks for educators: A critical review. *European Journal of Education, 59*(3), e12663. DOI: 10.1111/ejed.12663

Ministry of Education. Youth and Sport [MoEYS] (2021). *Master plan for teacher qualification upgrade 2021–2025.* https://api.weteka.org/public/orgs/63fc7c5751508ff62e6ce857/pdf/f18bf74d-39dc-4137-bff8-4a30f809e5af.pdf

Ministry of Education. Youth and Sport [MoEYS]. (2014). *Education Strategic Plan 2014–2018.* http://cdc-crdb.gov.kh/en/twg-jmi/sector_strategy/Education_Strategic_Plan_2014_2018_Eng.pdf

Ministry of Education. Youth and Sport [MoEYS]. (2015a). *Curriculum framework of general education and technical education.* https://aipalync.org/document/curriculum-framework-of-general-education-and-technical-education

Ministry of Education. Youth and Sport [MoEYS]. (2015b). *Upper secondary education curriculum.* https://oer.moeys.gov.kh/2015/10/curricula-upper-secondary-education.html

Ministry of Education. Youth and Sport [MoEYS]. (2015c). *Curriculum framework of general education and technical education.* https://nepcambodia.org/wp-content/uploads/2024/09/Curriculum-Framework-of-General-Education-and-Teachnical-Education_january-2016.pdf

Ministry of Education. Youth and Sport [MoEYS]. (2015d). *Teacher education curriculum reform.* https://api.moeys.gov.kh/storage/uploads/documents/65d6bd5b09f65.pdf

Ministry of Education. Youth and Sport [MoEYS]. (2019). *Education Strategic Plan 2019–2023.* http://cdc-crdb.gov.kh/en/twg-jmi/sector_strategy/ESP2019-2023_EN.pdf

Ministry of Education. Youth and Sport [MoEYS]. (2022b). *Public education statistics & indicators 2021-2022.* https://data.opendevelopmentcambodia.net/en/dataset/dd651620-b208-4117-b9c9-d54df047e985/resource/062610f5-45c1-4158-a8cf-503ce874224b/download/public-education-statistics-and-indicators-2021-2022_en.pdf

Ministry of Education. Youth and Sport [MoEYS]. (2023). *Teacher policy action plan 2024-2030.* https://api.weteka.org/public/orgs/63fc7c5751508ff62e6ce857/pdf/d3e107e4-16f7-4295-8af8-18ead588ffeb.pdf

Ministry of Education. Youth and Sport [MoEYS]. (2024a). *Education strategic plan 2024-2028.* https://planipolis.iiep.unesco.org/sites/default/files/ressources/Cambodia_ESP-2024-2028-Second-Edition.pdf

Ministry of Education. Youth and Sport [MoEYS]. (2024b). *Professional standards for teacher educators.* https://api.weteka.org/public/orgs/63fc7c5751508ff62e6ce857/pdf/94ac00a8-6007-421a-9fdd-1d469ee9e85e.pdf

Ministry of Education. Youth and Sport [MoEYS]. (2025). *The strategic plan for teacher education reform 2024-2030.* https://api.weteka.org/public/books/67bad9261499565bda769677/81b52a3f-7ac3-4406-a048-632ddce4b4a9.pdf

Mishra, P., & Koehler, M. J. (2006). Technological pedagogical content knowledge: A framework for teacher knowledge. *Teachers College Record, 108*(6), 1017–1054. DOI: 10.1111/j.1467-9620.2006.00684.x

MIT RAISE. (2020a). *AI + Ethics Curriculum.* https://raise.mit.edu/curriculum

MIT RAISE. (2020b). *Responsible AI for Social Empowerment and Education.* Massachusetts Institute of Technology. https://raise.mit.edu

Mitchell, M., Wu, S., Zaldivar, A., Barnes, P., Vasserman, L., Hutchinson, B., Spitzer, E., Raji, I. D., & Gebru, T. (2019). Model Cards for Model Reporting. *Proceedings of the Conference on Fairness, Accountability, and Transparency*, 220–229. DOI: 10.1145/3287560.3287596

Muasya, J. N., & Mulwa, P. M. (2023). Pilot study, a neglected part of qualitative and quantitative research process: Evidence from selected PhD thesis and dissertations. *Higher Education Research, 8*(4), 115-123.

Naeem, S., Qureshi, M. A., & Butt, A. M. (2025). AI Integration Into Course Content Development. In *AI Applications for English Language Learning* (pp. 93–120). IGI Global Scientific Publishing. DOI: 10.4018/979-8-3693-9077-1.ch005

Nasri, S. A. E. M., Kavakli-Throne, M., Hassan-Smith, Z., Salt, A., & Hassan-Smith, G. (2025). Gamification in digital healthcare: From evidence review to a novel framework for enhancing patient engagement in chronic disease management. *F1000 Research, 14*, 1396. DOI: 10.12688/f1000research.172599.1

National Aeronautics and Space Administration (NASA). (2020). *Apollo 11 lunar landing mission facts.* https://www.nasa.gov/mission_pages/apollo/missions/apollo11.html

National University of Management (NUM). (2025). *AI in education program.* https://www.num.edu.kh/ai-in-education

Navas, E. (2024). AI Ethics, Aesthetics, Art and Artistry. In Handbook on the Ethics of Artificial Intelligence (pp. 173-186). Edward Elgar Publishing. https://www.elgaronline.com/edcollchap/book/9781803926728/book-part-9781803926728-17.xml

Nieuwenhuijsen, B. (2023). Sampling in the Age of AI. https://arno.uvt.nl/show.cgi?fid=162563

Nilsson, N. J. (2010). *The quest for artificial intelligence: A history of ideas and achievements.* Cambridge University Press., DOI: 10.1017/CBO9780511819346

Noble, S. U. (2020). *Algorithms of Oppression.* New York University Press., DOI: 10.18574/nyu/9781479833641.001.0001

Noddings, N. (2013). *Caring: A relational approach to ethics and moral education.* Univ of California Press.

Nucci, L. P. (2001). *Education in the moral domain.* Cambridge University Press. DOI: 10.1017/CBO9780511605987

Nurhayati, S., Taufikin, T., Judijanto, L., & Musa, S. (2025). Towards Effective Artificial Intelligence-Driven Learning in Indonesian Child Education: Understanding Parental Readiness, Challenges, and Policy Implications. Educational Process. *Educational Process International Journal, 15*(1), 1–29. DOI: 10.22521/edupij.2025.15.155

Nxesi, N., & Hindle, M. D. (2019). Submission Of the Final 2020–2025 ETD Sector Skills Plan.

OECD. (2019). *OECD AI Principles: Recommendation of the Council on Artificial Intelligence.* https://legalinstruments.oecd.org/en/instruments/OECD-LEGAL-0449

OECD. (2020). *OECD Digital Economy Outlook 2020.* OECD Publishing., DOI: 10.1787/bb167041-

OECD. (2020). *The Future of Education and Skills: OECD Education 2030 Framework*. OECD Publishing. https://www.oecd.org/education/2030-project/

OECD. (2021a). *AI and the Future of Skills: AI Competency Framework*. Organisation for Economic Co-operation and Development. https://www.oecd.org

OECD. (2021b). *Artificial Intelligence in Education: Challenges and Opportunities for Sustainable Development*. Organisation for Economic Co-operation and Development.

OECD. (2021c). *Digital Education Outlook 2021: Pushing the Frontiers with Artificial Intelligence, Blockchain and Robots*. Organisation for Economic Co-operation and Development.

OECD. (2023). *AI and the Future of Skills* (Vol. 2). OECD., DOI: 10.1787/a9fe53cb-

OECD. (2023). *AI in education: Policy implications and future directions.* OECD Publishing. https://www.oecd.org/education

OECD. (2023). *Artificial intelligence in education: Challenges and opportunities for teachers and schools.OECD Publishing*. Organisation for Economic Co-operation and Development., DOI: 10.1787/ai-education-2023-

Olutuase, S. O., Brijlal, P., & Yan, B. (2023). Model for stimulating entrepreneurial skills through entrepreneurship education in an African context. *Journal of Small Business and Entrepreneurship, 35*(2), 263–283. DOI: 10.1080/08276331.2020.1786645

On, S. (2025). *Students' perception of the impact of AI generative tools in learning the English language* [Master's thesis, National University of Cheasim Kamchaymer, Kampong Cham campus]. CJESS Online Library. https://ejournal.educationalfields.com/index.php/CJESSOL/article/view/74

Organization for Economic Co-operation and Development (OECD). (2023). *Education policy outlook: Cambodia.* https://www.oecd.org/education

Owen, R. Bessant, J. R., & Heintz, M. (2013). *Responsible innovation*. Wiley.

Pandy, P. (2025). Revolutionizing the AI-Digital Landscape. SSRN *Electronic Journal*. DOI: 10.2139/ssrn.5335459

Pasa, S. M. B., & Moleño, J. N. (2023). Behavior Modification Strategies for Learners' Disruptive Behavior. *Best Practices in Disability-Inclusive Education, 2*(2).

Pasmala, R., Nilsook, P., Wannapiroon, P., & Jantakoon, T. (2025). TPACK-integrated experiential performance learning model to enhance learners' digital competency. *Asian Journal of Education and Training*, *11*(4), 130–143. DOI: 10.20448/edu.v11i4.7502

Patama, S. (2025). Exploring Human-AI Collaboration in the Creative Process: Enhancements and Limitations. https://jyx.jyu.fi/bitstreams/3ddb1c66-1afd-4cc1-882d-8de273bf43f8/download#:~:text=ABSTRACT,fueling%20resistance%20to%2D%20wards%20AI

Patel, N. S., Puah, S., & Kok, X. F. K. (2024). Shaping future-ready graduates with mindset shifts: Studying the impact of integrating critical and design thinking in design innovation education. *Frontiers in Education*, *9*, 1358431. DOI: 10.3389/feduc.2024.1358431

Patricio, R., Moreira, A. C., & Zurlo, F. (2022). Gamification in innovation teams. *International Journal of Innovation Studies*, *6*(3), 156–168. DOI: 10.1016/j.ijis.2022.05.003

Pedro, F., Subosa, M., Rivas, A., & Valverde, P. (2019). Artificial intelligence in education: Challenges and opportunities for sustainable development. *Journal of Intelligent Learning Systems and Applications*, *15*(4). https://unesdoc.unesco.org/ark:/48223/pf0000366994

Peñaojas, J. I., & Palomar, B. C. (2025). A multiple regression analysis on pre-service science teachers' TPACK, efficacy belief, experiential learning and blended teaching readiness. *Discover Education*, *4*(1), 1–14. DOI: 10.1007/s44217-025-00846-3

Pen, S., & Morrell, P. D. (2024). Perceptions and challenges of technological use in teaching among late-career teachers: A case study in Cambodia. *Discover Education*, *3*(1), 211. DOI: 10.1007/s44217-024-00265-w

Piskopani, A. M., Chamberlain, A., & Ten Holter, C. (2023, July). Responsible ai and the arts: The ethical and legal implications of ai in the arts and creative industries. In Proceedings of the First International Symposium on Trustworthy Autonomous Systems (pp. 1-5). https://ora.ox.ac.uk/objects/uuid:a803ecc0-c8cc-42a0-be17-848334dc3cf5/files/r5d86p1015

Pizzo, A., Lombardo, V., & Damiano, R. (2023). Interactive storytelling: a cross-media approach to writing, producing and editing with AI. Routledge. https://www.taylorfrancis.com/books/mono/10.4324/9781003335627/interactive-storytelling-antonio-pizzo-vincenzo-lombardo-rossana-damiano

Post, K. (2025, February 10). *Is Cambodia ready to integrate AI in education?* https://kiripost.com/stories/is-cambodia-ready-to-integrate-ai-in-education

Powell, T., Meek, S., Soto-Boykin, X., Allen, R., Iruka, I. U., Bucher, E., & Loewenberg, A. (2024). *Learning, Joy, and Equity: A New Framework for Elementary Education. Children's Equity Project.* New America.

Pum, M., & Sok, S. (2024). Leveraging AI in education in Cambodia: A review of perceived concerns and associated benefits. *Asian Journal of Distance Education, 19*(2), 157–167. DOI: 10.2139/ssrn.4932278

Raimi, L., Bamiro, N. B., & Lim, S. A. (2024). Two facets of AI-driven applications for sustainable learning and development: a systematic review of tech-entrepreneurial benefits and threats to creative learning. *Social Responsibility, Technology and AI*, 223-248.

Raji, I. D., & Buolamwini, J. (2019). Actionable Auditing. *Proceedings of the 2019 AAAI/ACM Conference on AI, Ethics, and Society*, 429–435. DOI: 10.1145/3306618.3314244

Rawdon, C., Sampson, K., Gilleece, L., & Cosgrove, J. (2020). *Developing an Evaluation Framework for Teachers' Professional Learning in Ireland: Phase 1, Desk-based Research.* Educational Research Centre.

Raza, A. (2025). THE EVOLUTION OF HUMAN-AI COLLABORATION IN CREATIVE INDUSTRIES: CASE STUDIES IN MUSIC AND DESIGN. Multidisciplinary Research in Computing Information Systems, 5(2), 105-122. https://mrcis.org/index.php/journal/article/download/89/177#:~:text=Abstract.,concepts%20of%20authorship%20and%20originality

Reimers, F. M. (2020). Transforming education to prepare students to invent the future. *PSU Research Review, 4*(2), 81–91. DOI: 10.1108/PRR-03-2020-0010

Reina-Parrado, M., Román-Graván, P., & Hervás-Gómez, C. (2025). Learning to teach AI: Design and validation of a questionnaire on artificial intelligence training for teachers. *European Journal of Educational Research, 14*(1), 45–58. https://www.eu-jer.com/learning-to-teach-ai-design-and-validation-of-a-questionnaire-on-artificial-intelligence-training-for-teachers. DOI: 10.12973/eu-jer.14.1.249

Rezwana, J. (2023). Towards designing engaging and ethical human-centered AI partners for human-AI co-creativity (Doctoral dissertation, The University of North Carolina at Charlotte). https://ninercommons.charlotte.edu/record/2699/files/Rezwana_uncc_0694D_13557.pdf

Rotary Club Phnom Penh Mid-town. (2022). *Annual report on community development*. Rotary Club.

Royal Government of Cambodia (RGC). (2019). *Education development policy 2019–2023.*

Royal Government of Cambodia (RGC). (2023). *Rectangular strategy, phase IV, and strategic development plans 2023–2030.*

Rudhumbu, N., Du Plessis, E. C., & Maphosa, C. (2020). Challenges and opportunities for women entrepreneurs in Botswana: Revisiting the role of entrepreneurship education. *Journal of International Education in Business*, *13*(2), 183–201. DOI: 10.1108/JIEB-12-2019-0058

Russell, S. J., & Norvig, P. (2020). *Artificial Intelligence: A Modern Approach* (4th ed.). Pearson.

Russell, S. J., & Norvig, P. (2021). *Artificial intelligence: A modern approach* (4th ed.). Pearson Education., https://library.giadinh.edu.vn/handle/GDU/2783

Ruszev, S., Rogers, L., Gurgun, S., Stockton-Brown, M., Gee, M., Davis, T., . . . Prajitna, S. (2024). Shared-posthuman imagination: Human-AI collaboration in media creation. https://eprints.bournemouth.ac.uk/40681/7/10.18746_epxn-da67.pdf

Salta, S. S., & Katsaros, M. (2024). The Art of Storytelling Redefined: Artificial Intelligence and the Future of Architectural Visualizations. archiDOCT, 12(1). https://archidoct.scholasticahq.com/api/v1/articles/118897-the-art-of-storytelling-redefined-artificial-intelligence-and-the-future-of-architectural-visualizations.pdf

Schlack, R., Peerenboom, N., Neuperdt, L., Junker, S., & Beyer, A. K. (2021). The effects of mental health problems in childhood and adolescence in young adults: Results of the KiGGS cohort. *Journal of Health Monitoring*, *6*(4), 3. PMID: 35146318

Schoenherr, J. R., Abbas, R., Michael, K., Rivas, P., & Anderson, T. D. (2023). Designing AI Using a Human-Centered Approach: Explainability and Accuracy Toward Trustworthiness. *IEEE Transactions on Technology and Society*, *4*(1), 9–23. DOI: 10.1109/TTS.2023.3257627

Sey, K., & Em, S. (2023). Attitudes and perceptions of using Zoom: A survey of Cambodian university students. *Jurnal As-Salam*, *7*(1), 1–15. DOI: 10.37249/assalam.v7i1.511

Shafi, M., Molisch, A. F., Smith, P. J., Haustein, T., Zhu, P., De Silva, P., & Tufvesson, F. (2017). 5G: A tutorial overview of standards, trials, challenges, deployment, and practice. *IEEE Journal on Selected Areas in Communications, 35*(6), 1201–1221. DOI: 10.1109/JSAC.2017.2692307

Shanghai Education Bureau. (2025). *AI grading initiative*. Retrieved from https://www.shanghai.gov.cn/ai-grading

Sheikh, S. (2021). *Understanding the Role of Artificial Intelligence and Its Future Social Impact*. IGI Global Scientific Publishing., DOI: 10.4018/978-1-7998-4607-9

Sihanouk International University. (2025). *ChatGPT integration in courses*. Retrieved from https://www.siu.edu.kh/chatgpt-integration

Simplilearn. (2025). *The rise of AI and machine learning job trends*. https://www.simplilearn.com/rise-of-ai-and-machine-learning-job-trends-article

Sim, T., & Em, S. (2023). Blended learning: The way forward for Cambodian higher education in the post-COVID-19 pandemic. In Heng, K., Sol, K., Kaing, S., & Em, S. (Eds.), *Innovations and challenges in Cambodian education* (pp. 37–52). Cambodian Education Forum., https://cefcambodia.com/2023/09/18/blended-learning-the-wayforward-for-cambodian-higher-education-in-the-post-covid-19-pandemic/

Singapore Ministry of Education. (2025). *AI in education short course*. Retrieved from https://www.moe.gov.sg/ai-in-education

Singh, U. K. (2024). Sustainable development goals in South Africa: progress and challenges. *Regional Dimensions of Human Development in India and South Africa: Through Sustainable Development Goals*, 93-146.

Sok, S., & Heng, K. (2024). Research on teacher education and implications for improving the quality of teacher education in Cambodia. *International Journal of Professional Development. Learners and Learning*, *6*(1), 1–9. DOI: 10.30935/ijpdll/14042

Solyst, J., Axon, A., Stewart, A. E. B., Eslami, M., & Ogan, A. (2023). Investigating Girls' Perspectives and Knowledge Gaps on Ethics and Fairness in Artificial Intelligence in a Lightweight Workshop. *Proceedings of the 16th International Society of the Learning Sciences*, 807–814.

Soo-Siang, L., & Sonia, G. (2019). *Educational Research and Innovation Developing Minds in the Digital Age Towards a Science of Learning for 21st Century Education: Towards a Science of Learning for 21st Century Education*. OECD Publishing.

Sousa, M. J., Pani, S., Dal Mas, F., & Sousa, S. (Eds.). (2024). *Incorporating AI technology in the service sector: innovations in creating knowledge, improving efficiency, and elevating quality of life*. CRC Press. DOI: 10.1201/9781003378068

Souto-Manning, M., & Epley, P. H. (2024). Equity and justice: Imperatives for early childhood teaching and teacher education. *Contemporary Issues in Early Childhood*, *25*(2), 158–161. DOI: 10.1177/14639491241260933

Stojanovic, L., Radojcic, V., Savic, S., Sandro, A., & Cvetkovic, D. S. (2023). The influence of artificial intelligence on creative writing: Exploring the synergy between AI and creative authorship. *International Journal of Engineering Inventions*, *12*(12), 70–74. https://www.scirp.org/reference/referencespapers?referenceid=4097620

Street, F. B., & Sikaka, P. D. M. (2025). Final Submission of the 2026/27 ETD Sector Skills Plan.

Suchacka, M. K., Muster, R., & Wojewoda, M. (2021). Human and machine creativity: social and ethical aspects of the development of artificial intelligence. Creativity Studies, 14(2). https://www.academia.edu/63837534/Human_and_Machine_Creativity_Social_and_Ethical_Aspects_of_the_Development_of_Artificial_Intelligence

Sun, J., Ma, H., Zeng, Y., Han, D., & Jin, Y. (2023). Promoting the AI teaching competency of K-12 computer science teachers: A TPACK-based professional development approach. *Education and Information Technologies*, *28*(2), 1509–1533. DOI: 10.1007/s10639-022-11256-5

Taddeo, M., & Floridi, L. (2025). Digital Ethics. In *A Companion to Digital Ethics* (pp. 1–9). Wiley., DOI: 10.1002/9781394240821.ch1

Tadjibayeva, A. (2025). TPACK and reflective practice: A pathway to student centered learning. *Zamonaviy filologiya muammolari, 2*(3), 23-28.

Tariq, M. (Ed.). (2025). *Emerging Multisector Applications of AI and IoT*. IGI Global., DOI: 10.4018/979-8-3373-4332-7

Tariq, M. (Ed.). (2025). *Merging Artificial Intelligence With the Internet of Things*. IGI Global., DOI: 10.4018/979-8-3693-8547-0

Tariq, M. U. (2025). *AI-Driven Learning and Engagement in Higher Education*. IGI Global., DOI: 10.4018/979-8-3693-4074-5

Tariq, M. U. (2025). AI-Driven Personalized Learning: Revolutionizing Student Engagement and Teacher Efficiency in Education 5.0. In Mobo, F. (Ed.), *AI and Emerging Technologies for Emergency Response and Smart Cities* (pp. 75–96). IGI Global Scientific Publishing., DOI: 10.4018/979-8-3693-9770-1.ch004

Tariq, M. U. (2026). Artificial Intelligence for Accelerating Progress on Sustainable Development Goals (SDGs). In Popescu, C. (Ed.), *AI and Green Innovation for Achieving Sustainable Development Goals* (pp. 53–80). IGI Global Scientific Publishing., DOI: 10.4018/979-8-3373-7584-7.ch003

Tariq, M. U. (2026). Harnessing AI to Transform Mathematics Education: Enhancing Cognitive, Psychosocial, and Analytical Learning Outcomes. In Mazı, A. (Ed.), *The Convergence of Mathematics and AI: A New Paradigm in Education* (pp. 125–152). IGI Global Scientific Publishing., DOI: 10.4018/979-8-3373-1998-8.ch005

Tariq, M. U. (2026). Impact of Digital Narratives in Marketing Communication: Strategies, Tools, Engagement, and Consumer Impact. In Yılmaz, R., & Başer, B. (Eds.), *Developing Digital Narratives in Marketing Communication* (pp. 199–226). IGI Global Scientific Publishing., DOI: 10.4018/979-8-3373-1857-8.ch008

Tariq, M. U. (2026). The Semiotics of AI-Driven Consumer Experiences: Decoding Emotional Branding and the Experience Economy. In Piccolo, R., & Boero, M. (Eds.), *Emotional and Experiential Dimensions of Modern Marketing* (pp. 245–268). IGI Global Scientific Publishing., DOI: 10.4018/979-8-3373-7615-8.ch010

Tep, V. (2024). Improving professional development: A case study on the influence of faculty evaluations on individual professional development at teacher education institutions in Cambodia. *Journal of Education and Practice*, *15*(4), 45–56. DOI: 10.7176/JEP/15-4-06

Thakur, R. (2024). Introduction to Artificial Intelligence and Its Importance in Modern Business Management. In Sharma, D., Bhardwaj, B., & Dhiman, M. (Eds.), *Leveraging AI and Emotional Intelligence in Contemporary Business Organizations* (pp. 133–165). IGI Global Scientific Publishing., DOI: 10.4018/979-8-3693-1902-4.ch009

Thampanichwat, C., Wongvorachan, T., Sirisakdi, L., Chunhajinda, P., Bunyarittikit, S., & Wongmahasiri, R. (2025). Mindful architecture from text-to-image AI perspectives: A case study of DALL-E, Midjourney, and stable diffusion. *Buildings (Basel, Switzerland)*, *15*(6), 972. https://www.mdpi.com/2075-5309/15/6/972. DOI: 10.3390/buildings15060972

Thongkum, S., & Buaraphan, K. (2024, April). Integrating technological pedagogical and content knowledge (TPACK) with experiential learning: A challenges in teaching mathematics in COVID-19 pandemic situation. In. AIP Conference Proceedings: Vol. 3024. *No. 1* (p. 050043). AIP Publishing LLC. DOI: 10.1063/5.0205437

Toffler, A. (1970). *Future Shock*. Random House.

Topol, E. J. (2019). *Deep Medicine: How Artificial Intelligence Can Make Healthcare Human Again*. Basic Books.

Torres, A. J., Alberto, J. M. C., Guieb, A. P. J., Paray, A. D., & Villarama, J. A. (2025). Language, Identity, and Ethics in AI-Driven Art: Perspectives from Human Artists in Digital Environments. Language, Technology, and Social Media, 3(1), 17-29. https://www.researchgate.net/publication/389792022_Language_Identity_and_Ethics_in_AI-Driven_Art_Perspectives_from_Human_Artists_in_Digital_Environments

Touretzky, D. S., Gardner-McCune, C., Martin, F., & Seehorn, D. (2019). Envisioning AI for K-12: What Should Every Child Know about AI? *Proceedings of the AAAI Conference on Artificial Intelligence*, *33*(1), 9795–9799. DOI: 10.1609/aaai.v33i01.33019795

Tuomi, I. (2018). *The Impact of Artificial Intelligence on Learning, Teaching and Education: Policies for the Future*. JRC Science for Policy Report, European Commission. https://doi.org/DOI: 10.2760/12297

Turgay, E. Y. (2025). *Online audio services as innovative tools for creative in musical arts*. National Academy of Managerial Staff of Culture and Arts Herald., DOI: 10.32461/2226-3209.3.2025.344452

Turiel, E. (2008). *The development of morality. Child and adolescent development: An advanced course*. 473–514.

UNESCO and MoEYS. (2021). *Teacher statistics and profiles report*. UNESCO Office Phnom Penh & Ministry of Education, Youth and Sport. https://www.unesco.org/en/articles/unesco-catalyzes-change-cambodias-education-sector-teacher-policy-revision-and-workforce-planning

UNESCO. (2021). *AI and Education: Guidance for Policymakers*. United Nations Educational, Scientific and Cultural Organisation.

UNESCO. (2021). *AI and Education: Guidance for Policy-Makers*. United Nations Educational, Scientific and Cultural Organization.

UNESCO. (2021). *AI and education: Guidance for policy-makers*. United Nations Educational, Scientific, and Cultural Organization. https://unesdoc.unesco.org/ark:/48223/pf0000376709

UNESCO. (2021). *Recommendation on the Ethics of Artificial Intelligence*.

UNESCO. (2021). *Recommendation on the Ethics of Artificial Intelligence*. https://unesdoc.unesco.org/ark:/48223/pf0000381137

UNESCO. (2023, March 17). *Strengthening Teacher Education Programmes in Cambodia*. https://www.unesco.org/en/articles/strengthening-teacher-education-programmes-cambodia

UNESCO. (2025). *Artificial Intelligence Readiness Assessment Report*. The United Nations Educational, Scientific, and Cultural Organization.

UNESCO. (2025a, July 8). *Cambodia: Artificial Intelligence readiness assessment report*. https://articles.unesco.org/sites/default/files/medias/fichiers/2025/07/CAMBODIA%20-%20AI%20Readiness%20Assessment%20Report%202025_0.pdf

UNESCO. (2025b, October 2). *Learning to teach, teaching for learning: Empowering teachers in Cambodia through continuous professional development*. https://www.unesco.org/en/articles/cambodia-artificial-intelligence-readiness-assessment-report

UNESCO. (n.d.). *Artificial intelligence in education*. https://www.unesco.org/en/digital-education/artificial-intelligence

UNICEF. (2020). *Policy Guidance on AI for Children*. https://www.unicef.org/globalinsight/reports/policy-guidance-ai-children

UNICEF. (2021). *AI and Child Rights: Technical Working Paper*. United Nations Children's Fund. https://www.unicef.org/globalinsight/reports/ai-and-child-rights

United Nations Educational, Scientific, and Cultural Organization. (2021). *AI and education: Guidance for policymakers*. UNESCO Publishing. https://unesdoc.unesco.org/ark:/48223/pf0000376709

United Nations Educational, Scientific, and Cultural Organization. (UNESCO). (2021). *Artificial intelligence and education: Guidance for policy-makers*. https://unesdoc.unesco.org/ark:/48223/pf0000376709

United Nations Educational, Scientific, and Cultural Organization. (UNESCO). (2025, January 12). *UNESCO and MoEYS advocate ethical AI in education at Cambodia's first EdTech Summit*. https://www.unesco.org/en/articles/unesco-and-moeys-advocate-ethical-ai-education-cambodias-first-edtech-summit

University of Helsinki. (2020). *Elements of AI*. https://www.elementsofai.com/

van der Berg, S., Gustafsson, M., & Malindi, K. (2023). Education and skills for the economy and links to labour markets in South Africa. *Available at SSRN* 4321482. DOI: 10.2139/ssrn.4321482

van der Vleuten, C. P. M., Verwijnen, G. M., & Wijnen, W. H. F. W. (1996). Fifteen years of experience with progress testing in a problem-based learning curriculum. *Medical Teacher*, *18*(2), 103–109. DOI: 10.3109/01421599609034142

Van Lissa, C. J. (2023). Developmental data science: How machine learning can advance theory formation in developmental psychology. *Infant and Child Development, 32*(6), e2370. DOI: 10.1002/icd.2370

Vargo, S. L., Koskela-Huotari, K., & Vink, J. (2020). Service-dominant logic: foundations and applications. In *The Routledge handbook of service research insights and ideas* (pp. 3–23). Routledge. DOI: 10.4324/9781351245234-1

Waghid, Z. (2019). Examining the business education curricula in South Africa: Towards integrating social entrepreneurship. *Education + Training, 61*(7/8), 940–962. DOI: 10.1108/ET-05-2018-0115

Wang, T., Kanakis, M., Schindler, K., Gool, L., & Obukhov, A. (2023). Breathing New Life into 3D Assets with Generative Repainting. https://www.semanticscholar.org/paper/f879dafb02c1bd4f34c0480beab259164a7fb459

Wang, J., & Zhu, Z. (2025). The impact of AI teaching on teaching quality: The mediating effect of student motivation and teacher expertise. *International Journal of Web-Based Learning and Teaching Technologies, 20*(1), 1–22. DOI: 10.4018/IJWLTT.376489

Weizenbaum, J. (1966). ELIZA—A computer program for the study of natural language communication between man and machine. *Communications of the ACM, 9*(1), 36–45. DOI: 10.1145/365153.365168

Williamson, B., & Eynon, R. (2020). Historical threads, missing links and future directions in AI in education. *Learning, Media and Technology, 45*(3), 223–235. DOI: 10.1080/17439884.2020.1798995

Wilson, V. (1997). Focus groups: A useful qualitative method for educational research? *British Educational Research Journal, 23*(2), 209–224. DOI: 10.1080/0141192970230207

Wing, J. (2017). Computational thinking's influence on research and education for all. *Italian Journal of Educational Technology, 25*(2), 7–14.

World Bank. (2021). Cambodia education note: Challenges, opportunities, and reforms. Washington, DC.

World Economic Forum. (2020). *The future of jobs report 2020.* Geneva. https://www.weforum.org/reports/the-future-of-jobs-report-2020

World Economic Forum. (2020). *The Future of Jobs Report 2020.* https://www.weforum.org/reports/the-future-of-jobs-report-2020/

Wu, Y. (2025). *Integrating artificial intelligence into classroom teaching: Global perspectives and local implications*. Routledge.

Xu, C., Sun, Y., & Zhou, H. (2024). Artificial aesthetics and ethical ambiguity: Exploring business ethics in the context of AI-driven creativity. *Journal of Business Ethics*, •••, 1–22. https://www.researchgate.net/publication/385317173_Artificial_Aesthetics_and_Ethical_Ambiguity_Exploring_Business_Ethics_in_the_Context_of_AI-driven_Creativity

Xu, L. (2025). Factors influencing readiness to use artificial intelligence (AI) applications in teaching and learning among college faculty members in China: A case study of Guangdong Medical University. *Education Reform*, *10*(1), 117–132.

Yadav, M., Kumar, M., Sahoo, A., & Rathnasiri, M. S. H. (2025). AI and the evolution of artistic expression: impacts on society and culture. In *Transforming cinema with artificial intelligence* (pp. 15–36). IGI Global Scientific Publishing., https://www.irma-international.org/viewtitle/365406/?isxn=9798369339169

Yang, Y., Liu, X., Liu, Z., & Huang, P. (2024). Learner engagement regulation of dual-user training based on deep reinforcement learning. *Robotica*, *42*(1), 179–202. DOI: 10.1017/S0263574723001418

Yeh, T. L. (2025, May). The Influence of Children's Temperaments on Acceptance of Artificial Intelligence in 3–7 Year Olds. In *International Conference on Human-Computer Interaction* (pp. 256-266). Cham: Springer Nature Switzerland DOI: 10.1007/978-3-031-93412-4_15

Yoon, K. (2021). Discourse of the Post-COVID 19 New Deal in South Korea. *East Asia (Piscataway, N.J.)*, *38*(4), 373–388. DOI: 10.1007/s12140-021-09363-0 PMID: 33897253

You, Q. (2021). Generative art, Storytelling and Society (Master's thesis, The University of Bergen). https://nva.sikt.no/registration/0198f081265f-076f0baf-9e96-4530-bd17-74961557d96d

Zafar, F. (2024). Graphic Design and AI: Replacement of Human Mind? *Journal of Arts and Linguistics Studies*, *2*(2), 1063–1077. https://jals.miard.org/index.php/jals/article/view/145

Zawacki-Richter, O., Marín, V. I., Bond, M., & Gouverneur, F. (2019). Systematic review of research on artificial intelligence applications in higher education – Where are the educators? *International Journal of Educational Technology in Higher Education*, *16*(1), 1–27. DOI: 10.1186/s41239-019-0171-0

Zazzaro, C. (2024). Charting a Paradigm Shift: The Impact of Christie's Auction of AI-generated Edmond de Belamy on the Evaluation of Art (Doctoral dissertation, Utrecht University). https://studenttheses.uu.nl/handle/20.500.12932/48553

Zhai, X., Chu, X., Chai, C. S., Jong, M. S. Y., Istenic, A., Spector, M., Liu, J.-B., Yuan, J., & Li, Y. (2021). A Review of Artificial Intelligence (AI) in Education from 2010 to 2020. *Complexity, 2021*(1), 8812542. DOI: 10.1155/2021/8812542

Zhang, K., & Aslan, A. B. (2021). AI technologies for education: Recent research & future directions. *Computers and education. Artificial Intelligence*, *2*, 100025. DOI: 10.1016/j.caeai.2021.100025

Zhang, R. E., Ringland, K., Paan, M. C., Mohr, D., & Reddy, M. (2021, May). Designing for emotional well-being: integrating persuasion and customization into mental health technologies. In *Proceedings of the 2021 CHI Conference on Human Factors in Computing Systems* (pp. 1-13). DOI: 10.1145/3411764.3445771

Zhao, J., Li, S., & Zhang, J. (2025). Understanding teachers' adoption of AI technologies: An empirical study from Chinese middle schools. *Systems*, *13*(4), 302. DOI: 10.3390/systems13040302

Zhou, M., & Song, P. (2025). The Usage of AI in Teaching and Students' Creativity. *Behavioral Sciences (Basel, Switzerland)*, *587*(5), 587. Advance online publication. DOI: 10.3390/bs15050587 PMID: 40426365

Zimmerman, M. (2018). *Teaching AI: Exploring new frontiers for learning*. International society for technology in education.

About the Contributors

Muhammad Usman Tariq has more than 17+ year's experience in industry and academia. He has authored more than 300+ research articles/book chapters/case studies and 4 patents. He is founder and CEO of The Case HQ, a unique repository for courses and teaching case studies. His work has encompassed sectors in aviation, manufacturing, food, hospitality, education, operations, software and suppl chain. He has diverse and significant experience working with accreditation agencies of ABET, ACBSP, AACSB, WASC, CAA, EFQM and NCEAC. He is Certified Higher Education Teacher from Harvard University, USA, Certified Online Educator from HMBSU, Certified Six Sigma Master Black Belt, Lead Auditor ISO 9001 Certified, ISO 14001, IOSH MS, OSHA 30, and OSHA 48. He has been awarded Principal Fellowship from Advance HE UK, Chartered Fellowship of CIPD UK, and Certified business and management educator recognition.

***

Egi Dina Aulia is a Master student of Educational Management at the State University of Malang (UM) with the support of the Republic of Indonesia Education Fund Management Agency (LPDP) scholarship in 2023. Previously, she completed her undergraduate education at Physics Education from the State University of Semarang (UNNES). Her professional experience includes her role as Learning Content Administrator at Private Company, as well as being the member of Bersama Guru.id, a community that focused on the development of Teacher Competencies. Egi actively writes as a form of contribution in the field of educational research and innovation, especially those related to teachers job performance, leadership, organizational climate, and the development of healthy learning environment.

Saban Bon earned his PhD in English for Professional Development from Mae Fah Luang University, Thailand, and his Master of Education in Educational

Administration and Leadership from the Royal University of Phnom Penh, Cambodia. He is a Human Resource Department Officer, the Ministry of Education Youth and Sports, Cambodia, an associate editor with the Cambodian Education Forum(CEF), and an editor with the Cambodian Journal of Educational and Social Sciences (CJESS). His research publications and interests include intercultural studies, learning motivation, coursebook analysis, teaching and learning English as a lingua franca, teaching and learning with technology, and linguistic analysis.

Nurul Ain Chua Binti Abdullah is a Senior Lecturer at Universiti Malaysia Terengganu (UMT), where she focuses on teaching Mandarin as a foreign language to non-native learners. She is actively involved in research related to Mandarin language acquisition and educational technology in language learning. Dr. Nurul Ain has over 30 years of experience in education and has taught at various levels, from primary to tertiary. She has presented her research at numerous national and international conferences. Her research interests include technology-enhanced language learning, language pedagogy, and differentiated instruction.

Sereyrath Em is a Cambodian government teacher of English with a higher education degree, a university lecturer, and an educational researcher with 18 years of experience in teaching, instructing, and lecturing. He holds three doctoral degrees: PhD in Educational Science, PhD in Educational Administration, and PhD in Cooperative Education. He currently serves as an Editor at the Cambodian Journal of Educational Research (CJER) and is the Founder and Editor-in-Chief of the Cambodian Journal of Educational and Social Sciences (CJESS). He also serves as a reviewer for many well-known journals and publishers such as IGI Global, Cogent Education, Frontiers, MDPI, Taylor & Francis, and Palgrave Macmillan, among other Scopus-indexed outlets. So far, he has published around 100 scholarly pieces in highly reputable journals and publishers.

Chhun Hong is the Vice Dean of Faculty of Agriculture, Svay Rieng University, Cambodia

Hour Ry is the Dean in the Faculty of Business Administration and Tourism of the National University of Battambang (NUBB), a public university in northwest Cambodia, which he joined in 2008. He received his Master Degree in Business from Chamroeun University of Poly-Technology, Cambodia in 2006. In 2003, he graduated with Bachelor's degree of Science in Mathematics at the Royal University of Phnom Penh (RUPP). Currently, in 2025, Mr. Hour Ry serves as the Head of Procurement at the Second Higher Education Improvement Project (HEIP2) of NUBB, which is funded by World Bank's Cambodia Higher Education Improvement Project. He is presently serves as Project Manager of Official Development

Assistance (ODA) South Korea Project in Cambodia at The National University of Battambang (NUBB) in cooperation with Duksung Women's University supported by Government of Republic of Korea. The project name is "Establishment of a sustainable win-win model through the opening of the Department of International Trade And SCM at National University of Battambang and the Strengthening of cooperation with the local community In Cambodia". Mr. Hour Ry also serve as project Coordinator in Erasmus+ Project including Smart City Asian Learning Network (SCALe), Geomatics for Disaster Risk Reduction (GeoDRR). From 2018 to 2024, Mr Hour Ry served as the NUBB the Head of Procurement at NUBB for the World Bank-funded Higher Education Improvement Project (HEIP). From 2013 to 2016, Mr Hour Ry served as the NUBB Procurement Officer for the World Bank-funded Higher Education Quality and Capacity Improvement Project (HEQCIP). His email address is ryhour@gmail.com/hour.ry@nubb.edu.kh, and his mobile phone number is +855 (12) 312878

See Jasmine is a Senior Lecturer in the Department of Education, Faculty of Education & Humanities at Nilai University. She holds a PhD and specialises in Teaching English as a Second Language, curriculum design, and instructional development. Her research focuses on inclusive multilingual pedagogy — notably translanguaging approaches — and improving English proficiency for under-served learners. Dr. See leads projects that combine classroom intervention, teacher development, and AI-assisted instructional tools, and she has published on translanguaging pedagogy for refugees' volunteers.

Kim Ramet is a Professor at Svay Rieng University, Svay Rieng Province, Cambodia. His major is political science.

Kaushik Kumar holds a Ph.D. in Engineering from Jadavpur University, India, an MBA in Marketing Management from Indira Gandhi National Open University, India and a Bachelor of Technology from Regional Engineering College (Now National Institute of Technology), Warangal, India. For 11 years, he worked in a manufacturing unit of Global repute. He is currently working as a Professor in the Department of Mechanical Engineering, Birla Institute of Technology, Mesra, Ranchi, India. He has 23 Years of Teaching and Research Experience. His research interests include Composites, Optimization, Non-Conventional Machining, CAD / CAM, Rapid Prototyping and Quality Management Systems towards product development for societal and industrial usage and has received 45+ patents for them most of which are donated to Start-ups and Industrial fraternity through Jharkhand Small Industries Association (JSIA). He has published 60+ Books (They are referred as Text Books and Reference Books by 40+ Universities / Institutes in their academic curriculum), 100+ Book Chapters and 200+ Research Papers in peer-reviewed reputed national and international journals. Kaushik has also served as Editor–in–Chief, Series Editor, Guest Editor, Editor, Editorial Board Member and Reviewers for International and National Journals. He has been felicitated with many awards and honours including Distinguished Alumnus Award for Professional Excellence 2023 under Academic and Research from National Institute of Technology, Warangal, India. He has also received Sponsored Research and Consultancy Projects of more than 1 Crore from Govt. of India and abroad. Kaushik has delivered expert lectures as Keynote Speaker at International & National Conferences, Resource Person at Various Workshops, FDP's and Short-Term Courses. He has guided many students of Doctoral, Masters and Under Graduate programmes of his home and other institutions in India and abroad. He also has served as Reviewer and Examiner of Doctoral and Masters dissertation for institutes in India and abroad.

A'idah Muflichatul Maghfiroh is a student in the Biology Education Master's program at the State University of Malang (UM) with support from the Republic of Indonesia government's education costs through the Beasiswa Unggulan program in 2024. Previously, she completed her undergraduate education at the Biology Education Study Program, FKIP Jember Muhammadiyah University. His professional experience includes being a teacher of the Youth Scientific Work (KIR) extracurricular subject at SMP Negeri 19 Malang, as well as being a science tutor in a tutoring group.

K. K. Mishra is working as a Professor of Marketing at the University School of Business, Chandigarh University, Mohali, Punjab. He has published 54 national and international research papers in Scopus-indexed journals and book chapters and presented 31 papers at national and international conferences. He has four patent rights and three copyrights. He has 25 years of teaching and research experience. He has supervised two PhD scholars. He has twice qualified for UGC NET in Management. He has received the Best Faculty Award three times from the Indian Institute of Materials Management, National Head Quarters, Mumbai, in 2009, 2016 and 2018, respectively. He has been conferred the Best Paper Award for the paper titled "Harnessing AI: Unveiling Educators' Intentions and Synergy in Education", presented at the 8th International Conference on Information System Design and Intelligent Applications (ISDIS 2024) in Dubai, UAE, in 2024. He has chaired technical sessions of international conferences organised by the Indian Institute of Materials Management, Mumbai, in 2016 and 2018 and OP Jindal University Raigarh, in 2022 and 2023. He did his PhD in "Strategy formulation for marketing services in rural Uttar Pradesh" from Uttar Pradesh Rajarshi Tandon University, Allahabad. He can be contacted at email: kkmsitmbbk@gmail.com.

Froilan D. Mobo, DPA, Ph.D. is a distinguished Filipino educator, researcher, and academic leader known for his outstanding contributions to education, public administration, and development studies. He currently serves as a Full Professor II at the Philippine Merchant Marine Academy (PMMA), where he has devoted over a decade of service in shaping future maritime professionals. In addition to his academic role, he is the Editor-in-Chief of the International Journal of Multidisciplinary: Applied Business and Education Research (IJMABER), a reputable international refereed journal. Prof. Mobo is a strong advocate of lifelong learning, having earned dual doctorate degrees—Doctor of Public Administration from Urdaneta City University and Doctor of Philosophy in Development Education from Central Luzon State University—as well as triple master's degrees, including a Master of Science in Computer Science, Master of Business Administration, and Master of Arts in Social Studies Education from Bicol University Open University. He also holds a Diploma in Social Studies Education from UP Open University and is a Licensed Professional Teacher with a specialization in Social Studies.

Channthoeurn Ny is a researcher in Business Administration whose interests include digital transformation, operations management, information systems, and the strategic application of technology to organizational performance.

Bikash Panja holds a Ph.D. in Engineering from Jadavpur University, India an M. Tech in Production Engineering from Kalyani Government Engineering College, India and a B.Tech from Asansol Engineering College, West Bengal, India. With 13 years of academic and research experience in different renowned organizations, he is now a Professor in the Department of Mechanical Engineering at Swami Vivekananda University, West Bengal, India. Dr. Panja has over 13 years of teaching and research experience, specializing in composites, optimization, non-conventional machining, tribology etc. His contributions include publishing 01 books, 9+ book chapters, and 25+ research papers. Dr. Panja received a gold medal from The Institution of Engineers (India) for his best journal paper in 2016. He has also shared his expertise on mechanical engineering and diploma education trends as a guest speaker on DD Bangla's live program "Ki Hote Chai'' on 14th July, 2023, and 30th July, 2021.

Pawan Pant is working as an Assistant Professor of Management at the University School of Business, Chandigarh University, Mohali, Punjab. He has published two research papers, one national and one international journal. He has 10 years of teaching experience and worked as an Assistant Manager (Purchase) at Pacific Industries Ltd., Udaipur (Rajasthan) for one year. His area of specialization is Economics. email: pawanpant04@gmail.com.

Chikesh Ranjan is currently serving as a Project Engineer for Project SwaYaan – Capacity Building in Drone/UAS at the Department of Mechanical Engineering, NIT Rourkela, India. He holds a PhD in Mechanical Engineering from the Department of Mechanical Engineering at the Birla Institute of Technology, Mesra, Ranchi, Jharkhand, India, where he also completed his Master of Engineering (M.E.) in Mechanical Engineering, specializing in the Design of Mechanical Equipment. Additionally, he earned a Bachelor of Engineering (B.E.) in Mechanical Engineering from the Marathwara Institute of Technology, Aurangabad, Maharashtra, India, graduating with First Class with Distinction. Chikesh Ranjan has made significant contributions to the field of mechanical engineering through his research, having published 17 journal papers, authored 12 books, and written 16 book chapters. He has been actively involved in organizing 10 workshops and coordinating 13 events, in addition to participating in 31 training programs and attending 34 national and international workshops, seminars, and webinars. His innovative work has been recognized with 13 design patents and 8 foreign patents, underscoring his commitment to advancing mechanical design and technology. With 9 years of teaching and research experience, Chikesh has built a global reputation in his areas of interest, which include composites, non-conventional machining, CAD/CAM, 3D printing, robotics and drone technology. He is a proud member of the Institution of Engineers, India, and has received 7 prestigious awards and honors for his outstanding contributions to the field of Mechanical Engineering.

RATHA Virak Voan earned a PhD in Economics from the Royal Academy of Cambodia, demonstrating a strong academic and professional commitment to advancing knowledge in the field. He also holds Master of Art in Economics from Pannasastra University of Cambodia and Master of Health Administration from National Institute of Public Health, Cambodia. He currently serves at Securities and Exchange Regulator of Cambodia, where he is engaged in supervising and promoting financial innovation. His research interests center on Macroeconomic Policy, Human Capital Development and Digital Economy. Through his studies and regulatory role, he contributes to shaping policies that support Cambodia's sustainable economic growth.

Mardy Serey is an associate professor at Svay Rieng University, Cambodia.

Sanjiv Kumar Tiwari is an Assistant Professor from Birla Institute of Technology, Ranchi, India. His Ph.D. dissertation is about continuous improvement using lean six sigma philosophy manufacturing industries. His research interests include supply chain, quality engineering, decision support systems, continuous improvement philosophies like lean manufacturing, Six Sigma, etc. He has authored nearly 20 research articles in various journals and conference proceedings.

Yaredi Waruwu is an academic and education practitioner with a strong background in English language and educational science. He completed his Bachelor's degree (S-1) in English Literature at Santo Thomas Catholic University in Medan in 2005. Subsequently, he earned a Master's degree (S-2) in English Literature from the Islamic University of North Sumatra in 2015, and a Doctorate (S-3) in Educational Sciences from Padang State University in 2022. Since 2009, Yaredi Waruwu has served as a tenured faculty member at Nias University in North Sumatra and currently holds the position of Dean of the Faculty of Teacher Training and Education (FKIP). He also has academic experience as a faculty member at several universities, including Taman Siswa University in Padang and UIN Imam Bonjol in Padang. Beyond his academic work, he has professional experience in various national and international organizations, including in community empowerment and community-based economic development programs. He has also been involved in collaborative activities with government agencies. Yaredi Waruwu is active in research and scientific publications, both in national and international journals. He is also a frequent speaker at national and international seminars. Currently, he is a member of the Indonesian Association of Lecturers in Community Service (ADPI) and contributes as an editor to ISBN-registered books and reputable international journals.

Goh Ying Soon is a principal lecturer 2 at Nilai University after he retired as a senior lecturer at UiTM Terengganu. He teaches in Faculty of Education at Nilai University, Malaysia. He has experiences in teaching at primary, secondary and tertiary level for more than 25 years. He has been actively presenting papers in national and international conferences. His research interests are educational studies, educational management, the use of educational technology in teaching and learning, web-based instruction, translation, and etc.

Nofamataro Zebua is a young lecturer in the Biology Education Study Program at Universitas Nias (UNIAS), Indonesia. He completed his bachelor's degree in biology education from Universitas Nias Raya (UNIRAYA) and his master's degree from the Department of Biology at Universitas Negeri Malang (UM). He is a passionate researcher and writer who explores innovative topics in the field of education. His research focuses on biology, biology and science education, literacy, thinking skills, artificial intelligence (AI) for education, biodiversity, pedagogy, 21st-century skills, and ethnobiology to enhance student learning experiences and engagement. He is also actively providing valuable insights to educators, researchers, and students, as well as promoting digital literacy and environmental awareness through problem-based, project-based, and community-based approaches.

Yan Piter Basman Ziraluo is a permanent lecturer in the Biology Education Study Program at Nias Raya University with the functional position of Lecturer. He completed his bachelor's degree (S.Pd) at IKIP Gunung Sitoli in 2010, then obtained a Master of Management (M.M.) degree from HKBP Nommensen University in 2013, and a Master of Education (M.Pd) degree from Padang State University in 2015. Currently, he is pursuing doctoral studies (S3) in the Biology Education Study Program at Malang State University to deepen his expertise. His research and publications focus on biology education, cooperative learning strategies, literacy, learning models, teaching media and materials, and biodiversity studies, which he has published in SINTA and Scopus indexed national journals. In addition to being active as a lecturer and researcher, he also plays a role in developing the quality of education as Director of the Internal Quality Assurance Institute (LPMI) at Nias Raya University.

Index

Symbols

A

C

D

E

F

G

H

I

M

P

S

T

www.ingramcontent.com/pod-product-compliance
Lightning Source LLC
LaVergne TN
LVHW081529300926
849161LV00006B/1359